"In 2008, the search began to select an intervention to promote VA health-care when Congress mandated those eligible for the Department of Veterans Affairs Health Services have access to couple counselling. Selection criteria included strong empirical support, appeal to clinicians trained in either cognitive-behavioral or acceptance-based approaches, manualization, and developers who were enthused about collaborating with the VA. Integrative Behavioral Couple Therapy (IBCT) fit the bill, and thousands of veterans have now participated in the intervention, to great effect. The text here updates and expands IBCT in an accessible, engaging format replete with clinical wisdom and practical guidance."

—**Shirley M. Glynn, Ph.D.**, Research Psychologist, Semel Institute of Neuroscience and Human Behavior, UCLA

"Integrative Behavioral Couple Therapy is the premier couple therapy for addressing the central concepts of acceptance and behavior change in intimate relationships. Developed by internationally recognized leaders in the couple therapy field, IBCT is easy for therapists to learn, is well-received by couples, and has strong empirical support. This book includes the latest thinking regarding acceptance and behavior change strategies, along with innovative applications of the treatment to diverse populations and specific complex problems. This volume will be a classic."

—**Donald H. Baucom, Ph.D.**, Distinguished Professor of Psychology and Neuroscience, University of North Carolina at Chapel Hill, author of *Treating Relationship Distress and Psychopathology in Couples*

"*Integrative Behavioral Couple Therapy* is a book every therapist and student training to be a therapist needs to read. This book tells the story of one of the most important innovations in the therapy field the last few decades, and not just in the couples therapy field. The IBCT approach to helping partners improve their relationships and lives is based on over 40 years of research and clinical practice. The lead author is one of the most esteemed psychologists on the planet, whose work is widely respected and has had a positive impact on countless therapists and couples. The second author is one of the best and brightest young psychologists in the couples field, who is destined to continue to make outstanding contributions. The third author, who sadly passed away too young, is still seen as one of the most important contributors to clinical and family psychology, and his work lives on in this book. Partners will want to read this book to discover skills and principles that will help them as they put what they learn into practice. Your work with people struggling with relationship issues will be forever changed when you read this book."

—**Howard J. Markman, Ph.D.**, Distinguished
Professor of Psychology, University of Denver,
author of *Fighting FOR Your Marriage*

"This book is essential reading for anyone participating in couple therapy. Powerful case examples bring underlying principles to life. Reading session accounts is like being in the therapy room, watching these experts in action. *Integrative Behavioral Couple Therapy* challenges traditional ideas about couple therapy through integration with online programs, such as OurRelationship.com. In addition, it expands IBCT's applicability to diverse couples and high-stakes issues, including infidelity and violence. This book offers enormous wisdom for both seasoned and new couple therapists."

—**Gayla Margolin, Ph.D.**, Professor, Department of
Psychology, University of Southern California

INTEGRATIVE BEHAVIORAL
COUPLE THERAPY

INTEGRATIVE BEHAVIORAL COUPLE THERAPY

A Therapist's Guide to Creating Acceptance and Change

ANDREW CHRISTENSEN
BRIAN D. DOSS
NEIL S. JACOBSON

W. W. NORTON & COMPANY
Independent Publishers Since 1923

Note to Readers: Standards of clinical practice and protocol change over time, and no technique or recommendation is guaranteed to be safe or effective in all circumstances. This volume is intended as a general information resource for professionals practicing in the field of psychotherapy and mental health; it is not a substitute for appropriate training, peer review, and/or clinical supervision. Neither the publisher nor the author(s) can guarantee the complete accuracy, efficacy, or appropriateness of any particular recommendation in every respect.

To our families—
Andy's wife Louise and children Lisa and Sean
Brian's wife Mandy and children Abby and Matthew—
who have accepted us and changed us in ways both big and small

Contents

**   DELIBERATE CHANGE (AND ACCEPTANCE)**
Chapter 9   Deliberate, Client-Led Change   185
Chapter 10 Dyadic Behavioral Activation   221
Chapter 11 Communication and Problem-Solving Training   239

PART 5   SPECIAL CONSIDERATIONS AND
**   NEW DIRECTIONS IN IBCT**
Chapter 12 Diversity in Couples: Clinical Considerations in
              Doing IBCT   275
Chapter 13 Special Problems in Couple Therapy: Violence,
              Sexual Problems, Infidelity, and Psychopathology   299
Chapter 14 OurRelationship.com and IBCT:
              A Model for Integration   333

              Afterword   365
              Appendix   367
              References   371
              Index   382

Acknowledgments

SCIENCE IS CUMULATIVE. Any evidence-based knowledge necessarily builds on previous evidence; on previous information. However large or small the contribution that one makes to this body of knowledge, one owes the people who previously contributed. In addition, science is collaborative. Whatever any of us contributes, we are able to do so because we had mentors, role models, and colleagues who nurtured, supported, challenged, and inspired us. It would be impossible to acknowledge all the people who influenced me and this work, but I am going to try to mention the ones of whom I am most aware.

Of most importance was the late Neil S. Jacobson and Brian D. Doss, the co-authors of this book. Neil and I developed Integrative Behavioral Couple therapy, wrote the first book about it (Jacobson & Christensen, 1996), and did the initial research on it (see Appendix). Many productive, delightful, and sometimes even frustrating discussions, e-mail exchanges, and manuscript drafts led to these accomplishments. Neil was a dedicated, enthusiastic, and brilliant scientist who could advocate energetically for his views, but could look unsupporting data in the eye and not flinch! Tragically, he died an untimely death in 1999, soon after we began a major, two-site clinical trial of the impact of IBCT. His death was a major loss to the field as well as to his family, friends, and colleagues. Brian was a graduate student of mine some 20 years ago, assisted with the clinical trial of IBCT, and along the way did some important research on couple therapy in general and on IBCT in particular. Once he got his PhD and settled into a career in academia, he took IBCT in a direction that Neil and I never even dreamed of. Brian began a major dissemination effort to extend the reach of IBCT by adapting IBCT principles into an online program, www.OurRelationship.com. With major grant support, he demonstrated that this online program is beneficial for couples, including minority and low-income couples who are underserved with in-person treatment. It has been my pleasure to assist him in this effort. As a result, we have been able to make IBCT accessible to a wider audience of couples. Chapter 14 in this book is devoted to the OurRelationship program and discusses how it can be integrated with in-person IBCT.

There are many others that deserve acknowledgment and I will discuss them in more or less chronological order. There is Robert Weiss, one of the founders of behavioral couple therapy and my clinical supervisor of couple therapy during graduate school. Wise and wily, he was a living contradiction of any argument that behavioral approaches were mechanistic. I saw my first couple case, as well as a group for couples, with fellow graduate student, Gayla Margolin, as my co-therapist and Weiss as our supervisor. When Gayla and I ended up at separate universities in Los Angeles—Gayla at the University of Southern California and me at the University of California, Los Angeles—we collaborated on a major federal grant studying the impact of couple therapy and family therapy. Throughout our graduate career and the many years since, Gayla has been that ideal combination of friend and colleague. Early in my career at UCLA, I met the late Harold Kelley, an influential social psychologist who wanted to put the study of close relationships on solid scientific grounds, obtained funding from the National Science Foundation for this endeavor, and invited me to join him and a group of clinical and social psychologists to write a book giving this burgeoning field direction (Kelley et al., 1983; 2002). What an incredible opportunity that was, and what an impact on my thinking about relationships. Dan Wile, an astute clinician, influenced my thinking through his writings, even though he came from a dramatically different theoretical perspective. However, perhaps the most direct influence on my thinking about couples came from my extensive clinical work with couples, either directly through my private practice which I continued throughout my career, or indirectly through the therapists I supervised. The messiness of real couples and their difficulties is a constant reality check on our oversimplified theories and interventions.

For our clinical trials of IBCT, we selected experienced, reputable, licensed professional therapists and trained them in IBCT. During our first pilot clinical trial of IBCT, we worked with Steve Clancy, Peter Fehrenbach, Joan Fiore, Susan Price, and Deborah Wilk. During our major two-site clinical trial of IBCT, we worked with Alfredo Crespo, Shelly Harrell, Megan Sullaway, and Anthony Zamudio in Los Angeles, and Peter Fehrenbach, Carol Henry, Christopher Martel, and Deborah Wilk in Seattle. To conduct these clinical trials, we depended on the help of a group of talented graduate students at UCLA and at the University of Washington, all of whom are now PhDs themselves. They did clinical assessments of the couples and helped run the day-to-day operations: Brian Baucom, Katherine Williams Baucom, Lisa Benson, Brian Doss, Kathleen Eldridge, Krista Gattis, Janice Jones, Meghan McGinn, Felicia De La Garza Mercer, Mia Sevier, and Lorelei Simpson were graduate students with me at UCLA; David Atkins, Sara Berns, Jean Yi, and Jennifer Wheeler were graduate students on the project at the University of Washington. During graduate school and afterward, David Atkins served as our statistical guru, analyzing and helping us make sense of the data.

For the last 10 years, I have been working with clinicians in the U.S. Department of Veterans Affairs to train VA clinicians nationwide in IBCT. Dr. Shirley Glynn has been the coordinator of this effort as well as other training efforts in evidence-based treatments for VA families. I never cease to be amazed at her energetic competence at making things happen in the VA and keeping such good cheer while she does so. Her talented assistants, Anna Lui and Natasha Faber, have not only helped her, but also me, with this effort. I am also grateful to Susan McCutcheon, the Director of Family Services at the VA, for her support of IBCT in particular and evidence-based family treatments in general. To implement this massive training effort required me to bring in outside people who were trained in IBCT by me or by Neil to serve as IBCT consultants and supervise VA trainees: Jill Compton, Krista Gattis, Kelly Koerner, and Stacey Prince, as well as Peter Fehrenbach, who fortunately worked in the VA. We selected the best of the VA trainees to themselves be consultants for new trainees. These VA consultants included: Brian Abbott, Jennifer Atkins, Tamia Barnes, Kori Blitstein, Adele Brainard, Tracey Carson, Eric Clausel, Barbara Dausch, Michele Decremer, Blake Evans, Peter Fehrenbach, Jennifer Hosler, Greg Inman, Sam Korobkin, Ivette Malavez, Birgitte Miller, Angela Mitchell, Karen Petty, Laura Rautio, Billy Rutherford, Jenna Teves, Nate Tomcik, and Betty Shadish. With this skilled group of consultants, we have trained 20 cohorts of VA therapists and are in the process of training two additional cohorts.

Finally, there is my own family. One of the joys of studying and working with couples and families is that one sees applications to one's own family. Louise Macbeth, my wife, and our children Lisa and Sean, have taught me how love, acceptance, and change work in the day-to-day bustle of family life.

Andrew Christensen
Los Angeles, January 2020

IN HIS ACKNOWLEDGMENT FOR THIS BOOK, Andy wrote, "Whatever any of us contributes, we are able to do so because we had mentors, role models, and colleagues who nurtured, supported, challenged, and inspired us." Andy has been all of that for me: a mentor, a role model, and—in more recent years—a colleague. I am forever grateful for him taking me under his wing as a graduate student, for his ongoing mentorship after I graduated, and for continuing to provide me with exciting opportunities such as being a coauthor on this IBCT therapist manual. I also want to thank Julian Libet at the Charleston VA hospital and Doug Snyder at Texas A&M who exposed me to different couple therapy orientations while on internship and in my first faculty position (respectively).

It has been over 10 years since we first started work on the OurRelationship program—an online, self-help version of IBCT. As we describe in Chapter 14, the program has been quite successful in expanding the reach of IBCT while also maintaining most of its efficacy. I'm very excited to present here—for the first time—our ideas for how the online program can be integrated with in-person delivery of IBCT. I think those ideas have a lot of potential for making IBCT more accessible to therapists who have less experience working with couples as well as to couples who cannot afford an extended course of IBCT.

There have been multiple people involved in the OurRelationship effort that I want to thank. Andy, Kelly Koerner, Mark Harrison, and Cammy Bean were all central in its initial conceptualization. Additionally, multiple graduate students have help shape its evolution over time (and shouldered the burden of coaching, supervising, and keeping the project afloat on a daily basis): Emily Georgia (Salivar), Larisa Cicilia, McKenzie Roddy, Kate Nowlan, Karen Rothman, and Gabe Hatch. An additional thanks goes to McKenzie Roddy and Kayla Knopp who provided valuable comments on drafts of Chapter 14 of this book. I also want to acknowledge funding from the National Institute of Child Health and Human Development as well as the Administration for Children and Families; the program would not be possible without this support.

Finally, I want to express my appreciation and gratitude for my family: my wife Mandy and children Abby and Matthew. They are accepting of the tight deadlines and the ever-present laptop that accompanies projects like this. But I also want to thank them for making me take the time to throw a football, kick a soccer ball, watch a middle school theater performance, actually get a babysitter and go out for a nice dinner or a concert with friends, and escape on a much-needed vacation. They give my life meaning, enjoyment, and fulfillment—I'm so lucky to have them.

Brian D. Doss
Miami, January 2020

Preface

IT HAS BEEN ALMOST 25 YEARS since Andrew Christensen and the late Neil Jacobson wrote the first edition of this treatment manual for Integrative Behavioral Couple Therapy (Jacobson & Christensen, 1996). Many developments in IBCT have happened during that time; which more than justify a revision. The most important developments for a clinically-oriented book such as this one is that we have done extensive dissemination of IBCT, and that dissemination has forced us to elaborate IBCT in a way that makes it more accessible to clinicians and couples alike.

IBCT is a principle-based treatment for couples. As such, it does not provide treatment recipes, step-by-step procedures for each session, or elaborate flow charts or decision trees about what to do and when. Soon after we had written the original treatment manual, a colleague read it and complemented us on the book, but asked, "Do you also have a treatment manual to go with it?" He was a proponent of detailed treatment manuals that specified what therapist behavior was appropriate at each step of treatment and thought there must be a companion volume that did this. We had to inform him that this was indeed our treatment manual.

Because this original treatment manual was so principle-based, our first clinical trials involved extensive supervision of therapists. Therapists did video recordings of each session; Christensen and Jacobson watched some or all of these video tapes and consulted with therapists, and sometimes each other, prior to each session. As a result, we were able to clarify for therapists how to implement these principles across a wide variety of couples. Based on the positive results from these clinical trials, the United States Department of Veterans Affairs selected IBCT as one of its evidence-based treatments for couples. Starting in 2010, Christensen has been heavily involved in training therapists in the VA in IBCT. As of this writing, over 500 licensed mental health professionals have entered the VA's extensive training program in IBCT, which involves a several day workshop and at least 6 months of weekly supervision as the trainee does IBCT with two or more couples and gets feedback on audio recordings of at least 20 sessions with these couples. As with our supervision of the clinical trials, this training effort required us to articulate and illustrate in detail how to apply the principles of IBCT with couples. Starting in 2009, Doss led a major effort to adapt IBCT principles into an online program for couples, OurRelationship.com. In this effort the principles were concretized with text, animations, video illustration, and interactive material in which participants answered questions and got feedback from the program and were guided by the program in a series of conversations with their partner. As with the clinical trials and dissemination through the VA, this effort required that we articulate how the principles would be applied in diverse situations. Therefore, in this revised version of our book on IBCT, we have maintained the fundamental principles of IBCT but have elaborated them in greater detail and included a wealth of examples that should make it easier for the clinician to understand not just the principles, but the diverse ways in which they can be applied. About two thirds of the material in this book is new. If our colleague reads this version, perhaps he will not have the same question he had before.

In the last 25 years, there has also been extensive applied research on IBCT. The Appendix lists all of the current publications resulting from this research. The clinical trials, the dissemination effort through the VA, and the online program have all led to published research on IBCT. Although this is a book primarily for clinicians, we will summarize that research briefly at points in the book to show not just that IBCT leads to beneficial outcomes for couples but also to document how it brings about those outcomes and how important subgroups benefit from IBCT (e.g., minority couples, affair couples, couples with some level of intimate partner violence). We also briefly review some of the basic research that supports particular interventions in IBCT, such as empathic joining and unified detachment.

Throughout the book we illustrate our points by referring to specific couples. We typically mention these couples by name. In many cases these are composites of the couples we have seen directly or indirectly through our work in therapy, training, supervision, and research. However, we selected these composites as typical examples of the kinds of couples and kinds of issues that present themselves in couple therapy. For these couples, we often describe how an IBCT therapist *might* work with them. At other times we not only describe specific couples and their behavior, but also what an IBCT therapist *actually said or did* with them. At still other times in the book, we describe couples at length and include transcripts of some their therapy sessions, along with our commentary about the couple and the therapist. In both of these later cases, in which we say what an IBCT therapist did or provide extensive transcripts of the session showing what he or she did, we are referring to specific, real couples. However, we have anonymized these couples to protect their actual identity without sacrificing the clinical reality of the couple. The transcripts are verbatim what the couple and the therapist said albeit with some minor changes to remove identifying information and increase readability. Some of these cases are from the original book and some are new. Some come from our clinical trials and some from our own work with couples or our training of other therapists who work with couples. Our commentary on these transcripts discusses what the therapist did that was good as well as the mistakes the therapist made as we believe it is helpful to see positive examples of IBCT as well as missed opportunities or mistakes in IBCT. We have not mentioned the names of the specific therapists in order to further protect the couple's identity and also the therapists' identities.

We start off the book in Chapter 1 with a detailed picture of one composite couple, Hank and Maria. We will visit them throughout the book, showing how IBCT would conceptualize their difficulties and how IBCT might work with them.

PART 1

Overview of Couple Distress and Therapy

1

&

A Couple in Distress

LET'S CONSIDER THE STORY of one couple, Hank and Maria, their personal history, their relationship history, their first session of couple therapy, and the multiple challenges that they present to a couple therapist. A focus on this couple will provide an introduction to couple therapy and in particular to Integrative Behavioral Couple Therapy. However, the story of one couple is really two stories: each partner has a separate story to tell that usually differs substantially from the story that the other tells.

MARIA'S STORY

Ever since James, our first and so far only child, was born a little over 4 years ago, our marriage has gone downhill. James was a difficult baby, very fussy, a poor sleeper, easily aroused and upset. I found it exhausting taking care of him; it seems like I never got a good night's sleep the first couple of years of his life. Hank was of no help to me and actually made things worse. He wanted me not to comfort James so much and let him "cry it out." So not only did he not help me out but also he criticized me for a lot of what I did for James.

When James was around 2 years old, I realized he was not developing properly because he was not speaking much, usually just one-word sentences. I couldn't share my concerns with Hank because he would tell me I was overreacting and that I was "coddling" James too much. So he directly and

3

indirectly blamed me for James' problems. I took James to several pediatricians and psychologists. All agreed that he is delayed; his language development is clearly below normal. Also it's clear that he has behavior problems; he tantrums a lot, in part because he cannot communicate his needs and desires and gets frustrated. He doesn't play well with other kids and will take their toys or be aggressive with them. But he can also be very sweet and loving, particularly to me. No one can agree on a diagnosis for him or whether he should be diagnosed. He is in a special preschool program. I just want to give him as much help as possible so he can develop to his full potential, whatever that turns out to be.

Hank doesn't think much of the mental health profession and so gives little credence to what psychologists say about James. He was really reluctant to come in to couple therapy but our relationship has gotten so bad that he agreed to give it a try. His approach to James seems so strict and unloving. He gets easily irritated with him. His total approach to James is punishment: taking away his toys, putting him in his room, turning off the cartoons, yelling "no" at him. I feel I often have to protect James from his own father. I don't like to say this but I don't think Hank is a good father; he's selfish and unloving.

I feel so turned off to Hank that I don't feel like being close to him. Occasionally he tries to initiate sex or affection and I am just not interested. I would like to talk with him about my concerns about James but I know I would just get a lecture from him so I often avoid Hank. In the evening, I usually have to lie down with James to get him to sleep and then I fall asleep also. So I end up in his room for a good portion of the night. Then I don't have to be with Hank and deal with him when he goes to bed.

I would really like to have a second child. I always dreamed of having a daughter. But given how bad Hank's and my relationship is, I know it would be crazy to have another child now. At times I think the only thing to do is to separate, but that really scares me.

HANK'S STORY

I thought we had a pretty good marriage until our son James was born. Then Maria got overinvolved with James. I think she fancies herself a super mom.

She had to be there to do everything with James. She is also a worrier and an overreactor. Almost as soon as James was born, she thought something was wrong with him. She has taken him to all sorts of psychologists and pediatricians and they cannot agree on what is wrong with him, except that he is slow to develop. Kids develop at different rates. I remember my family was concerned about a cousin because he developed slowly and yet he turned out just fine.

If anything is wrong with James, it's because Maria lets him get away with so much. She doesn't push him at all. She doesn't insist that he do things for himself. She anticipates his needs so he doesn't have to use language. If kids don't have to learn, they won't. Right now he cannot even go to sleep by himself. She lies down with him at night and often ends up spending half the night with him. How long is she going to continue that? How is he going to learn to fall asleep by himself if she just coddles him that way?

Our relationship is nowhere. She doesn't seem to want to be with me, her own husband. If I try to initiate sex with her, she just blows me off. Or she'll occasionally have sex just out of obligation. She also doesn't even want to kiss me or snuggle on the couch or cuddle in bed. I thought women were supposed to like affection. But she's so neurotic about James that she can't even focus on me.

Maria used to talk about a second child. We had always planned on having two and James is now four. But you have to have sex to have a child! Also, I think she would just become even more involved with being super mom. And if the child weren't perfect, she'd spend all her time worrying about that child as well as James. I would just fall further down the totem pool, if that's even possible.

MARIA AND HANK'S RELATIONSHIP HISTORY

Hank and Maria met at an accountancy firm at which Hank was a junior partner. Maria worked in a clerical position there while she was saving money for college. Hank was immediately attracted to Maria physically but also to her personality. She was warm, was playful, was sensuous, and knew how to have a good time. Maria was attracted to Hank for his drive and ambition.

She was impressed with how he had worked his way through college and was the first of his cohort to attain junior partner at the firm.

Hank found in Maria a refuge from his work-focused life. He could relax with her, have fun with her, and feel truly renewed and refreshed. He loved to be at her apartment because it felt so "homey" in contrast to his sterile apartment. He resonated to her warmth.

For her part, Maria felt protected with Hank. He was a man who took care of the details, who had a clear vision for the future, and who would get ahead. He pushed himself and was strong and assertive.

They had a rapid and exciting courtship that led within 9 months to marriage. They had James a year after marriage.

MARIA AND HANK'S INDIVIDUAL HISTORIES

Maria came from a poor but close-knit family. Her parents worked at menial jobs and got most of their pleasure from family life. They were a child-focused couple that tended to sacrifice their own needs to those of their four children. One child was born with Down syndrome as well as a variety of physical problems. The family coalesced around his care, until he died at the age of 8 years. That death was a major tragedy for the family, one from which it took years to recover.

Maria was attractive and always had plenty of male attention. She had several relationships with men before she met Hank but she found them to be immature. They were just into having a good time, and she felt their career goals were either unrealistic or missing. She wanted a life that was more financially secure than the one she had with her family, and she was immediately attracted to Hank for his ambition and career trajectory.

Hank's dad died when he was very young and he was raised an only child by his mother. She devoted herself to him, giving him as many opportunities as her limited budget would allow, encouraging his successes, and showering him with love and appreciation. Even today, she is thrilled at any success he has at work, and he has often been distressed that his mother shows far more interest in his victories than his wife does.

Hank had a number of girlfriends before he met Maria but once the novelty of a new relationship wore off, he often found them selfish and shallow. He wanted the kind of warmth and generosity he had found in his own small family of origin. He thought he had found that in a previous girlfriend, Kate, and lived with her for almost a year. Previously married, Kate shared custody of her 6-year-old daughter, Allie, who lived with them half of the time. Hank enjoyed Kate when Allie was with her father but when Allie was with them, Hank felt excluded, like the proverbial third wheel. He felt Kate was preoccupied with Allie and favored Allie over him consistently; he never felt comfortable taking any kind of parental role with Allie. He decided that a half-time partner was not enough for him and ended the relationship. When he met Maria, he was instantly attracted to her. Apart from the physical chemistry he felt toward her, much greater than he had felt for Kate, Maria seemed to have the warmth and nurturance that he wanted. Plus she was unencumbered with any children from a previous relationship.

HANK AND MARIA'S CURRENT CIRCUMSTANCES

Hank and Maria continue to work at the accountancy firm at which they met. Hank has now achieved senior partner status and is often somewhat overwhelmed with the amount of work he has to do. He has cordial but distant relationships with other members at the firm. As during most of his life, he has few close friends. He keeps in contact with his roommate from college and his best friend from high school but both live across the country. His primarily source of social interaction is with Maria and with his mother, whom he talks to frequently by phone since she lives out of town.

Maria had achieved a staff management position at the firm but cut back her work to part time after James was born, even though doing so put some strain on their finances. They pay for child care and nursery school for James when Maria is at work. Maria's parents and Hank's mother would gladly help out but are too far away to be of regular assistance. Hank was agreeable to Maria cutting back to part-time at her job because he saw it meant so much to her to be with James but he also thought it would free up more of her time to be with him as a couple. When that did not happen, he was sorely disappointed.

FIRST SESSION OF COUPLE THERAPY

In response to the therapist's question about what brought them to couple therapy, Hank immediately began by acknowledging that it was Maria's idea to come to couple therapy, that he wasn't sure it would be much help, but their relationship was certainly not in a good place and if therapy could help, he would be open to it. He continued with a list of his complaints about the marriage—specifically the lack of affection, sex, and even time together. Maria defensively responded with an explanation of her concerns about James, the various challenges he presents, and the time it takes caring for him. Hank interrupted her and suggested that the problem was more her "neurotic anxiety about James" than any problem with James. The therapist tried to limit the interruptions and give each partner a chance to talk. Maria shifted from her concerns about James to the conflicts that she and Hank have about James, how Hank tries to take a hard line with James and is so harsh with him that it has made her wonder whether Hank really loves James. Hank defended himself by arguing for the value of having high expectations for children and saying he has never physically hit James or verbally abused him and that he would never do so. Maria acknowledged that there was no abuse but still felt Hank didn't understand James and had unrealistic expectations for him. That led to an argument about whose expectations were out of line. The therapist shifted the discussion away from this argument and asked if this kind of argument was typical of them when they tried to discuss James. They acknowledged that yes, they often argued when they discussed James but because the arguments went nowhere, they often avoided discussions of him. With further inquiry, the couple talked about their general avoidance of meaningful discussion. They still dealt with the practical matters of the household in a reasonably civil manner but more and more "lived together separately," Maria doing much of the child care and Hank bringing work home.

The therapist used that comment to shift the discussion to their relationship apart from James, asking Maria to comment on her view of their relationship since Hank had previously indicated his dissatisfaction with affection and sex. Maria acknowledged that they had little physical contact with each other but she focused on the cold emotional climate between them. She said she felt as if Hank were always angry or upset with her, because of James or the lack of sex or something. She wasn't always sure what he was angry about, only that he was angry and it was usually about her. His anger made her want to distance herself from him. Why would she want to be physically close to someone who seemed so angry with her? Hank acknowledged that he was sometimes angry at her but insisted that she kept her distance no matter what he was feeling. He said, "She has a wall around her that is a foot thick and the only one who gets in is James."

Challenges for the Couple Therapist

A couple like Hank and Maria present many challenges to a couple therapist. The first is whether they are even appropriate for couple therapy. Maybe James needs a thorough evaluation so the couple can decide once and for all if he has problems and if so, what they are. Maybe Maria should be referred for individual therapy to deal with her anxiety about James. Or maybe Hank needs therapy to deal with the ambivalence that Maria suggests he has about even being a parent. However, a couple therapist would not immediately recommend individual therapy for two reasons: first, the couple came seeking couple therapy and it is usually best to meet the client where they are and address their presenting problems; second, a referral for individual therapy for James or Maria or even Hank plays into the couple's conflict, by endorsing Maria's concern that James really does have psychological problems and needs psychological help, by endorsing Hank's view that Maria is "neurotically anxious," or by endorsing Maria's view that Hank is not fully on board with being a father. Thus, a couple therapist, and certainly an IBCT therapist, would consider Hank and Maria as having a couple problem and being candidates for couple therapy without necessarily dismissing any of the individual concerns that the partners presented.

Which couple problems? A distressed couple such as Hank and Maria present a plethora of problems on which a couple therapist could focus. The most obvious problem for Hank and Maria is their distressing disagreements about James and how to handle him. They also clearly have problems in their physical relationship and in general there seems to be an absence of much positive interaction. If we move away from the content of their difficulties—the specific disagreements they have—the process by which they deal with those difficulties is also problematic. They clearly have communication problems in that their discussions about James are marked by either disagreement or avoidance. Avoidance seems to mark their physical relationship also; they rarely have sex and they don't discuss it. Their thinking about their relationship is characterized by distrusting and sometimes suspicious views of the other. Hank speculates that Maria doesn't even love him; Maria wonders if Hank even loves James. Strong negative emotional reactions to the other characterize any discussion of their difficulties. If we try to look beyond those immediate, surface, negative emotional reactions that they each have, we might speculate that Hank feels extremely neglected by Maria and perhaps even jealous of the love she pours on James. Maria may feel abandoned in the difficult and challenging role of mother that she is having to navigate without the support of her husband.

It is not hard to see problems in distressed couples; they are usually many and obvious. What is the most important difficulty? What problem should the therapist focus on first? How should he or she conceptualize the problems and address them in therapy?

Couple therapies differ in their answers to these questions because each approach has a different theory of distress, a different set of ideas to explain how two people who chose each other out of love and who presumably chose each other because they got on so well are now facing such difficulties. In order to understand Integrative Behavioral Couple Therapy (IBCT) and its theory about couple distress, we will first describe how each of the major evidence-based treatments for couples conceptualize distress and treatment. That will enable you the reader to understand the context in which IBCT came about and how it differs from other approaches, particularly other behavioral approaches with which it shares considerable conceptual underpinnings. Therefore, in Chapter 2, we will describe the three approaches to couple therapy other than IBCT that have the most supporting evidence. We will discuss how they conceptualize distress and treatment, and we will contrast them with how IBCT conceptualizes distress and treatment. In Chapter

3, we will discuss in detail IBCT's unique way of analyzing relationship distress, what we call a DEEP analysis of distress. Both chapters will use Hank and Maria as our example couple. Then we get into the how-to of IBCT in Chapters 4 and beyond, discussing couple assessment, the feedback session in which information is shared with the couple, the active treatment phase of IBCT, termination in IBCT, and special issues in couple therapy. These chapters describe the specific strategies and procedures of IBCT. We end with a chapter describing a recent adaptation of IBCT principles into an online intervention, OurRelationship, and how this program can be incorporated into face-to-face IBCT. Although this is a book for clinicians, describing the strategies and procedures of IBCT, we also include throughout the book brief descriptions of the extensive research supporting IBCT, including the research in support of the recent online adaptation.

2

&

Why Lovers Make War and How Couple Therapy Brings Peace

AMONG THE MANY DIFFERENT approaches to treating couples, several have proven themselves in the most rigorous tests of effectiveness, namely randomized clinical trials. In these studies, distressed couples are randomly assigned to different treatments or to a treatment and a control group, and outcome is assessed at the end of treatment and often a follow-up period. Compared to couples in the control condition, couples in the treatment conditions typically score higher on measures of relationship satisfaction as well as other ancillary measures, such as measures of communication or commitment to the relationship. Or couples in a new treatment condition score as well or better than couples in an older treatment that has previously been tested against a control group.

Four distinguishable approaches to couple therapy have been tested in more than one of these randomized clinical trials: Traditional Behavioral Couple Therapy (TBCT, originally called Behavioral Marital Therapy; Jacobson & Margolin, 1979), Cognitive-Behavioral Couple Therapy (CBCT; Baucom & Epstein, 1990), Emotionally Focused Couple Therapy (EFCT; Greenberg & Johnson, 1988; Johnson, 2015) and Integrative Behavioral Couple Therapy (IBCT; Christensen, Dimidjian, & Martell, 2015; Christensen, Jacobson,

& Babcock, 1995; Jacobson & Christensen, 1996, the focus of this book. There are other approaches that have been tested in one randomized clinical trial, such as Insight-Oriented Couple Therapy (Snyder & Wills, 1989) and Integrated Systemic Couple Therapy (A. Goldman & Greenberg, 1992). Although this research demonstrates the efficacy of these approaches, it suggests that their effect sizes are roughly comparable and there are too few randomized control trials comparing treatments to conclude that one is better overall or for a particular subset of couples. (For further detail see Lebow, Chambers, Christensen, & Johnson, 2012; Rathgeber, Bürkner, Schiller & Holling, 2019; and Snyder & Halford, 2012.)

We will focus on the first four treatments above since they have the most evidence for their effectiveness and are the most widely practiced of the evidence-based couple therapies. We will first describe the similarities and differences in these couple therapies, with a particular emphasis on how IBCT is similar and different from the others To organize this discussion, we will describe six fundamental principles that we believe underlie all effective approaches to couple therapy. Specifically, all evidence-based couple therapies 1) operate from a coherent conceptual framework; 2) present a dyadic perspective of the couple's problems, 3) alter emotion-driven, dangerous, and disruptive behavior, 4) elicit avoided, emotion-based private behavior, 5) foster constructive communication, and 6) build upon strengths and encourage positive behavior. Within each of these principles, we will show some differences between therapies, with a focus on how IBCT differs from these other therapies, especially from the other behavioral therapies. Our analysis is based on Christensen (2010) and Benson, McGinn, and Christensen (2012). Then we will briefly describe the evidence supporting the effectiveness of IBCT.

FUNDAMENTAL PRINCIPLES OF EVIDENCE-BASED COUPLE THERAPY

1) Operate from a Coherent Conceptual Framework

Each of the evidence-based couple therapies has a coherent conceptual framework that it uses to understand the development and maintenance of couple distress as well as to intervene in that distress. The development of relationship distress has particularly challenged scientists because partners choose each other out of love and commit to each other because of the gratifications they get in the relationship. How does this early love and commitment deteriorate into dissatisfaction, separation, and divorce?

TBCT, which is based largely on Skinnerian principles of operant conditioning (Skinner, 1966) and focuses on the reinforcement that partners provide each other, suggests that the satisfaction that partners find in each other early in the relationship deteriorates because of two primary processes: reinforcement erosion (Jacobson & Margolin, 1979) and coercion (Patterson & Hops, 1972). Reinforcement erosion refers to a deterioration over time in the impact of the rewards that partners provide each other: the husband's jokes or the wife's compliments may lose some of their positive power through repetition. Coercion theory refers to an escalating process of negative and positive reinforcement that often occurs when partners have a conflict of interest. For example, a husband may pressure his wife to visit often with his mother, whom his wife does not like. The wife visits much more often than she would like because of negative reinforcement, which is the termination of an aversive stimulus (i.e., his unpleasant, pressuring behavior stops when she agrees to visit) and he continues to pressure her because of positive reinforcement, which is the onset of a positive stimulus (i.e., he gets rewarded for his pressuring behavior because she agrees to visit his mother). These behaviors may persist because of the intermittent reinforcement they provide (i.e., the wife sometimes but not always gives in to the husband's pressure). Also, escalation usually occurs in this process through the reinforcement principle of shaping: because the wife really does not enjoy visiting his mother, the husband may need to use increasing levels of pressure to obtain her compliance. From a reinforcement perspective, she is shaping him to be more and more coercive because her compliance comes only after higher levels of coercion. In addition, both members may use coercive processes (i.e., the wife may use coercive pressure to obtain compliance for her demands from the husband) so that over time, levels of negativity rise. Combined with reinforcement erosion, coercion leads to relationship distress. Based on this conceptualization of distress, TBCT employs treatment interventions to counteract reinforcement erosion by structuring more positive activities between partners and attempts to counteract coercive processes by teaching communication and problem-solving skills. Thus, a TBCT approach to Hank and Maria would note the loss of reinforcement, such as Maria's lack of appreciation for Hank's business success, and their coercive behavior toward each other, such as Hank's frequent pressure to get Maria to have sex. TBCT would directly counter these problems by assigning positive activities and by teaching better ways to communicate.

CBCT accepts much of the conceptual framework of TBCT but argues that TBCT provides an incomplete picture since it ignores the cognitive interpretation that each partner makes of their own and the other's behavior. CBCT suggests that attributions for behavior, expectations and standards for behavior, assumptions about behavior, and selective attention to certain behaviors influence partners' behavior and satisfaction (Baucom & Epstein, 1990). For example, partners may have unrealistic standards for relationship satisfaction, believing that the passionate days of early romance should maintain. Or when they face inevitable conflicts of interest, they may attribute their differences to a lack of love by the partner or to a fundamental incompatibility that means they aren't meant for each other. In a similar manner to how depressed people focus on the negative, partners may focus on the limitations of their relationship and their partner rather than on the positive parts of both. Therefore, in treatment, CBCT uses cognitive restructuring interventions, in which partners examine the evidence for their beliefs and assumptions, in addition to behavioral strategies designed to improve positive activities and train communication and problem-solving skills. Thus, a CBCT approach to Hank and Maria would note the possible unrealistic expectations Hank has about James and the attributions that Maria suggests for Hank's behavior (that he may not love James). In addition to the strategies of TBCT, CBCT would attempt to alter cognitions such as these.

Like TBCT and CBCT before it, IBCT is also based on a behavioral analytic model of relationships. However, IBCT differs from these two previous behavioral models in four important ways. First, IBCT focuses on broad themes and patterns in the couple's relationship rather than on specific behaviors and thoughts. For example, an IBCT analysis of Hank and Maria would note two important themes: the struggle over the parenting of James (i.e., Maria's anxious concern versus Hank's tough approach) and the struggle over intimacy (i.e., Hank wanting more attention and sexual intimacy from Maria while Maria is turned off to Hank as she struggles alone with her concerns about James). IBCT would also focus on the pattern of communication that characterizes both: Hank's critical approach to Maria regarding her child rearing and her lack of physical contact as well as Maria's avoidance and escape from Hank and involvement in child care for James.

Second, IBCT considers historical and distal causal factors as well as proximal causal factors. TBCT focuses on immediate proximal antecedents and consequences in the environment (e.g., the partner's angry comment is the antecedent for the other's withdrawal) while CBCT also includes cognitive antecedents and consequences (e.g., a partner's interpretation that the other is trying to humiliate him). Although IBCT does include these proximal antecedents and consequences, it also includes historical factors (e.g., one partner history of being cheated on) and distal factors (e.g., the culture of privacy that makes one partner embarrassed that the other told friends of their problems). For example, IBCT would note the history Maria had in her family of origin where the family was focused on the care of a special needs child. IBCT would suggest that this history plays a role, alongside the proximal factors of the special challenges that James presents, in Maria's focus on James.

A third difference between IBCT and both TBCT and CBCT is that IBCT puts greater attention on emotion and has a treatment goal of greater emotional acceptance between partners. Acceptance in IBCT refers to a change in the cognitive-emotional response that one partner has to the other. During an IBCT assessment, the therapist identifies emotional sensitivities in each partner and possible historical origins for those sensitivities and distinguishes the surface emotions that are likely most apparent to the partner from the hidden emotions that might not be apparent to the partner. For example, Hank was used to lots of attention and nurturance growing up from his mother, who tried to make up for the absence of Hank's father and had no other children demanding her attention. In his only other significant relationship, he experienced rejection from his girlfriend when her child was around and she wanted to focus on the child. These experiences have left Hank with sensitivity about being ignored and anxiety about being a priority for his partner. He often expresses anger and irritation (his surface emotion) when he feels ignored or rejected (his hidden emotion). For Maria's part, her family of origin focused heavily on the children, particularly because one child required so much extra attention. This history plus the difficulties that James has experienced has left her with lots of maternal anxiety. Is my child okay? Am I being a good mother and doing enough for him? Because Hank has dismissed and criticized her anxiety about James, she fears discussing it with him (i.e., hidden emotion) and instead distances herself emotionally from Hank (i.e., surface emotion). During the feedback session as well as through treatment, an IBCT therapist might highlight these emotional sensitivities so that Hank can look more sympathetically at Maria's anxieties about James and her fear of sharing it with him and Maria can look more sympathetically at Hank's anxieties about her connection to him. When partners are more empathetically aware of the other's emotional sensitivities and how they reveal these sensitivities in surface and hidden ways, they can often accept them more readily and handle the surface and hidden emotions more kindly. As a result, they are less likely to exacerbate those sensitivities, as they usually do before initiating couple therapy.

Although IBCT promotes emotional acceptance of partner's sensitivities and sometimes the behavior associated with those sensitivities, there is a limit to acceptance. There are certainly some actions in relationships that should never be accepted, such as violence. Also, partners have a right to define other actions as unacceptable, such as sex with another person. However, the garden-variety problems with which most couples have to confront are not based on unacceptable behavior but on action or inaction that is hurtful or upsetting to the other. Partners often unintentionally neglect the other, frustrate the other, fail to carefully attend to the other, or hurt the other's feelings. As Christensen, Doss, and Jacobson (2014) note: "The crimes of the heart are usually misdemeanors" (p. 68). With actions or inactions that are not egregious but still are painful, there are two ways to solve the problem: changing the actions or inactions or becoming more accepting of those actions or inactions. TBCT emphasizes changing the partner's behavior;

CBCT emphasizes changing both the behavior and the interpretation of the behavior (e.g., my partner is being selfish). IBCT puts an equal emphasis on the emotional reaction to the behavior as it does to the behavior itself. As we shall see later, intervention in IBCT can involve a joint exploration of each partner's emotional reactions that may help them differentiate, label, and thus understand their own emotional reactions and also understand their partner's emotional reactions, both of which can change the partner's offensive behavior and also modulate the receiver's reaction to it—that is, greater emotional acceptance.

A fourth difference between IBCT and both TBCT and CBCT is that IBCT emphasizes evocative and naturalistic shaping strategies of change [what Skinner (1966) called "contingency-shaped behavior"] while TBCT and CBCT both emphasize deliberate strategies of change (what Skinner called "rule-governed behavior"). To see the difference between the two, consider two ways of promoting reading in a child. In the first, you might explain to the child that reading will be very important for her and you set up a program where she is required to read a certain amount of time every night and then will get a valued reward. In the second strategy, you select books that are on topics that are already interesting for her and are easy for her to read, and you perhaps read with her initially but gradually remove yourself as she gets involved with the reading. Later you discuss her readings with her, so she can get a common reinforcement for reading, namely the ability to contribute to conversation. Both strategies could work. The first is more straightforward but can have the negative effect of making reading a chore for the child and under the control of external reinforcement (i.e., pressure by the parents) rather than internal reinforcement (i.e., the pleasure of reading itself); it is behavior governed by the rule the parents set up. The second is less straightforward and consequently more difficult to implement, but is more likely to bring about a child who likes to read and does read for her own sake. It is behavior shaped by the various contingencies in the situation (e.g., the funny story in the book, the engaging pictures in the book, the shared laughter with the parents over something in the book, the attention the child gets when she describes something she learned from the book). Certainly these two strategies could be combined, but they refer to quite different processes.

TBCT and CBCT rely on deliberate, rule-governed behavior-change processes to bring about change. TBCT helps couples define pleasing behavior that they could do for the other and gives them various instructions to increase the frequency of that behavior. TBCT also trains couples in communication and problem-solving communication and instructs them to use these skills when they are faced with difficulties. In addition to these strategies, CBCT helps couples identify problematic cognitions and goes about a deliberate process of altering these cognitions by having the couple look at the evidence for the cognition, by challenging the cognition, and by using other methods of cognitive restructuring. In contrast, IBCT relies primarily on contingency-shaped change through methods such as *empathic joining* and *unified detachment*, which we will discuss below. IBCT does sometimes use rule-governed strategies such as communication training, but there is a preference for contingency-shaped change for two reasons: (a) the change will likely feel more authentic to clients and less a function of instructions from the therapist and (b) the change is more likely to endure because the clients will feel more ownership of the change.

A newer version of CBCT, called Enhanced Cognitive-Behavioral Couple Therapy (ECBCT; Epstein & Baucom, 2002), reduces the theoretical differences between CBCT and IBCT. ECBCT gives greater attention to patterns and themes, includes a broader array of causal factors in its understanding of distress, and incorporates more emotional factors than does CBCT. However, the enhanced version doesn't focus on emotional sensitivities in the way IBCT does, and ECBCT maintains the strong focus on rule-governed strategies versus contingency-shaped strategies during treatment. Although ECBCT may be more reflective of how CBCT is practiced these days, there are no clinical trials we know of examining the efficacy of the enhanced version for couple problems or comparing it to other couple therapy approaches. Therefore, we will not refer to it further.

Although they have important differences, these three major behavioral approaches to couple therapy share a general, cognitive-behavioral theoretical framework. In contrast, the fourth major evidence-based couple therapy, Emotionally Focused Couple Therapy (EFCT), is based on attachment and systems theories. EFCT focuses on core emotional experiences that are usually conceptualized as "attachment injuries. . . . that damage the bond between partners and that, if not resolved, maintain negative cycles and attachment insecurities" (Johnson, 2015, p. 100). EFCT views distress in relationships as resulting from attachment insecurity and the consequent separation distress (Johnson, 2015, p. 103). EFCT would likely see attachment problems in both Hank and Maria. Hank may be anxiously attached and feel comfortable in relationships only when the other's affection is undivided and constant. As a result, Maria's attention to James and withdrawal from physical contact may be experienced by Hank as clear rejection. For her part, Maria may feel abandoned by Hank as she struggles with the anxieties and stresses of being a parent to James, which leads her to withdraw from Hank. EFCT would focus on the attachment injuries that have occurred in the relationship, such as Hank's sense of being rejected, especially sexually, and Maria's experience of being abandoned in her parenting, and attempt to bring about *soothing interactions* that can redefine the relationship and serve to heal some of the attachment injuries. The three major tasks of EFCT are to "1) to create a safe, collaborative alliance; 2) to access, reformulate, and expand the emotional responses that guide the couple's interactions; and 3) to restructure those interactions in the direction of the accessibility and responsiveness that build secure, lasting bonds" (Johnson, 2015, p. 105). Thus, EFCT has a very different conceptualization of couple distress than the three behavioral approaches and, as a result, somewhat different treatment objectives.

2) Present a Dyadic Perspective of the Couple's Problems

In western cultures, virtually all partners in enduring romantic relationships choose their partner voluntarily for the gratifications they currently experience and for future gratifications they expect or hope to experience. These partners love one another, or at least think so at the time (they may later decide otherwise), and try to maintain a rewarding relationship. They know that their intentions are good and their positive efforts sincere. However, they both inevitably experience firsthand the pain, disappointment or frustration that comes when the other acts on his or her own interests and inclinations that conflict with one's own. Although both are acutely aware of their own constructive actions to benefit the relationship as well as their negative reactions to their partner's actions or inactions, they are less aware of the other's constructive actions and of the impact of their own actions or inactions on the other. As a result, they each may go through a kind of reasoning like this: I loved him or her, I tried to make this relationship go well, and now I am in pain from what he or she has done (or not done). He or she must be doing something wrong—or not doing something right.

A common bias in our interpretation of events, called the fundamental attribution bias or the actor-observer hypothesis (Malle, 2006), is that we tend to explain our own behavior by referring to situational causes (e.g., I'm late because of traffic) but explain other's behavior by referring to dispositional or person causes (e.g., You're late because you didn't plan ahead). This bias is particularly strong when we explain negative behavior and when we explain the behavior of someone intimately connected to us (Malle, 2006). Thus, if we don't like some action of our partner, we are likely to explain this action by referring to characteristics of our partner rather than to situational factors, such as our own behavior. In unhappy couples in particular, partners tend to explain negative behavior by referring to undesirable traits in the other (Karney & Bradbury, 2000). Each blames the other for their difficulties. When they come to therapy, they may attempt to convince the therapist that their analysis of their difficulties—and their partner's culpability in those difficulties—is correct.

People unhappy in their relationship often conclude that their partner has one or more of the following three broad categories of undesirable characteristics that account for the relationship difficulties: their partners are (a) bad, such as selfish, untrustworthy, inconsiderate, or hostile; (b) crazy, as in mental or emotional characteristics such as personality problems, depression, anxiety, and addiction; or (c) inadequate, such as having deficits in important life skills such as having poor communication, poor parenting, poor money management skills, and an inability to love or be intimate. In short, and in rhyme, they see the partner as bad, mad, or inad-. For example, Maria wonders whether Hank is selfish or doesn't love James; Hank sees Maria as neurotically overinvolved with James.

These theories about the partner are never completely false; they almost always contain at least a grain of truth—and often much more than a grain. Unless one is delusional, a view that the partner is selfish probably means that the partner, at the very least, is not on the short list for sainthood. Likewise, a view that the partner is too emotional probably means that the partner has not achieved Buddha-like levels of mindfulness and peace. Thus, the problem with these theories is not that they are utterly false but rather that they refer to static characteristics of the other and ignore all other variables, particularly the interactional dynamics between the partners. Even selfish partners have at times been loving and giving; even overly emotional partners have at times been calm and reasonable. A true analysis of each partner's behavior would consider the dynamic interplay between them that elicits selfishness and emotionality at some points and love and calmness at others.

Another problem with partners' theories about their problems is that these theories lead to overt or covert accusation and blame, as each partner lets the other know the purported cause of the objectionable behavior and their evidence for their causal analysis. The partner of course is usually resistant to this analysis and offers their own competing, opposing analysis. Partners now are faced with two problems: the existence of some problematic behavior on the one hand and conflict about the causes of that behavior on the other. Sometimes the anger and argument about the causes of the behavior are more intense than the anger and argument about the problematic behavior itself because the conflict about the causes speaks to the worth and value of each: is he a selfish person or not? Is she emotionally disturbed or not? Anger and defensiveness over these issues can drown out any anger or defensiveness about a particular objectionable behavior.

As a counter to this individualistic view of the couple's problems, each of the evidence-based treatments offers a systemic, dyadic analysis of couple problems (principle number 2) that emphasizes how both partners may contribute unwittingly to their difficulties and how each is in some ways a victim and architect of the system they have jointly created. All three of the behavioral approaches have a combined formal feedback and treatment-planning session right after a short assessment phase. In this session, the therapist offers an alternative, dyadic analysis of the couple's problems. TBCT was based in large part on social exchange theory (Thibaut & Kelley, 1959), and therapists might discuss the mutual reinforcement that partners have in the past obtained from each other and how they have gotten into a pattern of *negative reciprocity* in which they are exchanging negative behavior (negative actions begetting negative actions) instead of the positive actions that characterized them in the past. CBCT therapists would also discuss these negative interaction patterns but would in addition describe the cognitive factors, such as partner's attributions, that play into the difficulty the couple is having. IBCT also offers the couple an analysis of their core concerns, an analysis that explains how individual factors, such as fundamental differences between them and emotional sensitivities that each has, along with contextual factors, account for the pattern of interaction in which they are stuck as they struggle with their core issues. Later we will describe this analysis in depth. EFCT doesn't have a formal feedback session as in the behavioral approaches, but early on in therapy highlights to the couple the negative interaction cycle in which the couple is involved and the attachment-oriented emotions that they believe underlie the cycle. When EFCT therapists discuss the therapy contract, they discuss the purpose of therapy as shifting this negative cycle so partners can have discussions that feel emotionally safer and more supportive. In various ways, each of the evidence-based couple therapies moves the discussion away from faults in one or both partners to a discussion of interaction cycles and the factors that contribute to those interaction cycles.

A second important way that evidence-based couple therapies foster a dyadic understanding of relationship problems between partners is by developing a strong alliance with each partner, so that both partners experience understanding and support from the therapist and don't experience the therapist as allied with one versus the other. This process means shifting partners away from their individualistic analysis, such as not encouraging or validating their view that the other is selfish or emotionally immature. Instead, this process refocuses them on their interaction while simultaneously validating each partner's emotional distress about their interaction with their partner. This way, partners can not only understand cognitively that their problems are mutually created and maintained but also experience the therapist as validating them both.

3) Alter Emotion-Driven, Dangerous, and Disruptive Behavior

Intimate romantic relationships often create people's most positive and most negative emotional reactions. Love, attraction, and caring are bedfellows with anger, repulsion, and resentment. Distressed couples are often characterized by emotional dysregulation (Snyder, Simpson, & Hughes, 2006) so that strong negative emotions are particularly evident in these couples. Sometimes these negative emotions lead to dangerous acts of physical violence, sexual coercion, physical destruction, or restrictions on the other's freedom, such as not letting someone leave the room or house, controlling their money, or limiting their contact with friends and family. Substantial proportions of community samples of young couples report physical violence by one or the other or both. For example, a representative sample of couples with young children from a county in New York State indicated that 37% of males and 44% of females had been physically aggressive in the last year (O'Leary & Williams, 2006). Relationship discord is a risk factor for violence (Stith, Rosen, McCollum & Thomsen, 2004), so we might expect even higher levels of violence in clinical samples. Indeed, O'Leary (2008) writes that, based on a series of studies, 40% to 70% of couples who seek marital therapy report some physical aggression in their relationship.

Because couple therapy addresses each partner's concerns and the conflicts that they confront, therapy can trigger some of these strong emotions. Although is unlikely that one partner would physically assault the other, sexually coerce the other, destroy the other's property, or restrict the other's freedom during a therapy session, the strong emotions that therapy arouses could continue after the session has ended or increase as partners continue to discuss their difficulties after leaving the session, setting the stage for one or more of these dangerous acts. In that case, couple therapy could have unintentionally facilitated some dangerous and disruptive act. Because of this chance, there is some consensus in the field that couples with dangerous levels of violence should not be treated in couple therapy until the violence is under control (Simpson, Atkins, Gattis, & Christensen, 2008). Couples should be assessed early on for the presence of dangerous levels of violence, and partners in those couples should be referred to individual therapy or couple therapy that is specifically focused on dealing with violence (Epstein, Werlinich, & LaTaillade, 2015; Stith & McCollum, 2011). Later we will discuss assessment procedures used in IBCT to ascertain violence and destructiveness and the criteria that IBCT uses to determine if couples are unsuitable for therapy because of violence or destructiveness.

Less serious than physical violence but still disruptive are acts of verbal abuse, yelling, interruption, and refusal to talk or listen. All couple therapies must exert some control over these behaviors or else therapy cannot proceed effectively. Controlling these behaviors in the session is easier than controlling them out of the session. In the session, clients are more likely to contain themselves because they are in the presence of the therapist and want this therapist to view them in a positive light. Also, the therapist can refocus a conversation away from criticism and attacks or referee the conversation so partners don't interrupt or shout over each other. Therapists can ask the clients to talk directly to the therapist rather than to each other so the therapist can translate some of what each is saying in a way that the other can hear. Also, by talking directly to the therapist, the clients may be less likely to be as strident or as attacking as they might be if talking directly to the other. In addition, the partner listening to the other talk to the therapist may be less inclined to give negative reactions such as rolling eyes and shaking his or her head. Even if the listening partner does give those negative nonverbal reactions, the partner talking to the therapist may be less affected by them. Finally, as a last resort, the therapist can separate the pair and talk to each individually in a way that calms them down before bringing them back together again.

Controlling disruptive behavior outside of the session is more difficult than controlling it in the session. The therapist may guide the couple through an analysis of how their conflicts typically escalate and have them problem solve ways they could prevent that escalation. A common practice is to discuss *time-out* with the couple and come up with a plan for how they will end discussion of a conflict that is getting out of control. For example, the couple may agree about ways to terminate an interaction without further inflaming it (e.g., by indicating an intent to discontinue the discussion temporarily without imparting a final attack), agree that they will return to the interaction at a later point so the partner wanting further discussion does not feel shut out, or agree to postpone the discussion until the next session of therapy.

TBCT and CBCT both take a rule-governed approach to third principle of altering emotion-driven disruptive behavior. For both behavior in and outside the session, they provide guidelines for communication, such as using *"I" statements* to talk about their feelings and not interrupting their partner or not engaging in character assassination. These therapies teach time-out to control behavior outside of the session. EFCT certainly attempts to *restructure interactions* but not in a rule-governed way. EFCT therapists don't usually give guidelines and rules for good communication nor teach time strategies. Instead, they attempt to restructure interactions in the sessions by helping partners focus on their own emotional reactions and explore those reactions, eventually getting in contact with their more vulnerable reactions related to attachment, voicing these vulnerable emotions, and facilitating a positive partner response. By helping the couple experience a different interaction in the session that results in a *bonding event*, EFCT theory is that couples will have more productive and less destructive interaction outside of therapy.

The preferred strategy in IBCT to alter emotion-driven behavior, as in EFCT, is experiential or contingency-shaped change. IBCT tries to bring about a different interactional experience using strategies such as empathic joining and unified detachment that we will describe below. Additionally, IBCT can use the rule-governed strategies of other behavioral approaches, such as teaching time-out strategies or doing problem solving. However, rule-governed strategies in IBCT are more client generated than therapist generated. For example, IBCT might lead a couple through a behavior chain analysis of how their conflicts get out of control. The therapist might seek the couple's ideas about what they might do to prevent escalation at different points in the interaction, given the emotional arousal they are likely to feel in those moments. Then the therapists might encourage the couple to try to implement the ideas that they themselves generated.

4) Elicit Avoided, Emotion-Based Private Behavior

It is a natural and usually adaptive human tendency to avoid painful and scary events. We avoid getting too close to a fire or instinctively duck when something comes hurling our way. Although beneficial in the short run, avoidance can often be maladaptive in the long run. We can avoid going to the dentist or doctor because it is unpleasant and thus let a dental or medical problem worsen. This human tendency to avoid, in both its adaptive and maladaptive ways, can affect our communication with our partner. We may wisely avoid discussion of unpleasant topics with our partner, such as politics or religion, because the discussion would just lead to unnecessary tension and disagreement. However, we may avoid discussion of topics upon which we could and ideally should act. Consider a couple that is facing a painful reality, such as financial difficulties or an increasing distance and alienation between them. Discussion could be risky in that it could lead to accusation and defensiveness, but avoiding discussion could prevent any ameliorative actions, causing the issue to intensify over time. Consider also a couple that is facing a problem in one partner, such as his alcohol or drug use, her alarming physical symptoms and reluctance to visit a physician, or his sexual performance difficulties. Discussion of these topics could be uncomfortable at the least or at worst lead to accusation and blame by the partner without the problem and denial and resistance from the partner with the problem. Yet without discussion, serious problems may go unattended and increase in magnitude or severity.

Another kind of avoidance occurs around discussion of everyday emotional reactions to the vicissitudes of intimate life together. In partners' daily lives, there will inevitably be times of disconnection, miscommunication, lack of responsiveness, rejection, injury, and rebuff. Partners may be hesitant to discuss these everyday incidents in order to protect the other, to avoid a potential conflict, or to avoid revealing how vulnerable they are to the other. Jill may be reluctant to tell Josh that she doesn't like the aggressive way he drives because she doesn't want to hurt his feelings or start a fight. Marcus may only react with anger and distance after he sees Beth at a party flirting with another man, never voicing his simmering concerns that Beth doesn't find him attractive. Ben may only distance himself from James after James reacts with lack of interest when told about an incident at work that was significant for Ben; Ben may never reveal how badly he feels that something important to him seemed so unimportant to James. In the case of our couple Hank and Maria, Hank reacts with anger and distance to Maria's lack of interest in sexual contact but doesn't reveal how rejected he feels. Maria withdraws from Hank and struggles with her concerns about James alone but doesn't reveal to Hank how alone she feels as a mother. They each have strong, hidden emotions that they don't share.

All of the evidence-based couple therapies attempt to address these avoided issues (principle number 4) but in different ways. TBCT relies on the rule-governed approach of communication training with couples, which teaches couples how to make appropriate feeling statements. These statements ideally follow the format of "I feel X when you do Y in situation Z." For the "feel X" part of the model, the couple is taught about emotions and how to label them through didactic instruction, such as information about the distinction between thoughts and feelings and the use of feeling charts to assist in the labeling of feelings. For the "do Y" part of the model, the couple is taught how to distinguish between specific behaviors versus broad character traits and to focus on the former rather than the latter. Finally, for the "in situation Z" part of the model, the couple is taught to identify specific occasions when the problematic behavior occurs and refer to those occasions rather than saying or implying that the partner does these behaviors "all the time" or in every situation. The couple is also taught a formal *speaker and listener* structure in which to voice these feelings so both get a chance to speak and get heard by the other (we will discuss communication training in more detail in Chapter 11).

CBCT borrows this strategy of communication training from TBCT and additionally encourages couples to include thoughts in their statements of feelings. An ideal feeling statement in TBCT might be "I feel neglected when we are at a party and you talk with other people and don't include me in the conversations." Adding thoughts to this might include an additional comment: "It makes me think that you don't believe that I have much to contribute to the conversation."

EFCT doesn't do communication training at all but, as its name implies, puts a major emphasis on emotion because emotion is key to understanding attachment. "Emotion is primary in organizing attachment behaviors and the ways self and other are experienced in intimate relationships" (Johnson, 2015, p. 105). Not all emotion is emphasized. "[I]t is important to distinguish between different types of emotions, and understand which emotions need to be acknowledged and expressed to resolve conflict, which need to be bypassed, contained or soothed, which need to be explored, and which need to be transformed" (R. N. Goldman & Greenberg, 2007, p. 123). EFCT therapists focus on emotions that are related to attachment needs, attempt to get one partner to voice those emotions, and encourage the other partner to be supportive of that disclosure. This process can lead to a softening, which "involves a vulnerable request, by a usually hostile spouse, for reassurance or comfort, or for some other attachment need to be met. When the other, now accessible spouse, is able to respond to this request, then both spouses are mutually responsive and bonding interactions can occur" (Johnson, 2008, p. 123).

IBCT addresses avoided emotion-based topics primarily through a strategy we call empathic joining. This strategy, which we will describe in detail in Chapter 6, involves attention to the emotional reactions and emotion-based language of each partner. IBCT therapists attend first to the surface emotions partners reveal, such as Hank's evident frustration at the lack of sexual contact or Maria's frustration that Hank criticizes her approach to James. However, IBCT therapists try to move the partners to also reveal hidden emotions that they may have rarely or never discussed with their partner at all or at length, such as Maria feeling alone in her struggles as a young parent and Hank feeling rejected as a partner. This new emotional material may alter the interaction between partners and their view of one another in a contingency-shaped way. Empathic joining in IBCT is similar to the way EFCT approaches emotions but with several key differences: (a) IBCT doesn't assume that attachment-related emotions underlie all relationship problems and thus does not struggle to find attachment-related emotions, (b) IBCT takes a functional approach to understanding emotional expression and thus seeks expression of emotions that aren't a regular part of the couple's pattern of interaction and could alter that interaction (e.g., although the expression of soft, vulnerable emotions often alters interaction in a new and better direction, sometimes hard, angry emotions can do the same), and finally, (c) IBCT is also open to doing communication training even though that is not its first line of intervention.

5) Foster Constructive Communication

One of the most common presenting complaints in couple therapy is communication problems (Doss, Simpson, & Christensen, 2004). Often couples get into distressing and fruitless arguments when they deal with particular issues, such as money, sex, and in-laws. Therefore, a common goal in couple therapy is to improve communication. This goal, reflected in principle 5, focuses on everyday problems and their resolution and thus goes beyond the efforts in the third principle to alter disruptive and destructive behavior and beyond the efforts in the fourth principle to elicit avoided, emotion-based private behavior. Certainly the ability to discuss everyday problems constructively could be beneficial in limiting disruptive and destructive behavior, but the focus is on the communication around these problems rather than on the disruptive and destructive behavior. Also, discussion of everyday problems may be affected by strong emotions that are sometimes avoided, but again, the focus is on the everyday problems and problem solving around them rather than on the avoided emotions.

A key intervention in TBCT is problem-solving training. As discussed above (and in Chapter 11), couples are taught to express their feelings about an issue by using the strategies of communication training. Once couples have achieved some mastery of these communication training strategies, they are taught the rational approach of problem-solving training. This process involves defining the problem clearly, offering a variety of possible solutions by *brainstorming solutions*, evaluating the pros and cons of these solutions, negotiating a particular solution, trying out this solution, and then evaluating it and possibly revising it based on the outcome. CBCT adopted problem-solving strategies, as well as communication-training strategies, from TBCT.

EFCT does not focus on negotiation or problem solving. "Change in EFT is not seen in terms of the attainment of cognitive insight, problem-solving or negotiation skills" (p. 113, Johnson, 2015). The emphasis on communication is to create softening and responsiveness by the partners that will in turn lead to bonding events. As a result, partners are believed to engage in a different interactional dance that will lead to more effective couple functioning.

IBCT can include problem-solving training and discussions, but IBCT is careful to avoid those discussions until the emotional climate will facilitate them. Often couples attempt to engage in problem solving when they are angry and resentful of each other (i.e., showing their surface emotions). Engaging in problem solving in those situations often leads to coercive attempts to impose solutions and, at best, begrudging agreement with the solution. Once chosen, these halfhearted agreements often end in failure to implement the solution or, even if implemented, failure for the solution to make a meaningful difference in the relationship—often because it solves a derivative problem rather than the central, underlying problem. Couples are much more likely to achieve some workable solution to their problems when they feel emotionally safe with each other and can open up about their hidden emotions—which in turn helps couples identify the core problem to be addressed. This emotional safety also helps create a collaborative set, a cooperative attitude in which they both seek a solution acceptable to both. However, we find that when couples have reached the point at which they feel emotionally connected to one another and have a collaborative set to work on problems, they can often solve the problems on their own; they don't need a separate communication intervention. If still needed at that point, IBCT therapists can engage in the formal problem-solving strategies of TBCT, but a more informal approach that adjusts to the style of the couple is preferred. For example, rather than carefully separating the problem-definition and problem-solution phase as required in TBCT, IBCT allows couples to vacillate between the two, perhaps discovering that a potential solution they are considering doesn't solve the problem because they haven't really zeroed in on the problem of concern.

6) Build upon Strengths and Encourage Positive Behavior

All evidence-based couple therapies try to build upon strengths and encourage positive behavior. However, the manner in which they do this and the kinds of strengths and positive behaviors they emphasize differ. All of the behavioral couple therapies, TBCT, CBCT, and IBCT, ask about strengths during the assessment phase, such as what attracted partners to each other and what keeps them in the relationship despite its difficulties, and review those strengths during the feedback session. This communicates some hope to couples: despite their difficulties, they still have some strengths worth preserving. It also communicates that a focus on positive behavior will be part of the treatment. Although EFCT does not have a formal feedback session, during assessment, EFCT therapists often ask about what attracted partners to each other, thus highlighting the positive characteristics that each sees in the other.

During the treatment phase of couple therapy, all of the evidence-based approaches try to facilitate positive behavior between partners, but the kinds of positive behavior they emphasize differs. During the early days of TBCT, long lists of discrete, pleasing behaviors that partners could do for and with one another were developed through the Spouse Observation Checklist (Wills, Weiss, & Patterson, 1974) and were focused on during treatment. Some items referred to behaviors that "I did" with comparable items referring to the same behaviors by spouse while other items referred to things "we did." Example items of each of these categories are: "I comforted my spouse when s/he was upset," "Spouse prepared a favorite food for me," and "We engaged in sexual intercourse." The emphasis was on discrete, concrete, everyday behaviors rather than general or abstract actions (e.g., My spouse was loving to me) or rare behaviors (e.g., I gave my partner an expensive gift). CBCT adopted this emphasis on concrete, discrete behaviors but added a cognitive element. For example, Baucom, Epstein, and Rankin (1995) describe a case in which a husband agreed to talk more with his wife after dinner and complied with that request; the wife reported that these conversations were not gratifying because she believed the husband did not really want to talk to her but complied only to look good in front of the therapist. This discovery "initiated a discussion of her attributions for her husband's recent behavior changes that were more relationship focused" (Baucom et al., 1995, p. 76). Because of its focus on attachment, EFCT tries to promote attachment-related positive events, in particular partner-bonding experiences that result from the expression of vulnerability by one and responsiveness by the other.

Rather than these lists of discrete, positive behaviors or attachment-related positive events, IBCT emphasizes the positive behavior that is related to the fundamental themes and struggles that bedevil the couple and that are conceptualized in the IBCT analysis we will describe below. Even the most distressed couples sometimes handle their difficult issues better, and those occasions are instructive for the couple. For example, if Hank and Maria had a more productive discussion about James or had an occasion when they were more physically affectionate or sexually responsive to each other, the IBCT therapist would discuss those positive events in detail with Hank and Maria, helping them see how and why they were able to have more meaningful interaction in their areas of difficulty. As another example, consider a couple that often gets into a pattern of argument in which the wife tries to give her partner corrective feedback and he gets defensive. IBCT would highlight those interactions in which the couple handles this struggle better, so that the couple learns from their own experience how they interact in ways that make the husband feel more competent and that he has a say in things and that make the wife feel like she can voice her opinions and get heard. IBCT therapists believe that the fundamental conflicts with which couples struggle mask important vulnerabilities in each (e.g., a husband's sense that he can't do anything right in her eyes; a wife's sense that she never gets heard) and that if these conflicts are addressed successfully, the way is opened for greater intimacy between them and thus more positive interaction. For some couples these fundamental conflicts may be related to attachment issues, and for some couples they may be related to items on the Spouse Observation Checklist, but for IBCT the fundamental conflicts and any positive events related to them are the focus.

Not only do the various evidence-based couple therapies focus on different kinds of strengths and positive events, they attempt to promote these strengths and positive behaviors in different ways. TBCT and CBCT tend to use rule-governed strategies. In the behavior exchange strategy of TBCT, there are three phases: a generation phase in which lists of positive behaviors are created, an implementation phase in which partners are encouraged to engage in these behaviors, and a review phase in which partners discuss the impact of these behaviors and express appreciation to each other. In the first phase, partners are often asked to make a list of behaviors they could do for or with the other that would be pleasing to the other, often using lists such as that from the Spouse Observation Checklist (Wills, Weiss, & Patterson, 1974). Partners then react to those lists, indicating which ones in fact are most pleasing to them. In the implementation phase, partners are encouraged to engage in these behaviors by designating certain days as each one's *caring day,* when the other tries to increase those positive behaviors, or by getting partners to agree to increase the frequency of those behaviors over the next week. In the final phase, the partners in therapy discuss their experience with this assignment, discussing the impact of these positive events and expressing appreciation to the other. CBCT has largely adopted this strategy from TBCT, but may reject the term behavior exchange since the interventions don't usually involve an explicit quid pro quo agreement. These strategies can be seen as a kind of couple-level behavioral-activation strategy.

In contrast to the rule-governed approach of these behavioral therapies, EFCT and IBCT employ a more experiential approach, or what IBCT would call a contingency-shaped approach. Both approaches attempt to create meaningful positive events in the session by creating a safe emotional space where partners can disclose deeply held feelings that they may not have disclosed before (or at least so clearly) and where partners can not only hear those emotional reactions but respond to them supportively. In IBCT, this is achieved through the intervention called empathic joining. During treatment, the IBCT therapist also is careful to spend some time in all or most sessions focusing on the most positive or most meaningful interaction between the two of them since the last session. This discussion gives the therapist a chance to highlight what is still positive in the relationship that happens naturally between the pair outside of the session. However, IBCT can also include the strategies of TBCT and CBCT although usually not as a first-line interaction.

EVIDENCE BASE FOR IBCT

The empirical evidence supporting the effectiveness of IBCT in improving relationships comes from four sources: (a) basic scientific research that supports specific interventions used in IBCT, (b) randomized clinical trials that examine the efficacy of face-to-face IBCT, (c) effectiveness research on the impact of IBCT when implemented in the U.S. Department of Veteran's Affairs mental health system, and (d) clinical trials of the efficacy of the online program OurRelationship.com, which is described in Chapter 14 and which is based on IBCT principles. When we discuss specific IBCT interventions, such as empathic joining in Chapter 6 and unified detachment in Chapter 7, we will review some of the basic scientific research that supports the impact of these interventions. Here we will only review applied research that looks at the impact of IBCT (or the online OurRelationship program) as a package.

There have been several studies on the impact of face-to-face IBCT. Two early, small, randomized clinical trials indicated that IBCT brings about better outcomes than a wait list control condition (Wimberly, 1998) and that IBCT is equal to or better than the most researched treatment for couple therapy at the time, TBCT (Jacobson, Christensen, Prince, Cordova, & Eldridge, 2000). Subsequently, we conducted a two-site study comparing IBCT to TBCT that is unique in two ways: (a) it is the largest randomized clinical trial of face-to-face couple therapy for relationship distress ever conducted and (b) it has the longest follow-up of any clinical trial of couple therapy. Based on initial results at post treatment (Christensen, Atkins, Berns, Wheeler, Baucom, & Simpson,, 2004), 2-year follow-up (Christensen, Atkins, Yi, Baucom & George, , 2006) and 5-year follow-up (Christensen, Atkins, Baucom, & Yi, 2010), IBCT demonstrated that it is as effective as TBCT at termination and shows significantly better maintenance over 2 years of follow-up. Also, the effect size for IBCT at post treatment (Cohen's $d = 0.90$) is higher than the range (Cohen's $d = 0.59$ to 0.84) typically found in couple therapy studies (Shadish & Baldwin, 2003, 2005).* Based on this body of research, the U.S. Department of Veterans' Affairs adopted IBCT as its evidence-based couple therapy for relationship distress in 2010. In the

---

* The effect size for IBCT is a within-group effect size while those from the meta-analyses are between-group effect sizes, typically comparing treatment to no-treatment controls. Thus, these results should not normally be compared directly. However, a review of 17 studies (Baucom, Hahlweg, & Kuschel, 2003) showed no change over time in control groups, so a comparison between the two types of effect sizes is reasonable.

10 years since that time, approximately 500 VA therapists have gone through an extensive training program in IBCT, consisting of a several-day workshop followed by 6–8 months of weekly supervision while they see couples in their home setting. As part of this supervision, the therapist trainees audio record at least 20 sessions of couple therapy and get feedback from their IBCT-trained supervisor. Over a thousand couples have been seen by these therapists during their training period and many more couples have been seen after the therapists completed their training. Data collected from couples during the training period show that these IBCT therapists were able to bring about improved functioning in their couples even though the therapists were learning as they went along. Not surprisingly, the effect sizes for these couples is somewhat smaller than the effect sizes seen in the clinical trial (Christensen & Glynn, 2019), even when couples have approximately the same number of sessions (e.g., effect sizes around Cohen's $d = 0.50$).

Finally, there are three clinical trials of the online program OurRelationship.com, which is based on IBCT principles (Doss et al., 2016; Doss et al., 2020; Roddy, Rothman, & Doss, 2018) and which will be described in Chapter 14. These studies include over 1400 couples and thus represent the largest clinical trials ever conducted on a couple intervention for distressed couples. Furthermore, these studies have been done with the most diverse sample of couples, including one study of only low-income couples (Doss et al., 2020), to ever participate in a randomized clinical trial. These studies, which we describe in more detail in Chapter 14, have documented the effectiveness of OurRelationship.com to improve couple satisfaction as well as to positively affect individual functioning, such as depression and anxiety. In addition to these overall effects of IBCT and OurRelationship.com, there are additional studies that look at specific effects of these interventions, such as their impact on violence or infidelity. We will mention this research as we discuss those particular topics in later chapters.

This book is meant for clinicians who want to learn about IBCT. Therefore, we don't dwell on the research literature, with its varied methodologies and assessment instruments. Our goal at this point is simply to show that a substantial body of research documents the effectiveness of IBCT and of the online OurRelationship program that is based on IBCT principles. For those who want to take a deeper look into this literature, we have included an Appendix, which provides citations to all of the current research literature specifically on IBCT and OurRelationship.com.

SUMMARY

In this chapter we have focused on how IBCT is similar to and different from three other evidence-based couple therapies: TBCT, CBCT, and EFCT. All of these evidence-based couple therapies, including IBCT, rely on six fundamental principles. They all (1) operate from a coherent conceptual framework; (2) present a dyadic perspective of the couple's problems; (3) alter emotion-driven, dangerous and disruptive behavior; (4) elicit avoided, emotion-based private behavior; (5) foster constructive communication; and (6) build upon strengths and encourage positive behavior.

The behavioral approaches naturally share a similar behavior-analytic theoretical background. IBCT differs from the other behavioral approaches in several ways: (a) a greater emphasis on broad patterns and themes versus specific behaviors and thoughts, (b) the inclusion of historical and distal causal variables as well as proximal causal variables in its analysis of these themes and patterns, (c) a greater emphasis on emotional reactions and emotional acceptance versus concrete behavior change, and (d) a greater emphasis on contingency-shaped change (i.e., experiential change) versus rule-governed change (i.e., deliberate change). In contrast to CBCT, ECBCT, which we briefly mentioned earlier, gives greater attention to broad patterns and themes, historical and distal variables, and emotion than traditional CBCT. However, it gives less attention to emotion than IBCT and relies primarily on rule-governed strategies in its treatment approach rather than on the contingency-shaped strategies of IBCT. Beyond these broad differences in emphasis, IBCT differs from each of the other approaches in the specific ways that it implements these principles above.

Unlike the behavioral approaches, which share a common theoretical framework, EFCT is based on quite different theoretical grounds, namely attachment theory. Although IBCT recognizes that attachment issues may be predominant in some couples, it considers a broader range of issues and patterns that may plague couple's lives. IBCT and EFCT do share a similar emphasis on evocative, nondeliberate change, what IBCT therapists call contingency-shaped change. Some of the strategies of IBCT can seem in practice to be almost identical to those used in EFCT. However, while EFCT rejects rule-governed strategies such as communication training, IBCT does incorporate these strategies when appropriate, although not usually as its first line of intervention.

Now that we have seen broadly and conceptually how IBCT is similar to and different from other evidence-based couple therapies, we can focus exclusively on IBCT. In Part 2 we describe how IBCT therapists evaluate and conceptualize couple difficulties and provide feedback to the couple about their difficulties. In Part 3 we describe how IBCT therapists treat those difficulties through acceptance-based strategies, and in Part 4 we describe how IBCT therapists treat those difficulties through change-oriented strategies. In Part 5 we describe how we adapt IBCT for populations that differ in gender, sexual orientation, culture, ethnicity, race, and income as well as how we adapt IBCT for special problems such as violence, sexual problems, infidelity, and individual psychopathology. Finally, we describe new developments in IBCT, specifically OurRelationship.com, our online IBCT-based program for couples and individuals, and how this program can be integrated into a condensed, eight-session format of IBCT. First, in the next chapter, we examine specifically how IBCT therapists understand how partners who love each other and voluntarily chose each other become so distressed and upset with each other.

PART 2

Assessment, Clinical Formulation, and Feedback in IBCT

3

❧

Couple Distress from an IBCT Perspective

TO UNDERSTAND HOW IBCT therapists view couple distress and the causes of it, we will first briefly consider four broad questions: (a) what is a relationship, (b) what is relationship distress, (c) what factors influence relationships, and (d) what factors create relationship distress. We draw from the influential work of a group of nine social and clinical psychologists, including Christensen, who set forth a conceptual framework for understanding relationships in the early 1980s (Kelley et al., 1983; reprinted in 2002).

WHAT IS A RELATIONSHIP?

We can think of the stuff of each person's life as being a complicated string of public and private behavior. Public behavior would include anything observable by someone else, such as actions, words, and even subtle physiological responses, such as blushing and perspiration. Private behavior would include anything that the person is aware of or could be made aware of but that is not directly observable by others, such as thoughts, feelings, sensations, imaginings, and so on. These strings of private and public behavior can influence each other as when a sensation of being hot initiates behavior to move to a cooler spot or when talking to someone triggers feelings about that someone.

We define a relationship as existing between two people to the extent that they have interaction, meaning they directly influence each other through their public behavior. We assume there is no such thing as extra sensory perception, so we can only be affected by what the other observably does. This definition of relationship fits the normal intuitive sense about what a relationship is; no one would reasonably argue that two people who had never met or communicated have a relationship. However, this definition also excludes what some might call an extremely one-sided relationship. If a teenager follows a pop star on social media and is affected by what the star does but the pop star is not affected by anything the teenager does, we would not call that a relationship. This definition also does not propose any boundaries about what amount of interaction is required for a relationship. We might intuitively believe that partners must have a certain level of interaction in order to call that interaction a relationship. Partners sometimes argue about whether they are indeed in a relationship because they have so little interaction. However, such boundaries are arbitrary. One can have a meaningful relationship with the most limited of interaction (e.g., someone saves you from a fire, you never see them again, but you forever remember their face and feel grateful) or a relatively meaningless relationship with considerable interaction (e.g., you see and acknowledge the letter carrier frequently over many years but don't even know his or her name).

Although relationships are defined by interaction, and interaction is by definition observable, some of the most important features of a relationship, particularly a romantic relationship, are the private behaviors triggered by that interaction. The back and forth between one person and another can trigger strong feelings of love and attraction as well as anger and jealousy. This private behavior—the thoughts and feelings and sensations that partners have—can in turn trigger interaction, as in Figure 3.1 below.

WHAT IS A DISTRESSED RELATIONSHIP?

Now that we understand what we mean by a relationship, we can define what we mean by a distressed or dissatisfied relationship. It is simply a relationship in which (a) some significant portion of the interaction regularly leads to

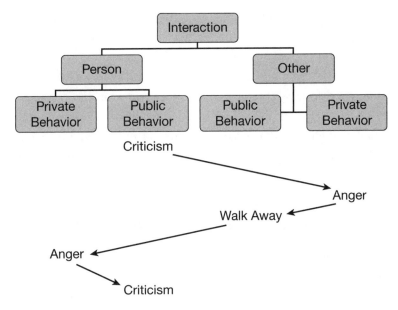

Figure 3.1: Example of a Conflictual Interaction

negative emotional reactions and the associated negative appraisals in one or both and/or (b) some significant portion of the interaction regularly leads to an absence of expected positive reactions and the associated appraisals in one or both. Thus, a distressed relationship is one in which a significant portion of the interaction regularly or repetitively leads to emotions such as anger, resentment, and disappointment, and/or a significant portion of the interaction regularly or repetitively leads to an absence of emotions such as joy, love, and anticipation so that one or both partners conclude that they are unhappy or dissatisfied. We say *significant portion* and *regularly or repetitively* because couples don't expect everything to always be fine but if, for example, they regularly argue about money or if their sex life is unfulfilling, they may conclude they are unhappy. Normally, partners in distressed relationships experience both a surplus of negative emotional reactions to their interactions and a paucity of positive emotional reactions to their interactions. However, distressed relationships may be characterized more by the presence of negative or by the absence of positive reactions. For example, a couple may be relatively free of conflict and work well together but feel they've "lost that loving feeling"—they feel just like platonic friends or roommates. Note also that the way we define relationship distress is always in terms of each person's judgment or appraisal. Partners within a couple and across couples have different emotional reactions to the same interaction and different tolerances for negative emotional reactions and different expectations for positive emotional reactions, so that what one couple or partner in a couple might conclude is an unhappy relationship, another couple or the partner might conclude is an okay or even good relationship.

WHAT CAUSAL FACTORS INFLUENCE A RELATIONSHIP?

What are the broad factors that influence the functioning of a relationship and by extension contribute to a dissatisfied relationship? Kelley and colleagues (1983; 2002) suggested five broad categories of causal factors that influence the relationship between two people: (a) the characteristics of Partner 1, (b) the characteristics of Partner 2, (c) the external physical environment in which their relationship exists, (d) the external social environment in which their relationship exists, and finally (f) emergent features of the relationship itself. The characteristics of the partners refer to obvious factors such as their personality, their physical attractiveness, their social skill, their social status, and their interests and preferences, but it also refers to the less obvious factor of their interpersonal history, such as one partner's history of being cheated on in previous relationships or the other partner's history of being physically abused by their parents. In short, the personal characteristics and individual history are factors partners bring to their relationship and that can influence that relationship. The external physical environment refers to such features of their circumstances as the poor neighborhood in which they live while the social environment refers to such features as the noisy in-laws that they have frequent contact with and also the cultural environment, such as the gender roles that influence how they structure their relationship. Finally, the emergent properties of the relationship refer to important developments in the relationship that influence subsequent interaction between the two of them, such as an agreement they make to share their finances, a norm they develop that he cooks and she cleans, or a shared joke they have that brings smiles to their faces when they encounter things that remind them of it.

The associations among these five components are not unidirectional; each can influence the other. For example, the physical and social environment could be very stressful for the couple but they could move and thus change both. One partner's characteristics, such as distrust because of a history of being cheated on in previous relationships, could lead to trust issues in the current relationship, but the reassuring nature of their interactions around trust could resolve those issues and lead to greater trust in the previously distrusting partner.

HOW DOES IBCT CONCEPTUALIZE DISTRESS AND ITS CAUSES?

With all of the above as background, how do we understand relationship distress in a particular couple through the lens of IBCT? We first identify the main issues that trouble the couple. Although unhappy couples often are unhappy about many things in their relationship, they are often primarily concerned about one or two central areas. For example, a couple may be primarily distressed about his work life: she is unhappy that he works so much and she has to take primary responsibility for taking care of their kids after her own day at work, while he is unhappy that she doesn't understand the demands of his work and appreciate all of his sacrifices to excel at his job. Other problems that they have, such as tension when managing the details of the day, may be a result of the tension around their central issue. While some couples have a relatively circumscribed problem like the one above, others have a number of different problems that center around a broad theme. For example, Ben may want a closer relationship with Raymond (e.g., more time together alone, more affection and sex, and more intimate sharing of the feelings they have for each other) while Raymond wants more independence (e.g., more time alone, more time separately with friends, and more privacy in general). As another example, Dave and Rachel may have difficulties over the division of labor in the household, with frequent arguments about who does what cooking, cleaning, and child care. In each of these cases the IBCT therapist identifies the target issue or issues of concern to the couple. Consider Hank and Maria, the couple we described in Chapter 1. For them, there seem to be two main areas of concern: parenting or child care and physical intimacy.

Once one or two central issues have been identified, we try to discern the most important causal factors, based on the casual factors we discussed above, that contribute to the problem. We do this by conducting what we call a DEEP analysis of the issues. Although suggestive of an in-depth rather than a superficial analysis, the term DEEP is an acronym that refers to four crucial aspects of an interpersonal problem: **Differences** between partners that contribute to the problem, **Emotional sensitivities or reactions** in each partner that contribute to the problem, **External circumstances, particularly external stressors** in their lives that exacerbate the problem, and the **Pattern of communication** that they get into when they try to discuss the problem.

Of all the individual characteristics that each partner brings to the relationship that might influence their core issue or issues, usually the differences between them are what create difficulties, whether these differences were there to begin with (e.g., he was always more sociable and extroverted than she was) or developed over time (e.g., she has grown unhappy with his parents and now wants less contact with them than he wants). When couples separate or divorce, it is often because of what are formally termed "irreconcilable differences." Sometimes similarities between partners cause difficulties, as when both are risk averse, miss out on important opportunities, and blame each other for the outcome; but it is usually differences, rather than similarities, that create problems. Another characteristic in partners that creates problems in their relationship is emotional sensitivities, which are the strong emotional reactions that they have to certain events because of their genetic endowment and learning history. For example, he may have abandonment issues and may be easily triggered when she travels on business or goes out with friends, while she is triggered by any attempt to limit what she considers her freedom to live life as she chooses. These sensitivities often provide emotional fuel to the differences between partners. If he wants a closer, more connected relationship while she wants more independence in the relationship, his issues with abandonment and her issues with being controlled may make this difference at times emotionally explosive. Of all the physical and environmental factors that affect their relationship, it is usually the external stressors that contribute most to their problems, whether those stressors are physical (e.g., they must live in tight quarters with little privacy) or social (e.g., they have a difficult and challenging child). When under stressful circumstances, the couple may experience their differences as more problematic and their sensitivities as greater. Because it is so distressing to one or both and central to their lives, they must somehow deal with their central issue or issues. They interact about it but, in distressed couples, this interaction isn't able to resolve the issue or improve upon it sufficiently. They may repeatedly argue about it or they may have such difficulty discussing the issue that they avoid discussion but still are affected by the issue and still think about the issue, usually in ways that are not particularly sympathetic to the partner. Even this avoidance can be interaction, as when one is reminded of the issue and shuts down and is short and distant from the other, and the other responds in kind. The couple has a repetitive pattern of problematic interaction with regard to their central issue or issues, a pattern that doesn't ameliorate the problem and often makes it worse. In short, they are stuck in a problematic pattern of interaction that leads to one or both feeling unhappy.

Below, we go over this DEEP analysis in more detail, discussing each component of the DEEP.

D: Differences between partners

No matter how carefully we select our partner, we will inevitably find someone who is different from us and is different in a way that is problematic. The first reason for this is very straightforward: no one is fashioned to suit another perfectly. Our unique genetic endowment and unique life history do not shape any of us to accommodate perfectly to someone else, who also has a unique genetic endowment and personal history. The second reason is more complicated. Most human characteristics have both a positive and negative side to them. An ambitious person may get ahead in his or her career but have limited time for family. A strong-willed person may stand up for the partner and the family but be difficult to deal with at times. What complicates the differences between partners is that sometimes what attracts us to someone may also repel us at times. For example, we might be attracted to someone who is decisive because we often have difficulty making up our minds but then be upset that our partner makes all the decisions.

Whatever the basis for the differences between partners, whether those differences were an unwanted feature of an otherwise attractive partner or were intimately related to the attractiveness of the partner, there are a number of areas in which partners can be different in ways that create problems for them.

First, partners are likely to be different in their personalities. Using the well-known five-factor model of personality (L. R. Goldberg, 1993) as a guide, we can imagine partners being different in openness to experience (e.g., one is more adventurous while the other is more conventional), conscientiousness (e.g., one is more organized and efficient while the other is more easygoing), extraversion (e.g., one is more social and energetic while the other is more detached), agreeableness (e.g., one is more friendly and cooperative while the other is more suspicious and cynical), and neuroticism (e.g., one is more confident while the other is more anxious) in ways that could create difficulties for them.

Second, partners may be different in their libidos, with one more desirous of sexual intimacy than the other. Third, partners may be different in their connection to their family of origin and in their views of their family of origin, with one wanting greater contact with his or her family than the other wishes. Fourth, partners may be different in their ways of dealing with stress, such as one partner wanting to discuss stressful events at length and understand them in detail while the other wants to escape and just put them in the past as quickly as possible. Finally, partners may be different in some of their interests, such as one being more of an outdoor person and the other more of an indoor person. This list of areas of possible difference is hardly complete and is somewhat overlapping, but it gives an indication of the diverse ways in which partners can be different in ways that could create problems for them.

We should note that sometimes it is similarities rather than differences that create problems for couples. For example, both partners may be shy and unassertive, may be unable to establish a friendship network, and may get upset that the other doesn't have the characteristic that they are missing. However, it is usually differences rather than similarities that create difficulties for couples.

With regard to Hank and Maria, there are some obvious differences between them on both of their major issues. Maria focuses more on their child James than does Hank, possibly because she came from a child-focused family that gave lots of attention to a special needs child. In contrast, Hank gives more attention to the marriage and less to James, possibly because he was an only child who got his mother's full attention and never had to share attention. In terms of the love-versus-limits continuum, Maria emphasizes love with James and Hank emphasizes limits. In terms of their sexual issue, Hank clearly has a greater desire for sexual intimacy than Maria at this point in their marriage.

E: Emotional Sensitivities, Vulnerabilities, and Reactions

As a result of our genetic vulnerabilities and learning history, all of us have certain emotional sensitivities or vulnerabilities that lead us to react strongly to certain interpersonal events. What may seem like a minor criticism to others can hit us hard. What may seem like a simple oversight to us may feel very rejecting to someone else. Of course, these emotional sensitivities and the related emotional reactions can range widely in intensity, from the intense pain that someone with borderline personality tendencies might experience in response to an interpersonal rejection or the intense anger that someone with narcissistic personality tendencies might experience in response to an interpersonal slight to the minor rejections that most feel in regard to a partner who is not attentive to us, or forgets an important event for us, or is not interested in physical contact or connection when we desire it. The point is that all of us have these sensitivities; none of us has achieved Buddha-like equanimity so that the ups and downs of daily life have no negative emotional impact on us. These sensitivities help make us human; there is probably a reason we don't hear much about Buddha's romantic relationships.

There is no universally agreed upon list of emotional vulnerabilities, but common ones that affect relationships are the following: (a) abandonment issues that make us especially sensitive to our partner being away from us or disconnected from us or possibly interested in someone else, (b) thin skin that makes it hard for us to take even minor criticism or constructive criticism well, (c) a fragile sense of our own importance or value that can make us question ourselves if we are not getting enough attention, (d) a need for recognition that makes us uncomfortable when we are not getting praise and adulation, (e) concerns about our own attractiveness if our partner is not interested in physical contact with us, (f) issues with being controlled by others so that we resist if our partner tries to influence us, and (g) concerns about our own competence that make us bristle when our partner seems better at handling life tasks and tries to teach us how to handle them better. There are also sensitivities related to our socioeconomic status (e.g., one partner may have a well-earned sensitivity about debt since her parents had their home go into foreclosure), gender socialization (e.g., the man may be especially sensitive about his ability to be the breadwinner in the household; the woman may be especially sensitive about her ability to be a good mother), and culture (e.g., someone raised in a culture that emphasizes family responsibility may feel it incumbent upon them to have their widowed mother live in their home, even if there is money available for other options). These sensitivities may have existed prior to the current relationship, which then exacerbates or ameliorates those sensitivities. Or the sensitivities can result from the relationship. In the first case, Susan was sensitive to criticism before she met Bart, but Bart's tendency to lash out made her even more sensitive. In the second case, perhaps Susan was no more sensitive to criticism than most other people but after living with Bart and his explosive temper, she has become sensitive to criticism and cautious around Bart.

These sensitivities are often related to the differences we have with our partner and provide emotional fire to the problems created by those differences. If two people differ in how much closeness versus independence they want in their relationship, they must work that out. If the one who wants greater closeness has abandonment issues while the one who wants greater independence has issues with being controlled, then the conflict about time together and connection could be intense. Similarly, if one partner feels that she is not a good daughter unless she brings her widowed mother to live with her, while her partner has tried to free herself from the oppressive family responsibilities she felt growing up and now cannot imagine living with a mother-in-law that she never really liked, the couple will be severely challenged. Finally, if one partner is distrustful because of his history of being cheated on, while the other enjoys what she sees as innocent flirtation, they may have intense conflict about her behavior.

Emotional sensitivities lead to a variety of emotional reactions, some that are clear and easily observed (i.e., surface emotions) and others that are less obvious (i.e., hidden emotions). The former are often what we call hard emotions such as anger and resentment that reveal the self as strong, while the latter are often what we call soft emotions, such as disappointment, rejection, and shame that reveal the self as vulnerable. For example, the distrustful man above may react with anger and criticism when he sees his partner being flirtatious (i.e., surface emotion) but may also feel small and unimportant to her (i.e., hidden emotion). She may react to his anger and criticism with anger and criticism of her own (i.e., surface emotion) but may also feel some guilt or shame at her behavior (i.e., hidden emotion). These surface and hidden emotions are not always so distinct, nor is the former always hard and the latter always soft. An unassertive man may seem intimidated (i.e., his surface emotion) and respond compliantly when his partner calls him to task but also feel angry inside (i.e., his hidden emotion) that he was treated this way. The point is that our emotional sensitivities lead to strong emotional reactions to relevant events. Some are hard and others are soft; some are surface and obvious and others are hidden and less easily observed or acknowledged.

Consider the emotional sensitivities that trouble Hank and Maria. Having gotten a lot of nurturing attention as a child and during the early days of their marriage, Hank now feels upset at the loss of attention from Maria and competitive with the attention that James gets from her. Given James' developmental challenges and Maria's cultural and family experiences that have made her into a responsible, caring mother, she feels a great deal of anxiety about James and a desire to protect him and assist him. These sensitivities bring into stark contrast the differences in child rearing that Hank and

Maria endorse and provides some emotional fuel to those differences. Hank's sensitivity about attention pales in comparison to his sensitivity about sexual contact with Maria. She seems not interested in being with him as a lover so he feels rejected but may reveal anger to her or an emotional shrug, as if he no longer cares. For Maria's part, her anxiety about James and the pressure and criticism she hears from Hank are hardly aphrodisiacs. Sex seems more of a chore to her than a pleasure. She may reveal lack of interest or active distaste to his initiations but also feel guilty that she is rejecting her husband.

E: External Circumstances, Particularly External Stressors

External circumstances can affect couple distress in either a positive or negative way. For example, if Sue is more connected to her family of origin than is Rick, living far from her family could maximize conflict over the time and cost to visit whereas living near her family might minimize those conflicts. The circumstances that normally create difficulties for partners are external stressors, such as poor housing, long commutes to work, job demands, illness, and difficult social relationships including problems with children. Anything outside of the dyad that creates challenges for either partner is a potential stressor that could affect their relationship.

External stressors often affect couple conflict by exacerbating existing differences and sensitivities. Assume that Raymond has a higher libido than Jane and that for him sex provides many benefits, including a relief from stress, while for Jane sex doesn't work for her unless she and Raymond are both relaxed and emotionally connected. External stress of any sort may increase his desire for sex while reducing hers. If Raymond has any sensitivities about Jane's attraction toward him or if Jane has any sensitivities about being used for sex, external stress could increase the differences in their respective libidos and exacerbate the sensitivities that each has.

The biggest external stressor that Hank and Maria face is James. The demands of parenting put some stress on most couples, but James has been a particularly stressful experience for Hank and Maria. The fact that James is experiencing some developmental problems that have not been easy to diagnose or treat has increased Maria's anxiety about James and her role as a mother and pulled her into greater contact with James and away from contact with Hank. Their natural differences with regard to parenting, that Hank emphasizes limits more than Maria and that Maria emphasizes love and nurturing more than Hank, have been exacerbated by James' problems. Maria feels protective of James because of his limitations and wants to be more nurturing toward him. Hank sees part of James' limitations as a result of too few demands placed on him so wants to put more limits and demands on him. Similarity, the problems with James have exacerbated their differences in libido. Maria's caretaking of James has made her less interested in sex while the demands of James and their intrusion into the couple's intimate life have made Hank more interested in sexual intimacy. The experience with James has also heightened some of the sensitivities that each has. Maria's concern about being a good mother and protecting her child has been triggered by James' problems while Hank's concern about whether he is loved and the focus of Maria's attention is heightened by her attention to James.

P: Patterns of Communication or Interaction

The final part of the DEEP analysis is the pattern of communication or interaction. We can think of the first three parts of the DEEP—the natural differences between partners, their emotional sensitivities, and the external stressors they face—as being the relationship problems in living that the partners face. The last component of the DEEP—the pattern of communication or interaction—is their efforts to solve this problem. The couple discusses the problems, avoids discussion of the problems, or otherwise interacts about them as a way of dealing with the problems. However, for couples who are distressed, these efforts to resolve the problems through their communication or lack of communication are not successful and often make the problems worse.

When partners first face the difficulties defined by the DEE components of the DEEP, often early in the relationship, they usually try to discuss them reasonably and constructively. However, they are often not successful at truly resolving them, since the differences are often fundamental, the emotional sensitivities are well established, and the external circumstances are at best uncooperative. The partners, in their frustration, then resort to less constructive strategies. They may move against the partner, criticizing the other for the way he or she is and demanding change. They may move away from the partner, avoiding discussion of the topic and distancing themselves emotionally from the other. Or they may move toward the other, anxiously and inappropriately, such as by appeasing the other or invading the other's privacy. Each of these strategies may be successful and thus gets reinforced occasionally or in the short term. For example, a partner may respond to blame or demands for change by making some temporary changes. Avoidance and withdrawal at least prevent or terminate an uncomfortable interaction in the short term, so it can be reinforcing. Appeasement may bring about a reduction of tension, and invading the other's privacy may reveal some valuable or reassuring information. Each of these strategies of moving against the partner, moving away from the partner, or moving anxiously toward the partner can lead to some short-term benefits.

If partners are not able to come to some workable resolution, either through constructive discussion or by occasionally moving against the partner, moving away from the partner, or moving toward the partner anxiously or inappropriately, then partners often get stuck in a repetitious pattern of interaction in which they both do the same dysfunctional behavior or each does different dysfunctional behaviors. For example, couples commonly get stuck in a symmetrical pattern of interaction where they both move against the other, criticizing, blaming, demanding changes, and threatening the partner if they don't get those changes. Another symmetrical pattern of interaction occurs when both partners move away from each other by avoiding discussion of a particular issue. They have been unsuccessful in talking about the issue so they give up on that direct method of resolution and withdraw from the other, often communicating their dissatisfaction in various nonverbal ways, such as by not initiating affection or otherwise being unresponsive to the partner. Couples can also get stuck in an asymmetrical pattern of interaction in which they each do different kinds of dysfunctional behavior. One partner may move against the partner by trying to discuss the problem and criticizing the other during those discussions, while the other moves away from the partner by avoiding discussion or withdrawing and being defensive when any discussion takes place. Or one partner may pursue the other anxiously while the other avoids and withdraws.

These descriptions of dysfunctional cycles of communication are oversimplifications. Even though one partner may take on a blaming and demanding role while the other is in a withdrawing and avoiding role, the interaction may intensify so that at some point the withdrawer gets angry and is blaming and critical of the blamer, who then withdraws and shuts down. That may be followed by avoidance and distance by them both before the cycle repeats again. Or consider the specific example of Mark and Ben's trust issue. Because Mark is more outgoing and flirtatious than Ben (i.e., the difference), because Ben has a history of being cheated on (i.e., Ben's emotional sensitivity), and because Mark's job involves extensive travel away from home (i.e., the external stressor), Ben often questions Mark about his behavior on his trips and tries to find evidence, such as credit card receipts or phone records, that might reassure him or be a means for questioning Mark's credibility. These interrogative discussions are especially unpleasant for Mark, so he often avoids or withdraws from these discussions and tries to hide information that might upset Ben, even if Mark has done nothing to violate their understanding about fidelity. Mark's reluctance to talk and efforts to disguise his tracks alarm Ben and make him think something wrong is really going on, thus increasing his investigative and interrogative efforts. This pattern can escalate until Mark gets furious at Ben's efforts to investigate; Ben feels despair at the relationship and withdraws and distances from Mark, who then fears the loss of the relationship and pursues Ben to reassure him. A period of calm is then followed by the cycle again.

Dysfunctional cycles of interaction often leave partners frustrated and angry. However, unless they break up or divorce, the couple recovers from the stress of the interaction. They get back to their normal way of relating, even though they may carry some emotional residue from the negative interaction. The process of this recovery, this return to the couple's normal way of relating to one another, can also be difficult for couples. As they try to recover, they may inadvertently ignite the argument again or get into a related dispute for several reasons. First, partners often have different methods of recovery. One partner may want to talk about the conflict and try to resolve it while the other just wants to move past it. Second, partners often have a different timing for recovery. One partner may heat up quickly in a conflict but also recover quickly while the other takes a while to get emotionally charged but then a while to recover. Third, partners often differ in their desire or need for specific acts of repair, such as acknowledgement of fault, apology, commitment to change, or confirmation of love (e.g., kiss and make up). For example, one partner may think apologies are necessary while the other doesn't see the need for apology, or the partners may differ on who needs to apologize for what. Because of these differences in the way partners recover, it is easy for couples to struggle about their recovery. One may push for discussion while the other resists. One may blame the other for "holding onto it" if the other doesn't recover as quickly as he or she would like. Each may insist that the other needs to apologize. Then the couple gets caught in a struggle over their recovery that can interfere with that recovery, bring back the conflict that upset them in the first place, or create another argument related to the recovery.

Rohrbaugh and Shoham (2015) describe these vicious cycles of interaction as "ironic processes" because even though they are designed to solve the problem or recover from a bad interaction about the problem, they not only fail in that effort but actually make the problem worse. These ironic processes thus apply to both the pattern of interaction in which a couple gets stuck as they deal with their differences, emotional sensitivities, and external stressors and to the pattern of interaction in which they get stuck as they try to recover from a difficult interaction. In the example above, Mark's interrogation and Ben's avoidance may provide some short-term satisfaction, but they don't ultimately reassure Mark about Ben's trustworthiness or reassure Ben that he can behave comfortably without critical scrutiny. Let's further imagine that after some of these difficult encounters, Mark himself shuts down and distances himself, which alarms Ben, who tries to be positive and light as a way of leading Mark back to their normal way of relating. If Mark is not responsive because it takes him longer to get over a conflict, Ben may criticize Mark for "hanging onto his feelings" and "not letting it go." Mark may then respond to that criticism with criticism of his own that impairs the recovery process at best and reignites the original conflict again at worst.

There are several ways in which dysfunctional patterns of interaction around the problems presented by partner's differences, emotional sensitivities, and external stressors may make these problems worse. First, the vicious cycle of interaction typically escalates and becomes more intense as that interaction achieves the goals of neither partner. Emotions intensify and voices rise. Second, the interaction may polarize the partners and the positions that they take. Consider Daren and Sylvia's disagreement about sexual frequency. Daren wants to have sex more often than Sylvia and pressures her sexually while she avoids and withdraws from his contact. Over time he feels more and more deprived and his desire for sex increases while the pressure from him is hardly an aphrodisiac for her and dampens her already lower desire for sex. Thus, as a result of the interaction, an initial difference in sexual desire becomes a greater difference in sexual desire. Third, the partners may begin to vilify each other. Rather than Daren and Sylvia seeing themselves as having a difference in sexual desire, they may start seeing the other as deficient or deviant in some way. Daren may see Sylvia as being uptight and frigid regarding sex while Sylvia begins to see Daren as having a sex addiction. Both may see the other as needing therapy. Fourth, the conflictual interaction in one area of the relationship may expand to other areas. Daren may be so frustrated with Sylvia, or she with him, that one or both is short or curt or unresponsive to the other when they go out to eat together, which is normally a good time for them. Finally, the conflictual interaction may lead to estrangement between the pair, as they begin to question the relationship and consider what alternatives they have. At this point, the couple may feel hopeless and helpless because their efforts to ameliorate the problem don't help and even make the problem worse.

Our example couple, Hank and Maria, have two central issues, parenting and sex, and have different patterns of interaction around each. Maria has considerable anxiety about James and has tried to share her concerns with Hank. When she does so, Hank typically minimizes her concerns or suggests that the problems James experiences are partially or wholly a result of her coddling of him. As a result, Maria shares less and less with Hank about her concerns about James. Hank still occasionally criticizes her behavior with James but because she shuts down and distances when Hank does so, they have less and less discussion about this important little person in both of their lives. When Hank attempts to discipline James, which Maria sees as often too harsh, she does not counteract Hank directly but often tries to comfort James and otherwise mitigate the impact of Hank's discipline. Their pattern of interaction around James has not provided any relief for Maria's concerns but rather increased them and has subtly undermined Hank's disciplinary efforts with James, giving both partners less and less of what they would like and creating distance and alienation between them around their important roles as parents.

The pattern of interaction around sex has in the past consisted of Hank as the pursuer and Maria as the reluctant participant. Occasionally Maria directly declines his advances but more often she avoids the situation by putting James to sleep and falling asleep with him so she does not come to bed until Hank is asleep. Hank complains about their lack of a sex life but initiates less and less as he senses her obvious reluctance when they do have sex and her frequent avoidance of situations that might lead to sex. At this point Maria is fairly turned off to sex with Hank. Although Hank still finds Maria sexually attractive, he has frequently given up his pursuit of her. As a result of this interaction, the pleasure and connection that sex can provide has declined for them both and they are more distant emotionally from each other.

SUMMARY

In this chapter we defined a dyadic relationship as occurring when any two people mutually influence each other through their interaction. We defined a distressed relationship as one in which a significant portion of that interaction regularly or repetitively leads to distressing emotions, such as anger and disappointment, or the absence of expected positive reactions, such as affection or love or sexual attraction. Five broad categories of causal factors influence relationships: the characteristics that each partner brings to the relationship, the social and physical environment in which the relationship exists, and emergent features of the relationship itself, such as the agreements partners make or the routines they establish. Of the characteristics that partners bring to the relationship, it is usually their differences, such as differences in their personalities and interests, and their emotional sensitivities that are most likely to create conflict and distress. Stressors in the social and physical environment are the most likely external factors that lead to distressed relationships. Finally, it is the stuck patterns of interaction that don't resolve their problems and usually make them worse that are the emergent factors most likely to lead to distress.

Because of this way of thinking about distress, IBCT uses the DEEP analysis to understand the causal contributions to a couple's dissatisfaction. IBCT therapists identify one or two core issues which trouble partners and then attempt to understand the natural **D**ifferences between partners that contribute to the issue, the **E**motional reactions and sensitivities that make the issue especially problematic for one or both partners, the **E**xternal stressors that contribute to the issue or impede thoughtful analysis of it, and finally, the **P**atterns of interaction in which the couple gets stuck as they try to deal with the issue or recover from a difficult interaction around the issue. We illustrated this DEEP analysis with several example couples, but especially Hank and Maria, whose case was presented in detail in Chapter 1.

With this information as background, we can now look in the next chapter at the specific assessment and evaluation procedures in IBCT that lead, among other things, to a DEEP analysis.

4

魯

Overview and Assessment
in IBCT

IBCT IS A PRINCIPLE BASED THERAPY rather than a protocol based therapy. There is no fixed length to the therapy nor is there a detailed protocol of what to do in each part of each session. Therefore, in this book we describe the principles of IBCT and how to implement them based on the challenges that couples present, rather than providing a session by session protocol of what to do. However, there are distinct phases of IBCT and particular tasks to accomplish during those phases. In this chapter we give a brief overview of these phases of IBCT and discuss at length the first phase, Assessment.

OVERVIEW OF IBCT

Integrative Behavioral Couple Therapy (IBCT) consists of four sequential phases. In the first phase, the assessment phase, we discover the presenting problems of the couple, gather information to understand and conceptualize those problems, and evaluate whether the couple is appropriate for IBCT. This phase includes an initial conjoint session and subsequent individual sessions with each partner. In the second, feedback phase, we meet conjointly once with the couple and describe our conceptualization of their problems by sharing our DEEP analysis of those problems. We present our analysis tentatively and invite clients to elaborate or modify this analysis as needed. During the feedback phase, we also provide a detailed description of the active intervention portion of IBCT, including the goals for therapy and the methods designed to achieve those goals. Therefore, at the end of the feedback session, the couple can go home, discuss their reactions to the conceptualization of their problems, the proposed methods to address those problems, and the comfort and confidence they feel in us, and then make a decision about whether to commit to a course of active intervention. The third phase is the active intervention phase, which almost always consists solely of joint sessions. IBCT does not have a fixed length for therapy, and therefore there is no minimum or maximum number of sessions for the active phase. Typically, therapy consists of at least a dozen sessions. Our major clinical trial on couple therapy limited the total number of sessions to 26 (Christensen et al., 2004). Termination begins when the couple desires it or when the therapist suggests it because the couple has reached a comfortable place in their relationship where they can now address their difficulties on their own. This phase ideally consists of spaced sessions at longer intervals that ensure that the couple can manage on their own and then a final termination session that reviews the DEEP analysis with an emphasis on the changes that have been made and the possible challenges in the future. We now focus in the rest of this chapter on the assessment phase of IBCT.

ASSESSMENT

There are several goals for the assessment phase: (a) to establish rapport with each partner and have an initial therapeutic impact, (b) to evaluate whether the couple is appropriate for IBCT, and (c) to gather information relevant for a DEEP analysis of the couple's core issue or issues. A couple is appropriate for IBCT if they have an established, committed relationship, their goal is to improve the relationship (or determine if it can be saved), and they can participate safely and competently in couple therapy. IBCT is not a program to match partners for a relationship based on their personalities or other characteristics; it is for couples who are already in an established, serious relationship. They don't have to be married or even living together but they do have to have regular, significant interpersonal contact with each other. Also, IBCT is not separation or divorce therapy or mediation leading to divorce. It is couple therapy for partners who are committed to improving their relationship. They can certainly be ambivalent in that commitment, as many distressed couples are, but their goal for therapy must be improvement in the relationship—not termination of the relationship. Finally, IBCT is only for couples who are free of dangerous levels of intimate partner violence and intimidation. Couples must also be mentally and emotionally competent enough to participate in couple therapy. Thus, they cannot be actively psychotic or so affected by drug and alcohol problems or suicidal impulses that they cannot safely or effectively participate in couple therapy.

Although the assessment phase in IBCT normally consists of an initial joint session followed by individual sessions with each partner, special circumstances can lead us to alter that process. If a couple is in crisis and cannot tolerate a more leisurely assessment procedure, an immediate intervention may be necessary. For example, a couple may present in the initial session as so distressed from the discovery of an affair that one or both want at least a temporary separation and planning for that is the immediate priority. More extreme examples include homicide or suicide risks, intimate partner violence, child abuse, or psychosis in one or both partners that are apparent in the initial session. In each of these special circumstances we may need to see each partner alone for part of the initial session. We may need to intervene in this first session, such as by helping the couple plan for a temporary separation, making referrals for individual treatment, or discussing possible hospitalization. Or we may need more evaluation sessions than usual. We describe some of these special situations, such as intimate partner violence, sexual problems, infidelity, and individual psychopathology in Chapter 13. Now however, assuming there are no special circumstances that would lead us to alter our usual plan, we describe how we use the initial joint session, the questionnaires we give to clients, and the two individual sessions to meet the goals listed above.

Initial Joint Session

Although sometimes one partner will enquire about couple therapy and request an initial individual session, we insist on an initial joint session so that both partners get to present their views to us and neither partner feels disadvantaged because the other got to us first. This first session is important in that it will give the couple a partial indication of what couple therapy will be like and thus determine whether they even come back for further sessions. It can be challenging for us as therapists because each partner will usually try to persuade us of his or her perception of the problem, a perception that often differs substantially from the partner's. We must show that we can understand both but not side with either.

Consider the typical couple sitting in the waiting room before the initial couple therapy appointment. They know that they are about to air their dirty laundry to a stranger, something that makes many people uncomfortable—especially those who have not been in therapy before. Moreover, by the time couples seek therapy, their problems have been festering for a long time, perhaps for many years. Although some partners may have unrealistic positive expectations about what therapy might accomplish for them, many partners are skeptical about therapy in general or about whether couple therapy can really help their long-standing problems. Because of this discomfort and skepticism, they are often ambivalent about being in the waiting room in the first place. We cannot assume that they are fully committed to therapy; in fact, one or both may have come with great reluctance. They are often confused, because they don't know what to expect. They may have never been in therapy before; or, if they have been in therapy, it has not been couple therapy; or, if it has been couple therapy, it was likely unsuccessful and was perhaps from a different theoretical orientation. They are uncertain as to how the process works.

With awareness of the couple's likely state of mind, the six goals of the initial interview are: (1) to socialize them into the twin processes of therapy and assessment, (2) to honor and respect their likely ambivalence, (3) to develop rapport with each partner, (4) to gather information about their core issue or issues that can be used to develop a DEEP analysis of those issues, (5) to make the session as therapeutic as possible, and (6) to give out questionnaires for each to bring back completed to the individual session. Some of the socialization into couple therapy may be done at the initial phone call with a client. He or she may ask about the process of couple therapy, but even if he or she does not, we think it is a good idea to use the phone call to give them some information about what to expect. Certainly we would indicate that the first session will require both partners to attend and that we will follow up with individual sessions with each. Based on these joint and individual interviews as well as questionnaires we will ask them to complete, we will provide them with feedback in the fourth session. We will give them our impressions of their concerns and information about how we would address those concerns in the active phase of couple therapy, which would follow the assessment and feedback phase and would be done conjointly. Even if we provide that information to the member of the couple that calls about therapy, we would want to repeat that early in the initial session so both partners are aware of the process. For example, after introductions and when partners are comfortably seated in the office, we might start off with something like the following:

Let me tell you a bit about how I work with couples so that you know what's in store for you over the next couple of weeks. I first try to get to know you and your concerns for three sessions that we call the *assessment period* or the *evaluation period*. Today's interview with the two of you is the first step in that evaluation. At the end of today's session, I will give you some questionnaires to complete and bring to your next session. Then I will meet with each of you alone in turn for the next two sessions. In these individual sessions, I look over these questionnaires you have completed and collect additional information to help me determine if I can be helpful to you and to help you determine if you feel comfortable working with me. In the fourth session, or what I call the feedback session, both of you will come in and I will give you the results of my evaluation, telling you how I understand your problems and concerns and how I will work with you in therapy—the goals of that therapy and the methods I will use to help you meet those goals. After that session, the two of you can go home and talk about what I have said and what your experience in these sessions was like. You can decide if you think I understand your concerns, if my approach makes sense to you, if you feel comfortable working with me, and thus if you want to begin the active phase of couple therapy where we work together on those goals. During the active phase of therapy, I typically see you together for almost all the sessions. How does that sound? Any questions before we begin?

With an opening like this, partners are socialized as to the evaluation phase and the active therapy phase. Even though the difference between therapy and assessment is clear to mental health professionals, it may not be intuitively obvious to clients. Some clients may expect us to find about their problems in the first part of the session and give them recommendations toward the end of the session. An opening like this will usually adjust their expectations appropriately. If one or both partners seem disappointed that they are not going to get help right away, we might add something like the following:

> At times couples are disappointed that we can't start therapy right away. I can certainly understand that disappointment. You are tired of these problems and understandably eager to get some immediate help. I wish I had the miracle cure that could benefit you without this thorough evaluation. Unfortunately, every couple is different, and any help I tried to give you today would be general advice that may or may not be a good fit for your relationship or your situation. I would possibly lead you astray. I need the time and contact with you to come up with a treatment plan that fits your needs.

Honor their ambivalence. When evaluation and therapy are distinguished, and partners are reassured that they are not necessarily committing themselves to couple therapy simply by showing up for this conjoint interview, they are often relieved. They are allowed and in fact encouraged to take some time in which to get to know us and the process before committing to it. They are also reminded that we are not making any commitments until we determine that this approach could be helpful. Thus, couples' understandable ambivalence is normalized and, in fact, built into the structure of the evaluation phase.

Develop rapport with each partner and with the couple. Before coming into therapy, each partner will likely think about what and how they want to present their concerns to us. They may have rehearsed their story of their concerns in their head. There is a danger that each partner will tell a long and detailed story of their concerns, leaving us in a position of being an audience to that story and an implicit supporter of that story and leaving the other partner waiting for a chance to tell his or her competing story. It is helpful to establish early on that we will be an active participant in the therapy rather than a passive listener and that we are aiming for dialogue, not monologues. In order to establish this pattern and prevent long opening monologues, it can be helpful to say something like the following:

> I would like to hear about the concerns that brought you here, but rather than hearing a detailed explanation or story from each of you, I would like to get a little piece from one of you and then get the other's reaction to that piece, and so forth so that we build the story by getting frequent input from each of you.

A comment such as the one above may not be sufficient to set up the pattern of dialogue that we want. We may need to interrupt a partner and get the other's response by saying something like "You made an interesting point there, Bill, so I want to get Susie's reaction to it. Do you see it that way also, Susie?"

When discussing their concerns, each partner will often implicitly or explicitly blame the other by recounting negative actions that the other has done. The challenge for us as therapists is to support both without alienating either. We can do that by focusing on the reaction rather than the action. Susie may talk about how Bill is so domineering and controlling and has to make all the important decisions. Rather than focus on Bill's actions by finding out details about his domineering actions, we can shift the focus to Susie's reactions, that she wants to have more of a voice in the relationship and sometimes feels powerless with Bill. We can be empathic with that experience of powerlessness and that goal of a greater voice in the relationship without necessarily alienating Bill, who probably does not see himself as controlling and domineering or, if he does so, views it as a reaction to her passivity. In IBCT we say "Focus on the wound, not the arrow." Partners will, metaphorically speaking, focus on the arrows that the other has shot at them. Therapy will be more effective when we can focus on the wound instead.

In the initial session, sometimes partners describe their concerns in vague and general terms because they are embarrassed by their concerns, because they want to avoid blaming the other for them, or because they are genuinely unclear about the source of their discomfort. They may talk about a lack of connection or a loss of love or the spark having left their relationship. We will need to probe for specific details and examples in order to understand their concerns. For example, if a couple mentions a lack of connection, we can follow up with a request for more information: "Could you say more about what you mean by lack of connection?" Or we might ask, "Are you talking about a lack of physical or sexual or emotional connection between you?" Or if a partner indicates that there is no emotional connection between them, the therapist might ask, "Can you give me an example of what happens when the two of you are together and what you would like to happen?"

Sometimes partners at the initial session will describe their problems in impersonal terms that imply obligation, duty, or moral requirements. "Men should be the one to initiate sex" or "Women should be the ones in charge of the children," or "Couples shouldn't argue as much as we do." In response to these kinds of comments, we should make the impersonal personal, by saying for example in response to the above comments, "You would like Ben to be the one to initiate sex" or "You would like Debra to be in charge of the children" or "You wish that the two of you wouldn't argue so much."

Gather information about their core issue or issues that can be used to develop a DEEP analysis of those issues. During the initial session partners will describe their primary problems or concerns. Sometimes these concerns are very specific, as when they struggle over their sexual relationship or parenting or in-laws. Other times, couples will describe their concerns more generally, such as "We can't communicate well" or "We are just not in love anymore." In fact, communication problems and problems with emotional affection (e.g., lack of love or intimacy) are the two most common problems partners list for seeking couple therapy (Doss et al., 2004). When couples describe these more general issues, we should of course try to clarify what is the core concern. Even very distressed couples can communicate about many things reasonably well; it is usually one or two content areas that really challenge their communication. Even if much of their communication is negative, most of that negativity may derive from the hurt and anger they feel about certain core concerns. For example, Susie may be irritable and blaming about many issues, primarily because she is so resentful that Bill is never around and the housework and child care are left to her. Frank may be so negative and withdrawn because he feels sexually rejected by Harold. When couples describe a lack of love or intimacy, it is often because of anger and resentment about some core issues or issues (e.g., feeling ignored or neglected by the other, feeling unattractive to the other or unattracted to the other). Based on what the couple says and how they respond to our questions and reflections, we can usually ascertain the core concerns of each partner in the first session.

Not only can we identify the core concern or concerns in the first session, but also we can usually get some information about key components of a DEEP understanding of those concerns—the **D**ifferences, **E**motional sensitivities, **E**xternal stressors, and **P**atterns of interaction around those concerns. For example, in talking about their relationship, Hank, from our initial case study, describes how "Maria is obsessed with James" but says with some emotion that "She will hardly give me the time of day, and any intimacy is out of the question." Maria responds by defensively mentioning her concerns about James and then says, "I have to deal with this on my own; I can't even talk to my own husband about it—he just dismisses any concerns I have." In this simple exchange, we get hints of the difference between them (e.g., her focus on the child and him on their relationship), their emotional sensitivities (e.g., his feeling of neglect and her sense of aloneness in dealing with James), the external stress that James has caused in their relationship, and even something about their pattern of interaction regarding James (e.g., that Maria brings up concerns and Hank dismisses them).

Use the initial interview to improve the relationship and learn about their strengths. Although we clearly define the first three sessions as assessment and evaluation and not as active intervention, this initial interview should be as therapeutic as possible. This therapeutic impact comes from first being able to discuss relationship problems openly with a therapist who does not take sides or cast blame but understands both partners' positions and their emotional distress. The second benefit comes from a review of the couple's relationship history, with an emphasis on what attracted them to each other and the strengths that still keep them together despite their problems.

After discussing the problems for a period of time, often one half to two thirds of the way through the session, we typically summarize our initial understanding of their concerns. This summary targets the core issues that have been identified and provides an early and limited version of a DEEP analysis. For example, we might say to Hank and Maria:

> I think I have a good initial understanding of your concerns. Clearly, James is a major point of contention between you. Both of you love him but have different views of him. You, Maria, have some serious concerns about James and feel that you can't share them with Hank without it getting into an argument. Hank, you feel that Maria's concerns are excessive and you try to show her that, but it leads to conflict between the two of you. And with all this difficulty about James, it seems your relationship has taken a back seat, which has been really hard for you, Hank. You miss the sexual intimacy and closeness you once had. And Maria, you feel alone in your concerns about James and wish you could be on the same team with Hank about James. Does that sound on track?

After this summary we typically indicate that we want to learn about the couple's history, particularly what attracted them to each other and what keeps them together despite their difficulties. This line of inquiry into their developmental history helps us see the basis for their attachment to each other and learn of the strengths they still have. Partners probably have not reflected on why they became a couple for a long time, since their focus has been on what is wrong with the relationship. It may be that they have never discussed their developmental history together, let alone in front of a stranger. As partners discuss what attracted them to each other and describe their courtship, the affect in the therapy room often becomes quite positive. We can sometimes build on that positivity by asking them what their relationship is like when they are getting along. Then this discussion can lead into the positive changes they would like to see in their relationship.

Some couples use this history-taking period as an opportunity to minimize their attraction to each other and to blame each other for the problems. Instead of thwarting such efforts or forcing them to discuss the positive aspects of their relationship, we take such blaming statements as a sign that the partner or partners are in too much pain to talk about positive aspects of the relationship, we relinquish making this part of the initial session, and instead we validate where they are emotionally. Indeed, the validating stance of the therapist is a constant throughout IBCT. If the partners are in too much pain to discuss happier times without blaming and accusatory remarks, we must be prepared to validate that pain.

Give partners questionnaires to bring back completed at their individual session. Some therapists may give the couple forms to complete prior to their first session, such as demographic questionnaires that ask about identifying information or consent or confidentiality forms about the therapy itself. We prefer to give questionnaires about the relationship itself at the end of the initial session, with a request that partners fill them out and bring them to their individual session. This way they will not complete the questionnaires until they have had an initial interview with us and we hope they will feel more comfortable disclosing information to us. Also, we can give them some basic instructions about the questionnaires, such as that they complete them independently and also confidentially if either fears that their answers might create an argument. In addition, we can let them know that we will look at their questionnaire responses and discuss them at their individual session and integrate them as part of our feedback to them both in the feedback session.

There are many questionnaires available for use with couples. In the table below, we have listed the questionnaires that we typically recommend for IBCT. These are certainly not the only questionnaires that you could use when doing IBCT. However, we recommend these for several reasons: (a) they are freely available without charge (links to the questionnaires are in the table), (b) they require minimal psychometric knowledge, (c) they require little time and effort by the couple, and (d) they cover areas that we believe are essential to evaluate before undertaking couple therapy. These essential areas are:

- level of distress
- level of commitment
- presence of violence
- problem areas
- strengths

Title of Questionnaire	Description of Purpose	Citation and Location
Demographic Questionnaire	Demographic information on both partners	Christensen, 2010; https://ibct.psych.ucla.edu/wp-content/uploads/sites/195/2018/12/demographic-question-naire-for-couples.pdf
Couple Satisfaction Index (CSI-16)	Normative data on relationship satisfaction	Funk & Rogge, 2007; https://www.researchgate.net/publication/299432196_The_Couples_Satisfaction_Index_CSI-16
Couple Questionnaire	Information on violence, commitment, satisfaction, and positive and negative interactions	Christensen, 2010; https://ibct.psych.ucla.edu/wp-content/uploads/sites/195/2018/12/couple-questionnaire.pdf
Problem Areas Questionnaire	Ratings of problem areas	Christensen, 2010; https://ibct.psych.ucla.edu/wp-content/uploads/sites/195/2018/12/problem-areas-questionniare.pdf

We will review these questionnaires in more detail below when we discuss how they are used in the individual sessions.

Possibly ask partners to read *Reconcilable Differences*. In addition to giving the partners questionnaires at the end of the session, we may recommend to them that they read the IBCT self-help book, *Reconcilable Differences* (Christensen et al., 2014) as they go through treatment. This is not a requirement and may not be appropriate for couples who would be burdened by such reading or who are uninterested in reading a book as they go through therapy. However, the book takes them through the processes of IBCT and we believe can only enhance their therapy experience. Even if only one partner wants to read the book, that could be helpful as long as the book is not presented in such a way as to lead partners to believe that the one reading the book is somehow the more committed or cooperative one.

Part I of *Reconcilable Differences* describes three ways of thinking about problems ("three sides to every story," p. 3): from the perspective of one partner or from the perspective of the other, which are often fault-filled explanations, as well as from a more objective perspective. Part II of the book describes the DEEP analysis and helps the reader define a core problem and conduct a DEEP analysis of it. Therefore, at the end of session 1, we may encourage partners to read Parts I and II of *Reconcilable Differences* prior to the fourth or feedback session.

Individual Sessions

There are a number of important goals for the individual sessions. Although some material relevant to these goals can be obtained in the initial joint session, the individual session is key to determining (a) whether couple therapy can proceed safely and (b) whether partners have sufficient commitment for couple therapy to proceed appropriately. The individual session also provides additional information for the DEEP analysis.

Honest information about violence and commitment can sometimes only be obtained if partners are assured of confidentiality from disclosure to the other. Therefore, our disclosure forms indicate that material disclosed in therapy can be kept confidential from the partner. In addition, we typically start off the individual session with a statement about confidentiality, indicating that normally topics discussed in the individual session can be brought up in the joint sessions but that confidentiality from the partner can be provided if specifically requested. For example, we might say:

> Even though I am seeing you alone, this is couple therapy. Therefore, I will assume that the information you provide can be brought up in our joint sessions. However, if there is something you want to tell me that you don't want your partner to know, please explicitly tell me that and I will keep it confidential.

Assess for violence in the relationship. As we discussed in Chapter 2, violence is common in couples that come to therapy, occurring in 40–70% of those couples. Thus, it is mandatory to assess for violence and evaluate whether couple therapy can proceed safely. Because partners may be embarrassed about the violence, or may not want to embarrass their partners by reporting it, or may be afraid of their partner's reactions if they do report it, violence is best assessed in the individual session. The Couple Questionnaire asks partners about any violence that may have occurred in the relationship in the last year and about any physical intimidation that the respondent may experience. Although there are certainly more detailed questions about violence, such as contained in the Conflict Tactics Scale (Straus, Hamby, Boney-McCoy, & Sugarman, 1996), these questions, created in consultation with intimate partner violence experts*, are what we believe are the minimum questions that should be asked via questionnaire:

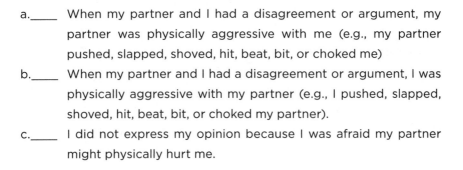

Many people, at one time or another, get physical with their partners when they are angry. For example, some people threaten to hurt their partners, some push or shove, and some slap or hit. Please indicate approximately *how many times* the behaviors in a, b, and c have occurred in the **last year**. Therapists will review your responses and discuss them with you as relevant.

a.____ When my partner and I had a disagreement or argument, my partner was physically aggressive with me (e.g., my partner pushed, slapped, shoved, hit, beat, bit, or choked me)

b.____ When my partner and I had a disagreement or argument, I was physically aggressive with my partner (e.g., I pushed, slapped, shoved, hit, beat, bit, or choked my partner).

c.____ I did not express my opinion because I was afraid my partner might physically hurt me.

---

* These questions on IPV were created in consultation with Drs. Richard E. Heyman, Katherine M. Iverson, and Daniel O'Leary.

If partners indicate zero in each of the items above, we will usually follow up with a confirming question such as "So there has been no violence between the two of you, or no fear of violence?" If either partner indicates that one of the first two items has occurred, we follow up with a series of questions to determine the specific acts that occurred and whether they led to injury. Violence has many degrees of severity so it is important to know, for example, if the partner hit the other in the face and left a bloody nose, or slapped the other in the face with an open hand that left a mark, or slapped the other on the shoulder in a way that neither hurt nor injured the other. If there has been violence in the relationship in the last year, it is useful to find out about the history of violence as it may have existed throughout their relationship, perhaps getting worse over time. If either partner indicates fear, we follow up to get more details on that fear. Sometimes partners are afraid of the other's reactions if they bring up a topic or voice a particular viewpoint, but it is a fear of the other's strong emotional reaction not a fear of physical reprisal. During the violence assessment, we are interested primarily in fear of physical reprisal.

Our general criteria for a couple being able to participate in couple therapy safely is that (a) there has been no violence leading to injury in the last year *and* (b) there is no fear of physical reprisal. These criteria should be applied with a strong dose of good clinical judgment. For example, perhaps there has been violence that did not lead to injury but could easily have (e.g., the partner tried to hit the other but the other ducked just in time) or there was slight injury but only because the partner lost her balance when the other shoved her and then the aggressive partner was mortified and apologetic. Depending on the circumstances, the first couple might be one that cannot proceed with couple therapy safely but the second couple might be one that could. If the couple is thought to be one for whom therapy cannot proceed safely, this feedback is usually given during the feedback phase to be discussed later, with a suggestion that the anger or violence issue needs to be addressed first. The exception to this might be the rare case in which the partner reveals the serious level of violence in secret, fearing reprisal by the other. In that case the therapist must take all reasonable steps to protect the potential victim and not reveal anything that might put the victim at risk. We discuss intimate partner violence in more detail in Chapter 13.

Fortunately, most couples who come to therapy and are violent have low-level, occasional violence driven more by an escalating argument than by a desire to hurt the other or control the other through force. Previous research on IBCT has shown that we can treat those couples effectively without increasing the risk of violence (Simpson et al., 2008). However, with these couples, as with all couples, we monitor violence throughout treatment and take it seriously whenever it occurs. When we discuss active treatment in IBCT, we will see how we monitor violence and address it.

Assess for commitment in the relationship. IBCT is a therapy for couples who have an established relationship and are committed to each other, even if ambivalently so. IBCT is not an intervention for dating couples to determine if they are compatible or a good match for each other; nor is IBCT a separation therapy or mediation therapy for couples who have decided to separate before beginning treatment. It is for couples who want to improve their relationship through therapy. These couples may feel hopeless at times that the relationship can be improved. They may have seriously considered separation as the only viable alternative. However, both partners must want to improve the relationship and be willing to try to improve the relationship. Neither partner can have firmly decided that he or she is done with the relationship. However, we will accept into IBCT couples in which either partner has decided that therapy is a final step—if the relationship doesn't improve in therapy, then they want to separate.

During the initial conjoint session, partners will often give clear indications that they want to improve the relationship, along with their doubts about whether that is possible. However, partners are more likely to be open about their true intentions and motivations in the individual sessions. For example, one partner may be afraid to tell the other that they are done with the relationship or may be fearful of the impact of that decision on the partner or on the children. Sometimes partners want to use couple therapy as a place to reveal their true intentions. That is certainly a reasonable way to use couple therapy and we are confronted with that issue occasionally. In that unusual situation, our feedback session and treatment sessions may be focused on the decision by one partner to leave, the reaction of the other, and the steps they want to take as a result. However, the strategies and tactics of

IBCT that we describe below are intended for couples who want to improve their relationship.

A jumping-off point for a discussion of commitment during the individual session can be the client's response to two items on the Couple Questionnaire, in which clients are asked to rate their commitment to the relationship on the following two scales:

	Not at all	A little	Some-what	Mostly	Certainly
a. I want my relationship to succeed	O	O	O	O	O
b. I will do all I can to make it succeed	O	O	O	O	O

Sometimes a simple reflection of what they rated, such as "You indicate that you certainly want your relationship to succeed" or "You indicate that you are not sure at all whether you want your relationship to succeed," will lead the client to discuss in more detail his or her feelings about the relationship. Obviously a strong desire for the relationship to succeed and a willingness to do one's part in that effort are good signs; however, IBCT is effective even with couples with lower levels of commitment (Atkins, Berns, et al., 2005).

A common barrier to commitment is the presence of competing relationships. IBCT offers clients confidentiality, even from their partners, so that clients can be open about competing relationships as well as about violence. Often we may ask directly about such relationships by making it easy for them to acknowledge such. For example, we may say, "When couples are having serious trouble in their relationship, one or both partners may secretly seek the comfort or the companionship or a connection with another person. Do you think your partner is involved in a secret relationship? Have you been or are you involved in another relationship?" If the client has had a secret emotional or sexual relationship with another but has ended that relationship, then we take a neutral position about whether the partner should or should not tell the other about this past relationship. We can and do certainly discuss what the client feels about that and what he or she thinks are the pros and cons of such a revelation, but we don't recommend what they should do. It is an existential decision, and we don't know what is better for the relationship. However, if the client is in a *current*, secret, competing relationship, whether emotional or physical or both, we take a strong position that the client needs to terminate that affair, reveal it to the partner, or both. We don't think one can focus on improving the presented relationship when there is a secret, competing relationship, and thus it would violate our implicit contract with the couple, which is to improve their relationship. Additionally, the evidence suggests that IBCT is not as effective when partners do not disclose an ongoing affair (Atkins, Eldridge, et al., 2005; Marín, Christensen, & Atkins, 2014).

Partners understand this position, and it is rare indeed that one will insist on both couple therapy for the current relationship and simultaneous continuation of a secret relationship. For the rare partner who does insist on that, we indicate that we cannot do therapy with them and they must handle that as they see fit. We will still preserve their confidentiality: if the partner asks us why we aren't doing therapy with them, we will refer them to the other for an explanation. The partner is unlikely to contact us because the client having the affair will likely indicate something about us (e.g., they don't think we will be helpful to them) or therapy (e.g., I don't want therapy now) that discourages such contact.

If the partner agrees to reveal the affair, then we can proceed with IBCT. If the partner agrees to end the relationship but wishes to keep it secret, we can also proceed with IBCT. However, that case presents a number of problems. Is the partner really prepared to end the relationship? What will be the obstacles to doing that? For example, the affair partner may be resistant to terminating the relationship and retaliate by revealing it to the partner. Maybe the client intends to end the affair but fails to do so. In Chapter 13, we discuss the special issue of infidelity and how IBCT deals with it.

Discuss the client's views of the presenting problems. Although the couple discussed the presenting problems in the first session, we always follow up with further discussion of those problems in the individual sessions. We may reference an important comment or concern that the partner revealed in the earlier session, such as "Bill, I noted in the first session that you were very concerned about how the two of you parent your two boys." Such a comment invites further discussion and clarification of that concern and is often a good jumping-off point for further discussion of the presenting problems.

Partners may provide more frank detail about the presenting problems in their individual sessions than they did in their joint sessions. They may even introduce new problems that were never mentioned in the joint session. The Problem Areas Questionnaire can assist us in this inquiry; it lists common problem areas for couples, asks respondents to rate their satisfaction or dissatisfaction for each of these areas, and asks them to circle their top three areas of concern. For example, a client may indicate on this questionnaire that sex is a major problem in the relationship but have never mentioned it in the joint session.

The following item on the Couple Questionnaire also assists with this inquiry into the presenting problems: "Please describe a recent interaction between you and your partner that is typical of the problems for which you have come to therapy." By discussing this incident, we can often get material relevant for our DEEP analysis. For example, if Bill describes in detail a troubling argument about the children, we may get information that he has a much stricter, discipline-focused approach to parenting than Susie has, that he was emotionally upset in the argument because he felt Susie was suggesting that he didn't really love the children, that he has little time with the children because of his demanding work schedule, and that their common interaction pattern is for Susie to be critical and Bill to be defensive. Throughout our discussion of the presenting problems, we are trying to focus on the one or two major concerns of the couple and gather information for a DEEP analysis of those concerns. We focus on this limited number of concerns for both practical reasons (i.e., the feedback will be too scattered if it includes multiple problems) as well as theoretical reasons (i.e., often just one or two core issues underlie a number of different surface or derivative problems).

If at the first session, one or both partners were interested in reading the self-help book on IBCT, *Reconcilable Differences,* we might enquire about their progress in reading the book and their reaction to it. Assuming they have read far enough to have decided on a core issue, we can find out about what they think that core issue is. If they have progressed through all or some part of the DEEP analysis of that issue, we can find out what they thought were the differences, emotional sensitivities, external stressors, or patterns of interaction that were behind their core issue. Such a discussion provides us not only with helpful information on the DEEP analysis and how the client is thinking about their problem but it also gives us an opportunity to broaden the client's thinking about the problem in the direction of a more adequate DEEP analysis.

Assess client's history, including family history and psychiatric history. Each client's individual history provides information relevant to the DEEP analysis, particularly the differences between partners and their emotional sensitivities. If Edith was raised in a deeply religious environment with strict limitations on sexual activity, her resistance to Daren's desire to be more adventurous sexually makes sense. If John remembers a critical father or critical first wife whom he could never seem to please, his sensitivities to Sue's critical comments makes sense. If Baron has struggled with depression most of his life, then it is hardly surprising that he is often depressed about his marriage.

An exploration of the client's history does more than fill in the DEEP analysis. It can provide information for treatment decisions. IBCT may not be appropriate for a particular couple at the time they seek couple therapy. If one partner struggles with alcohol or drug addiction and has not been able to control his or her substance use, referrals for addiction treatment should be the immediate treatment priority, with couple therapy being a later priority. Similarly, if one partner is seriously suicidal, a focus on that partner is necessary even if the relationship contributes to the suicidality. Finally, there may be issues that seem central to the couple but are better treated elsewhere. A common example is sexual problems. IBCT can be appropriate for conflicts about sexual frequency or type of sexual activity and can help a couple struggling to renew their intimate sexual relationship after periods of avoidance and neglect. However, IBCT is not a treatment in and of itself for sexual dysfunctions or paraphilia; at the very least, collaboration with an expert in these areas is needed. (We discuss the treatment of sexual problems in Chapter 13.) Another example of a common issue for couples that might require additional treatment beyond IBCT is parenting. IBCT can be useful for parents who have conflicts about parenting and who undermine each other, and it can certainly incorporate parent-training strategies. However, IBCT is not a treatment in and of itself for problematic parenting.

In discussing the client's history, we also find out about what attracts them to their partner and keeps them in the relationship despite their problems. Sometimes distressed partners can be more open about their positive feelings as well as their negative feelings when the partner is not present. The following question on the Couple Questionnaire can help us assess the kinds of positive interactions that exist currently: "Please describe a recent interaction between you and your partner that is typical of the positive features that are still part of your relationship." By reading what they have written and asking them to elaborate, we get additional material on the strengths in their relationship.

SUMMARY

In this chapter we provided a brief overview of IBCT and reviewed the evaluation or assessment phase in IBCT, which consists of an initial joint session followed by individual sessions with each partner. The goals for the assessment phase are to establish rapport with each partner and have an initial therapeutic impact, to evaluate whether the couple is appropriate for IBCT, and to gather information relevant for a DEEP analysis of the couple's core issue or issues.

The initial joint session is important because it provides a foundation for the therapy to follow. We establish early on that the process will be interactive and collaborative in that we are actively seeking input from both partners and redirecting the conversation so that neither partner is allowed to rant and berate the other. We typically redirect partners from discussion of the actions that the other does that cause them pain and instead focus on the pain that they genuinely experience, whatever the partner's intentions or actions were. In the initial session we also enquire about the couple's relationship history, reviewing what attracted them to each other initially and what still keeps them in the relationship despite its problems. In this way, we get initial information about their strengths as well as their problems.

The individual sessions are best for determining if the couple can safely and appropriate participate in couple therapy. In an individual session, partners are more likely to be open about the level of violence in their relationship, particularly if the therapist has assured them of confidentiality. Similarly, partners are more likely to be open in an individual session about their level of commitment to the relationship, letting the therapist know if there is a competing, secret relationship or if they have decided they want to end the relationship. Thus, the individual sessions are crucial for determining whether couple therapy is even appropriate for the couple. In addition to this evaluation, the individual session provides more information on the presenting problems and information about the individual's history that can help determine the appropriate course of treatment and inform the DEEP understanding of the couple's problems. It also provides additional information on the strengths in the current relationship.

After this evaluation period, we consider the information we have gathered from the interviews and questionnaires and we organize it for presentation to the couple in the joint feedback session, which is typically the fourth session of IBCT. In the next chapter we discuss that crucial session.

5

Feedback Session and Treatment Overview in IBCT

AFTER THE THREE EVALUATION SESSIONS, we consolidate the information obtained from the initial conjoint session, the two individual sessions, and the questionnaires and organize the feedback session. This session is central in IBCT, as it provides us with an opportunity to present a conceptualization of the couple's problems in a way that is true to the facts of the two individuals and their relationship but is less blaming of either of them than their own views and is more conducive to positive change. It also allows us to outline the nature of the active phase of treatment, in which the three of us can work together to create a more harmonious and fulfilling relationship. Thus, the feedback session consists of two phases: conceptualization of the couple's concerns and their strengths and a description of what the active phase of treatment will look like. The first phase is usually longer than the second phase.

The feedback session is a dialogue between therapist and client, not a lecture. We present our notions tentatively and elicit the clients' feedback. We view the partners themselves as experts on what they experience and invite them to contribute actively to the working formulation. The purpose is to arrive at a mutually acceptable understanding of their concerns and of the treatment plan to address those concerns. At the end of this feedback session, each of the two partners will have had three sessions with us and have heard extensively our views of their concerns and of the way forward. They can go home, discuss their reactions with each other, and make a decision about whether to commit to the active phase of this therapy.

CONCEPTUALIZATION PHASE OF THE FEEDBACK SESSION

Feedback to the couple about their problems and their strengths is organized around the answers to five questions: (a) How distressed is this couple? (b) How committed is this couple to this relationship? (c) What are the one or two core issues that they struggle with? (d) Why are these issues such a problem for them (i.e., what is the DEEP analysis of these issues)?, and (e) What are the strengths that still remain in the relationship? Let's consider these each in turn.

Level of Distress

The severity of a couple's distress may determine how therapy actually proceeds. If couples are mildly to moderately distressed, the assessment phase can proceed without interruption. However, if the couple is in crisis or cannot tolerate a more leisurely assessment procedure, an immediate intervention may be necessary. As we noted in Chapter 4, a couple may present in the initial session as so distressed that they want to plan an immediate, temporary separation or one or both partners pose risks for suicide, homicide, intimate partner violence, or other urgent matters that require immediate attention. Even if the three sessions of assessment proceed as described above, which is almost always the case, we may discover information about the couple's level of distress in the assessment sessions that informs the feedback session and how we should proceed with therapy. For example, the level of distress may be so high that the first step in therapy will be to deescalate tensions rather than address long-standing concerns between the two of them. Or dangerous levels of intimate partner violence or serious suicidal risk may have been

discovered in the individual sessions that indicate couple therapy should not
be the priority at this time.

Both the conjoint and individual interviews provide information about
the couple's level of distress. Partners may reveal facts about their relationship that indicate high distress such as a recent separation, statements that
they need to separate to reduce the distress, and statements that they can
hardly ever interact without anger and argument. In addition to these factual
indicators, the manner in which partners discuss their problems can reveal
their level of distress. Some partners are so angry at one another that they
frequently interrupt and have a hard time listening. One or both may exhibit
extreme hopelessness about their relationship.

Questionnaires can be used to gain a more precise and normative measure
of distress. As we indicated earlier, we use the Couple Satisfaction Index
(16-item version; Funk & Rogge, 2007) because it is available free and has
extensive normative data showing the normal range of satisfaction as well
as the distressed range of satisfaction for couples. When used repeatedly, it
can document improvement in the relationship. There are other good couple adjustment scales such as the Dyadic Adjustment Scale (DAS; Spanier,
1976) and inventories such as the Marital Satisfaction Inventory (MSI; Snyder, 1997) that provide quantitative indices and normative data for assessing
a couple's level of distress. However, they are lengthier and although they
provide additional information about other facets of the relationship besides
distress, they require a cost to use, and IBCT does not require the additional
scales that these questionnaires provide.

When giving feedback to a couple about their level of distress, we often
tell them their scores and give them normative data (e.g., the cutoff point for
distressed couples) to help them interpret their scores. It can be reassuring
for couples to hear that even though they are unhappy, their scores are in
the range of couples who come to therapy and who benefit from therapy.
Sometimes it can be a helpful shock to couples to hear their scores and see
that their unhappiness is well below that of other couples. For example, we
might say something like the following in the appropriate situation:

Both of you questioned whether it was useful or valuable to come to
therapy. You have been married a long time, both of you are good peo-

ple, and neither of you have never been unfaithful or violent or done other horrible things to the other. Your relationship is stable and yet neither of you seems happy. And your scores on the Satisfaction Index that I gave you, which has been completed by thousands of couples in America, reveal that deep unhappiness. Your scores are definitely in the range of couples who come for therapy, even toward the low end of that range. So I think the dissatisfaction runs deep. And therefore, I think couple therapy was a good decision on your part.

Providing feedback about violence during the feedback session can be tricky. The couple has come seeking couple therapy and we don't want to deny them that but we can inform them that couple therapy is not appropriate right now because of concerns about their safety, suggest that they need to get the violence under control before proceeding with couple therapy, and suggest some referrals we have for them, such as anger management or violence-oriented programs. For example, we might say the following prior to making specific referrals in the feedback session when intimate partner violence has been openly admitted by both:

> You both came here seeking couple therapy, and based on the assessment that I have just described, you could clearly benefit from couple therapy. However, I don't think now is the right time for couple therapy; I think there is something more pressing, namely the violence that you both have described. I am concerned about the safety of both of you, not just for your physical safety if the violence leads to injury but also the emotional safety of you both. These intense arguments set you back emotionally and make you question each other and yourselves. You both get embarrassed that the neighbors have heard. So I think dealing with the anger and violence should come first and then later on, couple therapy could be appropriate. Does that make sense?

However, sometimes there are not good and appropriate referral sources for violence and the couple is likely to stay together despite the violence. In this situation, we might tentatively accept the couple for treatment as long as they commit themselves to a nonviolent relationship and accept that treatment will have a major focus on violence, including the development of safety plans and nonviolence contracts and alteration of patterns of escalation. In Chapter 13 we describe in more detail data on intimate partner violence, when couple therapy may be appropriate and effective, and how we adapt IBCT for some violent couples.

Commitment

We also give feedback to the couple about their level of commitment. Usually this feedback is encouraging. For example, we can say something like, "Despite the problems the two of you are having, you both remain committed to the relationship. Both of you want to improve it and you both are willing to do your part in that effort. That is always a good sign for a relationship, no matter what the problems." However, we don't want to give false or misleading feedback. If the couple is low on commitment, we will say so. For example, we might say something like "Coming to therapy seems like a last ditch effort for both of you. You have tried to improve your relationship on your own. You have even tried couple therapy before, but any improvement was temporary at best. So you both are willing to give it one more try, but neither of you is very hopeful. Does that sound accurate?" Not infrequently, partners in a relationship have vastly different levels of commitment and we give feedback about that. For example, we might say "Both of you would like the relationship to improve but I think you, Nick, are much more hopeless about that. You mentioned that you often have had one foot out the door." This kind of feedback can occasionally have a salutary effect of jolting a couple into greater commitment. It can sometimes move one or both partners toward greater realization of the challenge that faces them. However, our feedback is not done to have a strategic effect; it is done to provide the couple with honest feedback. In so doing, we show the couple that we truly understand their situation.

Even when we give this kind of sobering feedback to couples with one or both having low levels of commitment, we balance that with feedback about the strengths in their relationship and with comments on what is at stake for them. Typically, we summarize the couple's strengths after we have reviewed their problems, but we might put that piece right after feedback about commitment if we are summarizing their low levels of commitment. When we give feedback about what is at stake in their relationship, we summarize what they have built and thus what they stand to lose. For example, we might say something like the following:

> Both of you are pretty discouraged about your relationship and often feel hopeless about whether it can be improved, but I think you see how much is at stake here. Over the 10 years you have been together, you have had two children you both adore, you have bought a home you are proud of, and you have created a life together with strong connections with mutual friends and family. Breaking the family apart is a big deal for both of you. So alongside the discouragement you both feel, I think there is a hope, perhaps only a glimmer, that you can improve this relationship and maintain the good you have created. And that is why you came to couple therapy.

Core Issues and Theme

During the three assessment sessions, partners will usually mention a number of issues of disagreement or conflict or concern; usually one or two areas stand out as central because partners express the greatest concern over these issues or these issues create the most intense and frequent conflicts. These issues often correspond to the top three areas of disagreement that partners circled on the Problem Areas Questionnaire.

Couples sometimes present with broad complaints, such as problems with "communication," "intimacy," or "lack of love." In these situations, we find it helpful to get more specificity. For example, does "communication" mean heated arguments, trouble opening up and sharing emotions, lack of discussion about day-to-day events, or something else? Does "intimacy" mean emotional or physical intimacy? Even if the troubles span more than one of these more specific domains, it is helpful for both conceptual reasons and feedback to make these distinctions.

Once we have identified a couple's core issues, we can discern if there is a central theme that unifies these issues. For example, differences in desired intimacy or conflicts around closeness or distance are a common theme in couples, particularly couples seeking therapy. This theme describes a struggle over the optimal level of intimacy present in the relationship. One partner enters therapy desiring more closeness, while the other seeks to maintain what is for him or her an optimal level of distance. For a couple with a closeness-or-distance theme, that theme is always present whether the couple is fighting about whether they should combine or keep their money separate, what amount of time they should spend together, what is quality time together, or what their sex life should be.

Another common theme has to do with control and responsibility. Couples manifesting this theme argue about who is responsible, who is more knowledgeable or competent, and who is going to control which domains of family life. Whether the issue is handling the kids, doing the housework, or managing the budget, the couple clashes over responsibility and control. We see this theme sometimes in military families when the male soldier returns from active duty. During his time away, his wife has worked out routines and ways of dealing with the children that work for her and them. She wants him to take her lead and adapt to their way of doing things. However, he is used to the strict discipline of the military and is not used to handling the immaturity of children. He thinks the children need a strong dose of discipline and attempts to impose that but meets resistance by her and the children. He may feel the family is united against him and that his wife wants him in a secondary position to her. She may feel that he is upsetting the calm equilibrium they were able to achieve in his absence.

Identifying a theme and giving it a label is somewhat subjective. We try to come up with a label that seems to fit for the couple and is one to which they can relate. Consider Hank and Maria, whom we have been using as our example couple. They have one core issue about the parenting of James and one core issue around physical intimacy. We could describe this as a theme around intimacy, with Hank longing for physical intimacy with Maria and Maria longing for emotional intimacy—especially for Hank's understanding and support of her concerns about their son, James. Or we could describe this as a theme centered on whether their relationship should be child focused or adult focused. Or we could describe two themes, a struggle over how James should be parented and a struggle over intimacy between them. Probably the best label would be the first, a struggle around intimacy, assuming that that label made sense to Hank and Maria. The advantage of that label is that it shows both partners wanting and needing a positive connection with the other.

The theme points to what contemporary behaviorists refer to as a response class, a class of interconnected behaviors that serve similar functions. For example, the function of *demanding* more time together, seeking more intimate conversation or sexual activity that includes more affection and foreplay, or arguing for combining finances may be greater connection and union. Conversely, the function of withdrawal, arguing for separation of finances, and seeking time alone may be to maintain or create more psychological distance and independence.

In this important sense, the theme can be thought of as identifying the function of each person's behavior in the prototypical conflict. Because behaviors that serve similar functions are often maintained by similar contextual variables, when the context changes to support a shift in one behavior, other behaviors in the response class may change in a similar manner. For example, if a therapist is able to create a discussion in session about parenting, in which Hank experiences Maria as struggling with how to deal with James and needing his support rather than as abandoning him to focus on James, he may engage in some behaviors out of session that involve moving toward her and James, such as showing concern about how she is feeling or taking a kindlier position toward James. In short, one useful function of identifying a theme is that it helps focus on behaviors such that a shift in one area can generalize to other areas in the relationship. As we will show, efforts to change the context in which particular conflicts occur are fruitful in both acceptance work and more traditional change interventions.

The theme ideally identifies a central struggle in the couple's relationship. If the therapist is successful in reducing that struggle during the session, then positive behavior change can sometimes result outside of the session. For example, if the therapist has a session like that described above and Hank moves toward Maria and James outside the session, Maria may also show more physical affection toward Hank. She is in less of a struggle with him, does not feel so resistant to him, and then naturally moves toward him. In this way, positive actions in one can beget positive actions in the other.

DEEP Analysis of the Core Issues

In this portion of the feedback session, we try to explain why the couple is struggling with their core issues by explaining to them the DEEP analysis of those issues. We often introduce the acronym DEEP and define its components before launching into the DEEP analysis for the couple. As with other aspects of the feedback session, we take a tentative, provisional approach, always seeking feedback and modification from the couple.

The DEEP analysis can be done for the theme itself or for the core issues that make up the theme. For example, if a couple is struggling with a central theme of closeness versus independence, it might be useful to do a DEEP analysis of that theme. For a case like Hank and Maria, it would be better to do separate DEEP analyses on their two core issues of parenting and sex, in that they have separate differences, sensitivities, stressors, and patterns of communication that come into play for each. We might describe the central theme for them, its two component core issues, and the DEEP analysis for each of those issues. See Chapter 3 for the DEEP analyses of those two issues.

Use of the Book Reconcilable Differences

If the couple has been reading our self-help book (Christensen et al., 2014) as they proceed through treatment and one or both have gotten through Parts 1 and 2 and have thus defined a core issue and done a DEEP analysis of it, we want to get their views before stating ours. As noted in Chapter 4, we check in about their reading in the individual sessions and thus get information about their thoughts about the core problem and a DEEP analysis of it, which can influence our own DEEP analysis. We can also guide them in these sessions about their DEEP analysis, leading them to a more accurate analysis. Therefore, what they tell us in the feedback session about what they developed in terms of core problems and the DEEP analysis of them should not be a surprise for us. We can incorporate what they say and build upon it. If couples generate their own DEEP analysis in part, guided by the book and our help, they are likely to feel more ownership of it than if we merely presented it to them as our conceptualization.

Strengths

In preparing to give a couple feedback about their strengths, we consider the information obtained in the interviews and questionnaires. During the initial interview, we reviewed the couple's history including what attracted them to each other and what they still enjoy and appreciate in each other. During the individual interviews we may have gotten additional information about strengths by, for example, following up on an open-ended item in the Couple Questionnaire: "Please describe a recent interaction between you and your partner that is typical of the positive features that are still part of your relationship." We consider four categories of strengths: (a) characteristics of each that the other admires, such as intelligence, or beauty or parenting skill or ambition; (b) characteristics of their relationship that are positive, such as their mutual commitment to the relationship, their devotion to their children and the broader family, their ability to limit heated arguments so that violence or verbal abuse doesn't occur, or their ability to compartmentalize some of their conflicts; (c) positive interactions that they are still able to have, such as an active sex life, positive coparenting, or support of each other during stress or illness; and (d) positive interactions observed in therapy, such as the willingness to listen to the other's point of view even when it is very different from one's own point of view, the willingness to acknowledge personal responsibility for some of the problems, and the ability to contain their negative reactions. We don't necessarily include factors in each of these categories but simply describe the strengths that genuinely have been revealed as a result of our assessment.

Feedback about strengths in the relationship can be uplifting for the couple and thus we usually place it after the discussion of the problems. However, feedback about strengths will only be effective if it reflects the experience of the couple and is not just an attempt to present a positive image. Sometimes distressed couples are so entangled in conflict that they have a hard time acknowledging any current features of the other that are positive. In this case, we can acknowledge some of the past positive features of the relationship, their desire to restore some of that positivity and thus their willingness to come to therapy, and their difficulty in now seeing much beyond their current conflicts.

DESCRIPTION OF THE INTERVENTION PHASE OF THE FEEDBACK SESSION

In this second phase of the feedback session, we describe for couples the goals of treatment as well as the procedures for achieving those goals. The goals include a combination of acceptance and change that are linked to the DEEP analysis. Partners' natural differences and emotional sensitivities are usually well-baked in by their genes and personal histories so that they are stable characteristics. These characteristics can certainly change over the course of a long-term relationship, but they are unlikely to change dramatically during the relatively brief course of therapy. We describe that one goal of therapy is to help partners understand those differences and sensitivities and thus view them with less blame and accusation and thus enable a greater acceptance of those characteristics. The stressors in the couple's external environment can sometimes be changed, but often a change in them, such as quitting a stressful job, can bring even greater stress; as a result, external stressors sometimes have to be accepted. However, it is possible for clients to change the way they deal with stressors and especially the way they deal with each other about their stressors, which brings us to the pattern of interaction. We indicate that a primary goal of therapy is to change the pattern of interaction so that the couple at a minimum does not make the problems created by their differences, emotional sensitivities, and external stressors worse. Ideally, their interactions make these problems better, because the couple is collaborating on their resolution. Our goal is to have them interact around their difficulties in a more constructive way, which usually means not falling into their usual pattern of interaction.

In addition to discussing these general goals of acceptance and change, we may discuss specific goals related to the presenting problems, such as improved collaboration around parenting or greater openness as a way of enhancing trust, or greater emotional and sexual intimacy. However, it is important to frame those goals as being achievable through an improved emotional environment between the two rather than as a behavioral target that the two should achieve and that could heighten the struggle between them. For example, we would not indicate that more sex is a goal of treatment when sex is a source of struggle between the pair and when indicating that as a goal could energize the partner who wants more sex to invoke the therapeutic goal as a coercive weapon to achieve more sex. See how we might give feedback about treatment to Hank and Maria, including feedback about the goals related to sex:

Our goals in this therapy is greater acceptance between the two of you for who you are as well as change in the way you relate to one another. As we discussed, the two of you differ in the types of emotional and physical intimacy you want in your marriage. We have also discussed your emotional sensitivities related to these natural differences. Maria, you are understandably concerned about James and anxious about his development. And Hank, you are understandably concerned about the neglect and distance you feel in the marriage, both the neglect of positive attention and sexual intimacy. There is certainly no way anyone can suddenly make you, Maria, less anxious or you, Hank, less concerned. And James, as both a joy and major stressor in your life, is here to stay. But I believe we can change the way you two relate to each other. Right now, Maria, you are not getting the support and connection you want with Hank about your concerns with James and right now neither of you are getting the positive connection that both of you would like in your marriage. And without that positive emotional connection, the sexual connection has suffered. I really believe this marriage can provide what both of you want—a supportive context for your child, a supportive context for each other, and an emotional connection that naturally leads to more sexual intimacy. And next I want to talk about how we will go about achieving that.

Figure 5.1: Weekly Questionnaire

Name _____   Date _____

Please circle the number corresponding to how you have felt about your relationship with your partner *since the last session. (Items 1-4 from Funk & Rogge, 2007, used with permission)*

1. Please indicate the degree of happiness, all things considered, of your relationship.

Extremely Unhappy	Fairly Unhappy	A Little Unhappy	Happy	Very Happy	Extremely Happy	Perfect
0	**1**	**2**	**3**	**4**	**5**	**6**

	Not at all TRUE	A little TRUE	Some-what TRUE	Mostly TRUE	Almost Com-pletely TRUE	Com-pletely TRUE
2. I have a warm and comfortable relationship with my partner	**0**	**1**	**2**	**3**	**4**	**5**

	Not at all	A little	Some-what	Mostly	Almost Com-pletely	Com-pletely
3. How reward-ing is your rela-tionship with your partner?	**0**	**1**	**2**	**3**	**4**	**5**
4. In general, how satisfied are you with your relationship?	**0**	**1**	**2**	**3**	**4**	**5**

5. Since the last session have there been (circle yes or no for each):

Any incidents of violence or destructiveness?   Yes   No
Any incidents/concerns involving alcohol or drug use?   Yes   No
Any major events or changes (e.g., losing or getting a job)? Yes   No

6. What was the most important, positive interaction that you had with your partner since the last session? Jot down a couple of notes (e.g., discussion about kids, romantic evening).

_____

_____

_____

_____

7. What was the most important, difficult interaction that you had with your partner since the last session? Jot down a couple of notes (e.g., trust incident, disagreement about money).

_____

_____

_____

_____

8. Any upcoming events that could be challenging? Jot down a couple of notes (e.g., visit by in-laws, business trip, weekend away).

_____

_____

_____

_____

9. In this session, it would be most helpful to discuss (rank each; 1 is most and 4 is least helpful):

    ___ Positive incident above   ___ Negative incident above
    ___ Upcoming event above   ___ Issue of _____

10. Homework (if any)

_____

_____

_____

_____

_____

_____

After this introduction to the goals of treatment, we describe the methods and procedures of treatment. We explain that clients will provide the material we will discuss in treatment, which will consist of the salient positive and negative events in their lives, important issues of concern, and upcoming events that could be challenging for them. We will be active participants in helping them discuss these salient incidents, issues, and upcoming events so that their interaction about them can be more constructive than it might be without our participation. In discussing this process, we introduce clients to the simple one-page Weekly Questionnaire (see Figure 5.1) and ask them to each complete this questionnaire prior to each session. They can complete it in the waiting room immediately before the session or at home the night before or the day of the session. Completing the questionnaire as close in time to the session is desirable. The reason that completing this questionnaire at the last minute is a good thing is so that clients will think about their interactions together since the last session and provide key information about their most salient positive and negative interactions and issues, some of which may have just come up prior to the session.

The first four items on the Weekly Questionnaire are rating scales about the level of satisfaction and comfort in the relationship since the last session. By looking at these ratings, we can see how the period since the last session was for them. (This measure can also be used for monitoring treatment progress over time.) The fifth item asks yes or no questions about the occurrence of violence, the occurrence of problematic alcohol or drug use, or the occurrence of any major change. If clients answer yes to any of these questions in item 5, that will be the first focus of therapy. Usually clients answer no to these items so that the remaining items on the Weekly Questionnaire provide the material that will be discussed in therapy. Item 6 asks about the most important positive interaction partners had since the last session; item 7 asks about the most important difficult interaction partners had since the last session. Item 8 asks about any upcoming events that might be challenging for the couple and item 9 asks partners to rank order these three events (e.g., positive, difficult, and upcoming challenging) as well as any issue of concern such as finances or parenting—even if there were no recent events related to the issue—in terms of which would be most helpful to discuss in therapy.

Often a session cannot cover all of these incidents and issues so it is important to discuss those that would be most helpful to the client. Item 10 refers to any homework that emerges from the discussion in therapy.

By going over the Weekly Questionnaire in the feedback session, we show clients how *they* will determine the content of therapy. We also emphasize that we will be active participants in these therapeutic discussions about the salient incidents and issues so that the couple can discuss them more constructively than they might be able to do on their own. Specifically, we will help them discuss this content without getting stuck in their usual pattern of interaction. We also explain how we will help them have more constructive discussions about these important topics by asking them to initially talk through us rather than directly to each other. By having them talk through us, we can slow down the interaction, make sure we understand what each wants to communicate, and help them communicate more clearly their views and feelings to the other.

If one or both partners have been reading our self-help book, we can encourage them to read the next section, Part 3, IBCT Strategies for Promoting Acceptance (and Change). This section will help them understand each other better and move away from their adversarial stance. This reading may facilitate their ability to accept the natural differences and emotional sensitivities that each has, which often trigger conflict between them.

After explaining the process of therapy, introducing the Weekly Questionnaire, and encouraging further reading in the book for those couples doing this reading, we ask for questions. Although we may solicit questions at various points throughout the feedback session, it is important to see if there are final questions once the feedback is complete. After answering these questions, we ask the couple to go home, discuss their reactions with each other, and decide whether they agree with the conceptualization and approach and wish to commit themselves to a course of couple therapy. The specifics of that commitment depend on the couple. Usually it is a good idea to ask the couple to commit to at least 10–12 treatment sessions. In that period of time, progress should be clearly apparent even though the couple may stay for longer treatment. The therapist can explain that in the primary clinical trial of IBCT, which led to significant clinical improvement in about 70% of moderately to severely distressed couples, couples received a total of about 25 sessions. However, it may be better for some couples to commit to a smaller number of sessions. A couple that is skittish about therapy may be willing to commit to 4 intervention sessions, which we believe is the minimum commitment that should be made. In our work with couples seeking help through the US Department of Veteran's Affairs (described in Chapter 2), we ask for an initial commitment of only 4 treatment sessions since veteran patients have high dropout rates from all forms of therapy. We tell couples that after this initial period of therapy, we will conduct a mini-assessment of progress to see if therapy is helping and if the couple wants to commit to another set of therapy sessions. In this way, couples see that they are making only a limited commitment to therapy and that we all will evaluate periodically whether it is helping them.

OVERVIEW OF THE INTERVENTION
PHASE OF TREATMENT

As noted in our feedback to clients, the goals of IBCT are both acceptance and change: primarily acceptance for the natural differences between partners and their emotional sensitivities; usually acceptance for their external stressors, although occasionally these can be changed; and primarily change for their patterns of interaction. We attempt to achieve these goals by focusing on emotionally salient material that the couple provides us with their Weekly Questionnaire: the positive and negative events that have happened, the issues of concern, and challenging upcoming events that they may fear or dread. However, the most salient material is what happens between the couple in the session. As partners discuss these emotionally salient incidents and issues, they will invariably be triggered by these discussions and engage in some variation of their problematic interaction patterns. A discussion about a negative incident in which partners were critical of each other will likely lead to a discussion in therapy in which partners exchange criticisms. For example, as Hank and Maria discuss an incident when they got into an argument about James triggered by Hank's criticism of Maria for her "excessive concern" about James, Hank may again criticize Maria about the way she handles James. Or as they discuss their sex life, Maria may start to shut down or withdraw. These responses by couples during the session, which resemble their problematic interaction patterns outside of therapy, offer the most salient targets for interaction because the couple is enacting the problem of concern. These illustrations of the problem during therapy sessions offer couple therapists the opportunity and challenge of bringing about change on the spot.

What is the change that we IBCT therapists seek to bring about? In place of the couple's problematic interaction, we seek to facilitate some combination and variation of three kinds of discussions: a compassionate discussion in which partners share deeply held feelings, an analytic discussion in which partners share nonjudgmental perspectives and views, and a practical discussion in which partners discuss concrete changes or attempt concrete changes. The couple's natural tendency will be to revert back to their usual pattern of interaction, which has become their default interaction when dealing with the particular issue under discussion. However, the extent to which we can repeatedly move them away from their problematic pattern of interaction and into a more constructive interaction consisting of some combination of these three discussions is a measure of how successful we are.

Through a compassionate discussion, we are focusing on emotional or affective change and trying to achieve the IBCT goal of *empathic joining*. Through an analytic discussion, we are focusing on cognitive change and trying to achieve the IBCT goal of *unified detachment*. Through practical discussions, we are focusing on behavioral problem solving and trying to achieve deliberate behavioral change. We devote separate chapters to empathic joining, unified detachment, and direct change respectively. We categorize empathic joining and unified detachment as primarily acceptance-focused interventions because the discussion in these interventions is not focused on what each partner could or should do to get along better. The focus is on what the partners feel (i.e., empathic joining) and what the partners think and observe (i.e, unified detachment); the goal is for partners to understand and accept their differences and sensitivities and by doing so, reduce the adversarial relationship between them. Thus, although behavior change is not the focus of the discussion, successful empathic joining and unified detachment often bring about positive changes in partners' interaction with each other.

These two acceptance-focused interventions are usually the initial focus of therapeutic interventions and will be discussed first in Part 3 of this text. We also describe tolerance interventions, which can sometimes facilitate both empathic joining and unified detachment. The change-focused interventions discussed in Part 4 of the book are usually a later focus of therapy. We focus on empathic joining and unified detachment first because real, long-lasting change is much more likely when partners first understand and care about what each is feeling and how their interaction prevents both of them from getting what they want. The compassionate discussions in empathic joining and nonjudgmental analytic discussions in unified detachment can on their own lead to positive change without the therapist or clients ever specifically targeting things to change or engaging in deliberate change efforts. We think this kind of *spontaneous change* is more likely to be meaningful to couples and persist in couples. Furthermore, an early focus on deliberate change efforts may be met with resistance or strained negotiations as partners push for what they each want and try to get the best deal possible, a process that doesn't mobilize their love for each other.

The typical format of an intervention session starts with a greeting and collection of the Weekly Questionnaire. If one or both partners did not complete the questionnaire, we have the questionnaires available so they can complete them on the spot. As previously described, we glance quickly at the questionnaires to see how the period of time was since the last session (the first four ratings on the questionnaire) and whether there were any "yes" answers to item 5, which asks about the occurrence of violence, the occurrence of a problematic drug or alcohol incident, or a major change. If there was an item 5 incident, the first order of business is to debrief that incident or change.

For most sessions, we typically start by discussing the most positive event that the two of them experienced (item 6), which may have been the same or different events. If the positive event(s) was significant, we give it detailed attention. A positive event can be significant because the couple handled an issue or event that is normally difficult for them in a better way (e.g., they had a more constructive discussion about money than they usually have or they handled a visit by relatives better than they usually do) or it can be significant because it marks a change in the relationship (e.g., they had sex for the first time in a long time) or it can be significant because it was especially positive (e.g., one partner supported the distressed other in a way that made them both feel good). For such significant events, we review the incident to help the couple understand what they did that made things go well and to give them opportunities to acknowledge what each did or express appreciation for what each did. If the positive event was not particularly significant, such as a fun movie or a nice dinner with the neighbors, we don't give the positive event a lot of attention but perhaps comment that the couple is still able to enjoy things together despite their problems.

If the couple had a very bad time since the last session and come to therapy in a negative mood toward the other, a focus on what was positive is often not a wise choice. The couple may be anxious to discuss the negative events of the week and any discussion of positives would be forced at best or actually be negative. For example, when partners are angry at each other they may thinly disguise a criticism in a presumably positive statement (e.g., "It was positive that I didn't have to see her much last week") or they may easily turn a genuine positive from the week into a negative event (e.g., "He got up in the middle of the night to take the baby—which is a rare exception"). When a couple is in this negative mood, it is usually best to focus first on the incidents that trouble them from the week.

Once the discussion of the positive event has concluded, or if we believe that a discussion of a positive event would not be helpful given the couple's angry or negative state, we set an agenda with the couple. There may not be time to discuss all the negative incidents, issues, and challenging upcoming events that both partners list, so we briefly mention what each listed on the questionnaire and their ranking of those items. We see if they still want to talk first about their top-ranked items; they may feel differently about the ranking at this point. If they have different top-ranked items, we see if they can agree on what should be discussed first. If they both are anxious to talk about their top-ranked item, we tell them that we will make sure to discuss both items this session and will give approximately equal time them to both.

Before starting the discussion of negative or challenging incidents or issues, we typically ask the couple to talk to us and through us. Rather than talking directly to each other, they should address their comments to us. With this format of interacting, we have the most influence over the interaction. We can slow down the interaction, prevent partners from interrupting each other or talking over each other, and ensure that each partner gets a hearing for their point of view. We can guide or prompt them away from accusation and blame and toward more disclosure of their feelings and views. We can ignore unhelpful comments and highlight helpful ones. We can make transitions between partners that minimize defensiveness and maximize the likelihood of disclosure.

For example, if we were discussing an incident during the week, when Hank and Maria had a negative discussion about James, and Hank was talking to us, he might initially mention what he sees as Maria's excessive concern and anxiety about James. We would guide him away from those kinds of comments and perhaps enquire about his observations of what happened when the two of them tried to discuss James. He might again criticize Maria for "the crazy fears" she voiced in that discussion, but we might try to focus him on his observations about how the conversation derailed so quickly. Or we might guide him toward voicing his concerns about James (e.g., maybe Hank has some also but is afraid to voice them for fear it would exacerbate Maria's), his feelings about his parental role (e.g., perhaps he feels left out of the parenting), or his frustration and hopelessness that they so quickly get into an adversarial positions regarding James. Once we have guided Hank into more revelatory communication, in which he talks about his feelings and views, and away from accusatory communication, in which he attacks Maria, we can transition to Maria. When we do that transition, we would try to prompt her to voice her own feelings and observations rather than defend herself (e.g., claiming she is not overly concerned about James), or counterattack (e.g., saying it is Hank who doesn't care about James). We might prompt her to talk about her feelings about the issue, such as her sense of having to deal with James on her own. For example, we might say "Maria, Hank has mentioned some of his feelings and views, but I know that an issue for you is that you sometimes feel alone in dealing with James and feel overwhelmed by the responsibility. Would you talk about that?" We might also ask her about her observations of their interaction: "Maria, Hank mentioned that you two quickly escalated into a negative discussion about James. Did you observe that also? Would you describe what you saw?"

This format of talking through us gives us more influence to guide the conversation in a constructive direction and decreases the chances that the couple will get into their usual pattern of interaction. However, the couple may have trouble following this format and, despite our efforts, get into a version of their usual pattern of interaction. In these cases, we make an important decision about whether it will be more helpful (a) to pause the discussion of whatever incident was the initial focus and instead debrief what just happened between them right now in the session or (b) to just encourage them to return to the format of talking through us and continue the discussion of the incident or issue. Often it is helpful to do the former because the emotions and dynamics of their interaction are on full display. We will discuss later how we use IBCT treatment strategies to discuss the couple's incidents and issues as well as the emergence of the couple's problematic interaction in the session.

Once we have established an agenda, we spend most of the session using the strategies described in the chapters below to help the couple discuss the incidents and issues they listed on the questionnaire as well as occasions when the discussion of the incident or issue leads to the problematic pattern emerging in the session. However, we leave some time at the end of the session for a wrap-up summary of the important take-home messages from the session, messages that may lead to a more constructive interaction between the partners. This summary may include observations by one partner or by us, emotional reactions by one or the other partner, practical suggestions that were made, or agreements on a decision or on an experiment to try. As we discuss the therapeutic strategies in the chapters below, what we mean by *important take-home messages* will become clear. If discussions during the session led to some specific decisions, agreements, experiments, or actions that partners decided to take, we can, if helpful, have them write these down on their Weekly Questionnaire as homework. Otherwise, their usual homework is just to bring in the completed Weekly Questionnaire.

If the conversation in session got heated, which can often happen, we want to allow time at the end of the session for the couple to cool down, to achieve some limited closure on the problem, and to make a decision about continuing the discussion after the session. Are they too heated to have a constructive discussion after leaving the session? Would it be better to postpone further discussion until the next session? Is that possible for them to do?

In order to help the couple cool down, we may say something like "We are getting near the end of the session and it looks as if we are not going to resolve this issue today. I want to give each of you a chance to make some final comments on the issue if you want, so you don't feel that you got cut off." After the couple has made some final comments, then we may say something like "I think we need to decide whether you two can leave this topic in here until we discuss it next session or whether you want to continue the discussion outside of therapy." If the conversation has been very heated and partners seem angry, they may not want to or be able to leave the topic in session. If we know that heated conversations between them outside of our presence are usually painful and unconstructive, we will encourage them to discontinue the discussion for a period of time until they can cool down. We may do some minor problem solving with them about what they will do on the ride home or for the rest of their time together that day. Of course we cannot control what couples do outside the session, but we may be able to limit some conflict escalation and the resultant pain for them both if we do a little joint planning with them.

SUMMARY

In this chapter we reviewed the feedback session as well as provided an overview of treatment intervention sessions. The feedback session consists of two parts, the first being a conceptualization of the couple and their difficulties and the second being an overview of treatment. In the conceptualization phase, we provide the couple with feedback about their level of distress, their commitment to the relationship, the issues that they struggle with and the central theme those issues reflect, our DEEP conceptualization of those issues, and the strengths in their relationship. In the second phase of the feedback session, we describe for the couple what treatment intervention will look like. The couple will provide the material that will be discussed in therapy through the Weekly Questionnaire: the most significant positive incident and difficult incident that occurred between them since the last session, any issue of concern to them even if a relevant incident didn't happen, and any upcoming event that could be challenging for them. We will actively participate in discussions of these incidents and issues with the goal of helping them have a more constructive and meaningful discussion than they normally have. Their natural tendency will be to revert back to their problematic pattern of interaction when they discuss difficult incidents and issues. Instead of allowing that problematic pattern to continue, we will try to facilitate some combination of three kinds of constructive discussions: a compassionate discussion in which the couple shares important feelings that they experience, an analytic discussion in which the couple shares their nonjudgmental views and perspectives, and a practical discussion in which the couple engages in deliberate problem solving to resolve concerns between them.

The content of a typical intervention session in IBCT consists of the following: (a) collection of the Weekly Questionnaire and a check-in on how they have been doing; (b) discussion of any major issues of concern that may have happened such as violence, problematic drug or alcohol incidents, or major changes in their life; (c) discussion of the most significant positive event that occurred between them since the last session; (d) an agenda-setting phase in which the topics of most salience for the couple (e.g., a negative incident, issue of concern, or upcoming event) and the order of discussion of those topics is decided, (e) discussion of those topics with us the therapists playing an active role in facilitating a constructive discussion; and (f) a wind down and summary toward the end of the session. The format of a typical intervention session, at least early on in treatment, has conversation going through us. Rather than clients talking directly to each other, they talk directly to us so that we can have greater influence to guide them in more constructive ways and make transitions that reduce the chances of defensive or counterattacking responses. However, as we shall see below, we may sometimes direct the couple to talk to each other, especially in later sessions. Whatever format we use, the couple will often default to some version of their usual pattern of problematic interaction. At that point, we can abandon the topic of discussion and focus instead on the problematic interaction that is happening in front of us, with the goal of altering that interaction in the moment.

With this overview of IBCT intervention in mind, we now discuss the specific treatment interventions that IBCT uses, both the acceptance-focused interventions in Part 3 and the change-focused interventions in Part 4. We begin with empathic joining in the next chapter.

IBCT Strategies for Promoting Acceptance (and Change)

6

&

Creating Acceptance and Change Through Empathic Joining

COUPLES USUALLY COME to therapy because they have repeated conflicts around a theme or set of core issues. Their immediate objective may be to resolve the conflicts; however, they want a relationship that is more than just free of conflicts. Partners got into the relationship for the emotional and physical intimacy they experienced with each other. Now they would like to resolve their conflicts and restore or enhance that intimacy.

The treatment strategy of empathic joining described in this chapter attempts to foster a fundamentally new experience of problems as a means for connecting with the other. Although couples might still prefer to be free of their problems entirely, these problems offer promise of greater closeness as well as the peril of greater distance. Their problems provide a window into their emotional sensitivities and the emotions, both surface and hidden, that these sensitivities activate, as well as their deeply rooted differences. Therefore, these problems can be an opportunity for them to learn more about each other and be more responsive to each other. In this way, problems can sometimes be vehicles for greater intimacy, for new sources of strength and closeness. This combination of openness, responsiveness, and emotional intimacy is the primary goal of empathic joining.

THEORY AND EVIDENCE FOR EMPATHIC JOINING

The Interpersonal Process Model of Intimacy (IPMI), proposed by Harry Reis and Philip Shaver (1988), describes how intimacy develops as a result of a series of interactions between partners. In this model, partners disclose personal information about core aspects of themselves, including both factual information (e.g., "My last boyfriend cheated on me") and emotional information (e.g., "Something about you makes me feel that I can trust you to be honest with me"). However, for the interaction to feel intimate, this information must be received by a responsive partner who provides understanding, validation, acceptance, and caring. Furthermore, the person who disclosed must perceive the partner as being responsive. If these three pieces play out repeatedly between partners, so disclosure and responsiveness go both ways, then partners will feel emotional intimacy with each other. Empirical evidence has garnered support for this model (e.g., Caprariello & Reis, 2011; Laurenceau, Rivera, Schaffer, & Pietromonaco, 2004; A. E. Mitchell et al., 2008).

As we shall see below, what we try to promote in couples through empathic joining is both factual and emotional disclosure but primarily emotional disclosure. However, unlike a developing relationship in which emotional disclosures usually are clear and positive (e.g., "I love when you do that"; "I looked forward all day to seeing you"), the emotional disclosures related to conflict may be more complicated because the feelings are painful, ambivalent, confusing, negative, or some combination of these. Thus, partners are not as easily able to disclose their emotional reactions or to be responsive to the other's disclosures. However, if the therapist can help them both disclose to the other and be responsive to the other, the conflict can be a means of achieving greater emotional closeness.

In addition to the emotional closeness that empathic joining can facilitate, research has shown that the experience of empathy is a powerful predictor of helping behavior (see Dovidio, Piliavin, Schroeder, & Penner, 2006, for a review). We want to help those we feel empathy toward. Thus, empathy for the partner can trigger supportive behavior toward the partner. This behavior may be particularly powerful because the behavior typically comes about spontaneously and autonomously, rather than being driven by obligation or pressure, and thus may feel more loving to the receiving partner. Consider the title of a recent research article that investigated the motivation for helping when there is empathic arousal toward the other, a title that captures one of our goals in empathic joining: "I help because I want to, not because you tell me to": Empathy increases autonomously motivated helping (Pavey, Greitemeyer, & Sparks, 2012).

Empathy affects the attributions that we make for another's behavior. Experimental laboratory studies have shown that getting participants to take an empathic stance toward a negative act increases the chances of them making a situational versus a dispositional interpretation of that act (reviewed in M. H. Davis, 2018). These situational attributions cast less responsibility onto the actor and thus lead to less blame of the actor. Perhaps as a result of this process, empathy is linked via attribution to forgiveness of the partner (J. R. Davis & Gold, 2011), although some research has shown direct links between empathy and forgiveness (Fincham, Paleari, & Regalia, 2002). In either case, empathy can facilitate the restorative process of forgiveness.

Forgiveness typically refers to a response to a transgression by the other. Emotional acceptance, as we use it, is both a broader and narrower term. It is broader in the sense that it refers to a large class of behaviors rather than a specific act. John can accept Angela's anxiety about company coming over and Angela's tendency to be short with John as Angela tries to organize for the event. However, John might forgive Angela for a particular act, such as calling John a "self-centered narcissist." Emotional acceptance is also a narrower term in that it refers to less egregious behaviors whereas forgiveness is usually reserved for more serious transgressions. John might accept that Angela is preoccupied, anxious, and short in advance of company but forgiveness would be more appropriate if Angela was extremely critical or dismissive (e.g., angrily telling John "You never help. You are a total failure as a husband"). We believe that empathy facilitates acceptance through similar processes by which empathy facilitates forgiveness. Our clinical trial on IBCT showed that IBCT led to much more emotional acceptance than the comparison treatment of TBCT, even after controlling for the frequency of the partner's behavior (Doss, Thum, Sevier, Atkins, & Christensen, 2005).

Romantic partners often experience their most positive and most negative emotions for each other. The hallmark of distressed couples is negative emotion, with one or both partners in distressed couples often demonstrating emotional dysregulation (Snyder et al., 2006). Because of this excess of negative emotion, partners have difficulty feeling empathy for each other. Although it is easy for most people to feel empathy for another when they see that other experience an obviously painful event, such as a bad fall or a public humiliation, partners have difficulty experiencing empathy for the person they love when the painful event is caused in part by the partners themselves. The reasons are several. First of all, partners are often not fully aware of the behavior in themselves that is painful for the other. For example, Debra may not realize how short and irritable she sounded when she declined Mark's attempt at physical affection. Or Mark may not realize how distracted he was when Debra told him of the doctor visit she had that concerned her. Second, partners often react to painful events from the other with anger or withdrawal that unfortunately decreases the chances of empathy from the other. Mark may make a critical comment to Debra (e.g., "You seem to have lost any ability to be loving") after she responds with irritation to his attempt at physical affection. Debra may just shut down and withdraw after Mark's distracted response to her description of her doctor appointment. Third, partners are often not fully aware of all of their mixed emotional reactions to their partner. Mark may be aware of his anger at Debra's response but be less aware of his sense of rejection or his discomfort at the strength of his emotional reaction. Debra may be aware of her upset at Mark's distracted response but be less aware of how dismissed and unimportant she felt with his lack of response. In IBCT we distinguish between the surface emotions, which occur more or less openly and are often obvious both to the person experiencing them and to the partner (e.g., Mark's open anger, Debra's angry refusal to talk), and hidden emotions, which are additional, less obvious, and more complicated emotional reactions (e.g., Mark feeling rejected, Debra feeling dismissed and unimportant). Fourth, even if partners are fully aware of some of their hidden emotions, they may react negatively to the possibility of being open with the partner about them. Mark may be hesitant to reveal how rejected he felt because it might make him look weak in her and in his own eyes. Debra may be hesitant to reveal anything to Mark about feeling so dismissed by him for fear of getting further dismissal from him, such as accusations that she is "overreacting." Fifth, it may be hard for partners to be empathic with the other because it can question their own views of themselves. If Debra were to empathize with how hurt Mark is by her lack of affectionate responsiveness, she might wonder if she is cold or unloving. If Mark were to empathize with Debra, he might wonder if he has not been a good husband. Finally, partners' own emotional experiences can get in the way of empathy. If Mark is preoccupied with his own upset at Debra's lack of affection, he may not be open to Debra's concerns about his responsiveness to her medical concerns. If Debra is preoccupied with her medical concerns, Mark's desire for affection may seem a petty nuisance.

Because of all of these factors, we often have to work with clients in the ways we describe below to bring them to a place where they can have a compassionate discussion and thus feel more naturally feel empathic with each other. As part of this work, we help them label and differentiate their emotional responses. Apart from the empathy that this process may engender in the partner, research has shown that labeling and differentiating emotions tends to reduce the intensity of these emotions and help regulate them. For example, Torre and Lieberman (2018) reviewed the research on "affect labeling" ("putting feelings into words") and how this process serves as implicit emotion regulation. A number of studies have shown that this process affects brain regions associated with emotional activation (e.g., decreased activation of the amygdala). In addition, helping a client differentiate negative emotions from one another also may modulate this emotion, reduce the likelihood that it leads to problematic behavior such as aggression or substance use, and lead to more adaptive behavior (e.g., Erbas, Ceulemans, Lee Pe, Koval, & Kuppens, 2014; Kashdan, Barrett, & McKnight, 2015; Starr, Hershenberg, Li, & Shaw, 2017). Thus, there is considerable empirical support for several specific benefits of promoting empathy between partners: it can promote greater closeness between partners, it can lead to supportive behavior by the partner who is feeling empathy, it can lead to acceptance and forgiveness, and the process of unpacking emotional experience by labeling and differentiating emotions can not only lead to an empathetic response by the partner but also to a down-regulation of emotion by the one unpacking his or her emotions.

STRATEGIES FOR PROMOTING EMPATHIC JOINING

The first step in promoting empathic joining takes place during the assessment and feedback phase. During the assessment, we highlight the painful reactions that each partner experiences, emphasizing the wound versus the arrow. Then during the DEEP analysis in the feedback session, we reformulate their problems in terms of natural differences between them that affect their emotional sensitivities in ways that are often heightened by the external stressors in their lives. We underscore the pain that each experiences and their efforts, however unsuccessful, to alleviate that pain. We show how these efforts led them to be stuck in a pattern of interaction that gives them at most temporary relief from the pain they experience with each other. As a result, when partners start the active intervention phase of IBCT, they should be more aware of the emotional experience that each has, setting the stage for empathic joining.

During the active intervention phase we discuss salient incidents and issues in the couple's life, such as the most positive and most negative incident since we last saw them, an emotional incident that develops between them during therapy, an upcoming event that could be challenging for them, or an issue of concern. Discussion of these events is likely to bring strong feelings to the fore. To process these feelings and increase the chances of an empathic response by the partner, we guide couples in a different way of talking about these feelings. Often partners' tendency is to focus on the other's behavior that triggered their feelings. Instead, we focus on each partner's own emotional reactions rather than what the other has done or said that caused those reactions. We encourage partners to talk about their own experience rather than attempting to describe what the other feels or what may have motivated the other. Thus, we may make comments that direct partners away from a focus on the other and onto themselves. For example, we may say something like "Cal, you are providing your thoughts about what Tanya may be feeling when her mother visits. Would you talk about what is going on with you when your mother-in-law visits?"

We know that partners are often not fully aware of or in touch with how they are feeling and thinking, so we don't want to bombard them with variations of the question "How does that make you feel?" However, because we have some knowledge of the client based on our assessment, because we know the situation that the client is in, and because we observe the client when he or she talks about a difficult situation, we can take educated guesses at how the client may be feeling and thinking. Therefore, to help focus clients on their own subjective experience, we may suggest tentatively what is going on with them. For example, we might say "Cal, I wonder if you feel put upon or that you don't have a say in what happens." Or as another example, "Tanya, it sounds as if you may be a little angry at your mom, but may be hesitant to voice that to Cal, for fear it might strengthen his already strong dislike of your mom."

When clients talk about their experience, we often encourage what we call *soft disclosures* rather than *hard disclosures*. Hard disclosures reveal the self in a stronger, more dominant position visa-vis the partner. They often involve expressions of anger and resentment that convey assertion, power, and control (e.g., "I will not let myself be taken advantage of"; "I will get what I want"; "I won't be controlled"). Soft disclosures reveal the self as vulnerable to the partner. They reflect feelings of hurt, fear, and disappointment or convey doubt, uncertainty, and danger (e.g., "I wasn't sure she cared about me"; "I didn't know if I could go it alone"; "I thought he would get upset"; "I was afraid she'd be disappointed in me"). Hard disclosures are sometimes easier to make because they don't reveal the self as vulnerable, but they are harder for the partner to hear because they imply blame and dominance over the partner. In contrast, soft disclosures are often more likely to promote closeness because they reveal vulnerability and pain.

We assume that when partners are upset with the other, their emotions are usually mixed. Although they are upset with the other, they love the other and can be troubled that they are so upset or that the partner who presumably loves them would do what they did. Even though they are upset at what the other did, they may have some sense that they were complicit in it. As a result, their emotions may be something of a jumble. Even if the emotions expressed are clear, such as strong and unmistakable anger, we can safely assume that other emotions may be present under the surface—hurt, betrayal, jealously, or others. Thus, we assume that there are soft counterparts to most hard expressions. Hurt usually accompanies anger; disappointment often comes with resentment; fear and insecurity often breed assertion and aggression. When we encourage self-disclosure, hard disclosures are most likely to come first. These disclosures are important because they are accurate reflections of the speaker's experience. However, they are likely to push the partner away and are unlikely to generate empathy unless they are accompanied by and framed in terms of soft disclosures. Tim will not be able to empathize with Sharon if he sees her as just angry at him for letting his boss's expectations control his life. However, he may be able to experience empathy for her if he sees her loneliness, her desire to share the burden, or her sense of being overwhelmed when she is alone with their three young children. Sharon will not be able to empathize with Tim if she sees him as angry and blaming her for not being able to manage the household better, but she may be able to empathize with him if she experiences that he, too, is overwhelmed with all of their responsibilities and uncertain how to proceed.

The goal of empathic joining is to soften partners so that they can engage with each other in a more compassionate, supportive way. Empathic joining is a way of shifting partners from an adversarial or fearful stance with each other and toward an understanding and caring stance toward each other. In IBCT, we take a functional rather than a formal approach to empathic joining. We don't assume that there are universal strategies that always work to create empathic joining with any couple. Because of partners' unique genetic endowment and learning histories, the path to an empathic connection may also be unique. For example, in general, angry expressions harden the listener, but some partners soften in response to the other's expression of anger. Alex had avoided much direct expression of feeling for years so Hilda softened toward him during a therapy session when he lost his temper, because at least some emotional expression was occurring and his strong emotion showed her that he still cared about her—instead of being indifferent about her as she had feared. Anger, in other words, will not always harden the listener or push the listener away or be experienced as negative; it depends on the couple.

Similarly, the so-called soft emotions may not always have the expected impact. Some listeners may respond to expressions of hurt and sadness negatively, seeing such expressions as opportunities to regain or enhance their dominance. To take another example, some listeners soften in response to their partner discussing some of the strong emotions they experienced in their families of origin that are similar to the emotions they feel toward their listening partners. Behavior that has been reacted to as malevolent by the listening partners may be received more empathically when it is viewed as an inevitable consequence of a traumatic family history. However, not all listeners soften in response to such insight into the childhood roots of their partner's negative behavior. They might say something like "Yes, I agree that it is not okay that his dad did that to him, but that doesn't make it okay for him to do the same thing to me." In short, couples will respond idiosyncratically to particular experiences; one that works for a particular couple will not necessarily work for the next.

Given the inevitable variability in how couples might respond to a particular intervention, how do we go about exploring each partner's emotional reactions in ways that facilitate empathic joining? First, we have to decide on whom to focus initially. Who will be able to discuss their emotional experience, revealing their hidden emotions in a way that leads to a different, better, compassionate discussion between the two of them? We need to make that decision strategically, basing it on our read of what is happening in the room at the moment and our understanding of the couple's usual pattern of interaction. If one partner is experiencing strong emotion at the moment, no matter whether it is hard or soft emotion, we usually start with that person first. Ignoring someone who is already experiencing strong emotion usually heightens that emotion because the person feels ignored, passed over, or throttled from expression. If neither partner is experiencing strong emotion, we can be guided by their typical pattern of interaction and our judgment about who is most likely to be able to disclose their hidden emotions. For example, if Derek and Alysia's usual pattern of interaction is Derek expressing his anger at Alysia for not following through on some task and the negative incident they wish to discuss seems like another example of this, we might start with Alysia and her views and reactions to the incident. If we start with Derek, it is more likely to trigger their usual pattern. If, however, we have seen that Derek is able with our help to explore his complex emotions and disclose his hidden emotions while Alysia tends to shut down immediately, we might start with Derek and see if an initial focus on him may make it easier for Alysia to open up. However, let's say that Derek has a hard time moving beyond his hard emotions of anger at what he sees as Alysia's many failures. Furthermore, his emotional expression is so strong and dominant that he trumps any emotional expression by Alysia, leading her to what seems like her only possible response—shutting down. In that case, we might share our analysis with the couple and enlist their cooperation in altering it by starting with Alysia first. For example, we might say:

> I have noticed that when we talk about a difficult incident, you, Derek, are able to express your strong emotions easily and feel comfortable doing so. However, those emotions come across so strongly to you, Alysia, that you start to shut down immediately so that when Derek is done, you have nothing to say, which makes you feel, Derek, even more upset, because you have lost contact or connection with your partner. I would like to try to alter this pattern so Alysia has a voice and Derek has a partner. So, when we talk about an upsetting event, whether it happens at home or in here, I want to focus on you first, Alysia, and help you voice your reactions. I want to hear your reactions also, Derek, but I think you are so clear on your reactions that you can hold them and voice them after Alysia has had a chance. Let's try that and see how it works.

Having decided on whom to focus first, our second step is to shift clients away from providing accusatory details about an incident and from speculating on the partner's unsavory motivations or emotions and toward expressions of their own emotional reactions. We can accomplish this shift directly, by being curious about a client's reactions. Sometimes we may need to first acknowledge what the client has said that we don't wish to pursue (e.g., "Eileen, I see you have thought about why Debra did what she did, but I am curious about your reaction to her letting you know that she wanted to spend the evening by herself"). Other times we can simply ignore what the client said and just pursue their emotional reactions (e.g., "Eileen, I am curious about your reactions to Debra telling you that she wanted to spend the evening by herself.").

In pursuing client's emotional reactions, we often try to show that we already have a sense of their reactions rather than ask open-ended questions (e.g., "How did you feel when . . .") or open ended statements (e.g., "I am curious about your emotional reactions when. . . ."). We are attentive to each partner's emotional reactions, not just listening for emotional words that each may speak but observing their expressions and voice tones. We can observe their angry expressions even if they don't indicate they are angry. We also attentive to what their words imply. For example, accusations often imply anger. Explanations often imply defensiveness. Being attentive to expressions, voice tones, and implications, we reflect what clients may be feeling, even if they have not uttered those feeling words. We of course do that tentatively since we could be wrong, but often clients will feel validated that we have expressed more clearly what they felt but didn't express. For example, rather than the example comments above, we might say "Eileen, it seems as if maybe you felt neglected or rejected when Debra said she wanted to spend the evening by herself."

Third, we start with where clients are emotionally. If someone is obviously angry, we don't want to suggest or try to lead them into softer emotions too quickly or we will lose them. They will feel invalidated at best and judged for being angry at worst. We want to validate their hard emotions fully because they are just as real as their soft emotions, but we also don't want clients to feel any need to justify their hard emotions or be stuck in them. As we validate their surface, up-front emotions, we are always attentive to possible hidden emotions they might experience. We can enquire directly about these emotions. Or we can suggest and explore them by looking for the pain behind the provocations they accuse the partner of. Even though they talk about the wrongs their partner has done to them, we can explore the wounds that the wrongs have created. We can explore what is missing when they describe how messed up things are in the relationship. If they whine about the limitations in their partner, we can explore the wish behind that whining. When they discuss their hopelessness, we can explore the hopes that got dashed. In these ways, we shift the discussion to softer emotional experiences that are less likely to lead to counterattack or defensiveness by the partner and more likely to lead to an empathic response in the partner.

Consider an angry accusation such as "You never spend any time with me." We could certainly validate the obvious anger that the partner feels. However, that accusation also suggests the partner is missing the other and wants a greater connection to the other or wants to feel more important in the other's eyes. Or consider an angry accusation such as "You always criticize me; no one could ever please you." Besides the obvious anger, there are suggestions of a desire to be appreciated by the partner, a concern that they are not good enough for the partner, and a sadness that they disappoint the partner. Even in the angriest accusations, there are often leads to the yearning that the partner has and the sadness and disappointment they experience. These implications about the complex, hidden emotions that each experiences besides the obvious surface emotions they express provide rich material for therapeutic exploration.

Fourth, as we explore each partner's hidden emotions, we highlight and intensify those vulnerable emotions. We do this because we believe that these emotions are more intense than partners initially reveal. We may intensify the emotions by leading the partner into new territory and using stronger words to reflect their experience. For example, if Ben reveals that he doesn't think Kate is ever happy with him, we can lead him into his sense of inadequacy or failure as a partner. Or we can intensify the experience for him by revealing other experiences when he felt similarly. For example, if we explore how Ben feels he is never good enough for Kate, we might intensify that experience for him by mentioning some relevant history, such as how Ben felt he never measured up to his brother, whom he felt was more successful than he was. This mention of historical material may not only intensify the experience for Ben and bring about a more compassionate response from Kate, but it also suggests that Kate is not solely responsible for these strong feelings he has.

Fifth, we always express empathy toward both partners, even if neither partner expresses empathy toward the other. As we explore the emotional experience of each partner, particularly his or her hidden emotions that may not have been expressed previously, we may naturally feel empathic toward them. We must always be careful not to expect the partner to respond similarly, since, unlike us, they are involved in those emotions. For example, while we may feel empathic toward Ben, Kate may feel defensive about his feelings, realizing that she had some role in making him feel that way. She may also have anger toward him because she *is* disappointed in what he has done or not done. As therapists, we should always work toward communicating understanding and empathy for each partner's strongly held feelings but not expect the other to do so. Nor should we pressure them to understand the other or feel empathy toward the other. We don't want to say to Kate, "Well, so do you *now* understand how Ben feels?" We can be confident that exploring Ben's emotions in ways that haven't been done before and our being empathic with those emotions will have a positive impact on Kate, as long as she, too, feels understood.

Sixth, when we are exploring the emotional reactions of one partner and our observations suggest that the other, listening partner is not defensive or angry, we try to incorporate the listening partner into the discussion. We may ask the speaking partner to tell the listening partner directly some important message. For example, we could ask Ben to voice some particularly vulnerable emotion to Kate, such as saying directly to Kate that he feels he never measures up in her eyes. That could intensify the experience for Ben but also lead to a natural response from Kate. Even if we don't have Ben speak directly to Kate or if he resists doing so, we can ask Kate to summarize what she is hearing from Ben, so that we bring her into the conversation. Or we can ask Kate what is going on with her as she listens to Ben.

Seventh, as we explore the emotions of one partner, we must keep an eye on the other for signs of their emotional reactions. Sometimes the other person can attentively listen as we explore one partner's emotions, so we are free to continue that exploration. At other times, the other has strong reactions and needs some time to speak and express their own emotions. Whenever we switch from one partner to the other, whether it is because we have come to a natural stopping point with one or because we see that the other is having difficulty listening and needs to speak their piece, we try to briefly summarize what the one has said and transition to the other in a way that doesn't bring about defensiveness or counterattack. For example, we might say "Carl, I see how that incident had a big impact on you, making you feel kind of left out of the process. But, Dan, I know that you were also upset and were feeling a sense of urgency to get things done."

Let's consider how we might do empathic joining with a negative incident from our focus couple, Hank and Maria, that might appear on their Weekly Questionnaire. Hank and Maria got a sitter for James and went out together on a Saturday night, which is a rarity these days for them. They saw a movie that they liked and discussed it over dinner but also talked about Hank's work and some gossip about a friend that both knew. They were feeling close to one another and held hands on the walk back to their car and from their car to the house. When they got inside, the sitter told them that James may be getting sick. He was asleep now but had been fussy all evening and the sitter was concerned that he might be getting a fever. Maria immediately got concerned and went into his bedroom to check on him; Hank muttered, "There you go again" to Maria but paid the sitter and walked her out. Maria woke up James while putting her hand on his forehead to check for a fever. He didn't have a fever but was crying. Hank came in and expressed his annoyance that she had awakened him. She said angrily "Well, I am concerned about our child," implying that she may be the only one in the family who is. Hank responded in sarcastic agreement, "Yes, you are concerned about James—overly and only." Maria then stayed in James' room until he was asleep but decided to stay longer until she could be sure Hank was asleep, so she could avoid Hank's wrath. Hank went to bed angry that their good evening was being destroyed but half hoping that Maria would come in soon so they might rescue the evening. Then he, too, fell asleep.

Let's consider how we might debrief this incident between them. With Maria, we would highlight the positive feelings she had during the evening with Hank, her concern upon hearing that James might be sick, her fear and anger that Hank would get angry at her for attending to James and waking him, her hesitancy to return to their bedroom for fear that Hank would launch into her for being so anxious about James, and her fear that he would initiate sex, which at that point she had no interest in. With Hank, we would highlight the positive feelings that he had during the evening and his hope that they might be sexually intimate, his irritation and disappointment in hearing that James might be sick and their evening at home upended, and his anger and hurt that Maria seemed so much more concerned about James than about him.

Depending on how Hank and Maria responded as we were debriefing that emotional incident for them both, we might have them respond directly to each other. For example, after debriefing Hank's experience, we might have him tell Maria directly how the evening got his hopes up for closeness with her but then how disappointed he felt when that possibility was aborted. We might have Maria summarize his comments or respond to them, telling him how his expression affected her.

It is relatively easy to talk about the goals of empathic joining and the strategies used to achieve it. However, there is as much art as science to the process, and dealing with a real couple in distress always presents challenges to the therapist. In the section below, we provide transcripts of part of therapy sessions with a real couple receiving IBCT during our clinical trial. In our commentary we show what the therapist did that brought the couple into an empathic connection but also show the opportunities the therapist missed and the interventions that failed to achieve a positive impact.

Empathic Joining Interventions for Henry and Fran

When Henry and Fran entered couple therapy as part of our clinical trial of IBCT, he complained about her criticism and her temper, which, according to him, at times led to low-level violence. She acknowledged having trouble controlling her temper but said that his lack of sexual desire was what often set her off. She was also angry at his lack of communication and his emotional distance. The DEEP analysis of their core problem around emotional expression emphasized the differences between them in emotionality. She was dynamic, energetic, and emotional, with highs and lows. He was much more of a steady state emotionally. Early in their relationship they had discussed the synchrony between their emotional styles and at times saw the benefit of their differences. In terms of emotional sensitivities, her previous experiences had led to a sensitivity around her attractiveness as a woman, so she was especially reactive to a lack of sexual interest by Henry. In contrast to Fran's family of origin, whose negative emotionality was common and open, Henry was raised in a family that rarely voiced overt negativity, despite considerable tension at times. His dad seemed to handle tension by drinking and withdrawing; his mother was consumed with psychosomatic complaints. Thus, Henry did not know how to handle negative emotionality from Fran and found it very overwhelming. They had the stressors of two young children, and Fran was also dealing with continuing difficulties with her mother.

Henry and Fran's pattern of interaction was classic demand/withdraw, with Fran often in an angry, critical position and Henry disengaging and withdrawing. However, at times he would get so upset by the conflict that he would be destructive, throwing a glass and breaking it, but never at her.

Early on in the active intervention phase of therapy, the couple had the following exchange, in which they talked about their difficulties and possible separation. Fran had threatened that if Henry did not change, she was going to leave. Henry added that their fights and anger and frustration were not good for them or their kids and that things had to get better or end between them. In the transcript below, Fran is speculating why Henry is connected and sexual with her for a while but then is not. She wonders why he has changed some habits to her liking but doesn't seem to be able to maintain a routine of intimacy.

Fran: And the thing that I'm thinking is that it's because either we get hectic at what goes on and you forget. It's not part of your routine. You always like to have things in your routine. Or else I see it as you're slacking off. And then that's how come it goes back to the same pattern. So I figure I'd give you time to okay, maybe go catch himself. And did you notice I haven't been, you know, saying anything about the toilet up, the toilet down because you've been doing it on your own.

Henry: It's a matter of it becoming a habit.

Fran: Right. But you've done it so often, you know. You started but you don't continue. See the thing with the toilet seat going up, that was for a short time, but yet you continued it.

Henry: Yeah, because there is nothing—I mean other than when you get mad at me—there is nothing emotional about it.

Fran: But still, the fact is that I remind you of it. Okay, I reminded you those couple of times. Right?

Henry: Right.

Fran: Okay, and we got on to each other about it, so I stopped bugging you. And then you continued to put the seat, the lid down.

Henry: Right. I guess what I'm saying is that it is a mechanical deal, putting the toilet seat down. It's merely mechanical.

Fran: But you said it's still part of the routine. It should be the same thing when you communicate with me. It's a routine. You-you deal with me more than you deal with the toilet seat.

Henry: No, but what I'm saying is that dealing with the toilet seat as a habit is totally different. I mean you made the analogy to me quitting smoking; that's totally different from my perspective than dealing with you emotionally. It's very different. One has, one has absolutely no explosive content. It's just you make it a habit and that's all it is.

Fran: Then how are you doing to do a habit with dealing with me then? If you said you have to have a routine, you know, how are you going to put me into your routine?

Henry: Well, I can't do it by myself. And that's the, that's the part of it—

Fran: But see, you know what you need to have a routine. Just like you, how you remember to put the toilet seat down. Okay, I don't know whatever you do to do it. You have to tell me how that's going to work. You're the only one who is going to—who has to have it in this certain way.

Henry: Right, and I've told you that. I've communicated that to you. The thing that makes it hard is that I've told you that, that I'm afraid of you, I've told you that I'm shy sexually. Those are all things I've told you.

Commentary: Things have escalated between Fran and Henry and it is time for the therapist to intervene. Even though Henry's comments above were said defensively, this would be an ideal occasion to intervene. The therapist could interrupt the building negative tension and reflect Henry's statement about being afraid of Fran and being shy sexually. Using empathic joining, the therapist could then explore those feelings in a way that might soften the interaction. However, the therapist stayed quiet and the tension escalated.

Fran: Yes, I know. And then you started for like a 1-week period, and then all of the sudden it stops.

Henry: Right, because I need your help to continue also.

Fran [getting more and more agitated, pointing her finger at him]: I thought I'd been doing that. But see you have to take the initiative that—okay, this is what I need, this is what I need more—and it's your prerogative because it's on your side. I told you, I'm willing to help you. To be your partner and whatever you need to do. But it's your initiative for you to do it. Because I don't know your routine. I know what my routine is. And like I told you, I set a goal, and I know what I want and I know what my end objective is. You have to do that.

Henry: Right, I know that. And then something will happen, and I'll get angry at you.

Fran: Right. And then it just blows the whole thing, and it's like—then it tells me then, then you don't have that capacity of okay—I got off the track and so now I need to go back to it. It's like you stop, and then there's nothing else, there's nothing in you that pulls it back and goes, "Oops, I got off of the track. I need to go back." I don't see that at all and that's what pisses me off more than anything else.

Henry: I don't have that yet. It's true. I don't.

Commentary: At this point things have escalated so that Fran is extremely angry and shaking her finger at Henry. If the therapist were not present, Henry would probably shut down and withdraw. Instead he acknowledges that he doesn't do it right in her eyes but without any sense of hope that he could ever do it to her liking. It would have been better if the therapist intervened before it got to this heated, escalated point but now the therapist does intervene.

Therapist [to Fran]: What's really positive about this is that you're able to communicate and express how the rage comes out.

Fran: Probably because I'm tired.

Therapist: No, and so remember last time I was saying to show me what it's like. Now you are really showing this rage that comes out like "You know what you're supposed to be doing. Now why aren't you doing it?" I wonder if you—? Okay, so we know there is rage, we know that there is this volcanic rage that comes out. What other feelings are you feeling inside? If you tried to look behind the rage, what kinds of feelings do you discover inside yourself?

Fran: Behind the rage. I mean, if it's just to focus in on what's . . .

Therapist: If you just tuned into yourself. If you said, "Okay, I know I'm really just raging, volcanically mad at him." And you've told him that. Okay, and you've expressed it with a lot of genuine feeling. So we all know that Fran is just raging mad at Henry. But if you were to just kind of sit within yourself, and just kind of tune into, "Okay, besides feeling angry towards Henry, what other feelings do I have?" And could you try to tell him?

Fran: Okay, well, I've told him whenever I get angry there are other emotions into it. Basically, there's a sense of sadness.

Therapist: Okay, tell him about the sadness. Try to really tune into it if you could, and try to tell him as close to your heart, and as tuned into that part of you that also feels sad besides rageful—about the sadness.

Commentary: The therapist intervened by starting where Fran was emotionally, namely angry. The therapist validated that Fran was angry and that she is good at expressing her negative feelings. In an earlier session, they had discussed how Fran sometimes feels a kind of volcanic rage, so the therapist could reference that without offending Fran. The therapist's acceptance of Fran and her emotions in the moment kept Fran from feeling defensive about where she was emotionally and thus Fran did not feel a need to prove to the therapist that she had every reason to be rageful. Therefore, it was easier for Fran to move away from her rage and consider other emotions that she might also be feeling. Fran mentioned sadness, and the therapist immediately encouraged her to discuss her sadness and to tell Henry about her sadness. Sadness, which is a soft emotion, is very different from rage, which is a hard emotion. Sadness is much more likely to lead to an empathic response in Henry than is rage. Normally, we might work with Fran, exploring and heightening her sadness before bringing in Henry. However, the therapist thought that bringing in Henry at this point would heighten the emotion and connection between the two of them.

Fran: Well, one, I feel sad that we're always arguing. The other thing: feeling bad. I don't feel like I have enough. I don't feel like you give—that you take me—that you love me enough. You know, there are other parts from the past that, you know, I've worked hard with other relationships too, and this is the first time that I've had to feel like I have to beg, you know, for someone to be with me or to make love to me. And so that, you know, that I'm sitting here trying to understand that. Umm . . . a lot of it, you know, my mother, you know how I deal with mom, so there's a part that's like, almost like the real strict disciplinarian who is like, "This is what I need, this is what I need. And I want you to follow that rule." Just frustration from things from the day, thinking, well, you know, if we didn't have children maybe the relationship would have been better. Feeling inadequate as far as, you know, I'm not doing a career. Not doing the things I used to. Feeling—feeling shut down. Umm . . . what else? Just feeling like I'm in a box. That's about it.

Therapist: Okay, can you tell her the feelings that you heard that she's going through besides the anger—just try to feedback to her what you've heard.

Henry: I hear—I hear that hurt because you feel like I'm not putting enough energy into it in comparison to past relationships. It feels like that I'm either withholding or don't love you enough or whatever the motivation is, the actions aren't there. And so that hurts. I hear that because of essentially being trained to have low self-esteem from your mom that that feeds into feeling hurt. It becomes a rationale or reason of maybe, maybe that's why he doesn't love me enough.

Fran: I think the other biggest thing is that umm . . .

Commentary: Fran was able to discuss the many things in her life that make her feel sad; she is no longer in a finger-shaking, attacking mode, but rather sharing her sadness and disappointments. Toward the end of her comment on all the sad things in her life, she is sounding sad and wiping away tears from her eyes. The therapist sees that Henry is listening attentively and doesn't seem defensive and so believes, correctly, that he can summarize Fran's feelings on his own, without the therapist aiding him, such as by highlighting those feelings first. Even though Henry has not been trained in communication skills, he does a good job of summarizing her distress in a sympathetic way. That has an emotional impact on Fran, softening her further and bringing more tears. The therapists hands her some tissues. At this point Fran is so emotional she has a hard time speaking, but the therapist encourages her to share more of her feelings.

Therapist: Go ahead, like, just whatever way you can, kind of spill it out. It's okay. Try to get that out so he'll hear it.

Fran: My frustrating part is that I feel guilty because—that you're a good man and that I should be happy and lucky that I have you because of the things that you do and the things that you put up with. And I feel that I'm asking too much, so maybe I should just be happy with what I have, you know. And I just feel like maybe I'm asking too much, and just—you know, because I do want to be with you.

Commentary: At this point Fran is expressing her most tender and poignant feelings toward Henry—that she wants to be with him. She has now voiced both sides of her struggle: one side is that Henry does not love her enough; the other side is that he is a good man and maybe she is asking for too much. There is no substantive answer to the question of whether he doesn't love her enough or whether she is asking too much. Her voicing the other side and expressing her needs in the tender way that she is doing now is more likely to bring Henry to her side in the loving way she would like. He has been listening to her intently and most likely feels positively toward her. Ideally, the therapist would intervene at this point and have him share some of his feelings listening to Fran. She has been open and vulnerable with him and it would be good if he could be open with her about the impact on him and what he is feeling. For example, the therapist could simply have said "Henry, I wonder what you are feeling right now as you listen to Fran." Or the therapist could have prompted him with a comment, such as "Henry, it seemed like you were looking at Fran tenderly, could you say what you were feeling." However, Henry doesn't share his feelings but instead goes to his usual way of supporting Fran by trying to reassure her, in this case assuring her that she is not asking for too much.

Henry: But, see, I don't think you're asking for too much. I don't think it's . . .

Fran: Then how come? I don't understand that part that if you said I'm not asking for too much, then why not?

Henry: It's the interaction. That's what I've been trying to say all this time. It's not, it's not what you're asking for. It's that whatever you feel that's negative—whether it's frustration or anger or loneliness or whatever, whatever, whatever the base motion is—you express it in terms of anger, or that's the way it comes out.

Fran: Yes.

Henry: That's exactly opposite—that's exactly the emotion that I shy away from.

Commentary: Henry just expressed very succinctly the essence of their struggle and Fran agrees with him—that her negative feelings usually come out as anger but that is the emotion he shies away from. In the previous segment, the therapist was able to get them out of their usual pattern of interaction in which Fran is angry or rageful and Henry withdraws. For a brief period Fran became tender and loving and Henry moved toward her emotionally rather than shying away. The therapist did an excellent job of turning her rage into a moment of connection. Ideally the therapist would have been able to have Henry express some of his feelings toward Fran, rather than just giving her his blanket reassurance and explanation, and thus perhaps keep them in this moment of connection longer.

SUMMARY

In this chapter, we first reviewed the theoretical and empirical support for the IBCT strategy of empathic joining. Self-disclosure of vulnerable information to a receptive, empathic partner leads to emotional connection and closeness between partners. Promoting empathy between partners can lead to acceptance and forgiveness and spontaneously lead to supportive behavior toward the other. The process of self-disclosure of emotional material, which involves labeling and differentiating often complex emotions, can also lead to a reduction of emotional distress.

We next reviewed the strategies of empathic joining, which begin during the assessment and feedback phase as the therapist highlights the pain that each partner has experienced rather than the provocations that each has committed. Most of the work of empathic joining comes during the treatment phase when partners discuss emotionally salient events in their lives, including those that happen during the session. During these discussions partners will usually reveal their surface emotions initially, which are often hard emotions like anger and resentment. We assume that most strong emotions involving a romantic partner are mixed and thus we explore additional hidden emotions the client might also be experiencing besides these surface emotions. Disclosure of these hidden emotions often creates a different reaction in the partner than the partner's usual reaction of defensiveness, counterattack, or withdrawal.

The steps that we typically take in this process are as follows: (1) we make a strategic decision, based on what is happening in the room and the couple's typical pattern of interaction, about whom to focus on first; (2) we shift partners away from the actions of the other to their own reactions; (3) we start with where partners are emotionally, which is often with hard emotions, and move them into an exploration of their hidden emotions, reflecting and validating those emotional reactions; (4) as we explore their hidden emotions, we may try to try to highlight and intensify them; (5) we empathize with both partners but don't pressure them to be empathic, knowing that the experience of hearing their partner's hidden emotions and seeing us respond with understanding and support will have a positive impact; (5) if the listening partner seems receptive to what the speaking partner is saying, we may try to incorporate the listening partner into the conversation, having him or her summarize the speaking partner's experience or disclose current emotional reactions to the speaking partner; and finally, (6) we keep an eye on the listening partner to determine in part when we need to summarize the speaking partner and transition to the listening partner.

We considered how an IBCT therapist might conduct empathic joining with our sample couple, Hank and Maria. We ended the chapter with a real-life example of a couple in IBCT experiencing empathic joining. In this case, the therapist worked with Fran's anger in the session, leading her to experience and disclose other emotions than her go-to emotion of anger. Henry was able to listen and respond to her without his usual pattern of withdrawal. At the end of the exchange, Henry provided a succinct description of their interaction pattern, a description that leads nicely into our next therapeutic strategy of unified detachment, discussed in the following chapter.

7

⚌

Creating Acceptance and Change Through Unified Detachment

EMPATHIC JOINING COUNTERACTS blame, promotes acceptance, and facilitates change by engendering empathy and compassion in each member for the other. Unified detachment works for these same goals by promoting a nonjudgmental, descriptive, and joint view of the problem. Rather than eliciting emotional expression, particularly the expression of hidden emotions, this approach engages partners in an intellectual analysis of the problem. This analysis can and often does include a discussion of emotion, but the discussion is from a distance, for example, when the couple describes what emotion is elicited in an interaction but neither experiences nor explores that emotion in the moment. Typically, unified detachment takes the form of a conversation with the couple about the sequence of conflict between them, about what triggers each other's reactions, about their differences and sensitivities and how these affect their concrete struggles, about the interconnection between specific incidents and their theme, and about other possible perspectives on their themes and patterns. In these discussions, we avoid any evaluative analysis that might place blame or responsibility for change on one person and guide partners away from such evaluative analysis. The emphasis is on a joint, mindful description of the problematic sequence. The problem is not a "you" or a "me" but an "it."

The *detachment* part of unified detachment refers to the stance or vantage point that we take when viewing the problem and that we guide the partners in taking. Metaphorically speaking, we ask the partners to put down their weapons, to climb a nearby hill to get a better view of the battle, to pick up their binoculars, and to look at what is happening during their struggles. They detach from the struggle to look at it more objectively. They observe the interaction that goes on and the emotions that each is likely feeling. The *unified* part of unified detachment refers to the dyadic nature of this process. We try to get them to see the process of their struggle in a similar or unified way. We often describe unified detachment as dyadic mindfulness, in that we help partners look at their struggles together in a nonjudgmental, nonevaluative, and thus mindful way.

With this brief introduction to unified detachment, we now look at the theoretical and empirical support for this intervention, the strategies for helping couples achieve unified detachment, and clinical case examples of unified detachment.

THEORY AND EVIDENCE FOR UNIFIED DETACHMENT

Research on mindfulness and mindfulness-based psychotherapies has exploded in recent years. Mindfulness is a key part of several established, evidence-based therapies such as Acceptance and Commitment Therapy (S. C. Hayes, Strosahl, & Wilson 2012), Mindfulness-Based Stress Reduction (Kabat-Zinn, 2013) and Mindfulness-Based Cognitive Therapy (Segal, Williams, & Teasdale, 2013). Meta-analytic reviews of hundreds of studies involving more than 12,000 participants have shown mindfulness-based therapies to be effective treatments for a variety of problems such as addictions, anxiety, depression, pain, smoking, and stress (S. B. Goldberg, Tucker et al., 2018; Khoury et al., 2013).

Because mindfulness-based interventions have such documented effectiveness, research studies have also examined how they work. What happens during mindfulness interventions that may lead to improved outcomes? Several meta-analyses have looked at this body of literature. Mindfulness-based interventions reduce emotional reactivity, reduce negative affect and increase positive affect (Gu, Strauss, Bond, & Cavanagh, 2015; van der Velden et al., 2015). These interventions also affect cognitive variables such as reducing rumination, worry, and cognitive reactivity, which is the extent to which distress leads to negative thinking patterns (Gu et al., 2015; van der Velden et al., 2015). One meta-analysis found evidence that mindfulness improves emotional clarity, which is the ability to identify and describe internal experience (Cooper, Yap, & Batalha, 2018).

All of the research described above concerned individual therapeutic interventions, not couple therapy. Yet one can easily extrapolate the findings to couples. Reductions in emotional reactivity, decreased negative affect, increased positive affect, greater emotional clarity, decreased rumination and worry, and reductions in cognitive reactivity will benefit the relationship as well as the individual. If partners have reduced negative affect, if they don't get quickly aroused and go into negative patterns of thinking, and if they have greater emotional clarity, they are likely to be able to communicate and problem solve more effectively. Furthermore, the very act of mindfulness counteracts an essential characteristic of distressed couples, namely, the tendency to blame and accuse the other. Being mindful is being aware of what is going on without taking an evaluative stance toward it. Mindfulness interventions in the individual therapy literature primarily focus on a nonjudgmental view of the self, such as viewing an internal emotional experience as just a passing experience rather than an occasion for self-evaluation, such as "I shouldn't be feeling this way." In IBCT, the mindfulness intervention of unified detachment primarily focuses on a nonjudgmental view of interpersonal behavior, such as viewing a pattern of interaction as a difficult dance that they both get caught up in rather than a blameworthy behavior that one does to the other. Beyond these effects on interpersonal judgment, unified detachment brings the couple together by helping them take a similar, more objective view of their situation or difficulty. Thus, it promotes a common conceptualization or understanding between the couple, a common story about their difficulties, which can have a further positive impact beyond the impact of a nonjudgmental view.

There is one recent study that shows the effect of a mindfulness intervention on couple behavior rather than on individual behavior. Finkel, Slotter, Luchies, Walton, and Gross (2013) did a longitudinal study of a group of 120 married, heterosexual couples in the Chicago area who were assessed every 4 months over a 2-year period for a total of seven assessments. At assessments two through seven, which occurred entirely through the internet, partners described their most significant, recent disagreement. Procedures in the first year were identical for all couples, but at year 1, couples were randomly divided into two groups, with one group being asked to engage in a conflict-reappraisal task at assessments four, five, and six. In this task, partners were asked to think about the conflict they described from the perspective of a neutral third party who wished the best for them both. They were asked how the third party might think about the conflict and how that third party might find good that could come from it. The couples were told that it could be helpful although at times difficult to take this perspective about one's own relationship and were asked what obstacles they might have in taking this perspective. Finally, the couples were encouraged to take this perspective over the next 4 months during interactions with their partner. In addition, couples were sent this reappraisal task as a reminder midway between the assessments. Results showed that both sets of couples decreased in marital satisfaction during year 1, as is usually the case, and the control condition continued that decrease in year 2; however, the appraisal couples did not decline in marital satisfaction in year 2. Furthermore, analyses showed that this effect was mediated by a decrease in conflict-related distress. Thus, simple, repeated instructions to take a detached, more objective perspective on their conflict seemed to ameliorate that conflict.

Like all studies, this single study is certainly open to critique. The study did not use distressed couples. There was no comparable task for the control condition, so perhaps any intervention that asked couples to think about their conflicts in a constructive way might have been helpful. However, the study does illustrate what we mean by detachment: the partners were asked to take the perspective of a neutral third party who wished the best for them. The study also shows its positive impact. In unified detachment, we try to get couples to take a detached perspective on their conflict, as in this study, but in contrast to this study we do it in a unified way, so that they see it jointly, together rather than individually. We believe that unified detachment or dyadic mindfulness can offer a greater benefit for couples than mere individual detachment or individual mindfulness.

Both separately and in combination, unified detachment and empathic joining may benefit couples through another important mechanism—exposure to emotionally arousing material. Arguably, exposure therapy for anxiety disorders, in which clients are gradually exposed to fearful stimuli in a safe situation and experience a reduction in their anxiety, is the most successful of all psychological treatments (Kaplan & Tolin, 2011). However, exposure therapy can be applied to other emotional disorders as well, such as depression (A. M. Hayes, 2015). For example, in Exposure-Based Cognitive Therapy for Depression (A. M. Hayes, Ready, & Yasinski, 2015), the therapist has the client identify events that are indicative of the client's harsh, negative view of self and describe those events in extensive and elaborate detail so the client can reduce the fear associated with the negative self-view and better integrate that experience more appropriately into a broader context.

Now consider what happens with distressed couples. They have difficulty discussing certain emotionally arousing, hot topics. Therefore, they may generally avoid discussing these issues until they are suddenly triggered. For example, a couple may have conflict over her mother and avoid discussing her until she calls with a plan to visit. When they do talk about a hot issue like this, they are likely to argue unproductively or withdraw without resolution but with resentment. These negative interactions then add to the emotional distress around the issues. However, if empathic joining and unified detachment lead to a reduction in emotional arousal and an ability to approach these topics without experiencing the negative outcomes of argument and resentful withdrawal, then the arousal may further be reduced as they experience a conversation about a hot topic that doesn't escalate negatively and is reasonably constructive. This new experience may also positively impact their thinking about the topic and their partner. Thus, empathic joining and unified detachment may also provide benefit through a kind of dyadic exposure therapy.

STRATEGIES FOR PROMOTING UNIFIED DETACHMENT

In IBCT, we promote unified detachment during discussions of the material the couple brings in on their weekly questionnaire, namely the negative or difficult incidents they experienced, the upcoming, challenging events they may face, the issues of concern they wish to address, and sometimes the positive incidents they experienced. We promote unified detachment with this material in a number of ways. Perhaps the most common strategy is to focus on the interaction sequence that (a) has already unfolded between partners during a particular incident; (b) will likely unfold during an upcoming, challenging event; or (c) actually unfolds during the session. Partners tend to view their own behavior as a reaction to their partner's behavior, which it usually is. However, they often don't see how their partner's behavior is also a reaction to their own behavior. Behavior is a continuous stream; any starting point is somewhat arbitrary. Bill may believe that a particular episode started when he arrived home: he was happy and greeted Susie cheerfully but she seemed distant and annoyed so he will likely perceive that any subsequent behavior of his, such as criticizing Susie or deliberately ignoring her, is just an understandable reaction to her initial behavior toward him. In contrast, Susie may start the interaction at a different time point. Perhaps she expected him to call during the day and check in with her, and she sees her distance and annoyance as a reaction to his behavior toward her. They are of course both right in their own way and they are likely to argue their own particular partial truth of the situation.

Clients typically report problematic behavior of their partner devoid of any context, as if it appeared unprovoked, out of the blue. As IBCT therapists we can take any behavior that a client reports to us and go forward and backward to get a fuller picture of what each partner is responding to. We can also go inside, getting partners to elaborate how they were seeing the situation and what they were trying to do. By elaborating what each is responding to and how they are construing it, we can make sense of both of their responses and perhaps have them see that both of their responses are understandable if not always desirable. We can do that even when one is responding to something other than the partner's behavior. Maybe Susie's distance and annoyance was not in response to Bill's behavior at all but to something that happened between her and her best friend that left her in a bad mood. We can also explore this and validate it as an understandable human response. However, even when the initial reaction was to something outside of the relationship, once the partners are together, they almost always are partially responding to each other. For example, even though Susie was distressed by her interaction with her best friend, she may anticipate how Bill will respond to her (e.g., by defending her best friend, by being uninterested, or by otherwise not supporting her) and that may prime her to be distant and annoyed when he comes home. Bill may see her upset, think that there is nothing he can do to help, and think that the safest thing to do is to withdraw and hope her storm will pass. Thus, even when an issue does not initially involve the partner, it soon does. By elaborating the sequence of interaction and discussing what each partner is responding to, we can help them step back and see how their interaction unfolded, even when it was initially triggered by something outside the relationship. This elaboration often reduces the blame that they impute to their partner, allowing them to see the interaction in a more unified and detached way.

When we analyze the sequence of interaction that occurred between the couple during a difficult incident they describe, members of the couple will often describe a particularly egregious behavior that the other did during the escalation or final stages of their interaction. We typically shift the focus away from this moment to the early stages of the interaction, where the origin of the conflict lies. Partners rarely enter an interaction wanting to hurt or upset the other unless they are reacting to a previous interaction that was difficult for them. Therefore, the early stages of an interaction usually reveal both partners in an easily understandable light, even if one was stressed by something that happened to them previously. With this understanding of where both partners started from, we can then examine the key first steps in the interaction—which are usually trigger points when one did something— often unintentionally—that was offensive to the other and how the other, in turn, responded in a way that was offensive. Then we can track key points in the escalation of the interaction as well as any points when one or both tried to right the interaction. Unless the interaction escalated to the point that one or both did something unusual or particularly hurtful, such as suggesting divorce when that is not the usual route of their escalation, we don't go over each bit of escalation. This is because at some point both partners are engaging in behavior that is easily blameworthy and we want to avoid a discussion of who did the most blameworthy act. Instead, we may make a comment such as "So at this point, you two are off and running, doing your usual dance." If an escalated interaction does lead one or both partners to say something very hurtful that is not part of their usual escalation, such as a mention of divorce or a comment like "I no longer love you" or "I hate you," then those comments and the reactions they cause need to be debriefed, usually with empathic joining. However, sometimes partners will mention some especially provocative behavior by the other, not because they felt threatened or especially hurt by the other but because they want to show the therapist some especially blameworthy behavior by the other. In this situation, we would want to shift away from that behavior, as it is likely just a variation of their blaming interactions.

As we discuss the sequence of interaction in a particular conflict and the key steps in that interaction, we will inevitably mention the emotions that each experiences because the key steps are usually actions or reactions that trigger strong emotions. However, we discuss these emotions in a different way than we do in empathic joining. We describe the emotions but don't explore them or have the clients express them as is done in empathic joining. For example, let's say the following sequence of interaction occurred between Debra and Ben. She told him of some difficulties she was having at work, hoping to get his understanding and support, but Ben tried to be helpful to her by offering her advice. We might talk about her reaction (e.g., anger at feeling patronized by his advice) and what that naturally led her to do (e.g., make a critical comment to Ben) and discuss Ben's emotional response (e.g., defensiveness, anger) and what that naturally led him to do (e.g., shut down). In this way, we help the couple delineate the key points in a difficult interaction but we don't attempt to heighten her emotional state in the therapy room or explore her emotional state, such as other, hidden, and soft emotions she might be experiencing, and we don't do that with his emotional state. Even if we did explore the emotions, it would be in a mindful way (e.g., what emotion did you notice yourself having) rather than in an expressive way, in which the client reveals the emotion, perhaps reexperiences the emotion to some extent, and gets a response from us as empathic therapists and possibly from the partner as an empathic listener.

In addition to analyzing the sequence of an interaction and identifying the key trigger points, a second way we promote unified detachment is by making ratings, comparisons, and contrasts of interactions. We can ask a couple to rate on the familiar 10-point scale how upset they were at different points in an interaction, how intensely the argument escalated, how similar this interaction was to their usual pattern, or how long it took them to recover. By asking them to make ratings of the interaction or of emotional upset, we are asking them to step back and view their interaction or arousal from a distance. For example, we may ask Karen and Frank to rate how upset each was at various points in an interaction that started when Karen saw Frank had not done the dishes. We discover that she rated herself a 3 when she saw the dishes and said something to Frank about them but that he rated her as a 6, seeing her as much more upset than she saw herself. However, she rated her response to his defensive reply about the dishes as a 7, so she was much more upset about his reply than she was about the dishes, but Frank rated her as similarly upset at the dishes as at his reply. Thus, we document how (a) she was more upset at his response than at the dishes, (b) his response to her upset led her to feel as upset as he thought she was to begin with, and (c) he experiences her as having very few gradients of emotional upset—she is either quite upset or not upset at all. Such information could lead to a useful analytic discussion, that is, unified detachment.

We can also ask couples to make comparisons or contrasts between their interactions and analyze the reasons for any differences in the interactions. For example, we might say to them "The interaction we discussed today seems very similar to the one we discussed last week but this one didn't seem nearly so intense. Why do you think that was the case?" In response, the couple might note that they had been getting along better, so neither wanted to get into an argument and they both made efforts to avoid escalation. Then we would discuss with them what specific things they did to avoid escalation. Or the couple might note some environmental factor, such as the fact that both were tired or stressed or had been drinking before the earlier, more negative interaction. In each of these cases, we guide the couple in stepping back and analyzing their interactions as normal human behavior with understandable variables determining it. In so doing, we help the couple understand the causal determinants of their interactions with each other.

A third way we promote unified detachment is by discussing the initial intentions of each partner and contrasting them with the impact on each partner. We noted in Chapter 3 the ironic processes in interaction, that partners often engage in behavior in order to achieve a particular outcome but that that behavior often leads to just the opposite of that outcome. Consider a common example: Roland comes to Mark extremely upset about an incident with his father, hoping to get validation and support from Mark. Mark wants to ease Roland's upset so explains to him why the incident is not really a big deal or explains that maybe his father had more benign intentions than Roland is perceiving, or that the incident is a bad one but that Roland is overreacting to it. Roland feels invalidated or criticized or both for his reaction and gets more upset and attempts to convince Mark that the incident really is as bad as he made it out to be, which makes it even harder for Mark to be validating, and both get upset with the other. Even though both wanted something reasonable and understandable from the other, they both did things that led to exactly the opposite results from what they were pursuing. If we as IBCT therapists can engage the couple in an analysis of how they each wanted something positive from the interaction but did things that inadvertently created something negative from the interaction, we can help them achieve some unified detachment from the interaction and learn something from it.

A fourth strategy for promoting unified detachment is to point clients to features of their relationship that may give them a different perspective on the relationship, a perspective that is more relationship enhancing than the perspective that they have. Typically, we focus on the differences between partners and how those differences may be beneficial as well as problematic for the relationship. For example, our focus couple, Hank and Maria, see themselves at odds with each other regarding attention to James versus attention to their own relationship. As IBCT therapists working with them, we might note that they each are guardians of one of the two important aspects of any family, the marital relationship and the parenting relationship. Hank is the guardian of the former while Maria is the guardian of the latter. They could potentially work together to create a balanced family in which both partners gave sufficient attention to both aspects of family life but they have gotten into a position where they are so polarized that each is holding up one aspect of family life on their own, leaving them both lonely and resentful. Consider another example of a couple that is polarized around emotion, with one partner being quite emotional and the other calm and steady. In that couple, we could engage them in a conversation about the benefit of each for the other: the emotional one needs the steadiness of the less emotional one while the steady partner needs the color and interest and energy that the emotional partner brings to the relationship. We can have this discussion while also acknowledging how the differences also create problems for them and thus have a both-sides-of-the-coin discussion. The therapist used this strategy of unified detachment with Fran and Henry, who were discussed in Chapter 6. They had mentioned that early on in their relationship they discussed the "synergy" between them because of their different styles, so the therapist could easily highlight or reference that as part of a unified detachment discussion.

Another way we discuss differences is to show how partners are often working toward the same goal and are on the same team even though they work in different ways. For example, consider a mother and father who are in conflict about how to handle their son Jimmy, with the mother focused on emphasizing the positive in Jimmy and the father focused on strict contingencies for Jimmy. We could help them discuss their common goals and the importance of both of their strategies. Certainly a single discussion about how the differences between partners are positive as well as negative is not going to dramatically change the relationship but it complicates partners' views of each other and of the relationship and may reduce the anger or resentment that partners have about the characteristics or approach of the other.

A fifth strategy for promoting unified detachment is to use metaphor, images, and humor to describe important features of the relationship, a description that may create emotional distance from those features. Some-times metaphors and images can capture the benefits and limitations of the couple's characteristics. For example, we could describe a couple as having a Tarzan and Jane dynamic, in which she is trying to civilize him and he is trying to get her to enjoy the wild. We can encourage couples to come up with humorous names for their patterns of interaction, names that may employ metaphors or images. A couple may decide they engage in a cat and mouse game with each other, an angry parent and rebellious teenager interaction with each other, a Goldilocks game in which each has to get it just right for the other, or a turtle interaction in which both partners withdraw into their shells. In a recent couple seen by an IBCT therapist, the wife would gladly take on household responsibilities until she felt over-whelmed by some urgent matter or the sheer load of the responsibilities, at which point she would approach her husband with anger and anxiety, which would prompt him into anxious and energetic action, but no matter what he did, it didn't seem as if it was enough. Her position was captured by some metaphors that she liked: "I am the only one rowing the boat" and "I am the only one with a fire hose." His position was captured by a metaphor that he liked: "I feel like I am in a game of 'whack-a-mole.'" With a recent case seen by another IBCT therapist, the couple was encouraged to generate a name for their pattern. The husband was good-hearted and cooperative but absentminded, so he would often not notice what needed to be done, such as a child needing a diaper change, dishes being stacked up, and so on. The wife was very on top of things and found her husband's lack of attention frustrating; she would often get angry at him for not jumping in and doing what in her mind needed to be done without her asking him. They gener-ated the clever name "red alert" since she "saw red" when he was not "alert." Another humorous way of injecting unified detachment into a conversation is to point out the irony in one or both partner's behavior. With a man who tries to help his partner's distress by offering her suggestions of what she should do, suggestions which upset her more because she feels blamed for not doing things right, we might note the irony in that he tries to help her so much that it hurts them both! These metaphors, images, and names can reduce conflict because (a) they detach the couple from the problem, (b) they clearly imply that both partners contribute to the problem, and (c) they often add a humorous lightness to the discussion.

When do we use each of these five strategies? We almost always go over the sequence of interaction during a particular incident, identifying key trigger points that cause upset or make the interaction take a turn for the worse. We use the other interventions when we think they can bring about some increase in unified detachment. For example, we use comparisons, contrasts, or ratings when we see differences that are worth noting and that may bring about greater awareness of relationship dynamics. If we see that a recent incident is much more or much less intense than another similar incident we have discussed with the couple, we may have them compare the two, analyzing why one was so much more difficult than the other. If we see differences in the emotionality of partners, we may call attention to that, perhaps with the use of ratings. For example, one partner may be worried about an external situation while the other is not so worried about the situation but is worried about the other's worry: Allie may be very worried about finances but Judy is not so worried about finances but is worried about Allie's worry about finances. We could then discuss that dynamic, maybe having Allie and Judy rate their worry about finances, in which Allie's score is much higher, and their worry about the other's worry, in which Judy's score is much higher! We might then talk about the possible process, that Judy not being worried about finances makes Allie feel more responsible and thus more worried about finances but then Allie's worry about finances makes Judy worry about Allie's worry. Then Judy tries to soothe Allie's worry by telling her there is nothing really to worry about, which doesn't work for Allie and may contribute to her further worry and thus Judy's further worry. When intentions and impact are so starkly at odds, as in Judy and Allie's case, when the efforts to soothe backfire, we call attention to the difference between what each is trying to achieve, which are worthy goals, and the impact they actually have. We use the strategy of calling attention to the differences between partners, especially when those differences were a source of attraction as well as distress or when those differences have positive as well as negative effects. We use metaphor, images, and humor when they seem appropriate for the couple but particularly when the couple themselves suggest or use them. In the earlier extended excerpt from Fran and Henry in Chapter 6, the therapist talked about Fran's "volcanic rage" because Fran had used that metaphor and because it captured her experience of sudden rage. The IBCT therapist above picked up on the client's metaphors of "whack-a-mole" and "only one with a fire hose" because the client had used that metaphor first. Just because a client has used a metaphor doesn't mean we automatically pick up on it. Sometimes clients use metaphors that are or are perceived as very attacking. For example, the "whack-a-mole" and "only one with a fire hose" metaphor could be perceived as attacking, in that the first implies that the partner can never be satisfied and the second that the partner never helps out with emergencies. However, the couple and the therapist used the metaphors as labels for the desperation that each felt at certain moments rather than a concealed attack on the other, so they helped achieve unified detachment in that they communicated in shorthand: you were feeling like this so of course you behaved in the way you did. As can be seen from this discussion of how we choose the various strategies of unified detachment, there is quite a bit of art involved. We get to know our clients and make informed judgments about what might work with them. Of course, sometimes we are wrong, but often enough we are right and can bring clients to greater unified detachment.

All of these strategies of unified detachment help couples look at their problems jointly without getting into an argument about them and without blaming each other for them. They do more than that. They are a way of teaching partners more about their interaction. Through these strategies, partners see how they do things that upset the other and how the other does things, unintentionally, to upset them. This kind of learning can often create *contingency-shaped change*: partners start doing things differently without us as therapists assigning homework to either. When partners come to a more objective understanding of the causes of their interaction pattern, they will sometimes spontaneously make some changes. In fact, we want to leave open that possibility, so we usually refrain from following unified detachment with immediate suggestions of what each can do differently. We know that change during ingrained patterns of interaction is difficult; we do not know where the best place to institute change is or which one is more capable of acting. Also, we don't want to create additional therapist pressure on an already pressured situation or create additional opportunities for blame, such as one partner blaming the other for not instituting the change that the therapist recommended. We let them sit with greater understanding, confident that it will lead to some additional acceptance of each other and possibly change in their way of dealing with each other.

Unified Detachment Examples on Video

The American Psychological Association has a series of videos illustrating different types of therapy. There are two videos that illustrate IBCT, one in which Christensen works with a young, white heterosexual couple with a trust issue (https://www.apa.org/pubs/videos/4310904.html) and one in which Christopher Martel, a therapist in the clinical trial of IBCT, works with an African American gay male couple with issues about how out to be in the world (https://www.apa.org/pubs/videos/4310939.html). In both cases the therapists are working with a real couple but spend only one session with the couple that lasts just short of an hour.

In the Christensen case, the couple describes a trust issue in which the girlfriend worries that the boyfriend may become interested in other women. They describe an incident when the boyfriend describes some juicy gossip to his girlfriend, an incident which triggers them both. In going over the sequence of this incident and exploring what each was thinking and feeling, Christensen shows that the boyfriend is cautious around his girlfriend and tried to tell her this juicy gossip in a way that would not upset her. He did that in part by avoiding any mention of the gender of the person who told him the gossip because it was a woman who told him and he was concerned that his girlfriend might think that he was interested in this woman. As he put it, he avoided saying "the definite pronoun" when referring to the source of the gossip. However, Christensen explores how the girlfriend is on alert and has her antenna up for any indication of distrustful behavior on his part. When she senses that he is avoiding telling her something, such as the gender of the source of the gossip, then she gets suspicious that there is something going on with another woman and that therefore he is hiding information about the other woman. As a result of this discussion, the couple came to have a common view of their dynamic—that he is cautious, she is on alert, and he does things out of his caution to avoid triggering her but that paradoxically do trigger her.

In the Martell case, two gay men discuss their differences over being out. One of the men is more comfortable being affectionate in public than the other, who is uncomfortable with such a public display of their sexual orientation. Martel explores with these men some of the background for these differences. The more out partner had an easier time coming out, is very political, and is now a journalist determined to reveal some of the untold stories of the harassment of gays. The other man came out later, had been exposed to more taunts and harassment, and has had to fight physically for appropriate respect in the past. He was both more scared of confrontation over his sexual orientation and also more willing to get into physical fights if disrespected. The more out man was aware of his partner's anxiety and discomfort but he did not respond sympathetically to it. Instead, it made him angry—his partner was not on the same team with him, fighting for gay rights. In the discussion Martell helped them see that they were both on the same team fighting for gay rights but each in a different way: the one with political and public action and the other by standing up against anyone who would disrespect them as a couple. This way of looking at their differences had a particularly strong impact on the more out partner. He spontaneously volunteered that he might not be so overtly political in the presence of his partner, knowing that now he saw that they really were on the same team.

Now let's look at a transcript of a session with a couple in therapy in which the therapist uses unified detachment with the couple's repetitious struggle. We include our commentary on what the therapist is doing and how the couple is responding.

Unified Detachment with John and Mary

Mary was an energetic, take-charge partner who ran the family business while John made a living as a schoolteacher. In contrast to Mary, John was a passive, somewhat forgetful man who waited for others, Mary in particular, to take care of family affairs. Their relationship worked well enough until the family business started to crumble and John developed some medical problems. In the middle of the business difficulties, without consulting Mary, he decided to take early retirement from teaching. Mary was angry at John for retiring at a financially stressful time and even angrier about the fact that he made the decision unilaterally. Nevertheless, after the family business went bankrupt, Mary, being a take-charge person, started a new business, with John as reluctant junior partner. She resented his lack of involvement in the business. He resented being told what to do. When she expressed her resentment, he attributed it to hysteria and believed her menopause had resulted in a chronic PMS condition. She complained about not having a partner who shared with her both their failures and their successes. He complained that his lack of expressiveness was being mistaken for noninvolvement. Oftentimes, he would be planning to take action, only to be beaten to the punch by Mary, whose energy level was such that she tackled tasks before he got around to them. She insisted that she had no way of knowing that he planned to help, because he was so silent about his intentions. His frequent refrain was, "I love you; that should be enough." Her response was, "I'm glad that you love me, but your love isn't doing me much good these days. I am constantly overworked and overwhelmed; yet, if I didn't take care of business, business would not get taken care of." As a Christian, John emphasized forgiveness but used this notion to insulate himself from her attempts to change him.

A DEEP analysis of Mary and John is relatively straightforward. Their primary issue is control versus responsibility about the family business and household tasks. A key difference between them relevant to this issue is that Mary is much more active and John more passive and reactive, Mary more communicative and John more circumspect. A key emotional sensitivity for Mary is her feeling overwhelmed and alone, that the responsibility is all on her shoulders, while a key sensitivity for John is being controlled and told what to do. The external circumstances that have made this issue even more difficult for them are the financial difficulties they have faced with the failure of the old business and the launch of a new one, John's retirement from teaching, as well as his ongoing medical problems. Their pattern of interaction is one of Mary's increasing activity and John's increasing passivity, along with her anger and resentment at his passivity and his resentment and withdrawal in the face of her resentment. The more passive he becomes, the less interest she takes in him as a man and a husband. She withdraws from him sexually and concentrates her efforts on getting help from him in running the business. These efforts fail, as his inhibitions have generalized to the point where he has become a silent partner, spending much of his time watching television. He shows life only when he plays golf or loses his temper because she is "overreacting" or "becoming hysterical again."

During a 2-week break between therapy sessions, John and Mary took a short road trip. The day before the trip, Mary noticed that the brakes on their car weren't working. She mentioned this to John, who replied, "They're fine! They just take a few blocks to kick in." Mary was not satisfied with that response, and she assumed that he was going to ignore her concerns and put them both in danger rather than getting the brakes fixed. John said nothing to Mary, which led her to believe that he did not take her or the brake problem seriously. She often felt as if she were being humored, as if she were a hysterical female who needed to be patronized. In the meantime, John silently went and got the brakes fixed.

As they were driving to their destination the next morning, he mentioned in passing that he had tried the brakes himself and discovered that, indeed, they were not working. She blew up at him when she heard this, because if he had validated her concerns the day before by revealing this information she would not have felt so disqualified. She was furious at him for dismissing her concerns and not even revealing to her his discovery that they were, in fact, valid. He was confused by her anger. After all, he had gotten the brakes fixed. Wasn't that the important thing? Here is how the therapist handled the discussion of this incident.

John: The part that I have trouble with is when we were driving down the road and she talks to me about this situation, and as far as I was concerned, it was already all taken care of. I went out and did what we needed to do to get the car fixed.

Therapist: You thought you'd solved it. You thought you responded to what she needed. She made it clear what she needed. You did it. You thought, "Okay, it's fine now."

Commentary: Here the therapist is simply describing John's thought processes in descriptive, nonblaming language. She describes his thinking as natural, understandable, and even inevitable.

John: Right.

Therapist: Do you understand why she was still upset even though you had the brakes fixed?

John: Well, I was mulling it through my mind. We had one car that was laid up and this is the other car. Now, how are we going to deal with the cars? And I thought at this point, "We really didn't need to fix the other car because the brakes warm up after a little while and I can drive it."

Commentary: Although John did not answer the therapist's question, he provided her with an opening for unified detachment. By his use of the term "mulling it over," he was implying that, even though he did not visibly respond to her concerns, he was taking them seriously. He was, according to his statement, "mulling over" the problem. This is exactly where this couple begins to polarize, when his passive behavior is viewed as nonresponsiveness. The therapist's goal is both to reformulate his apparent nonresponsiveness as quiet concern and to describe each of their reactions and counterreactions in neutral, nonblaming language emphasizing naturalness, inevitability, and reciprocal causality. The therapist uses his term "mulling" as the entry.

Therapist: Okay, so you're mulling this over.

John: So the alternative is that we could get it fixed. But it was Saturday.

Therapist: It took you awhile to process all of that.

John: Yeah, but then I took care of it and took most of the day to do it.

Therapist: It seems as if you needed time to sort through a dilemma: "Here is the car situation. This one is even worse off. The other one's got this brake problem, but my experience is that it gets better as you drive it. What should we do?" You were mulling all of these facts over in your mind. It was a factual dilemma.

Commentary: Using terms like "dilemma" and "factual," the therapist emphasizes, perhaps with some hyperbole, the activity underlying the observable passivity. She turns the brake problem into a complex information-processing task requiring a great deal of active problem solving and demonstrates how seriously John was taking Mary's concerns. As she does this, Mary is listening intently, gradually leaning forward, and becoming less angry at John. Note that the therapist spends most of the time in this section focusing on John, but in so doing, she is altering their usual pattern of interaction. Instead of Mary actively talking and John listening passively as a silent partner, John is talking and Mary is listening with interest.

John: And I was apprehensive about going out to get the brakes fixed because it was Saturday and I would have trouble finding a place. But I found one.
Therapist: So you were concerned that there wouldn't be a place to fix them.
John: I went to several places.
Therapist: So you were mulling all that over! You were thinking, "I don't even know if I can get the brakes fixed on a Saturday."
John: Yeah.
Therapist: So you were really processing a whole bunch of information inside yourself.
John: Yeah.
Therapist: You are kind of thinking the facts through of what can we do to solve this dilemma about the car. You're thinking, "Will it even be open?"
John: I even contemplated the possibility of a rental.

Commentary: Now John is making his own contributions to the view that he was engaging in active, complex problem solving. He is adding the consideration of a car rental as another possibility. Perhaps he is responding in part to the therapist's reformulation: it is probably reinforcing for him to hear himself described as an active information processor and problem solver. That is certainly not how Mary sees him or describes him. Now the therapist brings Mary into the conversation by capturing her understandable dilemma in this situation.

Therapist: So you were thinking about a whole bunch of stuff over there. And you're [to Mary] clueless to this. You were thinking that he's just kind of ignoring the situation. This is your fear—that he's ignoring the situation.

John: The rental idea was kind of dubious.

Therapist: But you were very actively, busily in your brain trying to solve this problem. Right?

John: And decide which was the best solution since it was a Saturday.

Therapist: So you were busy trying to respond to her dilemma, which was, "This car is in bad shape." You heard that, obviously.

Mary: But he didn't believe it because he remembers when he drove it and it wasn't in such bad shape.

Therapist: Well, that was part of his factual analysis. You're right. He was incorporating his memory of last driving it.

Mary: "Oh, she's overreacting again."

Therapist [to Mary]: You felt that he saw you as overreacting, and you became understandably irritated, and you [to John] saw her reaction, didn't understand it, and did indeed interpret it as overreacting.

John: But then when I went out to drive the car I realized that it really was bad.

Therapist: And that's the part that bothers her, but let's put that aside for a moment. It is important that you hear her concern, which she thought you discounted.

John: I didn't discount it, but I was a little befuddled for a while.

Therapist: You were a little befuddled because you didn't understand why it bothered her so much because your memory of driving it wasn't so bad.

John: Yeah.

Therapist: Okay, you didn't know until later when you drove it.

John: Well, that and the fact that I wasn't quite sure what we were going to be able to do.

Therapist: So you have two dilemmas now. You've got Mary's experience of this car which seems different from yours. And you have to decide what to do about solving the problem: "It's a Saturday. I don't know if I can get the brakes fixed." So you are just processing all of this information, but what I think is important for Mary to hear is that there was a whole bunch of activity going on inside you that she didn't know was happening. You don't say a lot of things. But you're saying them now. You were not, as it appeared, ignoring the situation or her. You were processing it. It's just that you were doing it all inside yourself, so it was invisible. Make sense?

John: Now it does.

Therapist: Okay, so Mary is over here, still anxious about the car, still wondering what's going to happen about it, feeling like she tried to express her concern to you: "I'm scared, concerned about driving this car." And she's looking over at you. She thinks her feelings don't matter to you.

John: I kind of figured that out a little bit, but I didn't know exactly what to do with it.

Therapist: Exactly. You were actually trying to respond to her need. You heard it. You thought about it. You considered various options. But meanwhile, Mary is over here feeling ignored. She can't see all this activity going on in your head, so she thinks you really don't care. You are just ignoring her, her feelings aren't important, her safety isn't important. She doesn't feel respected, or special. What else, Mary?

Commentary: The therapist tried to bring Mary into the conversation above but John kept adding comments. The therapist could have made a more definitive switch to Mary but given John's usual reticence to talk, the therapist let John temporarily dominate and now brings Mary's experience back into the conversation with her summary of Mary's experience and the question, "What else, Mary?" If Mary had indicated increasing upset at John's analysis above, then the therapist presumably would have included Mary earlier.

Mary: Why isn't he listening to me? Why didn't he tell me that the brakes were as bad as I knew they were? Where do I stand? What am I to him?

Therapist: You are thinking of all of those things, feeling all of those feelings as you watch him and all of the activity inside of him is invisible to you. So you get even more upset. The more you see his inactivity, the more upset you get. Meanwhile, [to John] you're really not inactive. You're really a busy little bee!

Commentary: The therapist is shifting into a little bit of empathic joining interventions by focusing on Mary's anxiety and fear, which was driving her anger at his lack of sharing with her. However, the episode is primarily an illustration of unified detachment in that the therapist helps the couple talk about the sequence of interaction without reliving that sequence (i.e., Mary expressing anger and John being resentfully quiet). The therapist did this in several ways. First, she is successful in making both partners' reactions and counterreactions seem natural, understandable, and even inevitable. Second, she detaches both of them from the interactional pattern and succeeds in getting both of them to look at it from a distance, together facing a common enemy. Third, she creates a different pattern of interaction in which John is sharing and Mary is listening, rather than the reverse. Finally, she injects a little empathic joining into the interaction to reformulate John's ignoring as quiet support and Mary's strong emotional reaction as the inevitable outcome of being ignored, unloved, and not respected. What the therapist doesn't do, consistent with IBCT's conceptualization of unified detachment, is follow these good interventions with suggestions that John needs to share more or that Mary needs to realize that John really is taking her seriously even though he does not visibly indicate that. She lets them experience this new understanding and see what impact it has.

Integration of Unified Detachment and Empathic Joining

We almost always start off treatment with empathic joining and unified detachment, as they follow naturally from the DEEP analysis we presented in the feedback session. Our discussion of their DEEP helps a couple come to a common, unified view of their problems that is more objective and thus more detached than their usually fault-focused, initial conceptualization. Our discussion of their emotional sensitivities and the emotions that are triggered in their usual pattern of interaction points them to the strong emotions that fuel the intensity of their conflicts.

Up until now, we have presented empathic joining and unified detachment as separate interventions because they are conceptually different. However, during the active phase of treatment, we typically combine these interventions. We can, for example, delineate a sequence of interaction but delve into the emotion that was experienced at key points. Sometimes the client leads us from one intervention to another. For example, we may be focusing on unified detachment, but the client may start to explore their emotional experience at a key point, leading us to follow that direction and pursue more of an empathic joining intervention. Or if we are focusing on empathic joining, the client may make a comment indicating unified detachment. For example, in the last chapter, we presented a lengthy segment from an empathic joining intervention with Fran and Henry. At the end of that segment, Henry spontaneously comments to Fran that "whatever you feel that's negative—whether it's frustration or anger or loneliness or whatever, whatever the base motion is—you express it in terms of anger, or that's the way it comes out." She agrees with him, and then he adds "That's exactly opposite—that's exactly the emotion that I shy away from." Here he beautifully describes the problematic dynamic in their relationship, including the emotional reactions of each, and she agreed with that description—a great example of unified detachment.

Let's consider how we might integrate empathic joining and unified detachment when we discuss the four frequent topics of the active intervention phase of IBCT: the most positive incident since the last session, the most difficult or negative incident since the last session, an upcoming event that will be challenging for the couple, and an issue of concern even if there have been no relevant incidents around that issue. With each of these topics, we are attuned to the emotional reactions of each, in that those reactions are key to understanding their difficulties and improving their relationship.

When we debrief a positive event, we are alert for emotional reactions that can tell us whether this event was important and alert for the pattern of interaction that unfolded to tell us whether something different happened. If the event was important and/or different, it may deserve detailed attention. If the event was positive but did not have much emotional impact or was typical of their usual positive interactions, we may not give it much attention. For example, if the couple mentions dinner with some friends that was positive, but a common positive, we would acknowledge their ongoing ability to enjoy each other and their friends and not to let their problems invade areas of pleasure. However, if they ordinarily have tension when out with friends, in that she thinks he dominates the conversation, giving her little attention or room to speak her views, a positive event with friends would merit detailed attention. With empathic joining, we would want to explore her emotional reaction. Maybe she was relieved that she got more airtime with their friends, maybe she appreciated that, but maybe she is hesitant to voice much acknowledgement, not trusting that the change will be consistent. Maybe he put in effort to give her space but didn't feel acknowledged for his effort. Or maybe it was a thoroughly positive event for each. With unified detachment, we would want to explore the sequence of what happened that made it go better. What did each do or not do that seemed to change the usual course of things?

Exploration of the most difficult recent event leads to a combination of empathic joining and unified detachment, but the order is often dictated by the couple's emotional state. If one or both is still upset by the incident or quickly gets upset as they recall the incident, we typically begin with empathic joining, trying to explore, elucidate, validate, and sometimes intensify the emotional experience of each. If discussion of the incident triggers emotion in the session (e.g., he reacts to her description of his "half-baked ideas"), then we also lead with empathic joining. If the incident has lost most of its emotional force over the course of the time since the incident, we can lead with unified detachment, helping the couple see the sequence of their interaction and how the incident was another example of their usual dance. We could discuss how it reflects their differences and sensitivities, we can help them make comparisons and contrasts, and we can engage in other strategies that bring greater unified detachment, such as humor and metaphor.

Discussion of an upcoming, challenging event also allows us to use and integrate both empathic joining and unified detachment. With unified detachment, we help the couple discuss the usual pattern of interaction that unfolds in that difficult scenario. With empathic joining, we discuss the emotions that are typically elicited. For example, in one IBCT case, the couple regularly had painful reactions when they visited her mother. Because they were only able to visit occasionally, the wife wanted to focus most of her attentions on her mother and adapt to her mother's cultural and religious patterns, which the couple did not themselves follow. The husband had a difficult and somewhat strained relationship with his mother-in-law and as a result of his wife's approach felt completely abandoned and alone during the visits. He would angrily retreat. His wife would get upset with him for not "allowing me to be with my mother . . . just once or twice a year." As a result, the visits were usually unpleasant for both and probably for her mother as well. We often follow empathic joining and unified detachment of an upcoming, challenging event with discussion about changes they might each make to increase the likelihood of them handling the event better than they usually do. Because it is easier to make a specific change, such as changing how you are during a weekend visit with family, than changing how you are in general, such as increasing how supportive you are of your partner, we often follow empathic joining and unified detachment around an upcoming event with discussion of direct changes each could make. We will address this focus on direct change in Chapter 9.

Discussion of an important issue, even if there were no recent events about this issue, usually begins with empathic joining but then often includes unified detachment. An issue of concern may objectively present challenges for a couple in that they want different things or different courses of action. However, their strong emotion makes the issue of even greater concern. For example, Rachel wants their child to go to one school while Barry wants the child to go to another. Her desire for the one school is driven by her strong desire for the child to attend a religious school; she would feel that she had let her children down or not been a good mother if she did not have the child raised in the religious environment she endorsed. Barry is not opposed to religious training but the religious school costs much more than the public school the child could attend. His worry about money and the cost of the religious school makes that a big deal for him. A focus on empathic joining does not solve the problem but brings to light the strong emotions that each has; thus, empathic joining may soften positions or allow for more constructive communication.

Unified detachment comes into the picture when we discuss with the couple how they usually discuss the problem. For example, in the case above, Rachel and Barry tended to operate somewhat secretly from the other, she going to the religious school orientations without him and not discussing it with him for fear of his rejection and ire and him acting as if the child would go to public school without discussing it with her. Of course, we don't just do empathic joining and unified detachment when we help couples discuss issues of concern. We also focus on changes they might make to better the situation. We will focus on how we do that in Chapters 9–11.

SUMMARY

In this chapter we first defined unified detachment and reviewed the empirical support for it. Unified detachment interventions engage couples in discussions of their salient incidents and issues in a way that is nonjudgmental, descriptive, and dyadic. It is a kind of dyadic mindfulness that helps couples develop a common story about their problems. The extensive theory and research on mindfulness interventions, which show that they can reduce negative affect and cognitive reactivity among other effects, provide some of the empirical base for unified detachment. This mindfulness research has been conducted on interventions for individuals, but the dyadic mindfulness of unified detachment may have an even greater power than its individual effects on the partners because it brings the couple together in a shared understanding of their concerns. As an illustration, we reviewed one study of a joint mindfulness intervention that had a positive impact on conflict in nondistressed couples. We also described how both unified detachment and empathic joining may bring about positive change in couples by exposing them to emotionally arousing material in the safe, nonblaming environment of therapy. With repeated exposure, partners may be able to discuss hot topics in a less heated way and thus handle them more effectively.

We discussed several strategies for promoting unified detachment. Our most common way of doing unified detachment is to engage couples in an analysis of the sequence of behavior during a particularly difficult episode between them. We highlight the key points in that interaction, which are usually points that trigger emotional reactions in one or both of them. Thus, we certainly discuss emotion during unified detachment but we don't explore or intensify emotions as we do in empathic joining. When we discuss a sequence of conflict, we typically focus on the opening phase of that sequence because partners act in ways that are more understandable and less blameworthy in the early phase of conflict than in the later, escalated phase. However, if partners say or do something that is particularly hurtful, we may focus on that, usually with empathic joining. We may also ask couples to rate their interactions and to compare and contrast them so they learn why some interactions go better than others. We may distinguish between the intent and the impact of certain crucial behaviors, showing how partners' usually benign intentions often lead to behaviors with a negative impact. We can engage couples in a discussion of their differences, showing how those differences have benefits and costs for each of them or reveal that the partners are part of the same team. We can also help couples distance from their conflicts by encouraging them to come up with metaphors, images, and names for their patterns or key roles in those patterns. Or we may suggest such metaphors, images, or names. These terms may capture some humor or irony in their positions or dynamics, enabling distance from them. All of these strategies also teach the couple about the determining factors in their conflict and suggest alternative responses that might lead to better outcomes. However, we are careful not to jump into suggestions and assignments for them to do things differently because we know how hard it is to change ingrained patterns and we don't know what or who is most able to change. Also, as couples sit with their newfound knowledge, they may spontaneously change in ways that improve their relationship and thus they will more fully own that change.

We provided two short descriptions of unified detachment that are available on video through the American Psychological Association and a detailed episode from a client in IBCT, along with commentary on what the therapist was doing and how the clients responded. Then we ended the chapter with a discussion of the integration of empathic joining and unified detachment. Even though the two types of interventions are conceptually distinct, we usually combine them in our work with couples. We discussed how this is done.

8

❧

Creating Acceptance and Change Through Tolerance Building

INTIMATE RELATIONSHIPS BRING many occasions for pleasure, satisfaction, and contentment but almost as many occasions for emotional pain. Our partner may rebuff our efforts to be physically close or sexually intimate because they are not in the mood when we are. Our partner may be distracted or not sufficiently interested in something that seems important to us. Our partner may get caught up in his or her own concerns and not be responsive to our needs. Our partner may have a different idea of how to raise children, a more negative view of our family, an alternative plan for vacation, or different standards for contact with past or potential future romantic partners. As previously shown, our differences, our emotional sensitivities, and our external circumstances, particularly external stressors, create conflicts in relationships: one or both partners may feel unloved or unappreciated or neglected; important wishes and desires of one or both get thwarted. In short, as the title of the old blues song suggests "You always hurt the one you love" (Doris Fisher and Allan Roberts, 1944).

We human beings, like all other organisms, find it hard to accept pain.

We are wired genetically to do all that is possible to prevent, avoid, or escape from pain. Often these efforts are successful. However, often these efforts to avoid or escape from pain in close relationships are only temporarily successful. They give us short-term relief but ultimately complicate the problem or make it worse. Short-term gain but long-term pain. As we have seen repeatedly with the patterns of interaction in which couples get stuck, their actions designed to solve a problem actually make it worse.

In IBCT we attempt to promote emotional acceptance in part to interfere with this process by which partners try to prevent or escape from a painful experience only to meet another version of that experience later, often in a more toxic form. If partners can be more emotionally accepting of each other in general and each other's imperfect behaviors, they may be less likely to behave in ways that grant immediate relief but make a painful problem more painful or more persistent in the long run. As we have discussed, IBCT's primary ways to encourage acceptance are empathic joining and unified detachment. An additional way to increase acceptance is to increase each partner's tolerance for the other partner's negative behavior. Acceptance is a broader and more positive term, emphasizing an embrace of the other, warts and all, while tolerance is a narrower term, emphasizing endurance of something unpleasant and implying less responsiveness to it. We use tolerance in IBCT similar to the way Dialectic Behavior Therapy uses the term *distress tolerance* except that our focus is interpersonal—tolerance of a loved one's actions that are not egregious, such as violence and infidelity, but are painful nonetheless. If partners can endure these behaviors without trying to change them, if they let go of the effort to convince the partner that these behaviors are wrong and shouldn't be done, then they often find that the behaviors occur less frequently or less persistently. Even if the frequency or duration of the behavior does not change, its toxicity may be reduced.

Tolerance training is also analogous to exposure therapy approaches to anxiety problems. The key to successful reduction of anxiety is nonreinforced exposure to the feared stimulus. During gradual exposure to whatever it is that scares the client, the therapist controls the context in which the stimulus is experienced, the client doesn't experience the fearful outcome, and anxiety is reduced. Thus, the exposure counteracts the client's avoidance, which served to maintain the anxiety. For example, a person who is afraid of snakes is gradually exposed to a harmless snake until the client can hold the snake without fear. In a similar way with IBCT tolerance interventions, the therapist exposes the client to the partner's upsetting behavior and prevents avoidance or escape or other counteracting behavior; as a result, the client may come to experience the behavior over time as less aversive even if not pleasant. For example, assume that Raymond gets upset with Chelsea when she reacts with strong emotion to some event in her world and he normally tries in vain to get her to calm down by showing her that her reactions are "over the top." If the therapist can help Raymond just listen to Chelsea and tolerate the aversiveness of her strong reactions rather than counteract them, he may experience that she calms down sooner. More importantly, he may experience that listening to her without counteracting her is not so aversive, even though it may always be somewhat unpleasant for him.

There are three primary techniques for promoting tolerance: practicing negative behavior in the therapy session, faking negative behavior between sessions, and self-care. To be successful, all three of these techniques require that the couple have first understood their pattern of interaction, have reached a level of unified detachment from it, and have some empathy for each other's experience in it. Otherwise, they might engage in the activities with hostility or view them as encouragement to do what their partner dislikes. Thus, the three techniques that we describe below are usually reserved for later in therapy and usually when empathic joining and unified detachment have not increased acceptance to a desired level. However, as we shall see, the first two also provide an opportunity for unified detachment and empathic joining discussions of the negative behavior that just occurred.

ROLE-PLAYING NEGATIVE BEHAVIOR DURING THE THERAPY SESSION

Role-playing or behavior rehearsal is a common strategy for improving communication in Traditional Behavioral Couple Therapy (TBCT). Couples practice new communication skills in the session so that they can use them later outside the session. These skills, which we will review in Chapter 11, focus on constructive ways of communicating about each one's needs and desires without questioning the validity of the needs and desires themselves; in other words, the needs and desires themselves are implicitly *accepted* in these communication or problem-solving training exercises. For example, if we help a couple communicate more effectively about their differences over the amount of time they want to spend together, we might have them practice clear, direct ways of signaling each other about their differing desires and constructive ways to negotiate time together and apart. However, change efforts are not directed at getting the one who wants more time for independent activity to want more time together—which the other may hope for— or at getting the one who wants more time together to be more interested in independent activity—which the other may hope for. Thus, even in these traditional, change-oriented procedures, the therapist promotes acceptance of the couple's divergent needs and desires while trying to change the way they communicate about them.

IBCT goes one step further. It promotes acceptance not only of partners' divergent needs but also of the notion that no matter how effective they are at making changes, they will at times slip up and lapse into old communication patterns. We know that we cannot eliminate dysfunctional patterns of communication completely. When we ask couples to rehearse negative behavior in the session, we are aiming to reduce the toxicity of that behavior by diminishing the sensitivity to it. By so doing, we may also lower the likelihood of escalation. If partners experience negative behavior less intensely, they are less likely to respond with avoidance, escape, or attack that leads to additional negative behavior. Both goals of reduced sensitivity and decreased escalation will enable a quicker recovery from the occurrence of that problematic behavior. However, the exercise may affect the partner who does the negative behavior as well as the one who receives it. The partner who engages in the negative behavior may decrease the frequency and intensity of these negative behaviors because he or she becomes more aware of the impact of his or her behavior on the other. Finally, if partners are prepared for these inevitable occurrences of negative behavior, they won't misinterpret them as an indicator of relapse—that all their efforts in therapy have been in vain.

We are up front with the rationale for role-playing negative behavior in the session. For example, we may introduce it by saying the following:

I am going to ask you to do something that may initially sound a little weird. You both understand this tense pattern of interaction that you often get into. Now that you are both calm and relaxed, I would like you to replay it in front of me, maybe getting into a particularly bad version of it. Why would I ask you to do something that crazy? Because when you are not emotionally triggered, you may be able to experience the interaction differently, not get so caught up in it, see it not from the inside but as an actor might see it, feel that it is not so horrible, and see alternatives for getting out of it. So, if you are willing to try that, let's first review the key parts of the pattern and then get you two started on enacting it right here.

With this rationale in place, we ask couples to role-play a common dysfunctional pattern of interaction in which they get stuck or, as a way of getting started, to role-play one of the behaviors that is provocative for the other and leads to the pattern. Consider John and Mary, the couple with issues around control and responsibility that we discussed at length in the previous chapter on unified detachment. We might ask Mary to role-play a situation in which she criticizes John for forgetting to take care of a business responsibility. Or we might ask John to roleplay a situation in which he attacks Mary for over-reacting. When Mary and John do these behaviors, they are responding in an entirely different context than the context that usually elicits those behaviors. They are engaging in these behaviors in response to a therapist request, not in response to some provocative situation. Therefore, the negative behavior is usually going to be a diminished or limited or partial version of what it normally is. Therefore, partners may respond with a smile or laughter at the effort required to produce something that is normally done naturally or at hearing only a faint resemblance to what they experience as "the real thing." That leaves open the possibility of a unified detachment discussion of the provocative behavior, since this occasion of it automatically led to a humorous response. Or, if the partner engaging in the behavior is able to produce a realistic replica of his or her usual behavior and the other has the usual response to it, the therapist can engage in empathic joining, often with greater ease, in that the negative behavior and reaction to it were somewhat diminished in magnitude because of the unusual context. Sometimes the most impactful aspect of this intervention is the discussion that follows the initiation of the negative behavior and the reaction to it—a discussion that can go in the direction of unified detachment, empathic joining, or both. With the therapist's assistance, spouses express their feelings in these scenarios rather than acting them out; they discuss their observations rather than making judgments about the other's behavior. Through this process partners become more conscious of their behavior that the other experiences as negative and they learn new information about the other's motives and emotions that may make that behavior less toxic.

The purpose of the therapist's interventions is to prepare the couple for future negative behavior and to reduce the impact of it, rather than to prevent the occurrence of that behavior. The distinction between preparing for and preventing negative behavior is extremely important. The therapist is clearly not trying to completely prevent a negative behavior that is a regular part of the couple's pattern of interaction; this would be an unrealistic goal. Moreover, the generation of therapeutic conversation between the partners, that is, getting them to debrief the experience of the negative behavior through empathic joining and unified detachment, is not necessarily expected to generalize to the home environment. Rather, the intervention leads to a contextual shift around that negative behavior: the greater understanding of the negative behavior and the dynamics that create and maintain it changes the meaning of that behavior for them both. As a result the partner engaging in the negative behavior may do it less frequently or intensely or may make an attempt to counteract it once he or she has done it; the recipient of the negative behavior may not respond with as much emotional intensity to it and or may be less likely to counteract it with negative behavior of their own. Thus, there will be a greater tolerance when such negative behaviors occur in the future, as they inevitably will. In short, the expectation is that couples will continue to engage in some of these negative behaviors, it is hoped less frequently and less intensely, but when they do occur, the couple is better prepared and the impact on the relationship will be less destructive. They will be able to recover from the incidents more quickly.

Sometimes the discussion in therapy makes partners so aware, so self-conscious about the negative behaviors that they do, that they stop doing those negative behaviors—at least in the short term. Although that is not necessarily the goal of the intervention, that is certainly a positive outcome. Let's consider an example of faking negative behavior in the therapy session from Randy and Ginger. Randy was a skilled laborer who often worked overtime because he was so concerned about the family having enough money. He insisted on a rigid budget and would lose his temper if Ginger exceeded the budget by even a few dollars. He also desired very frequent sex and felt hurt and rejected whenever he wanted sex and Ginger did not. Ginger loved Randy and felt guilty about her lower sex drive. However, she firmly insisted on her right to refuse, and Randy did not question that right. Ginger also acknowledged overspending her budget, but refused to discuss such issues with Randy when he lost his temper, because he used abusive language. When she refused to talk to him, Randy would get even angrier, and the argument would escalate. This pattern stopped during the course of IBCT, and the cessation seemed tied to the following intervention.

Therapist: I want you to have your discussion about money as if you were having it at home. Don't try to do it better because I'm here. In fact, do it as badly as you ever do it. Be the lousiest communicators possible.

Ginger: Can I do his part?

Randy: No.

Therapist: Do your own parts but let's see it as bad as it gets; in fact, you can even exaggerate it a bit.

Randy: Okay. We can do that easy.

Therapist: This better be bad.

Commentary: By directing the couple to do their communication badly and repeating that instruction, she is making it harder for each partner to be emotionally affected by the other, since they are so clearly responding to directions from the therapist rather than acting spontaneously.

Ginger [to Randy]: You had a problem with me going over budget by five dollars.

Randy: Well, you can't control your compulsive spending. And then you tell your family that I'm abusive, making it sound like I'm beating you or something. Can't you keep your mouth shut and your wallet closed? You're like a kid when it comes to money. Are you trying to send us to the poorhouse? Don't you care if your kids have enough money to eat? (Pause.) You're supposed to interrupt me now and change the subject.

Ginger: I only went over budget by a few fucking dollars. For God's sake—

Randy: A few fucking dollars add up, when it happens every month.

Ginger: You're nuts. It hasn't happened in 6 months.

Randy: Your memory is about as good now as it is when you forget to balance the checkbook.

Ginger: You're just being paranoid. You think I spend money and don't tell you about it. Get some help.

Therapist: You two surely can do worse than this.

Randy: It might follow us out of here.

Ginger: I'm not really mad at the moment, but that is what it sounds like. When we are tired we often create problems, especially you [to Randy]—

Therapist: Are we still doing lousy communicating?

Randy: She always gets the last blow, the last word.

Ginger: "Like you always do" is one of my favorites.

Therapist: Okay, are you both finished now? I'd like to go over it with you. When you were trying to be lousy communicators, what were you doing?

Commentary: Note that the therapist chides them at their difficulty in doing bad communication but when they start getting into it, she asks them "Are you still doing lousy communicating?" which reminds them they are to be faking their bad communication and that the communication that they are hearing from their partner is not real. This is an attempt to down regulate the intensity. However, the therapist makes sure that the bad communication does not continue or escalate and then stops them to discuss the process that just went on. Because they only got a taste of their provocative behavior, they are able to talk about what they did with some unified detachment.

Ginger: Talking and not listening. Being defensive.

Randy: Insulting her about her mouth. She's very sensitive about how much she talks.

Therapist: She called you "paranoid" and "nuts."

Randy: Yeah, those are about the rudest things you [to Ginger] can come up with as far as I'm concerned.

Ginger: It's a trigger for Randy. I'm questioning his mental health and he really goes off the deep end about it.

Therapist: Okay, so one thing you were doing is questioning his mental health. What else?

Randy: I was just getting warmed up. I was trying to get in the mood. Mostly I was just doing what we do.

Ginger: Accusing.

Randy: Yeah, accusing, I guess. Thank you, dear.

Therapist: What were you accusing her of?

Randy: Having a big mouth.

Therapist: Blabbing to everybody.

Randy: Sabotaging me with money and with gossip. Telling things out of context that make me look bad.

Therapist: Right, in a loud voice that everyone would hear.

Randy: Uh-huh.

Therapist: Okay, that was good. But what's it like when you are really in each other's faces, like when you're eye to eye and escalating?

Commentary: Because the couple is doing well talking about some of their provocative communications with unified detachment, the therapist takes a risk and asks them to talk about their most provocative behaviors and then to enact those behaviors.

Ginger: I stop talking and Randy starts yelling.

Therapist [to Ginger]: How would you do it? You would be quiet, but what does your face look like?

Ginger: I sneer.

Therapist: Okay, could you please just sneer the best you can? Can you [to Randy] rant just for a minute so I can see what your ranting looks like?

First, you [to Ginger] have to give him your best sneer. So look [to Randy] at her, because I won't be able to judge how good a sneer it is.

Ginger: [Demonstrates sneer, combined with flipping her hand upward] All I've got to do is go, "Whatever." That means I don't care, I'm blowing you off.

Therapist: Okay, so you have to wave your hand like, "Okay, whatever."

Ginger: It's an indication that I'm not going to listen anymore.

Randy: Yeah, "whatever" is a trigger.

Therapist: What does her hand movement mean?

Ginger: That I'm shutting you out.

Randy: Yeah, that's it.

Therapist: "I flip you off."

Randy: That sort of thing, yes.

Ginger: I won't deal with you when you're like that.

Randy: Yeah, I start cussing and the volume goes up. I look for about the meanest thing I can think of at the moment to say.

Therapist: Okay, what's the meanest thing he's ever said to you?

Ginger: "Worthless" and "lazy" are my least favorites.

Therapist: Would you [to Randy] mind doing those?

Randy [reluctantly]**:** Okay.

Therapist [to Ginger]**:** You have to get into your very best dismissive mode. Is that the right face?

Randy: She's getting close.

Ginger: Yeah, I don't know if I can create it.

Therapist: So, it has to be provoked?

Ginger: It develops naturally.

Therapist: What if he called you worthless and lazy first, would that help you get your face, or does the face come first?

Randy: The face comes first.

Ginger: I don't know. I just shut off at some point. I go someplace else if it gets loud. The face means "You're not going to be dealt with unless we can talk about this calmly."

Therapist: Okay, so you do the silent dismissal treatment. And so she goes silent. You [to Randy] go loud. How loud? Let's hear it. Could you just call her worthless and lazy as loud as you can? But first she has to give you the face. You [to Ginger] have to do your best dismissal.

Randy: I don't particularly want to because I guess I'm ashamed. I wouldn't want anyone else to hear it. It's bad enough that Ginger has to hear it. When it happens, I wonder, "Did just one neighbor hear it? Or did the entire neighborhood hear it? Do the fishermen on the lake hear it? Are the windows open?" Okay, here goes. You [to Ginger] stupid, lazy, worthless excuse for human being! What did you do this time? Where did all the money go? Where did it go? [To the therapist] That ain't loud but that's what I say.

Therapist: Okay, but that's the worst of it, calling her names.

Randy: "Stupid" gets her going a whole lot more.

Ginger: "Lazy" and "stupid" really get me.

Although the nonverbal body language is lost in a written transcript, during this segment the threesome engaged in unified detachment, alternating between playfulness and humor as they described the triggering behaviors that they do and receive from the other. They also engaged in a bit of empathic joining, as Randy revealed his embarrassment at saying some of the things he has said and Ginger heard that revelation. All of these factors probably contributed to this interaction sequence stopping immediately subsequent to this session.

Faked Incidents of Negative Behavior at Home

As a follow-up to the intervention above, we often ask couples to fake instances of the negative behavior at home when they are "really not feeling it." That is, partners are instructed to behave negatively at times when they would not otherwise be inclined to engage in such behavior. For example, John may purposely "forget" to accomplish a business-related task, even though he actually remembers that the task needs to be accomplished. Or Mary might react strongly to John's forgetting even though at the particular moment she is not angry at him.

We ask couples to fake negative behavior rather than wait until it occurs naturally because a faked behavior is devoid of any negative emotional experience on the part of the faker. Although fakers may feign negative emotion as part of the negative behavior, internally they are calm. This inner tranquility allows the faker to more clearly observe the partner's reactions and perhaps see their emotional pain; it is also likely to prevent the incident from escalating. In fact, we instruct the faker to reveal the fake soon after he or she initiates it to ensure that escalation doesn't occur. Then we encourage the couple to debrief this faked incident.

The instructions to fake are given in front of the partner, so that the partner knows that some negative behavior in the future may be faked. This knowledge may interrupt the partner's stereotypical reactions to negative behavior. For example, if Donna attacks Michael as not caring when she really doesn't feel that way, she can see his upset and defensiveness more clearly, since she is not angry. She may be able to empathize with him or at least see clearly how her actions don't bring about the response that she would like. Furthermore, the instructions cast a shadow of doubt in Michael over her attacks, which may then interrupt his defensiveness.

This task of identifying negative behavior and instructing partners to engage in it when they don't feel the emotional push to do so can be beneficial in several ways. The primary purpose of the task is to build tolerance in the partner who experiences the faked behavior. Through the process of identifying the negative behavior, role-playing it in session, and assigning it for homework, the therapist is treating the negative behavior not as some unacceptable and hateful actions that the actor does to the recipient but just as a troublesome behavior that can occur without the drama that is usually attendant to it. As a result of this process, as well as having the recipient experience the behavior under faked conditions, he or she may become somewhat desensitized to it and thus more tolerant of it. Also, the faking task makes behavior that was once contingency-shaped rule-governed. Now it is occurring at least in part because the therapist assigned it, rather than as a response to natural events in the environment that pull for the behavior. The potential recipient of the negative behavior may now wonder, every time the behavior occurs, whether this instance is the assignment or a spontaneous example of the problem. This shift in controlling variables can lead to a less emotional or negative response on the part of the recipient. To put it another way, the recipient of the faked behavior may respond with greater tolerance to all instances of the behavior because of the ambiguity in what variables are controlling the behavior.

A second purpose of the faking task is to make the actor who engages in the negative behavior more aware of the impact of his or her behavior on the other. People are less able to determine the impact of their behavior when they are emotionally caught up in it themselves. However, if they are not emotionally distressed and are primed to observe, they can see more clearly how their behavior has an impact on their partner that is often not what they intend. Therefore, as a result of the faking assignment, the actor may engage in the negative behavior in the future less frequently or less intensely or walk it back or even apologize for it, so that the negative behavior has a less serious impact on the other.

The third purpose of the faking task is to facilitate discussion by the partners after the task, during which they might be able to engage in some unified detachment or empathic joining on their own. If the task achieves any of these three outcomes, even partially, it will be helpful for the couple.

This faking assignment is similar to the technique of *prescribing the symptom* in strategic therapies. However, the primary goal with that technique is to reduce the likelihood of the behavior through a paradoxical directive. That is not our goal. If such reduction does occur, we are not displeased. However, our rationale for this assignment is greater desensitization and tolerance in the recipient, greater awareness and altered behavior in the actor, and more discussion between partners that leads to unified detachment and empathic joining. Unlike strategic approaches, this rationale can be shared with the couple.

Let's consider an example from Patrick and Michelle. Patrick was an engineer while Michelle was an unemployed real estate broker during the time of therapy. Patrick was very work-and-goal focused and initially complained about the disorganization in their lives and their lack of saving. Michelle was relationship focused and complained about their lack of romance and time together. She also struggled with depression, particularly during the long, wet winters in Seattle, and had been diagnosed with seasonal affective disorder. By the time the session below occurred, Michelle and Patrick's therapy was winding down. They had come a long way in accepting their differences and making some changes. For example, they had agreed to live in Seattle for no more than three years. If Michelle still found herself depressed during the Seattle winters after three years, Patrick agreed that they would relocate to San Francisco. They agreed to put some money each month into a "sun fund," which Michelle could use whenever she felt boxed in by the Seattle winters. She would take a vacation, and if Patrick could, he would join her. During the current session, they expressed a readiness to terminate. However, the therapist was concerned about a potentially destructive interaction pattern that he viewed as both inevitable and imminent, now that the winter rainy season was approaching. Michelle would complain about the weather in Seattle and Patrick would usually respond to her complaints by accusing Michelle of not trying hard enough to enjoy Seattle. This response would lead Michelle to be angry at Patrick and accuse him of being defensive. She would also blame him for having brought her to Seattle in the first place, which would of course make Patrick even more defensive. The therapist, wanting to prepare them for this inevitable transaction, proposed a homework assignment involving their faking negative aspects of this interaction cycle.

Therapist: Okay, here's the scenario that I want us to talk about. The scenario is that when you [to Michelle] feel blue about the weather, you make a remark that's not necessarily intended to be hostile or blaming. You make a remark about the weather.

Michelle: Stating a fact.

Therapist: But also reflecting depression. And you [to Patrick] notice that she's depressed. You feel guilty and responsible and then you make a defensive response.

Patrick [to Michelle, jokingly]**:** He knows how this works, doesn't he?

Therapist: If you look at that situation, both of your reactions are quite understandable. If you [to Michelle] feel blue, you are going to make a comment about the weather, and it's understandable why you would get angry at him for being defensive, because you weren't blaming him but he feels blamed anyway and so it's irritating to you that he reacts the way he does. Now in order to change that pattern it would require that you [to Michelle] recognize that you are feeling blue about the weather and moderate your response and that you [to Patrick] recognize that she's not blaming you and not get defensive.

Patrick [jokingly]: What if she is?

Michelle: I never do.

Therapist: The point is that no matter how hard you work, this chain is so automatic and happens so quickly that it's inevitably going to happen, at least occasionally. So, the question is, what can you do to minimize the harm that these exchanges do to the relationship? And Michelle, I would like you to try a little experiment over the next week. I would like to give you a task to do at home. At some point during the week when you don't feel badly about the weather, complain about it anyway. I want you to do this so that you can observe the impact that these complaints have on him at a time when you are not really feeling bad. It gives you a chance to look at his reaction when you are not emotionally involved in the discussion.

Michelle: Okay.

Therapist: I'm assuming that he's going to have the same defensive reaction he always does but you won't be upset and so you will be able to see his defensiveness. You may be more sympathetic to it because you are not upset. You may see the bind that he gets put in when you feel blue about the weather. Now, shortly after he begins his defensive response, I want you to say "I was faking. It was the assignment." I don't want it to turn into an argument. And you [to Patrick] won't know which behaviors are faked and which are real, so you may not respond as automatically as you usually do. But I'm trying to put Michelle in a situation where she can see your response—because it makes good sense to me—at a time when she's not upset and hopefully she will become more empathic with the bind that you are in during those situations. So, the purpose is not to get you [to Patrick] to stop being defensive or to get you [to Michelle] to stop making these remarks, but to help you [to Michelle] become more sympathetic to him when he reacts the way he does, so you don't get so mad at him when he gets defensive. So that's half the assignment. And the other half is something you [to Patrick] do.

Commentary: Unlike the strategic therapy technique of symptom prescription, we don't provide a bogus rationale but the true rationale of promoting understanding, sympathy, and tolerance. There is no therapeutic investment in changing this pattern. However, the therapist is setting in motion a series of processes that may make change possible. Now, whenever Michelle complains about the weather, Patrick is likely to wonder whether it is real or whether it is the assignment. This ambiguity may alter his typically defensive response or, at the very least, promote greater tolerance in him for her complaints.

Patrick: Okay.

Therapist: So, does that make sense to you [to Michelle]? Do you think you can pull it off?

Michelle: I just don't understand why he can't just do active listening and all of that stuff when I complain. I understand that it's humanly impossible for him but it sure would simplify the situation.

Therapist: Well, I agree. Presumably, Patrick will try to actively listen, but no matter how good he gets at it, he's not going to be successful 100% of the time. So I am trying to prepare you for those times when he is not successful.

Patrick: I have gotten better.

Michelle: That's true. You have.

Therapist: Okay, now here's your [to Patrick] assignment. At some point during the week, when you're not feeling defensive about the weather in Seattle, take a weather map and point out to her all of the places where the weather is worse than it is in Seattle.

Michelle: He did that this morning.

Therapist: Okay, but now do it at a time when you're not really feeling an impulse to defend our climate here in Seattle. Fake it. Do it because it is the assignment. And I want you to observe the impact on Michelle.

Patrick: I did that this morning. I couldn't believe it. It was so warm on the west coast and in the Upper Great Lakes, 4–5 inches of snow! And I was just pointing out the extremes, and she got very cold.

Michelle [playfully]**:** Oh, I did not.

Patrick: But next time I'll remember to say I was faking.

Therapist: Okay, so do you want to point out all the places in the world, or should we just go with the U.S.?

Patrick: Let's just go with the U.S.

Commentary: Ideally we want to give the *faking at home* assignment to both partners, asking them to each fake their behavior that is part of the pattern. Therefore, neither is likely to feel that they are primarily to blame or that they have the burden to understand the other without being understood themselves. Note that as they discuss the faking assignment, they review their pattern of interaction, discussing it in a way that promotes unified detachment from it. Interestingly, after this assignment, neither partner did the faking behavior nor did the pattern appear. This assignment did produce some immediate changes as well as acceptance. That of course is all the better.

SELF-CARE

Emotional acceptance and even tolerance of the other is especially difficult if one is feeling especially needy or vulnerable, and for whatever the reason, the partner is unable or unwilling to fulfill those needs or accommodate those vulnerabilities. One avenue toward greater tolerance is to increase each partner's self-reliance, so he or she can manage better when the partner doesn't come through. For example, it could benefit Michelle if she had other people with whom she could complain about the weather, or more importantly, discuss her sad feelings, no matter how much better Patrick becomes at dealing with her.

As IBCT therapists, we occasionally explore alternative means for need satisfaction when the spouse is unable or unwilling to respond in a satisfactory fashion. This exploration must be done sensitively, because alternative means are likely to be experienced as less than optimal. Consider Sally and Fred, who have a conflict about closeness and time together. Yes, Sally could have a good time on weekends with her friends, but what she wants is greater participation from Fred, not time alone with her friends. Also, these alternatives should be framed as something to supplement what the partner does rather than as something to replace what the partner could do; otherwise, the strategy could be seen as a way to absolve the partner of responsibility for attending to the wishes and desires of the other. For example, if Sally sees this exploration as a way of facilitating Fred's freedom on weekends so that he can spend more time alone on the boat or at his computer, she is bound to look askance at such exploration—and with good reason. However, if most of the attention in therapy is directed at building a closer relationship between Sally and Fred, the self-care techniques are likely to be received more favorably: within the context of a therapy focused on building greater closeness, a tactic that would help Sally take better care of herself when Fred is unavailable makes intuitive sense. Sally is likely to be more amenable to this exploration under such circumstances. Also, if Sally begins to see some of Fred's activities, such as being on his boat, as his own self-care actions, she may be less resistant to them. Her decreased resistance might make him more enthusiastic about spending quality time with her.

Because we are seeking greater acceptance between partners, this intervention can be successful even when partners do not make use of the methods of self-care discussed during therapy sessions. The discussion sensitizes partners to issues related to autonomy and personal responsibility, which form a core component of any intimate relationship. No partner, even in the best of relationships, is always available when needed. Personal life stresses, work demands, and even responsibilities to previous partners and children all have the potential to hinder the ability of even the most devoted partners to respond as expected in every situation in which the partner's need is involved. For example, even if Sally does not plan more weekend outings with just her friends, this discussion could move her toward acceptance of Fred as having needs which, even in the best of times, might make it difficult for him to be the family man that she wishes he would be.

Partners are particularly vulnerable to one another when they are stuck in their dysfunctional patterns of communication. When Sally accuses Fred of putting his own selfish interests ahead of his family—something his mother also accused him of—he is especially challenged because he has to deal not only with her anger but also with a concern that he has had about himself all his life. He is bound to escalate the situation further because the accusation is too provocative to produce good, constructive communication. Of course, his efforts only lead to Sally's escalating further, since her anger about his disengagement from family life has been part of an intense struggle that has lasted for years. Partners in the middle of such escalation need some means of protecting and caring for themselves. If we promote the idea that therapeutic efforts, however successful, will rarely eliminate all future occurrences of the problem, then we must prepare couples to face those incidents in ways that are self-protective and that minimize escalation.

Common means of protecting and caring for oneself in the face of stress include leaving the situation, seeking solace from others, or acting assertively to alter the situation. For example, in the face of Sally's accusations, Fred could leave the scene of the interaction, call one of his friends for comfort, or tell Sally assertively that he will not sit and listen to attacks on his character.

The self-protective strategy needs to be chosen in part based on the effect it is likely to have on the partner, since the last thing the self-protector wants is further escalation. For example, Sally may react even more strongly if Fred leaves the situation or calls certain friends. We help clients explore measures that will protect without further alienating the partner or contributing to further polarization. For some couples, taking a time-out will have dire consequences later, especially if it is unilateral. On the other hand, for couples who have a high risk of intimate partner violence, taking time-outs is preferable (we discuss time-outs in more detail in chapter 9 and 13). Assertive responses work very well with some couples but simply lead to further escalation with others. The same is true of seeking social support from outside the situation. The functional analysis is all-important when choosing self-care strategies, but so is the dyadic approach envisioned here. Partners consider alternatives together, with attention to what would work best for the other as well as for themselves. They are planning how each can take care of him or herself, but they are doing this as couple, as a team, making sure to protect their relationship as well.

As we noted above, exploring self-care possibilities in the session can promote acceptance even if the strategies are never used. In fact, the discussion can promote tolerance even if the partners can't come up with any effective self-care methods. In particular, the discussion itself promotes four notions that may further acceptance: (1) provocative behavior will occur at least on occasion even in the best of relationships; (2) during provocations, partners may not be able to provide what the other is seeking; (3) partners may need to take care of themselves during those moments of provocation; and (4) the provocative behavior does not necessarily imply that the relationship has fallen apart, only that it consists of two imperfect human beings.

SUMMARY

In this chapter we described the rationale for tolerance building and three strategies for promoting tolerance: role-playing negative behavior in the therapy session, faking negative behavior at home, and self-care. Although the idealism that is common among couple therapists pulls for techniques with loftier goals, such as empathic joining and unified detachment, tolerance plays a vital role in IBCT. For many problems, and with many couples, learning to tolerate what was formerly intolerable is a major accomplishment in and of itself. If that is all the partners get from therapy, they will have benefited greatly. However, tolerance strategies also provide occasions for discussions that promote unified detachment and empathic joining.

The primary rationale for the first two strategies, in which partners are asked to engage in negative behavior in the session or at home, is exposure to upsetting behavior by the partner—but under altered circumstances. Rather than the negative behavior coming about naturally, it comes about by therapist directive. Thus, the negative behavior is likely to be less intense and the response to it less intense, enabling partners to experience the negative event without engaging in their usual strategies of fight or flight, which in turn generates greater tolerance of the negative behavior. In addition, the conversation between partners after these incidents of instructed negative behavior often provides for unified detachment and empathic joining.

The third strategy of self-care provides clients a way for handling the inevitable limitations of their partners in fulfilling their needs. These discussions must be held sensitively so that partners do not experience them as exempting the other from their responsibilities. When done appropriately, partners jointly discuss how they will care for themselves in ways that don't exacerbate already challenging situations.

All three of the strategies should only be done later in therapy, when the partners have achieved some unified detachment about their patterns of communication and can easily identify the triggering negative behaviors in which each engages and when partners have achieved some empathic joining so they view the partner's needs sympathetically. Sometimes we introduce tolerance strategies even after we introduce some direct change interventions, the topic of the next part of this book, when those interventions don't bring about the changes the couple wants and when their patterns continue to bedevil them.

If we are using the self-help book, *Reconcilable Differences* (Christensen et al., 2014), as part of IBCT, we want to assign Part 4 of the book prior to our efforts to instigate deliberate change, the topic to which we turn now.

IBCT Strategies for Promoting Deliberate Change (and Acceptance)

9

❧

Deliberate, Client-Led Change

"There is nothing permanent except change."
—Heraclitus, quoted in Diogenes Laertius,
Lives of the Eminent Philosophers,
translated by Robert Hicks (1925)

"It is not the strongest or the most intelligent who will survive but those who can best manage change."
—Leon C. Megginson, a Louisiana State University
business professor at the convention of
the Southwestern Social Science Association
in 1963, subsequently misattributed
to Charles Darwin

THERE IS A SEEMING PARADOX about change. On the one hand, change is inevitable, the only true certainty. We see change all around us, but perhaps most obviously in relationships. People fall in love and are happy together at one point in time but then later are unhappy and question their love for each other. They may swear to never talk again to the person whom they once claimed was their soul mate or the best thing that ever

185

happened to them. On the other hand, change is difficult. Those unhappy partners may go through a long process of trying to change each other and themselves in order to improve their relationship. They may change temporarily only to fall back into old patterns. They may get stuck in the push-pull of change, with each pressuring the other to change and each resisting in turn.

Much change, both good and bad in relationships, happens naturally, unintentionally, and usually because circumstances change. The arrival of a baby changes the routines of the young couple dramatically. The presence of a new and attractive colleague may make one reconsider the current relationship or explore a new one. A parent gets sick, has to move in with her daughter and son-in-law, and the couple's life is dramatically altered. A new job opportunity allows a young couple to move back to the neighborhood where their families are and their struggles over how often to visit family and how to pay for it are suddenly over.

The change we are going to consider in this chapter is *not* unintentional change. Instead, we are focused on intentional, deliberate change—when partners try to change themselves or each other in order to better their relationship. The change is driven not by new circumstances that happen to them but instead by conscious, deliberate decisions driven by dissatisfaction with each other or the relationship. That kind of change is often hard—difficult to bring about and difficult to maintain if brought about.

Why is this deliberate change in the service of the relationship so difficult? First, we often want our partners to change their behavior when our partners (and often we) are stressed or otherwise emotionally activated. Bill may not want Sue to talk to him so curtly when she is stressed or not to have such anger in her voice when she is upset with him. Sue may want Bill to not retreat and shut down when he is feeling overwhelmed or upset. It can sometimes be difficult to bring about consistent change even when we are in a relaxed state; it is much more difficult to change how we behave when we are emotionally distressed. Strong emotion usually pushes us into well-worn paths of behavior rather than into creative explorations of new paths. Second, we may want our partners to experience emotions that they don't have. Bill may want Sue not only to talk to him differently when she is angry but also to not be angry with him. Sue may want Bill to be more sexually attracted to her, to lust for her in a way that he currently doesn't feel, or to not have an eye for other attractive women. We can't force ourselves to have an emotion, or not have an emotion, that we genuinely don't experience. Third, we may want our partner to view people or situations in a way that they don't. Bill may want Sue to view his mother as he does: as a kind, sweet, caring woman, while Sue views her as needy and demanding. Or Sue may want Bill to view her friends as interesting and engaging, although he views them as snobbish and off-putting. Certainly, each partner can try to convince the other, but Sue and Bill's separate experience of his mother or Sue and Bill's separate experience of her friends may overwhelm any efforts to convince. Finally, we may want our partners to change something fundamental about themselves. Bill may be more of an ambitious workaholic than Sue would like, but he has been that way for all his adult life. Sue may be more of a homebody than Bill would like, but she may have been that way for most of her life. Sue may wish that Bill were more impulsive and spontaneous rather than the plodding planner he is. In each of these cases, Bill and Sue want to change something fundamental about the other—something that has persisted through lots of prior changes in their lives.

Deliberate change is hard. It can be as hard to change long-standing patterns of dysfunctional interaction in relationships as it is to change long-standing patterns of individual dysfunction, such as addiction. Yet, if we don't engage in deliberate change, then the patterns may continue and get even more ingrained. The literature on addiction, particularly on Motivational Interviewing (Miller & Rollnick, 2013) and the Transtheoretical Model of Change (Prochaska, DiClemente & Norcross, 1992), can be instructive for dyadic change because the approach to deliberate change in IBCT overlaps somewhat with that in Motivational Interviewing. In fact, William Miller, one of the originators of Motivational Interviewing, and the first author of this book (Christensen) organized a symposium years ago that included the two of them and the renowned horse whisperer, Monty Roberts. The symposium, which was titled "Habits, Husbands, and Horses: The Dance of Relationships," examined some of the similarities between Motivational Interviewing, IBCT, and horse whispering.* Let's examine some of the similarities between IBCT and these approaches.

The Transtheoretical Model of Change indicates that there are different stages of intentional change as well as different processes of that intentional change (Prochaska & DiClemente, 1983). The earliest stage of change is pre-contemplation, when one is not aware of a problem and thus has no intention of trying to change it. The next level is contemplation, when one is aware of a problem but has not committed to action to change it. After contemplation is preparation, when one intends to take action and has taken some initial, often unsuccessful, action. The next stage is action, when one takes direct action aimed at the problem. After action is the maintenance stage, when one tries to consolidate change and avoid relapse. Finally, termination is when the problem behavior has ended and no active efforts are necessary to avoid relapse.

Even though these stages are hierarchically ordered, a fundamental tenet of this theory is that individuals may cycle through some of the stages, such as moving from contemplation to preparation to action, but having difficulty implementing action and then coming back to contemplation. The Transtheoretical Model of Change also suggests a variety of different change processes that are linked to these various stages of change. For example, in the contemplation stage, one is open to consciousness raising, in which one gets new information about the problem and the self, and dramatic relief, in which one experiences and expresses feelings about the problem and its solution (e.g., expressing distress that alcohol is ruining one's life and a hope that treatment might help). In the action stage, one might engage in stimulus control, where one avoids environmental stimuli that elicit the problem behavior, or counterconditioning, where one finds substitutes for the problem behavior (e.g., learning to relax rather than drink alcohol).

Although the stages of change and processes of change are not directly applicable to IBCT and its notions of intentional change in romantic relationships, IBCT shares two central tenets of this model: (a) there are stages of change, and

---

* Although the three of us thought that the symposium was innovative and creative, it was not accepted for presentation at what was then called the Association for Advancement of Behavioral Therapies but is now called the Association for Behavioral and Cognitive Therapies. This proposed symposium never happened!

(b) different change processes are linked to these stages. When distressed couples first come to treatment, they are often in a kind of precontemplation stage of change regarding the actual changes that may need to occur. They may think that the problem lies mainly with their partner and what would really improve the relationship is if their partner changed. Even if they endorse platitudes such as "it takes two to tango," they may strongly feel that the fault and the responsibility for change rests with the partner. They may feel that any change by them is dependent on change by the partner (e.g., if he or she would just do X or not do Y, then of course I would do more of A or less of B). Or they may have tried to bring about change on their own but found it wasn't helpful and so they are hopeless that there is anything they can do to solve the problem.

The three acceptance strategies we discussed earlier, namely empathic joining, unified detachment, and tolerance building, can certainly bring about unintentional change, such as when one feels more empathy for the other and softens their approach to the other or when one sees the humor in an interactional cycle and is less upset by it. However, these strategies can also move the couple toward more deliberate change. Through empathic joining, one may learn in detail how his or her behaviors affect the other. Through unified detachment, one may learn how his or her behavior is part of a vicious cycle of interaction. Tolerance interventions may lead to the consciousness raising of either empathic joining or unified detachment or both. Thus, the three strategies make it clear that there is something concrete that one could do that might improve the relationship. They may thus encourage the contemplation of change and may prepare the way for the deliberate change strategies that we discuss below, strategies that are like the action stage in the Transtheoretical Model of Change.

Motivational Interviewing (MI; Miller & Rollnick, 2013) is a counseling approach designed to elicit change, particularly in addictive behaviors. MI assumes that the client is ambivalent about the addictive behavior and it attempts to explore and resolve that ambivalence. MI posits that change can only come from the client and can best be brought about with collaboration rather than confrontation (e.g., "You really need to stop drinking"), education (e.g., "Drinking will take a toll on your liver"), or explanation (e.g., "See how drinking is ruining your life?"). MI attempts to evoke and reinforce change talk on the part of the client until the client comes to a clear commitment to change. Then the therapist may work directly with the client on an intentional action plan for change. At the many points along the way when the therapist meets inevitable resistance from the client about change, the therapist rolls with the resistance, taking an empathic approach to the client rather than pushing the client to change. Change is hard; there are strong pressures not to change. Yet the therapist supports and reinforces self-efficacy whenever it occurs, such as the client's efforts to change or efforts to limit the damage done by his or her addiction.

Similar to MI, IBCT assumes that partners have mixed emotions about the problems that beset them. As we noted in the chapter on empathic joining, the surface emotions that partners typically reveal when their problems come up often mask other hidden emotions. For example, Maria may feel angry and annoyed at Hank's sexual advances but also feel worried that she has lost her sexual feelings or feel guilty that she is not a more responsive partner or that Hank is being deprived of something that means so much to him. In IBCT we explore those mixed emotions in ways that highlight the hidden emotions, elaborate them, and thus move partners into ideally a more empathic stance toward the other. Even if empathy cannot be achieved, partners at least move into a less adversarial position, a position that makes them more open to change. Also, similar to MI and the Transtheoretical Model of Change, we don't engage with clients in planned behavior change until they are ready for it and committed to it. When they have difficulty with change and are resistant to change, we also take an empathic stance rather than a confrontational stance. We know change is hard and is marked by fits and starts, advances and setbacks, rather than by a steady progression.

With this context for deliberate change, we can now consider several principles for bringing about deliberate or intentional change in IBCT.

MAKE SURE YOU UNDERSTAND THE PROBLEM
BEFORE INITIATING DELIBERATE CHANGE

Couple problems are often not what they seem at first glance; they are usually more complicated than they appear and more resistant to solution. Our clients usually are not intellectually deficient people; often they have been trying to solve this problem for a long time, and there are two of them to generate potential solutions. If the problem were simple, one or both of them should have come up with a solution before coming to couple therapy. In fact, they often come up with what they term "simple solutions" but get into a conflict about those solutions, suggesting that the problem cannot be addressed easily with the simple solution.

Let's consider some examples. Jake and Chelsea have a parenting problem with their teenage sons, who are often disrespectful, particularly of Chelsea. Chelsea's simple solution is that Jake should be firmer with them and insist that they treat their mother better. Jake's simple solution is that Chelsea should not be so sensitive—they are just being teenagers. A therapist might think the simple solution is for Jake and Chelsea to negotiate over the issue, defining what behaviors constitute disrespect and how they will respond to them. Instead, IBCT therapists would want to be sure to explore fully the issues first. Let's consider those issues. Chelsea is angry at Jake, holding him responsible in large part for the boys' behavior. After all, she feels they learned how to roll their eyes or treat their mom's questions and comments dismissively from Jake, who often reacts to her that way. She doesn't feel that Jake has her back or is supportive of her role as mother. Being the only female in the family and with Jake and the boys sometimes taking a similar stance toward her, she feels isolated, as if it is her against the three of them. For Jake's part, he has often felt that Chelsea is too sensitive and comes on too strong with him and the boys. He sees her as reprimanding him as she does with the boys, and he has dealt with it by often dismissing her comments. He often smiles at the way the boys react to Chelsea, feeling some kind of validation in their response to her: "See, they feel the same way I do!" As IBCT therapists, we would use empathic joining to access some of the feelings that both partners have, such as Chelsea's sense of being ganged up on and Jake's sense of being treated like a kid. We would use unified detachment to help them describe the interaction patterns that occur when Chelsea makes requests of the boys or gives them negative feedback, showing how each of their understandable responses promotes the very thing they don't want. The lack of support Chelsea feels leads her to come on stronger than she might otherwise; Chelsea's strong response leads Jake to dismiss her and model that for the boys. If a therapist tried to negotiate a solution to this problem without the exploration that could lead to more understanding and unity between Jake and Chelsea, the therapist could easily get lost in elaborate definitions of what constitutes disrespectful behavior, how Chelsea is going to give her commands and reprimands, and how Jake is to respond. Even after such long negotiations, Jake and Chelsea might not follow through with their plans, leading to accusations between them.

As another example, consider Mark and Diane's trust issue. Although Mark is confident that Diane is not having an affair, he often accuses Diane of flirting with other men and leading them on. He will validate that she is not motivated by ill intentions but he insists that she does not understand men, that they will misread her and are trying to pursue her. For her part, Diane often accuses Mark of trying to control her. She says she is often uncomfortable in his presence when there are other men around, since he will be eyeing her and their every move. When she has drinks or meals with business colleagues and especially if she has to travel for business, she anticipates "the third degree" from Mark, with him interrogating her about the details of her interactions without any interest in the possible business opportunities that she may be developing.

Diane's simple solution to this problem is that Mark should "loosen up" and trust her. After all, she is someone of integrity who has never cheated before in any previous relationship. Mark's simple solution is that Diane needs to watch and curb her social behavior because predatory men are likely to misinterpret many of her social moves. A problem-solving therapist might think the solution involves discussion and negotiation over what is appropriate and inappropriate contact with potential romantic partners. Although that could be helpful at some point, as IBCT therapists we would first want to explore the issues fully through empathic joining and unified detachment. Mark never saw himself as very attractive or appealing to women and thought he would never be able to have a romantic relationship with a woman as attractive as Diane. From the very beginning of their relationship, he feared he could lose her to other men. That insecurity on his part was actually appealing to Diane early on since he so openly needed her and feared her loss. She would reassure him of her love and devotion. Now, well into the relationship, she experiences his insecurity as control and intrusiveness. She has always enjoyed the company of men, has been able to command their attention, and comes across as charming to most. Those very skills have contributed to her business success. She doesn't want to curtail her behavior since she views it as enjoyable, helpful to her success, and not a violation of her and Mark's commitment to each other. Empathic joining might explore Mark's fears regarding Diane as well as Diane's fears of being controlled by Mark and limiting what she views as beneficial and appropriate behavior on her part. Unified detachment might explore how Mark's intrusiveness pushes her away from him more than other men pull her away from him or how her dismissal of his comments about the intentions of other men makes him double down on those comments, escalating the cycle between them. An early negotiation of appropriate and inappropriate behavior, without due attention to the powerful factors in each that drive this conflict, could lead to highly detailed discussions that serve to make Diane feel more controlled and Mark to feel more on guard, watching carefully for violations of these rules.

In neither of these cases of Mark and Diane, nor of Jake and Chelsea, will the problem be simply or easily solved. Like most couple's core issues, the conflict is tangled and multifaceted. However, these couples, like most couples, have not reached the apex of their functioning. They can likely handle it much better than they have in the past. A focus on empathic joining and unified detachment first may be sufficient to ease the tension around this core conflict as well as prepare the couple for deliberate positive change. With these notions in mind, we proceed with deliberate change in the following ways.

REDIRECT DISCUSSIONS ABOUT CHANGE IF THE CLIENTS ARE IN A STRUGGLE ABOUT CHANGE

Couples are often in a struggle about change, with one pushing for specific changes and the other resisting them or countering with their own list of changes—even after some empathic joining and unified detachment. Couples in the midst of such a struggle are not in the mood to accommodate each other. If any change is made, it would likely require the therapist to come down on the side of that change, and the other partner may feel somewhat coerced to make the change. The resultant change may be only temporary at best or lead to other reactions that bode ill for the relationship. Consider a common example. Debra wants Michael to do more of his share of the housework and child care. She clearly does more than he does, even though both of them work full time. A therapist familiar with the data on male lack of involvement in household tasks—both the rates and their implications for the relationship—might join with Debra and push Michael to do more. However, Michael may feel ganged up on and agree reluctantly to do more. However, his resentment might mean a limited or temporary change or he might react by withdrawing from Debra and from therapy, which might have more negative relationship consequences than his earlier lack of involvement.

In a case like that of Debra and Michael, we IBCT therapists would want to postpone any discussions of deliberate changes, such as a discussion of household duties, until we had explored the issue more fully through empathic joining and unified detachment and Debra and Michael were in a collaborative mood about that issue. Behind even the most concrete desires for change is often the larger issue of "how you treat me." Even though Debra wants specific change in what Michael does in the household, she is likely also concerned with issues about her importance in the relationship (e.g., "Am I just a housewife?"; "Am I the one who has to do the scut work?"; "Is he the more important person who gets more free time?"). In IBCT we don't believe coercive means, either by the partner or the therapist, are a good way to bring about positive interaction. Certainly it can do so in the short term but, in the long term, partners will treat each other better if they understand the issues that each face and try to accommodate because they care about each rather than because they feel forced to change.

Some question IBCT therapists at this point, wondering what we do if empathic joining and unified detachment don't lead to a more collaborative and positive relationship. What if our best work still does not lead to Michael being willing to take on more housework or child care? Perhaps he has strongly patriarchal views and won't budge from that position. Or consider a more dramatic case, in which discussions of trust don't lead to a positive place. For example, let's assume Diane has cheated on Mark a number of times in the past, finds male attention and affairs too alluring to stop, and is unlikely to be the kind of trustworthy wife that Mark always wanted. What do we do in those cases?

Empathic joining is not guaranteed to bring couples to a positive place—only to expose the emotional issues that drive them. That exposure, when done well, usually leads to a softening of partners toward each other. It puts partners in a better position to work together on those conflicts because they have a greater understanding of them; however, it hardly ensures a resolution of the conflicts. Similarly, unified detachment enables partners to see how their interaction drives them apart and complicates their struggles rather than minimizing those struggles; but, it too doesn't ensure a better interaction. However, when couples fully understand the issues involved, we assert that partners are in a better position to make important decisions about whether to accommodate their partner or to leave their partner. People are always better able to adapt to their circumstances or to change those circumstances when they see the true contingencies operating in those circumstances. If Michael is truly unwilling to do housework or child care, it is better that Debra confront that and decide what she wants to do rather than take them both through a change process that leads to limited, resentful, and temporary change. Similarly with Mark and Diane; if she has no intention of curtailing her liaisons with men, it is better that Mark confront that rather than increasing his hopes through temporary and limited measures.

CATCH CLIENTS MAKING OR ATTEMPTING POSITIVE CHANGE AND DEBRIEF THOSE EFFORTS

Even the most distressed couples are likely to make some kinds of positive change: intentional or deliberate positive change and unintentional or spontaneous positive change. However, both these changes may end up being negative even though they start out as positive. Let's consider them both.

Unless members of distressed couples have decided to end their relationship or that it is only their partners who can and should change, they will periodically make deliberate attempts to be positive or to improve the relationship. That change may be as simple as trying to be nice to the other, suggesting some positive activity with the other, reacting less negatively to the other than they typically would, or even doing some piece of what the other has wanted. These changes can sometimes be noticed and reinforced and result in positive interactions; however, in distressed couples, they may be met with suspicion. If a previously angry partner is now nice, the other may wonder what he or she is up to, be suspicious of the change, and not respond to it positively. Therefore, the partner who was previously angry but tried to be nice may not only not get reinforced for his or her efforts but get punished for them—leading the partner to question the value of being nice or to conclude that nothing will work with the other. Meanwhile, the recipient of the nice behavior gets reinforced for his or her suspicion when the niceness goes away quickly; the recipient lacks knowledge that it went away in response to the recipient's lack of positive response or distrustful response. As a result, both partners get confirmed in their negative views of the other.

A second type of positive change is unintentional. No matter how deeply entrenched a negative pattern is in a distressed couple, there is always some variability in that pattern. Partners may be in a good mood and initiate something positive or don't respond as angrily to behaviors that they normally find offensive. Partners may be too tired to fight with the other over something that normally causes an argument. Partners may be preoccupied with something else and don't come across in the harsh way they usually do. As with the intentional behavior above, these positive changes may be met with a similar response and lead to a positive interaction. However, they are sometimes met with the usual negative response so that what starts out differently ends up in the same negative dynamic.

As IBCT therapists, we want to *catch* these intentional and unintentional positive actions, whether they lead to positive outcomes or not. Consistent with the behavioral principle of reinforcing positive behavior, we want to catch these incidents and debrief them. A common way that we catch these positive events is when clients report them on the Weekly Questionnaire in the item that asks about the most positive event since the last session. However, they may also show up in the negative events section of the Weekly Questionnaire because, despite the good intentions at their origin, the incident led to negative reactions. Or these events may not show up on the questionnaire but may be mentioned in passing by one or both partners or even happen in the session.

However they show up, they can be debriefed in a helpful way. If the positive actions resulted in a positive outcome, this debriefing is relatively straightforward. We help the couple identify and highlight the things that each did that made for a positive interaction, thus reinforcing those actions and making partners aware of what things they do that make a difference. If the initially positive action did not result in a positive interaction, we also debrief it to learn why. In that process we want to be sure that the initiator of the positive action gets appropriate credit for their positive action, particularly if it was intentional. They made the effort. We also validate that the other understandably may not have trusted the positive behavior or may have responded as if it weren't anything new or different. Such instances can lead to useful empathic joining and unified detachment. Consider the following scenario in which Anthony tries to make amends to Jada the next morning after an evening where he was late to an event at her work, disappointing and angering her. He feels guilty about it even though he had good reasons for being late and in their argument at the end of the evening, he voiced those reasons loud and clear. He is especially friendly in the morning and offers to make her breakfast, which he doesn't often do. She does not respond well to his offer, feeling he never sufficiently apologized for the previous evening and upset that he thinks he can slide past that evening by simply fixing her breakfast. The incident sets both of them back, making him feel that there is no redemption once he has wronged her and making her feel that he will never genuinely apologize to her or show her any remorse when he has hurt her feelings. In a therapy session following this incident, we would walk Anthony and Jada through the process they went through. We would acknowledge that Anthony tried to make amends by fixing breakfast but we would also explore how and why that effort, however laudatory, doesn't work for her. By so doing, we might engender some empathy in them for the other (empathic joining) as well as engender some understanding of how their best efforts sometimes backfire on them (unified detachment). These new experiences and understandings may enable their future efforts to be more successful.

BUILD ON CLIENTS INTERESTS AND MOTIVATIONS TO CHANGE, BUT CAREFULLY

As a result of debriefing of positive events, therapists might be inclined to suggest some obvious changes. Imagine that, in the above scenario, Anthony apologized the next morning and Jada accepted his apology gratefully and they genuinely kissed and made up. In that situation, the therapist might suggest that Anthony could apologize more often after a misstep and Jada could accept his apology graciously—and that would help buffer them against the interactional bumps that throw them off. Or, after an empathic joining or a unified detachment intervention, therapists might be inclined to suggest some obvious changes that would get them out of their interactional binds. For example, if the therapist had debriefed Anthony and Jada's situation in a way to show their understandable feelings and interactional binds, the therapist might be inclined to suggest quicker, genuine apologies by Anthony and greater responsiveness to those apologies by Jada with a kiss at the end as a way out.

There are several potential problems with such an intervention. First, it states something obvious and by so doing may implicitly suggest that the couple can't see that. After going through a scenario between a couple, it is usually not hard to see what made it go well—if it did—or what might make it go better—if it didn't. Presumably, the couple can see that also. Second, such suggestions imply that the couple can implement them in a rule-governed way: for example, just knowing that it is a good idea will somehow enable Anthony to routinely apologize quickly and genuinely and somehow enable Jada to accept those apologies graciously. However, most important solutions to couple problems can't be effectively implemented in a strictly rule-governed way. Anthony can't show genuine remorse and apology if he doesn't feel it. Nor can Jada accept his apology and kiss and make up if she doesn't feel it. Even if they could take those actions in a rule-governed way, the partner might attribute the action to the therapist rather than to the partner or use the therapist as a means of punishing the partner for lack of compliance. For example, Jada might respond to Anthony's apology with a comment that "You are only doing this because the therapist said to do so." Or Anthony might respond to Jada's lack of response to his apology with "I apologized as the therapist suggested but you won't accept it" (i.e., I did what the therapist asked, but you didn't). Third, by these suggestions, the therapist may get ahead of the client in the process of change and take away the client's initiative. For example, a good debriefing on an incident such as that between Anthony and Jada might get them both thinking about their response and the other's response and might lead at some point to a different and better response by one or the other. However, the therapist's urging of positive action can short-circuit that process of reflection and consideration that might, in a contingency-shaped way, alter their responses in future occasions. Rather than considering each other's reactions and their own reactions, they must focus on an explicit therapist directive. After someone has engaged in a genuinely positive action, getting the message "Why don't you do it more often?" by the partner, and especially by the therapist, is likely to reduce the likelihood of that action reoccurring.

As a group, therapists want to be helpful; for many therapists, suggesting solutions is the most obviously helpful thing to do. They can easily see solutions. Not being emotionally involved in the problem or seeing it in its complexity, they think that merely mentioning the solution to clients is a positive intervention. Therefore, they suggest solutions that are not easily implemented and thus fail to address the problem. As a result, the clients may not follow through. The therapist may feel frustrated, and in the worst-case scenario, take on a frustrated teacher or parent role with the clients, challenging whether they really want to change.

As IBCT therapists we want to trust our couples. We believe that they want a better relationship and will try to take steps to improve it, particularly if they don't feel defensive or pressured to change. If they don't want a better relationship or are unwilling to take steps to improve it, we are unlikely to be able to help them improve the relationship. When couples express a desire to change or actually change, we reinforce and support those efforts. However, if the change is likely to be difficult (e.g., Anthony apologizing when he anticipates criticism or experiences criticism or Jada accepting his attempt to make amends when she is still hurt by his actions), we help them understand what prevents each from doing the action that might be desirable while at the same time reinforcing their efforts to do so and their success when they are able to do so. Thus, we support positive actions on their part but also support their understanding, tolerance, and acceptance for when their partner is unable to do the positive actions that they might like.

FOCUS ON CHANGE AT POINTS
WHERE CHANGE IS POSSIBLE

As IBCT therapists, we always work based on our clinical formulation, namely the DEEP analysis. We know that we are unlikely to change important differences between partners or their emotional sensitivities. Not that they are immutable to change, but they certainly are unlikely to change in any quick, easy, or dramatic way. A couple's external stressors are also not usually subject to easy or dramatic change. What we can sometimes change is the couple's pattern of interaction. If we do change that pattern, we actually may have some positive influence on their differences and sensitivities because, as we described earlier, their patterns of interaction often accentuate those differences and sensitivities.

We can certainly change those patterns of interaction during the therapy session. In fact, if we cannot do that, if couples just replay their dysfunctional discussions in front of us, we are not doing effective couple therapy. However, even though we can usually help a couple have more constructive interactions about difficult topics in session than they do at home, it is not easy for them to generalize those more constructive interactions to situations where we are not present. What kind of change is possible in their natural environment?

Change During Specific Situations

Making a specific change in a specific situation is easier than making a general change across a number of unspecified situations. For example, Sophia may want Luis to be less critical and more complimentary of her in general across a variety of situations. However, perhaps she is especially sensitive if he is critical of her when the two of them are together with his mother, whom she fears is already somewhat critical of her. Luis would have an easier time changing his behavior in that particular situation than in changing his critical and complimentary behavior in general. Therefore, when couples list an upcoming, challenging event on their Weekly Questionnaire, such as Luis and Sophia taking his mother out to dinner, it gives us a wonderful opportunity for deliberate change. Typically, we use empathic joining to discuss the emotions that are typically triggered in these challenging situations and unified detachment to discuss the sequence of behavior that typically occurs. With this as background, then we can discuss with the couple what they think they might do differently, given the challenging circumstances, to make the situation better. For example, when Luis and Sophia spend time with his mother, Luis makes what he thinks are teasing remarks about Sophia, which she feels are critical and diminishing. She tends to get angry and withdraw, contributing little to the conversation. Luis gets frustrated that she "so sensitive" and withdrawn; even after they end the event with his mother and are again alone with each other, they are angry, resentful, and distant. A constructive discussion based on a shared understanding of these dynamics could lead Luis and Sophia to agree on specific actions that each might take when they are with his mother that could better the situation. At the session following the dinner with Luis's mother, we would debrief the experience with Luis and Sophia and see if their efforts to improve that specific situation were helpful. Usually they are. If they are not, we can use our typical strategies to help them understand why.

Change at Key Points in the Pattern of Interaction

If we are trying to bring about general change in a couple's pattern of interaction rather than change in a particular circumstance, we should consider the points at which change is possible. Most of the dysfunctional interaction sequences with which we work have three distinguishable phases: an early phase in which things get tense or distressing and start to escalate, a later phase during which things escalate to their high point (e.g., angry words, or one or both shut down), and a recovery phase in which partners try to return to normal after a bad interaction. There are rare exceptions, such as the couple that has distanced from each other and no longer engages on difficult issues. They don't escalate because they don't engage. However, most dysfunctional patterns of interaction have these three phases and we can potentially intervene at each of these phases.

Early intervention is usually ideal. When partners are not yet too emotional, they are more likely to be able to implement change that could prevent further escalation. Discussion of early intervention is always done in the context of a discussion about what usually happens between them. Then we can help them recognize trigger points that set each other off or red flags indicating imminent escalation. When we can lead a discussion about these patterns in a way that is collaborative, they may demonstrate some unified detachment from the pattern (i.e., they are not blaming each other for doing the triggering behavior or reacting so sensitively) and some empathic joining around the pattern (i.e., they show some understanding and sympathy if not empathy for the other's feelings). Then we can ask them what they might be able to do in that difficult situation that could make a difference. Sometimes they spontaneously offer those possibilities or request some actions by the other. If the conversation does not develop that way, we can certainly introduce that discussion. In doing so, we always acknowledge that it is difficult to change their behavior when they are emotionally triggered or tense or distressed. It is certainly helpful if they can do so, but they are unlikely to be able to do so always or consistently. We also always focus on dyadic solutions so that there are things that each partner could do that would better the situation. That way, both are empowered, since to wait in frustration for a partner to change is a powerless position, and one partner doesn't feel the entire blame for the problem or the sole burden of the solution. When partners mention something they might be able to do differently, we see how the partner thinks they would respond to that different behavior and whether that might lead to a different chain of interaction that would be better for them.

In discussing change, we try to be faithful to the complicated reasons and consequences of their dysfunctional interaction. For example, it is common, and often helpful, for one or both partners to ignore small annoyances by the other, but these annoyances may build up until the proverbial straw breaks the camel's back and they get inappropriately angry at a small event. These angry confrontations may serve a useful purpose in bringing a problem to the fore, allowing for a clearing of the air, and bringing about a useful discussion. Although letting things build up is not ideal, we would want to acknowledge that this pattern can be helpful for the couple and an angry confrontation may be better than no confrontation at all. An important variation of this pattern is when partners get emotionally distant from each other, one partner gets distressed by that distance and gets upset, they have an angry confrontation, and then they are emotionally closer afterwards. Distance followed by angry confrontation followed by positive engagement may not be ideal but it is certainly better than continuing distance. Therefore, we always intervene with full discussion of the pattern that goes on with a couple and the consequences of that pattern for the couple. We don't want our solution to be worse than the problem.

A second area where we can intervene is when things reach a high point of escalation. Often an argument can escalate to the point that partners are likely to do or say extremely hurtful things to the other. They may make personal attacks on the other, such as calling the other names or attributing negative characteristics to the other (e.g., "You are incapable of love"; "You have the emotional maturity of a 2-year-old"; "You are delusional"). They may threaten the relationship through implication (e.g., "We should never have gotten married"; "We are incapable of getting along"; "I don't love you anymore, if I ever did in the first place") or through direct statements (e.g., "I am no longer going to tolerate this craziness"; "I want a divorce"). They may do scary or hurtful things such as yelling or looking hatefully at the other, blocking the other from leaving the room, slamming doors or throwing things, or engaging in physical aggression toward the other. In Chapter 13 we will deal specifically with physical and verbal abuse. However, for our purposes here, we just need to acknowledge that arguments can often escalate to a point where partners say and do things that are hurtful and dangerous. Even if not physically dangerous, they can be dangerous to the ongoing relationship because they are so hurtful or because they raise doubts about the viability of the relationship.

When we talk with a couple in therapy about how their conflicts can escalate, our goal should be harm reduction or prevention of further harm. When couples reach a high point of escalation, it is unlikely that they can do anything positive to turn the argument around at that moment. They are too distressed to engage in constructive action. Even if they could, their partners would likely not respond to it well. If constructive change is hard in the natural environment early on in their dysfunctional pattern of interaction, it is even more difficult when the pattern has escalated. However, there is always something they can do to make a bad situation worse. That is what we want to prevent. We want to help them think through their process of escalation and talk about how they could prevent or reduce any potential harm that can come when their conflicts have veered out of control.

When conflict has escalated, the best harm-reduction or further harm-prevention strategy is usually a time-out or cooling-off period. Partners need a cease-fire for their angry comments. Further conversation will only make the situation worse; couples need to disengage. However, that is easier said than done. Sometimes one partner is happy to disengage while the other may believe the disengagement is what led to the escalation. Often partners want to disengage but only after making a final criticism or accusation. Or partners announce their disengagement with a provocative message, such as "Okay, you are out of control so I am going to put you in time-out."

To implement a plan for disengagement, we help partners discuss what options they think would be helpful and what they can actually implement, given the emotionally aroused state that they are in during those moments. We make it dyadic, so it is a joint plan rather than something either one of them does to the other, such as "putting the other in time-out." Common recommendations for time-out for couples is that the time-out be short, partners communicate the approximate length of the time-out, and partners reconvene to discuss the matter soon. Ideally, these parameters are discussed and agreed upon beforehand. However, sometimes partners need a lengthy time-out after an especially bad fight and cannot give any reasonable estimate of how long they will need. If one partner tends to feel abandoned during any time-out, it may be important for the other to indicate that they will return to this issue, even if they can't give a reasonable time frame. As always, we want to come up with strategies that are appropriate to the couple in that they address both what would work best for this couple and what this couple could actually implement in those challenging circumstances.

The third phase of dysfunctional interaction in which we can intervene is the recovery phase. As we noted in Chapter 3, unless partners break up, they return at some point to their normal interaction after a period of conflict. Even though the conflict may leave its memory and its hurt and resentment, the couple moves on. However, this process of recovery can itself be problematic and lead to a repeat of the previous conflict or an entirely new conflict. Couples often differ in (a) their timing of recovery, with one ready to return to normal before the other; (b) their methods of recovery, with one wanting to discuss the previous conflict and the other just wanting to move on; and (c) the role of repair, with one seeing the need for acknowledgement of responsibility and subsequent apology and the other not seeing any such need. Any one of these differences can lead to a new conflict, as when one complains that the other "won't let it go" or insists that the other "get over it." Or these differences can lead to a resumption of the previous conflict, as when a discussion about who should acknowledge responsibility and apologize leads to a replay of the original conflict.

Consistent with IBCT's focus on individualizing treatment to the specific couple, we want to tie any interventions in the recovery phase to what typically happens between the couple as they recover from the conflict. For example, if one gets over the conflict quickly and then pressures the other to get over it and kiss and make up, we see what each partner might be able to do in that period after an argument to avoid sparking a new conflict over recovery. Maybe the one who wants to recover quickly can voice a desire to reconnect rather than challenging the other with accusatory questions about whether the other is "over it yet." Maybe the one who is slower to recover can simply indicate that he or she is not ready yet rather than making an accusatory comment such as "Of course, you are ready to get over it. I wasn't mean to you like you were to me." If the couple gets into conflict about who should apologize for what, it can be helpful to discuss how a forced apology will probably not be soothing to either and that it can be better to state one's hurt rather than to demand an apology.

As we discuss changes in their pattern of interaction, we always rely on our understanding of what typically happens during their pattern of interaction. In addition, we always incorporate empathic joining and unified detachment into these discussions. We review how partners normally feel as the typical sequence of interaction unfolds between them. We know that this kind of discussion by itself is helpful for couples. With the formulation, empathic joining, and unified detachment as the backdrop, we explore what partners might be able to do early on in an interaction to prevent their usual conflict from occurring, what they might be able to at the points of escalation to prevent future harm, and what they might be able to do to recover more quickly and fully. We do this always with an awareness that change in times of emotional arousal is difficult. We explore, encourage, and support change as we also foster acceptance and understanding of those many times when change does not occur.

REPLAY INTERACTIONS THAT DIDN'T (OR DON'T) GO WELL

One important, direct way to bring about change is to ask clients to enact in therapy an interaction that didn't go well or doesn't usually go well and try to make the interaction go better. In the first case, we ask the clients to redo an interaction that didn't go well that they just had in the session or in the previous week (e.g., a negative incident on their Weekly Questionnaire). In the second case, we ask clients to enact an interaction that typically doesn't go well. In either case, we are asking clients to have the conversation they didn't have (Wile, 1981).

The interaction may go better simply because of the presence of the therapist. However, with a distressed couple that has an ingrained interaction pattern around a particular topic or issue, the couple is likely to revert to their usual pattern of interaction even in the presence of the therapist. To increase the likelihood of a better interaction, we often remind them of the pattern that they usually get caught in, including the key triggering behaviors in which they each engage, and the emotional impact that those behaviors have. Prior to this intervention, there should have been sufficient empathic joining and unified detachment so that both partners easily recognize the pattern and the associated feelings when we describe them.

Then we may ask them to redo the interaction in a more constructive way, avoiding the trap of their usual pattern. With this general prompt, we see how they do. We intervene to redirect them if they start getting sidetracked or stuck. For example, we may redirect them if they get off on an irrelevant topic. We may ask them to let each other speak without interruption, but we may encourage shorter talking turns if one tends to go on and on and the other has difficulty listening for so long. We may encourage them to talk about themselves, revealing their own feelings and concerns, rather than speculating on what the other feels or talking about how the other behaves. Thus, we may be quite directive but without training them specifically in communication skills or giving them rules for how to talk, a topic we address in Chapter 11. We trust that they are able to have good conversations about difficult issues, have done so in the past, and can do so now if they can avoid the usual traps that bring about their typical dysfunctional pattern of interaction.

With this kind of direction by us and the clients interacting in front of us, they are likely to have a better interaction. We don't assume that they can easily take this interaction and implement it regularly at home, but it can be a good step toward breaking their pattern and having better interactions. Even if they have difficulty implementing it at home, because they are usually provoked and emotionally aroused when they are at home, the experience can be helpful. They may be able to recover from those home interactions that go badly more easily or quickly because they know they didn't do it well; they understand what feelings in each got aroused; and they are more forgiving, accepting, and resilient.

Replaying a Difficult Interaction
Pattern with Jeremy and Dana

Jeremy and Dana came to therapy dealing with a trust issue. They had gotten married 6 months earlier despite a major trust violation 2 months prior to the marriage. Dana had met her previous husband and spent the night with him. That naturally caused great turmoil between Jeremy and Dana, but they decided to proceed with their marriage. Jeremy knew that Dana didn't want to be with her first husband. She had left him for many reasons, but primarily because of his drinking problems. She knew that he was wrong for her and she had no interest in returning to the turmoil of her first marriage. Yet Jeremy worried that her first husband was still interested in Dana and would try to contact Dana and that Dana would not tell Jeremy of those contacts—that she would hide these contacts with her former husband as she had done before their marriage.

We conceptualized this couple through a DEEP analysis. Jeremy was older than Dana, was responsible and the type who made plans, and took on a kind of parental role with Dana, who was girlish, coquettish, flirtatious, and somewhat impulsive. These differences were clearly a source of their appeal to each other. Because his first wife had cheated on him, Jeremy was sensitive about trust even before he met Dana. Her flirtatiousness and this incident with her first husband heightened these concerns. For her part, Dana was sensitive about her impulsiveness and desire for male attention and knew that it had gotten her into trouble before. The two had no children from previous relationships although Dana was close to a child her former husband had from a previous relationship which meant that she kept an indirect link with her former husband. Jeremy and Dana had some career and money struggles but weren't in a particularly stressful situation when they entered therapy. Their pattern of interaction was typical of those who face trust issues. Jeremy would question Dana when he became suspicious and she would roll her eyes and dismiss his concerns, which didn't ameliorate those concerns and often led into a big argument.

The segment below follows a lengthy discussion of their pattern of interaction, which enabled some unified detachment between them. The therapist suggested names for the roles that each played in the pattern: he was the interrogating district attorney and she was the hostile or uncooperative witness. They accepted and even adopted these terms as well as the interaction pattern that they described. With this background the therapist below tries to lead them into a different and better discussion when trust comes up. The therapist starts off by reminding them of key features in their pattern and gives them a general prompt to do it better.

Therapist: Let's try, with each of you being who you are, but would you try to do it better. If you [to Jeremy] try to do the interaction when you get concerned about her, and if you tried to do it in a less interrogative position and you [to Dana] tried to do it in a less defensive, rolling-eyes position, but still being yourselves. Let's try that. Let's say she's scrolling through the iPhone or whatever, and you're getting concerned.

Jeremy: Has what's-his-name tried to contact you?

Dana: No.

Jeremy: He hasn't tried to contact you at all or are you just trying to avoid a fight?

Dana: No, he really hasn't.

Jeremy: Are you sure he hasn't tried to call you or text you or email you or anything?

Dana: Yeah, babe. You're interrogating me. Stop interrogating.

Commentary: Clearly the therapist's first intervention did not change the behavior of Jeremy. Despite the reminder of the pattern and the general prompt to do it better, Jeremy reverted back to interrogation. The therapist must try something different, a more specific prompt to have Jeremy talk about himself and his emotions.

Therapist: Okay, could you, Jeremy, tell her what's going on with you? If you told her what's going on with you emotionally, what would you say to her?

Jeremy: I would tell her, like I do, 'cause I do communicate with her—

Dana: Yeah, we do.

Jeremy: My feelings with her. And I would tell her.

Dana: And I eventually communicate well back—

Jeremy: Eventually, but I mean—

Dana: After you're done yelling and I'm done, we're fine.

Commentary: Jeremy senses that he is isn't doing it better and gets defensive when the therapist prompts him to talk about his emotions. Below, the therapist ignores the defensiveness and repeats the prompt but suggests what he might be feeling.

Therapist: So, let's just for the sake of discussion—if you open the discussion with what's going on with you emotionally—I'm guessing you're getting concerned, you're feeling a little distrustful, you're a little worried—something in that domain is going on with you, justifiably. Is that fair?

Jeremy: Yeah, but I also—you know there's this part of me that since we got married so soon after that, that we—sometimes I'm scared. I guess you could say that we cast a bone that wasn't set, or we wrapped a wound that wasn't—

Therapist: Healed completely.

Jeremy: Wasn't scrubbed down properly. So, so I get fearful that we prematurely jumped the gun. And that's why I feel the way I do sometimes.

Commentary: Jeremy didn't go along with the therapist's suggestions of what he might be feeling when Dana scrolls through her iPhone but Jeremy didn't return to his usual pattern of questioning Dana. Instead, he started talking about some significant and meaningful emotions that he has about their relationship, so the therapist tries to support and encourage that.

Therapist: Okay. What you just said was very important.

Jeremy: That's why I said it.

Therapist: I think it's genuine. And what if you—what if you told that to her when you got upset. Some version of that—that you told that to her, and I'd like for you [to Dana] to respond to that. So why don't you [to Jeremy] try saying what you said to me to her?

Jeremy: I'm fearful that we jumped the gun and that—and that you're not completely looking at me as your husband and that's why I feel the way I do sometimes.

Dana: Well, what do you mean that you don't think I look at you as my husband?

Jeremy: Because I, there are times, there are times—there are times where, you know, where I think I'm justified and you, you downplay my justification for asking you questions.

Dana: But you are unjustified in them because I've changed my mind about that whole situation. I'm on your side—I wanna be, you know, I want this to work so . . .

Commentary: Jeremy said something quite revealing, that he fears Dana doesn't look at him as her husband. That definitely caught Dana's attention and she asked about it but Jeremy doesn't explore that further. The therapist could have, and probably should have, kept Jeremy on that topic, asking him to talk more about that and getting Dana's response.

Therapist: Keep going and talk about the unjustification, so you feel like that. Say more about that please. It's important.

Jeremy: Well, I feel like, that there was a point where you would say I was, there was a point where I was prodding you and you were telling me just like you are now that I was being ridiculous. And it came to a point where I was correct. And I'm just scared that when I ask you a question once that it's not getting answered honestly so I have to ask it 10 times because I found success with that method before. That's why I feel like I have to ask sometimes 10 times because I found success when I asked 9 times before I got the same answer I'm getting now.

Dana: That's justified. I understand that.

Jeremy: In a controlled environment she says this.

Commentary: Jeremy explains himself and Dana understands him and genuinely validates him. However, he doesn't trust it so he dismisses it somewhat by attributing it to the therapeutic environment. The therapist tries to keep the conversation going between Jeremy and Dana. Jeremy has revealed some important information about himself so now the therapist tries to get Dana to reveal something about herself.

Therapist: Okay, and Dana, what's going on with you because he's telling you something very different now than he normally tells you?

Dana: No, he tells me this.

Therapist: But doesn't normally when the issue of the iPhone or something come up it's more the questioning and interrogation?

Dana: Yeah, you're right.

Therapist: But what is your reaction when he tells you things like this?

Dana [defensively]: I understand that he feels that way. I understand that you have those feelings.

Therapist: And what—what goes on emotionally for you, though? So you understand he has those feelings—that makes sense.

Dana: I wish that he—I wish that I wouldn't have made that choice so that he wouldn't feel that way. I don't want him to feel that way.

Jeremy: Well, you can make a wish in your right hand and—

Dana: I know.

Therapist: Wait, wait just a minute so let me just stay with you [to Dana]. So are you feeling bad when he tells you that—bad that you did that?

Dana: Yeah, right.

Therapist: Bad that you ever did that?

Dana: Right. Yeah, I wish he could just know that I'm telling you the truth the first time because that would make things a lot easier for both of us.

Therapist: You certainly wish that, but you're also feeling bad that you ever did this that caused this nine times.

Dana: Right, yeah, because it causes, it causes—

Jeremy: Discord.

Dana: Yeah. Discord in our life and there's no reason for it. It's just like last night when you got that phone call. That was unneeded and that person brought, you know, discord into our life.

Jeremy: And then she's suspicious of me.

Commentary: Note in the above that Dana has a difficult time talking about how badly she feels about what she did. She is uncomfortable doing that and then switches to talking about a phone call that he got. The therapist knows that phone calls to Jeremy are not an issue for this couple so he tries to keep the couple on track.

Therapist: Okay, let me just stay with this though. So, what would you tell him if you told him about that? If you told him what's going on with you, which I think is—or let me check this out with you—I think what's going on with you is when he tells you his feelings like that, it makes you feel bad about what happened.

Dana: Yeah.

Therapist: And it makes you—let me check this out—you don't know how to reassure him or to get past—

Dana: Right, like I don't know if there's any way to reassure him of that because I understand that—

Jeremy: But see, she doesn't act like that. She gets frustrated with me.

Therapist: I understand. I understand. But that's why we're going to try to structure something a little bit differently. So, if you said all of that to him—why don't you try to say all of that to him now?

Dana: I feel horrible. I wish that there was something that I could do. I wish I would have made a different decision. I wish all these things, but I'm not lying to you. And I want to work on having a 100% honest relationship and that's why I married you.

Jeremy: Well, see—

Commentary: Dana said her statement above quickly, as if it was hard to say and she wanted to get it out quickly. The therapist wants to keep Jeremy from going back to the old pattern and find out the impact of what she said to him.

Therapist: Let's not go back to what typically happens. Would it make a difference for you to hear something like that?

Jeremy: No, because I don't even like how that sounded.

Therapist: Okay, well, what bothered you about that?

Jeremy: Because it's not remorseful. She's going through the motions. She's saying what she thinks she's supposed to say but she's not—

Dana: You know that I'm remorseful, though.

Jeremy: It doesn't sound like it.

Dana: You want me to be crying every time?

Jeremy: Yes.

Dana: And me, just be like on my knees and be like I'm sooo—

Jeremy: Yes, that's exactly what I want. Is that normal? Or do I need more therapy?

Therapist: I'm not concerned with what's normal or not. I'm trying to find out what's going on with you guys and what would help. So is that what you would really like from her? That when you're anxious, when you're anxious and concerned and you have a tendency to go on the district attorney thing but then what you really would like from her is a statement of her remorse?

Jeremy: Yeah, I'd like for the witness to just break down on the stand.

Therapist: But because what is that doing for you? What does that tell you?

Jeremy: I don't know. It's just certain—

Dana: It's not healthy.

Jeremy: It's just certain emotions can't be staged. And you know, like if she seems upset and regretful.

Dana [rolling her eyes and then acknowledging it]: I just did what I always do.

Jeremy: Yeah, see.

Therapist: What did she say?

Dana: I just had the response that I always have.

Jeremy: She just had her typical response, which is rolling the eyes.

Therapist: So this is what would—what would—

Jeremy: Right.

Dana: You can really expect me to break down and cry?

Jeremy: Well, we don't have these talks every day but whenever, whenever she does that it, it calms the situation.

Commentary: Genuine remorse by the perpetrator of cheating usually is soothing to the victim of that cheating because it shows that the act was upsetting not just to the victim but also to the perpetrator.

Dana: When I cry?

Jeremy: Like when she's genuinely upset about it. Like if we're talking about it. When we, when it escalates is when I ask her and she sloughs it off or acts like it's not important or that I have no reason to even ask her.

Commentary: In contrast to genuine remorse, when the perpetrator sloughs off, dismisses, or otherwise doesn't take the victim's concerns about cheating seriously, then that raises doubt and anxiety in the victim's mind that maybe it is happening or will happen again.

Dana: I can't just be like going about my day and then get into this mode of feeling like crying and saying I'm sorry and thinking back on it and bringing it back all the time. That's like acting.

Therapist: Dana, that's, you're absolutely right. You can't just—at the drop of a hat.

Dana: Yeah, I mean I'm not that good of an actress.

Commentary: The couple is now getting into a dead end, where he is demanding something—her remorse on command—that she cannot provide, and so she can dismiss his request. The therapist tries to open a path forward where they can avoid their usual district attorney versus uncooperative witness pattern and she can genuinely reassure him.

Therapist: Dana, what did he say though that really bothers him? He said something that escalates it for him. Did you hear that part?

Jeremy: She wasn't listening.

Dana: No, I was listening.

Therapist: Wait, wait just a minute. Because I think you were thrown by his statement that, you know, he wants you to do a big crying scene every time this comes up.

Dana: Yeah, it's ridiculous.

Therapist: But what really bothers him is the—did you?

Dana: Okay, go ahead and tell me.

Therapist: Yeah, it was the sloughing off was the word you used. And what was the other word you used? Or discounting.

Jeremy: She's just complacent sometimes.

Therapist: Okay, so there's a big difference between—there are many degrees in between sloughing off, discounting, and rolling eyes and going into a major crying episode. I'm exaggerating—I'm not saying you want that all the time. And what I think might be helpful is if you took him really seriously and tried to respond to him at the emotional level that he came and if you came at her at a more emotional level rather than an interrogation level. So I'd like you guys to try to do that. So I'd like you to talk to her as you did a little while ago, what's going on with you emotionally. I know it's a repeat and I know it's odd, but then Dana, I'd like for you to respond to him, so not sloughing off, not rolling eyes because that escalates it. But you—I'm not expecting you to go into a big tearful scene, but you can take him seriously.

Dana: Okay.

Therapist: And address him seriously. So why don't you take it from the start?

Jeremy: As if you know I'm asking her about the emails?

Therapist: Yeah—that you've gotten suspicious. You're feeling, for whatever reasons—the emails or whatever. You're feeling uncomfortably suspicious and you're going to—rather than going into interrogation—you're going to tell her what's going on with you.

Jeremy: Who is this person that wrote to you on Facebook with a smiley face at the end with a wink?

Dana: It was a former student of mine.

Jeremy: Former student?

Dana: Yeah.

Jeremy: Did you ever have sexual relations with him?

Dana: No. I never had any sexual relations with any of my former students.

Therapist: Tell her what's going on with you though—get to more of the emotional road.

Jeremy: Well, I can't help but ask because . . . [pause, nonverbally showing that he is experiencing some vulnerable emotions].

Dana: I love you and I am sorry. I am still sorry and I'm still sorry that you have to think about it and that it comes up in your mind. And that you hurt over it and that—

Commentary: In response to Jeremy's vulnerability, Dana responded immediately with genuine reassurance, but then, below, Jeremy goes back into interrogation. The therapist believes that Jeremy was uncomfortable with his vulnerability and her genuine support so reverted back to the usual pattern. The therapist tries to process what happened by seeing how Jeremy actually felt when Dana said what she said.

Jeremy: How do I know you're never going to do that again?

Therapist: How did you respond to what she just said?

Jeremy: How did I respond?

Therapist: Yes, how did you respond?

Dana: How did you feel?

Jeremy: How do I feel or how did I respond?

Therapist: That's a good distinction. How did you feel when she said what she said?

Jeremy: I felt that she was being remorseful.

Dana: And I am and you know that.

Jeremy: But she's really trying right now.

Dana: No, I'm not really trying right now.

Therapist: Well, by saying really trying—I want her to really try. I want both of you to try to do it differently. Are you worried that she won't do it in the natural world or something?

Jeremy: Right.

Therapist: Well, let's get it right here and then we'll talk about you guys' ability to take it out of here.

Jeremy: Okay.

Therapist: But did that feel differently to you?

Jeremy: Yeah, a little bit.

Dana: And then he comes back at me with, "How do I know you're not going to do it again?"

Therapist: Right, right. Because if you go back into the interrogation mode, that will get you guys out of a more meaningful discussion about this, that will be more reassuring for both of you. Reassuring for you that she's faithful, and reassuring for you that this is not going to go on and on and on and he's never going to trust you. So we want reassurance for both of you—we need reassurance for both of you. So why don't you kind of— let's come in on the end of what you were just saying. And why don't you try to respond differently? Just kind of get the last part.

Dana: I want you to know that I'll never do that again because that's why I married you. I want to build a family with you and if I made choices like that again I know that I'd ruin that. And I won't ever make choices like that again.

Therapist: Now how would you respond differently to that?

Jeremy: All right, let's go get an Egg McMuffin. (Laughter by both. Dana spontaneously reaches over and hugs Jeremy.)

Therapist: Now, let's put aside for a moment whether you guys are able to take that out of here. But is that more satisfying for you—to have a conversation like that?

Jeremy: Yes.

Therapist [to Dana, who is still hugging Jeremy]**:** Would you say that, too?

Dana: Yes, I don't like to close down. I mean, that's a healthier way to speak. I don't want to act like a child. I don't want to close down.

Commentary: The session was relatively early in the morning so Jeremy's humorous comment about getting an Egg McMuffin was appropriate. However, more importantly, what it communicated was that he didn't need to talk about this anymore. He felt reassured. The therapist, with lots of direction and guidance, led them away from their usual pattern of interaction and into a more meaningful discussion that was more reassuring for them both. In debriefing the interaction at the end, the couple acknowledges that this is a better way to talk, and Dana spontaneously offers that she doesn't want to do what she usually does, which is close down.

In this extended excerpt from a therapy session, the therapist did not do any didactic teaching of communication skills; we will discuss that approach in Chapter 11. However, the therapist was very active in intervening, redirecting, and prompting better communication. There is no expectation that this particular intervention will prevent Jeremy and Dana from getting into their usual cycle of interrogation and shutting down when this topic comes up. Even if we repeated this intervention a number of times in session, it would not serve to completely prevent a recurrence of that interaction pattern. However, the interventions led them into a more constructive communication that brought them together rather than pushed them apart emotionally. As a result, it reassured him in the moment of her commitment to him and reassured her that she can soothe his distrust. The interventions highlighted the triggering behaviors for each of them, which they experienced in session in a modified form, leading perhaps to greater mindfulness of these behaviors. Note that Dana even caught herself rolling her eyes. With this greater mindfulness of the pattern and experience of a more constructive discussion, partners may be able to prevent some of these interaction cycles, or not get into them so intensely, or be able to recover from them more easily—or some combination of these goals. In these ways, interventions like those above can help couples without necessarily removing a difficult interaction pattern completely.

SUMMARY

This chapter focused directly on change. We distinguished unintentional change, which always happens and usually without our noticing it, from intentional, deliberate change, which is often difficult to implement. We compared the difficulty of bringing about deliberate change in distressed relationships to the difficulties of bringing about change in addictive behaviors. We showed how IBCT has similar views of change and similar ways to bring it about, as do several related approaches to addiction, such as the Transtheoretical Model of Change, the Stages of Change, and Motivational Interviewing.

With this background on how IBCT conceives of deliberate change, we reviewed six important principles for bringing about deliberate change. First, make sure to understand the problem before initiating deliberate change. The DEEP formulation is our starting point for this understanding but there can be important additional nuances that we should understand before trying to bring about some specific change. Second, redirect discussions about change if the clients are in a struggle about change. Forced or coerced change is unlikely to endure, and the process of coercion may bring about negative side effects that outweigh any good that comes from the change. Third, catch clients making or attempting positive change and debrief those efforts. Most clients will attempt some positive actions during therapy; we want those actions to be noticed and debriefed so even if they don't go well, the couple understands why and the effort gets reinforced nonetheless. Fourth, build on clients' interests and motivations to change, but carefully. We want to capitalize on clients' readiness and interest in changing but we want to be sure that the change will have a positive impact. Fifth, focus on changing dysfunctional patterns of interaction at points where change is possible. Change in a specific situation is easier than change across a variety of situations. When couples list an upcoming, challenging situation, it gives us an opportunity to discuss what typically happens in that situation, how they typically react emotionally, and what they could do to handle the situation better. When our goal is to alter their general pattern of dysfunctional interaction around a core issue, we can intervene at three possible points in the pattern: (a) early intervention so the couple can prevent the pattern from playing out, (b) damage control when the pattern has escalated, and (c) recovery when partners are experiencing the emotional aftermath of an argument and want to repair the rupture and get back to normal. Finally, replay interactions that didn't—or don't—go well. If an interaction during the week or in therapy didn't go well or if couples regularly get stuck in a difficult interaction pattern, we can ask them to replay that interaction, reminding them of the pattern they got or typically get stuck in and coaching them to do it better so they don't go into their usual traps. We finished the chapter with a detailed excerpt from a therapy session in which the therapist coaches a couple through a replay of their problematic interaction pattern.

In the next two chapters, we will continue our focus on change. We will describe the change strategies that are employed by traditional behavioral and cognitive behavioral couple therapies. These change strategies tend to be more therapist driven and more rule governed than are those described in this chapter. Thus, they are not the normal, first-line interventions in IBCT but are still part of the strategies used by IBCT. In the next chapter, we focus on ways to promote positive activities between partners (Dyadic Behavioral Activation). In the subsequent chapter, we focus on communication and problem-solving skills (Communication and Conflict Resolution Training).

10

&

Dyadic Behavioral Activation

COUPLES COME TO THERAPY because of problems in their relationship. The most commonly reported problems are communication difficulties and lack of affection (Doss et al., 2004), but couple problems include a large range of concerns, such as disagreements about specific areas in the relationship (e.g., children, money, sex, and in-laws), concerns about how the other treats them (e.g., partner too critical, distant, demanding, unaffectionate, or unsupportive), and concerns about the other as an individual (e.g., drinking, drug use, infidelity, and depression). In almost all cases, these problems have created negative reactions in one or both, such as anger, frustration, disappointment, despair, or loneliness.

As we have seen, the focus in IBCT is on the presenting problems of the couple—seeking to understand these problems with the DEEP analysis and intervening in these components not just to ameliorate the problems but to strengthen the connection between the partners. By so doing, we reduce the negative affect and improve the relationship. In fact, in IBCT, the most important positive actions are those when the partners experience some empathy for each other in the context of their core issue, come to a greater understanding of how their interaction pushes them apart, and demonstrate some improvement in how they deal with the problem that bedevils them—all of which can bring them into a closer, emotional connection.

Other approaches to therapy, such as Traditional Behavioral Couple Therapy (TBCT; Jacobson & Margolin, 1979; Stuart, 1980), Cognitive-Behavioral Couple Therapy (CBCT; Baucom, Epstein, Kirby, & LaTaillade, 2015) and Solution-Focused Couple Therapy (SFCT; Hoyt, 2015) address the negative affect early on and directly by instigating positive activities between the partners. In the case of TBCT and CBCT, they may delay a focus on the presenting problems until the instigated positive activities have produced a more positive emotional climate between the partners. In the case of SFCT, the range of positive activities instigated is thought to address the presenting problems.

We can use these strategies in IBCT, but we typically don't rely on them as our first line of intervention. In fact, often we don't use them at all if the interventions we have described above bring about improvement in the relationship, including greater positive affect. However, they can be strategies at our disposal, particularly if our efforts bring about improvement in the couple's handling of their core issues but don't lead to much positive interaction. Couples want not just a relationship that is connected, supportive, and relatively free from conflict but also a relationship that brings pleasure and fun.

We have called this chapter Dyadic Behavioral Activation to link the strategies here to the work on Behavioral Activation in individual therapy, particularly for depression. In Behavioral Activation, therapists help their depressed clients schedule activities that counteract their avoidance behavior, engage them with their social environment, and are thus likely to bring about positive reinforcement. This reinforcement is thought to help clients further confront the important tasks and situations that they avoid, increase their involvement in their social environment, and counteract their depression. A large body of research has supported the efficacy of this approach (e.g., Ekers et al., 2014).

What helps individual clients increase their reinforcement and life satisfaction can also increase a couple's satisfaction. Of course, Dyadic Behavioral Activation is more complicated than the usual Behavioral Activation because the therapist is working with two clients rather than one. In Dyadic Behavioral Activation, the partners will always be reacting to each other in ways that can facilitate or impede their positive activities. For example, partners may wait for the other to start before they do anything positive. Or partners may be disappointed or critical of a step forward by the other because the other didn't do more or show more enthusiasm when doing it. Thus, therapists must not just encourage positive actions but manage the often complicated interactions between the partners about these actions.

With this background in mind, let us look separately at the behavioral activation methods from behavioral approaches and those from solution-focused approaches and then see how we can incorporate these methods into IBCT.

BEHAVIORAL ACTIVATION METHODS FROM BEHAVIORAL COUPLE THERAPY

TBCT used the term *behavior exchange* to describe its behavioral activation techniques. Instead of behavior exchange, CBCT uses the term *Guided Behavior Change* to describe these same techniques. CBCT rejected the term behavior exchange because it suggests a contingency contract involving a quid pro quo exchange (i.e., he does this if she does that). Behavioral treatment of couples used that quid pro quo approach early on; the first published study of an "operant-interpersonal treatment of marital discord" detailed an intervention in which husbands received tokens for talking with their wives and could redeem those tokens for sexual activity (Stuart, 1969). Needless to say, quid pro quo exchange as a way to improve positive interaction quickly fell out of favor, particularly if the exchange involved sexual favors (Jacobson & Margolin, 1979). However, the term behavioral exchange remained, implying that both partners are engaging in positive behaviors but not strictly via a contingency contract or quid pro quo arrangement. However, whatever the name, both TBCT and CBCT view this kind of behavioral activation as an intervention to apply early on in treatment because it does not require any skills training, such as the communication and problem-solving skills training we discuss in the next chapter. It only requires direct instruction. Both approaches see it as an effort to alter the ratio of positive behavior to negative behavior in the relationship and thus to increase relationship satisfaction and to move partners into a collaborative set where they are better able to communicate and problem solve their long-standing issues.

There are a variety of specific techniques that are included in behavior exchange or guided behavior change. The therapist can encourage the couple to do specific joint activities that they used to enjoy but have stopped doing or only do occasionally, such as going out on date nights. The therapist can encourage partners to engage in specific "love days" (Weiss, Hops, & Patterson, 1973) or "caring days" (Stuart, 1980) when each will treat the partner as special by doing things for her or him that are not ordinarily done. Weiss and Birchler (1978) originated the "Cookie Jar" strategy for unscheduled positive activities. As described in Jacobson and Margolin (1979), the therapist can have the couple create a cookie jar that includes a list of positive actions that each could do for the other on short notice (e.g., bringing flowers, making dinner, cleaning up a particular area of the house, taking over the partner's chores for an evening). The partners put their desired items on separate colored pieces of paper and into a jar so that the other, when moved to do something special, can pick the appropriate color item from the jar and do that positive event for the other. After implementing any one of these strategies, the therapist follows up in the next session, seeing whether the partners did the assigned task and debriefing its impact.

The actions specified in the cookie jar or done during the love days or caring days are assignments designed to increase positive activities between partners that are usually unrelated to problem areas. The activities should certainly not be controversial. For example, if certain sexual activities are a source of struggle between the couple, those actions would not be candidates for these interventions. Nevertheless, these behavioral activation strategies can address particular areas of concern. For example, if partners don't normally spend any one-on-one time together at the end of the day, the therapist might see if they could structure their evening to accommodate time together. Or if each partner wanted a night off during the week to be with friends, that might be incorporated as a behavioral assignment. However, these actions should also not be a source of major controversy. For example, if a night out with friends is threatening for a partner because of trust issues, that activity would not be a good behavioral assignment. Instead, the trust issues and concerns about a night out with friends would be addressed else-where in treatment.

Perhaps the most common dyadic behavioral activation strategy in TBCT is based on some variation of a wish list. We will describe one variation of this strategy in detail, showing how therapists get the list generated, how they instigate couples to engage in behaviors on the list, and how they debrief the couple's efforts to engage in those behaviors and get their reactions to them. Then we will describe how therapists deal with the issue of noncompliance or minimal compliance with dyadic behavioral activation strategies.

As a first step in the wish list, the therapist asks each partner to inde-pendently generate a list of all behaviors that would, if done more or less frequently, lead to greater relationship satisfaction in the other. The motto behind this assignment is "Ask not what your partner can do for you; ask what you can do for your partner." For example, a husband generates what might be considered his wife's wish list, without any input from her. His list is his best guess as to all of the behaviors in his repertoire that have the potential to make her happier on a day-to-day basis; and his job is to generate this list independently, without consulting her about it or telling her what is on the list. He is also asked to refrain from putting this hypothesized wish list into practice. The therapist doesn't want him to be inhibited in the generation of items by the concern that he might be asked to do some of these things. His wife will find out what is on his list in due course; in fact, he is asked to bring the list to the next session. Meanwhile, his wife is asked to generate her best guess of his wish list. To help them in this task, the therapist can give them a copy of the Frequency and Acceptability of Partner Behavior Inventory (https://ibct.psych.ucla.edu/wp-content/uploads/sites/195/2018/12/frequency -and-acceptability-of-partner-behavior.pdf), which lists categories of positive and negative behavior. They are not to complete the measure but just use it to give them ideas of specific behaviors that they think their partner might like. Or the therapist can give them other lists of possible spouse behaviors (e.g., https://www.psychologytoday.com/us/blog/living-the-questions/201402/58 -caring-behaviors-couples).

The assignment may strike some clients as counterintuitive; it may seem backwards compared to the way partners typically think, which is "What do

I want my partner to do for me?" If the assignment is given at a time when the partners are not too distressed with each other and have some degree of collaboration, then they are able to focus on themselves and their own role in determining how successful the relationship is. Although this assignment is only the first step in the task, it sends a message: both of them have the unilateral power to affect the quality of the relationship.

If the partners comply with the initial assignment, then the primary purpose of the next therapy session is for the therapist to talk with one partner and then the other to clarify items on their lists and make sure that the lists are comprehensive. Importantly, during this dialogue the other partner, the potential recipient of the behaviors on these lists, is silent: no input at all is allowed! The therapist wants the occasion to be an opportunity for the giver to devote full attention to the potential recipient's needs, without the recipient having to ask for anything.

As the therapist works with each partner, one at a time, while the other simply listens, the therapist asks the potential giver to read items from the list to be sure that they are adequately operationalized. For example, if a husband writes that "She would like it if I were to become more romantic," the therapist enquires as to what exactly that means: does she want more affection outside the bedroom, more touching and hand-holding while watching television, more flowers, all of the above, or none of the above? Whatever the outcome of this discussion, the result is that the item is stated in terms that are observable, so that objective determination of when it occurs and when it does not can happen. Then the therapist repeats this procedure with the other partner.

During these dialogues, the therapist makes sure that each person's list is as comprehensive as possible. Since the recipient is not providing input into the giver's list, the therapist is the only source of feedback regarding the extent to which the giver has included most of the major items from the other's wish list. The therapist may know from the initial discussions what things might be satisfying for the partner and can offer them as possibilities. For example, the therapist might say, "I seem to remember that Sally said that she likes when you initiate social activities for the two of you. Can you think of anything you might do in that area that would make her happier?"

Once each partner has successfully developed this list, the therapist asks each of them to try to increase their partner's satisfaction during the next week by doing items from the list, but without telling the partner what they are going to be doing and when they are going to do it. For example, the therapist might say something like the following:

> I would like each of you to use your lists to enhance your partner's relationship satisfaction between now and the next session. Specifically, each of you is to go through your lists, pick one or more items that you choose to increase or decrease, and observe the effects of these changes in your behavior on the other's relationship satisfaction. So, you [to Partner A] pick some items from your list. Don't tell him (her) what items you have chosen. Just implement them, and see what happens. Your goal is to increase his (her) happiness this week. But don't tell him (her) what you are doing or why you are doing it. And you [to Partner B] are simultaneously doing exactly the same thing with your list. Decide today or tomorrow which items you're going to work on; don't tell her (him) what they are—just do them and see how they work.
>
> Now listen carefully. At no time between now and the next session should you discuss these lists in any way or discuss the assignment. Neither of you is under any obligation to choose any particular item from the list. I don't care what you do, as long as you do something that you think will be positive for your partner. And most importantly, don't choose any item that will be difficult for you to do. Keep it simple and low cost. That's it. Then next week, bring the lists back to the session and we will discuss how things went. Questions?

There are several things to note in this assignment. First, the recipient is not asking the giver for anything. In fact, the recipient hasn't had any input at all in the generation of the lists. Whatever negativity that might have been associated with the recipient asking for positive activities or complaining about the lack of them is avoided. Second, the giver gets to choose what items to give from a wide range of options. This facet presumably provides the giver with some sense of freedom of choice that may make compliance easier. Both of these factors may actually increase the likelihood that the behaviors that are chosen will be well received by the recipient. In other words, to the extent that the giver appears to be choosing the positive behaviors without coercion from either the partner or the therapist, their effects are more likely to be reinforcing. It is generally true that people experience behaviors from another as more pleasurable when the giver appears to give freely, spontaneously, or because he or she wants to rather than has to. Third, the giver is specifically cautioned against attempting hard-to-do tasks. Giving high-cost items might make the partner happier, but it would be unpleasant for the giver and therefore self-defeating. Couples should focus on only those items from their lists that can be enacted without detracting from their own relationship satisfaction. With this instruction, the recipient is further prompted to view whatever behaviors they receive as freely given.

Of course, there is a downside to this way of promoting positive behavior. Because the recipient has up until now provided no input, the giver may choose behaviors that are ineffectual or even detract from the recipient's relationship satisfaction, despite the best of intentions. This risk is a real one. Givers sometimes do choose the wrong behaviors, with negative results, but that can be addressed in the follow-up session. However, at times, even if the wrong behaviors are chosen, the impact on the recipient is reinforcing because of the giver's obvious effort. The effort to please may be more important to some partners than the ability to immediately access the keys to their heart. In any case, this is a risk worth taking, because when the right behaviors are chosen the impact tends to be positive.

Whether or not this assignment has worked is sometimes obvious as soon as the couple steps into the therapist's office. When a good faith effort has been made, even if only partially successful, the partners may be lighter, more playful, and interested in telling what they each did. If the assignment did not work or other negative events have intervened, the partners may show that through their demeanor or tell the therapist early on during their report of the week. Let us examine how therapists might proceed during the subsequent session under each eventuality.

If the assignment was successful and relationship satisfaction was enhanced, the therapist begins by helping them describe which items from the list were attempted; of those attempted, which ones were noticed by the recipient; and of those that were noticed, which ones contributed to the increased relationship satisfaction. Thus, for the first time, the recipient is asked to provide input on the giver's behavior. Hearing which behaviors contributed to the enhanced satisfaction, the giver finally has some indication from the person who presumably knows best which behaviors are likely to maintain the enhanced relationship satisfaction experienced since the previous session.

The therapist also enquires as to how costly it was for the giver to provide particular positives or decrease particular negatives. At times, partners are able to muster up considerable energy for a week and create a honeymoon effect; when asked, they acknowledge that they do not envision themselves performing at this level on a regular basis. If the experience is a honeymoon effect, or if particular behaviors were performed once, never or seldom to occur again, it is important for the recipient to know that. Maybe those are discussed as special event items, namely behaviors that can be done occasionally when one wants to acknowledge a birthday or anniversary or other special event for the other. At other times, providing positives that seem costly to the giver in the abstract turn out to be easy. When behaviors that sound burdensome turn out to be relatively effortless, the positive changes that result can be fairly dramatic.

After the enquiry about what worked and what did not, the next step is to allow for systematic input from the recipient. First, the therapist asks the recipient to comment on each item from the giver's list. The recipient designates each item as either a "keeper," a "minor but still pleasing" behavior, or one that is "off the mark." Armed with this input, the giver now has more information that can be used to make the task work even better when it is reassigned for the following week. None of this input is to be interpreted as a prescription for what the giver *should* do. Rather, it is simply information to help the giver in making decisions about how to inject quality into the relationship on subsequent weeks. Finally, during this session the recipient has an opportunity to suggest items that the giver should add to his or her list. Once again, these items are not requests for increases in specific behaviors, simply missing items that, according to the recipient, would be useful additions to the list. The giver dutifully adds the items, without incurring any obligation to perform any particular one. The input is added to provide the giver with more information, in order to increase the likelihood that successful items will be chosen in subsequent weeks. The homework assignment from the previous week can be reassigned with a higher likelihood of success; even though no specific directives are delivered for changing particular behaviors, now each partner has more accurate information about what the other finds pleasing.

What if the assignment did not work? There are several potential explanations for why a task like this would fail. One possibility is that one or both of them did not comply with the task. Assuming that the therapist went through the process in a competent manner, noncompliance probably means that it was a mistake to assign the task in the first place. The couple was not in a collaborative enough place that they could implement such an intervention.

A second possible reason for failure is that the wrong behaviors were chosen. Each partner tried some behaviors from the list, but relationship satisfaction did not change. It is unlikely that the partner chose something so off the base that it was negative for the partner. More likely, the partner chose something that was easy to do but as a positive seemed paltry and lame to the partner. Often partners' expectations for positive behavior from the other are disappointed and thus any positive behavior from the other is viewed as negative. In this case, the problem can be addressed by getting input from the recipient about which behaviors would have worked better and whether the partner is willing to do those behaviors. If this process goes well, the task can be reassigned and the outcome should be better.

At times, the task falls flat because the couple does not really have a problem of an absence of positives. They may have two or three major issues that brought them into therapy, but on a day-to-day basis they get along quite well. Nevertheless, it is not always apparent whether or not a task such as this will be helpful until it is attempted. There are other instances in which a lack of positives is a problem, but the major problems are so prominent that until those are dealt with nothing that happens on a day-to-day basis will make much difference.

In any case, assuming compliance, the therapist typically gives the wish-list task two sessions to work. Generally, a task like this will work quickly or not at all. There is no need to dwell on any task that is not working. However, since dyadic behavioral activation is a generic category of techniques rather

than one in particular, one failure doesn't mean that behavior-change strategies should be abandoned.

Whatever particular strategy is used to create positive interactions between
partners, TBCT is often faced with minimal compliance or noncompliance
with therapeutic assignments. Therapists usually assume that minimal or
noncompliance means that either (a) the assignment was inappropriate for
the couple at this time or (b) the assignment was not delivered properly.
Sometimes therapists are quick to make interpretations such as that the
couple really doesn't want to change. In fact, some therapists often sound
suspicious of, rather than sympathetic to, their clients around the issue of
compliance with therapeutic tasks. Clients are accused of sabotage when
there are often much more plausible explanations. Unfortunately, these more
plausible explanations often have to do with mistakes made by the therapist,
and so it is easier to blame the noncompliance on sabotage or resistance.

Minimal or noncompliance means that the couple was not ready or appropriate for the task if a) they remembered what they were supposed to do, b)
they understood the instructions, c) the rationale was explained to them,
d) they were involved in the planning of the assignment, e) potential obstacles to compliance were discussed, and f) no major changes happened that
prevented them from doing the assignment—but they still did not do it.
Sometimes the couple is too distressed to genuinely engage in positive actions
or so distressed that they will receive any positive actions by their partner
with distrust and view their actions as trivial, manipulative, or otherwise
inadequate. Sometimes couples are too focused on their core issues to want
to attend to anything else. In these cases, dyadic behavioral activation should
not have even been attempted in the first place.

BEHAVIORAL ACTIVATION METHODS FROM
SOLUTION-FOCUSED COUPLE THERAPY

Developed by Steve de Shazer and Insoo Kim Berg (e.g., de Shazer, 1982;
Berg, 1994), Solution-Focused Couple Therapy is dramatically different from
IBCT in that it doesn't focus on the couple's core problems or issues and
doesn't try to understand these problems or issues. Instead, it uses a series
of questions to focus clients on actions that they can take in the future and

have taken in the past to create a better relationship and then gives them a series of directives to instigate these positive actions. Despite this fundamental difference from IBCT, some of these questions from Solution-Focused Couple Therapy are excellent tools to get partners to think about and engage in positive actions in their relationship.

A key question used in SFCT is the *miracle question.* The therapist asks the couple to imagine that during their sleep the night of the session, a miracle occurred and the problems that brought them into therapy were solved, but because they were asleep they didn't realize that the problems were in fact solved. Then the therapists asks each how they would gradually discover that the problem was solved, namely, what each would notice that was different, how each would react to that difference, how their partner would react, and so forth. In asking the miracle question, the therapist does not mention any specific problem that the client may have mentioned, such as their struggle over in-laws or their communication problems; that might limit the actions that the clients might offer as part of the miracle. In pursuing these questions, the therapist attempts to get specific details about what behaviors each would do differently and how each would react to those different behaviors. The therapist asks about how these changes would affect their feelings about the relationship and how their partner would know that they were feeling differently about the relationship. The therapist might also ask if they can remember a time recently when a little bit of this miracle happened, namely, when they were doing a few of the actions and feeling some of the positive feelings that they describe. The therapist might also follow up the miracle question with questions asking them to rate the status of their relationship in regard to the miracle. For example, if the day after the miracle is a 10 and the situation at its worst is a 1, what rating would you give to things today? Then the therapist might ask each what actions would move their ratings up a level from what their ratings are today. As a result of these series of questions and answers, the clients outline for themselves a list of specific acts that they could do and their partner could do that would enhance their satisfaction and would be concrete signs that their problem has been improved or resolved. They also highlight the fact that they have done some of these actions recently.

Unlike the items that typically go into lists for love days, caring days, cookie jar, or wish lists, the miracle question usually elicits behaviors relevant to the presenting problems, such as "He would talk to me before he invites his friends over" or "She would call my mother and chat with her." However, it usually includes a variety of positive behaviors that attest to a changed emotional climate between the two of them, such as "He would give me a hug and kiss before leaving for work"; "She would cuddle with me in the morning"; or "He would give me a call during the day to see how I was doing." The behaviors are anything the clients think would be part of a miracle cure to their problems.

SFCT usually includes a directive for the client at the end of the session. As a follow-up to the miracle question, particularly if the clients are in a "complainant relationship" (Hoyt, 2015, p. 313), in which they are focused on complaining about the other rather than on any positive actions they could take, the therapist might give the clients an observation task by asking each to keep track of what the other is doing to make things a little better in the relationship but not to tell the other what they are noticing. Instead, in the next session, the therapist will find out from each what he or she noticed that the other was doing to improve the relationship. Another directive that can be used after the miracle question, if the clients seem motivated to make change, is to encourage clients to pick a day during the next week without telling anyone and pretend that the miracle has happened or to implement a small piece of the miracle, noticing what is different as a result. Then in the subsequent session, the therapist would debrief that experience.

In debriefing how the couple initiated the therapeutic directive and what its impact was, SFCT continues its focus on positive activities. If partners didn't follow through with the directive because they were getting along too poorly or if one or both followed through with the directive but it didn't have much of an impact given the overall negativity in the relationship, the SFCT therapist doesn't try to understand why things went awry. The therapist may accept that they had a bad experience but focus them on what they did that kept their interaction from even getting worse.

With this information about behavioral activation methods in SFCT, TBCT, and CBCT, let's consider how IBCT would use these behavioral activation methods. First we describe how IBCT encourages certain positive behavior apart from any specific behavioral activation methods.

POSITIVE BEHAVIOR, DYADIC BEHAVIORAL
ACTIVATION, AND IBCT

During the assessment phase in IBCT, we gather information about existing strengths in the relationship and summarize those strengths in the feedback session. During the treatment phase of IBCT, we always track positive
behavior and give it therapeutic attention. An item on the Weekly Questionnaire asks partners to decide on the most important, positive interaction
that they had since the last session and jot down a brief description of it. In
almost every treatment session, we give some therapeutic attention to the
positive interaction or interactions if partners listed different ones. The only
occasions when we would not attend to positive interactions are when there
was a crisis demanding the full session or if partners were in such a negative
emotional state that any attention to positives would be perfunctory or rid-
dled with negative comments denigrating the motives behind or impact of
any positive behavior.

We view the most important positive actions as those related to the couple's
presenting problems and those that indicate a shift in relationship dynamics.
In the first case, the couple handles some recurrent issue in a better way than
they usually do or recovers from a recurrent argument in a more effective way
than they usually do. In the second case, partners engage with each other
in a way that they have not done in a while. For example, they have sex for
the first time in a long time. Or they have an emotionally close, engaging
discussion in a way that they have not for a long time. In all of these cases,
we would give detailed attention to the positive action. In the first case of
better handling of a difficult problem, we want to learn from the couple and
in so doing have them learn what exactly they did that was an improvement
and what enabled them to do it better. In the second case of a change in relationship dynamics, we want to highlight the importance of this change and
help them understand how it came about. When appropriate, we might also
do some relapse prevention. Just because a couple has sex or an emotionally
significant experience for the first time in a while does not mean their problems are over or that they will be able to repeat these experiences on a regular
basis. Yet the experiences are an important advance and mark the beginning

of a better relationship as long as the likely recurrence of their problems don't return them to despair that "nothing has changed."

Most positives listed on the Weekly Questionnaire are not as dramatic as a change in relationship dynamics or an improvement in their way of handling or recovering from a difficult issue. Often the positives are activities that continue despite the couple's problems, such as recreational activities alone or with friends and family. Regarding these positive activities, we acknowledge that the couple is still able to enjoy each other, and we perhaps note that this activity is one of their strengths as a couple. For example, a discussion of a positive family interaction might lead to comments that the couple gets along well with her family and are spared the usual in-law tensions. However, we do not give these positives additional attention unless they tie in with the presenting problems, even indirectly. For example, if she is unhappy that he tends to diminish her or criticize her in public when they are out with friends but he is very positive about her in the presence of his family, we might note this difference when discussing a positive interaction with his family. That might lead to a useful discussion of what is different for him and her about his family versus their friends. Maybe he feels a little threatened by her with his friends but wants to promote her to his family. As another example, if a positive event with friends happened to end an argument more quickly than usual, we might note that in discussing the positive interaction with friends. It might be helpful for them to reflect on the fact that they are able to both let an argument go quickly because of social demands and that letting go, whatever the reason, is beneficial to them both. We might comment facetiously that whenever they get into their usual argument, they should call their friends and arrange an immediate social event.

What we have discussed above is often the limit of what we do with positives in IBCT. We assume that couples come to therapy to address their presenting complaint and the related core issue or issues. We further assume that these core issues are the major barrier to a gratifying relationship but also a window into partners' vulnerabilities and thus the way to increase emotional connection. Particularly with empathic joining but also with unified detachment, we can strengthen the understanding, the emotional acceptance, and the bond between partners. A stronger bond may be the biggest positive that can come from couple therapy.

Apart from these assumptions about IBCT, we have seen clinically and in our research how addressing the core issues leads to greater relationship stability and satisfaction. That said, some couples want and need more in the way of positive engagement with each other. After our acceptance work, they may still lack positive activities with each other and seek greater positive engagement. In that case, we can pursue intentional, deliberate methods for increasing positive interaction. In so doing, we can consider three phases in that process: specification of positive activities, instigation of positive activities, and review or debriefing of positive activities. Let's consider each in turn.

In specification of positive activities, we get couples to consider what they might do to increase their positive interaction. Sometimes the simplest way to do this is to engage in a discussion with them about what they have found enjoyable in the past and would like to do and could realistically do in the future to improve their enjoyment of each other. Couples usually have ideas about what they like and could reasonably do. Most couples who come to therapy, typically with demanding jobs or children, are not looking for or do not have the time for exotic, untried activities. They would like to take a little time in the evening to curl up with a show or movie or have a date night on the weekend alone or with friends. Therefore, they can come up with ideas on their own. Of course, we can use some of the strategies above, such as the wish list or miracle question, to generate possibilities if we think that might be helpful for the couple.

Once some positive activities are specified, we want to facilitate the instigation of them. This can be as simple as talking with the couple about when they can and want to do the activity or activities. Discussing with the therapist and agreeing in this public setting to engage in some positive activity at a particular time, such as this weekend, increases the chances that the couple will do it. It is also possible to use some of the instigation strategies above, such as the caring days, the cookie jar, or instructions to do some positive activity, such as "a little piece of the miracle," on a day that one partner selects, without notifying the other partner in advance. These often seem a bit contrived and are thus unlikely to maintain. They also can engender high expectations in the receiver so that he or she is disappointed even if the giver does something positive. Thus, we often use the simpler strategy of talking with the couple to see what they want to do and when. Furthermore, this models the way that most couples instigate positive activities, by talking with each other and deciding what to do that is fun or interesting.

The final phase is debriefing or review of the positive activity. At the following session we see if the couple followed through with their plan for positive activities and how they experienced them. We might see them on the Weekly Questionnaire as their most positive event, or they may have done them early on and another spontaneous positive event occurred that ended up on the Weekly Questionnaire. Or the couple may not have done the activity or it may not have turned out positively. If the couple followed through with the positive activity and enjoyed it, we want to reinforce their efforts and see if they want to engage in that activity again or make it a regular part of their life. If the couple didn't do the activity or didn't enjoy it, we want to understand why without facilitating blame between them. Depending on what happened, such discussion may involve empathic joining and unified detachment. Sometimes some version of the couple's core issue infects their attempt at a positive activity. For example, if there is a pattern of domineering and resistance between the two of them, they may have struggled with that when they were trying to initiate the event, with the domineering one pushing to get going earlier and the other resisting and feeling imposed upon. Based on an understanding of what went wrong, the couple may be in a better position to plan a future event.

SUMMARY

In this chapter we examined strategies and techniques of dyadic behavioral activation, namely, getting partners to do positive activities for and with the other. Couples want a relationship that is not only free from conflict but also has companionship, support, humor, affection, and sex. Traditional Behavioral Couple Therapy and Cognitive-Behavioral Couple Therapy have similar methods for promoting positive behavior in couples. They first help the couple generate a list of possible actions, often by having each partner focus initially on what they could do that their partner would appreciate. Then they instigate these behaviors through homework that asks the couple to do items on that list by engaging in love days or caring days, by putting items in a cookie jar so partners can pick something they want to do for the other, or just by giving general directions to engage in items from the list. Therapists then debrief the homework assignment to see how it went and provide necessary corrections and modifications.

Solution-Focused Couple Therapy does not focus on exploring and understanding the presenting problems but on guiding couples toward positive solutions. Through such techniques as the miracle question and the associated follow-up questions, the therapist highlights positive actions that the couple has done in the past and could do in the future that would make their relationship better. Then the therapist may instigate these positive actions through a variety of strategies, such as observational tasks during which they notice any positive actions that the partner does, or tasks that encourage them to engage in some part of the miracle solution. At a subsequent session the therapists reviews the results of the task. Even if the couple did not do the task well or got caught up in their usual arguments, these therapists will often focus on the positive, such as by examining what the couple did that prevented an argument from being worse.

In IBCT we focus on the presenting problems, attempting to understand the core issues that these problems reflect and in so doing helping the couple understand each other and their relationship better. Through empathic joining and unified detachment around these issues, couples expose their vulnerabilities to each other and create a stronger, deeper bond. This deeper bond, along with a reduction in conflict, is the primary positive that emerges from IBCT. However, some couples may want and need additional focus on creating positive activities in their relationship. Usually we engage couples in a discussion in which they can talk about how they would like to enhance their relationship and what activities they want to do that are possible given their busy lives. Then we follow up to see whether they were able to implement these activities and how they went. We can certainly use the techniques of Traditional and Cognitive-Behavioral Couple Therapy or of Solution-Focused Therapy as part of this process of creating more positive interaction. However, they are almost never our first line of intervention.

11

Communication and Problem-Solving Training

COMMUNICATION AND PROBLEM-SOLVING training have been major components of traditional behavioral couple therapy (TBCT) since its inception (Jacobson & Margolin, 1979; Liberman, 1970; Weiss et al., 1973). Cognitive-Behavioral Couple Therapy adopted the strategies of TBCT, including communication and problem-solving training, as cognitive strategies were added to the mix. Many other approaches to working with couples include versions or variations of such training. For example, the Prevention and Relationship Education Program (PREP), a behavioral training program designed to prevent couple distress, relies extensively on training in these skills (Markman, Stanley, & Blumberg, 2010). The central ideas are that couples lack key communication skills necessary for a successful relationship, that these skills can be taught to them, and as a result couples will have a more satisfying relationship that is less troubled by conflict.

Traditionally, communication training is split into two overlapping but distinct sets of skills: training in general communication skills that involves sharing feelings, support, and understanding, often just called Communication Training (CT) and training in how to deal with difficult decisions, problems, and conflict, often called Problem-Solving Training (e.g., Jacobson & Margolin, 1976), decision-making or problem-solving skills in CBCT

(Baucom et al., 2015), and conflict-resolution training in early descriptions of IBCT (Jacobson & Christensen, 1996). We will refer to this as Problem-Solving Training (PST). Although related, CT and PST are really quite different and can be distinguished both conceptually and procedurally. CT teaches couples how to express themselves more directly but with less blame and accusation and how to be better listeners when their partner is speaking. PST teaches couples how to define problems, generate possible solutions, and then negotiate and implement those solutions. Both CT and PST train couples in a deliberate, structured interaction; there is no expectation that the couple will use these skills and the related structure for ordinary conversation. Rather, the idea is that couples should use CT and PST for those issues that are difficult for them and have led to arguments in the past.

In the sections below, we will first describe CT and then describe PST as they both are used in TBCT and CBCT. Following this, we will describe the empirical and clinical concerns we have with CT and PST and how we adapt them so we can incorporate them into IBCT.

COMMUNICATION TRAINING IN TBCT AND CBCT

CT makes an important distinction between the roles of the speaker and the listener. In fact, sometimes CT is referred to as speaker-listener skills. Partners decide who will begin as the speaker and who begin as the listener. Only one partner has the floor at a time. In fact, it is sometimes helpful to have a concrete item to serve as the *floor card* so each partner knows who has the floor. While the speaker expresses him or herself using the expresser skills. which we describe below, the listener pays attention using the active listening skills, also described below. The speaker holds the floor either until he or she is willing to relinquish it or until the listener requests it. Then the roles reverse with the listener becoming the speaker and the speaker becoming the active listener.

Both partners are trained in both speaker and listener skills. The goal of speaker skills is to train speakers to express their feelings and views in a non-blaming manner. To achieve this goal, speakers are trained to take responsibility for their feelings by using "I" statements of feelings and to indicate the specific behavior and situation that elicited those feelings rather than make "you" statements about the partner's undesirable behavior or characteristics. Thus, the speaker might say "I feel frustrated when you come home late from work" rather than saying "You are so inconsiderate; you never come home on time." The goal of active listening skills is to train listeners to attend intently to their partners so that the listeners can demonstrate through summary, paraphrase, or reflection that they have heard and understood what the speaker said. Doing so helps focus the listener on what the speaker is actually saying—rather than preparing a rebuttal—and circumvents arguments that "You're not listening to me."

Training in communication skills in TBCT and CBCT typically consists of some or all of the following components: didactic instruction, modeling, behavior rehearsal, and feedback. Sometimes therapists conduct the didactic instruction by assigning clients reading material about communication skills, such as in self-help books like *Reconcilable Differences* (Christensen et al., 2014) or *Fighting for your Marriage* (Markman et al., 2010). Or they may provide verbal instruction to couples in session.

Whatever the form of the didactic instruction, therapists propose a number of rules or guidelines and explain the rationale for those rules. Couples should pick an appropriate time and place when they are not distracted by other things such as television or children and when they are not in the immediate throes of a strong reaction to a provocative incident. They should clearly identify who is the speaker and who is the listener, keep to those roles so they don't interrupt or over talk each other, and then change those roles deliberately so each gets a chance to voice their reactions as well as listen to the other's reactions. When in the speaker role, clients should speak for themselves, articulate as best as they can their honest, subjective feelings, and state those feelings as such (e.g., make "I" statements of feeling). If they are talking about their emotional reactions to their partner, rather than sharing their reactions to some outside event with their partner, they should specify clearly the particular troublesome behavior of the partner and the situation in which that behavior occurs. They should edit their statements so they do not attack the partner's character or personality or speculate on the partner's motives for doing the troublesome behavior (i.e., mind reading). The ideal form of an "I" statement would be "I feel X when you do Y in situation Z," such as "I feel frustrated when you come home well before me but don't start making dinner," and "I feel isolated from you when we go the whole day without checking in with each other." Furthermore, neither speakers nor listeners are to problem solve during this conversation; problem solving comes later—only after both partners have a good idea of what the problem is. By just focusing on their emotional reactions to their partner's specific behavior, speakers are more likely to get heard by their partner. Speakers should also be brief, rather than going on and on about the issue; they should pause to let the listener summarize or paraphrase what they have said. Normally speakers should only say a few sentences; otherwise, the listener will not be able to summarize correctly. If the listener's summary or paraphrase is not correct, the speaker should clarify his or her message. Finally, speakers should willingly give up the floor and switch roles with the listener at a natural stopping point for them. To keep from going on and on, speakers are encouraged to only go two or three rounds of voicing their views and hearing a summary before switching roles.

For their part, listeners should attend to the speaker politely and communicate that attention with appropriate nonverbal behavior, such as by looking at the speaker, nodding, and saying "Uh-huh." They should not interrupt the speaker or engage in any nonverbal negative behavior, such as rolling their eyes or shaking their head or turning away. When a speaker has finished a thought or when he or she indicates a desire for the listener to show understanding, the listener should summarize or paraphrase what the speaker has said, without any attempt to rebut or discredit the speakers' comments. It is not simply enough for the listener to state that "I understand"—they must demonstrate this understanding by paraphrasing the speaker's key points. If possible, they should validate the feelings of the speaker even if they have different feelings themselves. Listeners can show understanding even if they don't agree. Listeners are not to offer solutions or make judgments, although they can ask questions for clarification if they don't understand what the speaker has said.

As part of this didactic instruction or immediately following it, therapists provide examples of the various speaker-listener behaviors so that clients see a model of what the appropriate behaviors look like. These may be written examples, videotaped illustrations, or therapist-generated examples. The therapist might use some topic from the couple themselves to illustrate the behaviors. For example, if the therapist knew that the husband didn't like that his wife teased him about his weight, the therapist might illustrate how the husband might express that as a speaker and how the wife might show she understood his feelings as a listener.

The heart and soul of CT is behavior rehearsal with coaching from the therapist. It is not enough to describe the skill. It always sounds easier in theory than it is in practice, especially since the material couples talk about is usually emotionally provocative. Distressed couples have typically gotten so used to trying to win arguments around their core issue that speakers have often lost track of their key thoughts or feelings, especially underlying soft emotions. Listeners have forgotten how to experience and convey empathy rather than becoming defensive or rebutting the speaker's point. The only way to shape the skills is for the therapist to have the couple practice them in the session and provide them with appropriate direction and feedback. When couples are given reading assignments prior to practice attempts, therapists sometimes warn the couple explicitly about the dangers of practicing the skills at home without first mastering them in the session under the watchful eye of the therapist. Premature practicing of the skills at home could lead to a difficult interaction that might make it harder for the couple to learn the skills correctly.

Typically, therapists have couples practice skills in small, incremental steps. They wouldn't start by having the couple discuss a major conflict. Depending on the couple and their judgment of what the couple might be able to achieve, therapists might not even start with a small problem. Instead, therapists might ask the couple to practice on a positive topic, with the speaker telling the other their positive feelings about something the listener does and the listener paraphrasing those feelings. Also, therapists may focus on just a part of the communication, such as paraphrasing. For example, the therapist might say:

"Okay, let's practice paraphrasing. Frank, you have the floor, and your job is to tell Cheryl your positive feelings about how she handles the children. But the focus is on you, Cheryl. Your job is to listen, maintain eye contact, and paraphrase. Don't exert your point of view. Just demonstrate that you are listening and that you understand, whether or not you agree.

Even though couples have typically read about these skills, practice sessions are preceded by prompts from the therapist such as the one above. The prompts are designed to minimize mistakes by reminding couples about the areas where they are most likely to slip up. Thus, the cues offered to one couple will differ from those offered to another. Some people can't state an affective experience without also making a judgment. For such a partner, the therapist might say, "Now remember, tell him how you feel, not whether he is right or wrong." Others have problems being explicit when defining problems; then the therapist might say, "Okay, when you begin, tell him exactly what he does that angers you." In short, the prompts and cues are tailored to the deficits of the particular couple. Depending on the specific deficits, the therapist might do additional remediation training. For example, if one or both partners in a particular couple had difficulty identifying their emotional states, the therapist might bring in a feeling chart to help them with that.

Early in the training, the rehearsals themselves should be brief. The structure of the practice session should be designed to minimize failure; the briefer the rehearsal, the less likely the client will be to forget to do something right or to add something wrong. Thus, the training sessions can be positive between them.

Therapist feedback and continued practice by the couple until competence is important. For example, when Jane began a communication exercise by saying, "It pisses me off when I come home and the house is a mess. You've got plenty of time to keep the house clean. I don't know what you do with yourself all day except have lattes with your friends," the therapist responded, "Your anger was very direct. That's good. The problem with the way you expressed it was all of that criticism at the end. Try it again without accusing him of wasting him time and being lazy. Just tell him about your experience when you come home." In her next effort, Jane said, "I get angry whenever I come home and the house is a mess." The therapist responded, "That was better. You got most of the baggage out of your statement. My only quibble is with the word 'mess.' Although you may feel that the word fits, it is not specific and may make it harder from him to hear you. Remember that your job is to make it easy for him to listen and not be tempted to respond defensively. You are more likely to succeed without that word. Try a different one. Or no word at all." On her third attempt, Jane said, "I find myself getting angry when I walk into the house and it is not as neat as I might have expected or hoped, such as the sink being filled with dishes."

As the above example indicates, Jane gets better and better at conforming to the rules with each attempt. However, if she does not practice being the speaker to the point where her statement conforms to the speaker rules, Jane is less likely to get it right when she tries to have a speaker-listener conversation at home. It is also important to note that the therapist is constantly teaching when providing feedback. In addition to correcting her, the therapist is repeatedly reminding her of the rationale for stating her concerns in a particular way. Therapists often take things one step further. They may drive the point home by bringing in the experience of the listener; for example, "Paul, did it make any difference to you how she said it, or did all three statements have the same impact on you?" Paul, being a well-socialized client, responded as expected: "Well, by the third time she said it, I was still bristling from the idea that I sit around and drink lattes all day. But if she hadn't done it the way she did it the first two times, and had led with the final statement, I wouldn't have felt this need to defend myself." In short, feedback includes restating the rationale for your corrective comments. It also includes verifying with the listener that the experience is truly different when the rules are followed.

Therapists allow couples to practice the skills at home only after they have mastered them in the therapy session. They caution the couple repeatedly against trying things at home before they are ready, such as trying to use the skills for a major issue at home when they have yet to master the skills for even minor problems during the session. The context of the therapist's office and the presence of the therapist invariably make the task easier in that environment than at home. It is a safe bet that if they haven't done it right in the office, they are not going to do it right at home.

When conducting any type of communication training, therapists become less directive as time goes on, leaving more of the work to the couple. By the time a couple completes training, the partners should be able to have their own conflict resolution sessions at home. Therapists may encourage couples to have these communication sessions regularly at home. During these sessions, they can share their positive and negative feelings with each other. They can also engage in problem solving once they have received that particular training, which we discuss later in the chapter.

Subtleties of Communication Training

The guidelines above may seem reasonable and straightforward, but there is room for lots of nuance in the execution. Let's first consider the speaker's role. Speakers can feel so strongly about something that they come off as if they are stating an absolute truth rather than a statement of how they, as individuals, feel. They may not qualify or condition their statement in any way or their tone may be so insistent that the listener feels immediately defensive and has a more difficult time paraphrasing the statement. A tentative voice tone or expressions such as "from my perspective" can make it easier for the listener to hear and validate. For example, consider the statement, "I can't believe you invited your mother over without asking me first. It really pissed me off." Although it is a direct expression of feeling about a specific behavior, if it were said in a strident way with an emphasis on the behavior that was done rather than on the emotion it triggered, it could easily communicate a message that "You committed a terrible wrong." A more qualified, less strident tone might lead to a less defensive listener. Such a tone can communicate generally that, "I recognize that we are different people. I'm sharing with you what I was thinking and feeling in that situation—which I recognize might be different than what you were thinking and feeling." Of course, partners don't usually think this way, let alone verbalize things this way. Nevertheless, at times interaction breaks down because each is challenged by the other's apparent attempts to assert a universal truth, along with an implication that the other has failed to abide by that obvious truth. It is as if they are heard to be saying, "I see the truth and you don't." Or, "I am right and you are wrong." Since strong statements with an air of apparent certainty can usually push conflict buttons in couples, sometimes training in making qualified statements or attending to voice tone is needed.

Now let's consider the listener's role—to listen to the speaker and demonstrate to the speaker's satisfaction that the speaker's message has been understood. That is all that is required and it seems so straightforward. However, there are four very different types of active listening, and their impact is likely to vary for a given speaker and from couple to couple. First, there is simple paraphrasing, whereby the listener attempts to communicate that he or she has been listening by simply summarizing what the speaker is saying. For example, a listener might summarize the speaker's message above as "So you didn't like when I invited my mother over without checking in with you first." At times, this level of active listening is reinforcing in and of itself, because for some speakers simply knowing that the other is listening is a vast improvement over typical conversations prior to communication training. However, speakers often want more from the listener than just a summary.

A second, more complicated form of active listening is reflection. Here the listener tries to capture the emotional state of the speaker as well as summarize the content of what he or she is saying. In so doing, the listener ideally validates those feelings as understandable. For example, the listener might say, "You get upset with me when I invite my mother over without checking with you first. It sounds like it may make you feel not considered or left out, as if your views didn't matter?" This response is often more gratifying to the speaker than mere paraphrasing because, when done appropriately, the speaker feels that the listener has connected with the emotional feeling underneath and may empathize with that feeling as well as understanding the simple content. Of course, with an incredulous tone of voice a speaker could capture accurately the content and the emotional state of the speaker and yet dismiss those emotions as inappropriate, excessive, or even pathological. That would constitute a reflection but with an accompanying judgment that would counter any positive impact of the reflection.

A third type of listening, validation, demonstrates that not only has the listener understood the speaker but that the speaker's point of view is valid and his or her feelings understandable. Validation can occur with simple paraphrasing or with reflection. Validation can be communicated verbally, such as by saying "You were upset that I invited my mother over without checking it out with you first. That makes sense—I understand." Nonverbally, the listener's tone can also communicate that the speaker's feelings and views make sense.

Sometimes speakers want something more, and something entirely different, than just paraphrasing, reflection, and validation. They want agreement with their position and as a result an admission of guilt and an apology. For example, they may want a comment like "You are right; I screwed up by inviting my mother over without consulting with you first. I am really sorry." Here is where one of the limitations of active listening becomes apparent. What if the listener does not see the validity of the speaker's point of view or feel any admission of guilt or apology is appropriate? Communication training teaches the speaker to make a direct statement of feeling about particular actions by the listener but without attacking the listener, thus making it easier for the listener to hear what the speaker is communicating without defensiveness. However, given the complicated interpersonal history that usually accompanies a speaker's comments, the listener's defensiveness is often not removed by carefully edited, direct expressions of feeling. The listener may read between the lines of what the speaker is saying and hear an implicit criticism or attack. Moreover, not all speakers are mollified by knowing that their partner listens and understands. They want the listener to acknowledge that they have a reasonable point of view, to agree with them, to admit their errors, or to apologize. It is not uncommon that, even after achieving a perfect expression followed by a perfect job of active listening, neither partner is happy. For example, the speaker is still waiting for validation, even though the listener does not find any validity in the speaker's point of view; the listener is waiting for the speaker to have a different feeling about the listener's behavior and reacts defensively no matter how the complaint is registered.

Behavioral and cognitive-behavioral couple therapists do not usually encourage validation on the part of the listener simply to mollify the speaker; however, they would encourage validation to the extent that the listener does see validity in the speaker's point of view. Similarly, these therapists would not encourage the speaker to be dishonest in order to pacify a listener; however, they do want speakers to speak in a nonblaming way and emphasize their own experience to see if the listener will become more validating as a result. Therapists may explain that the goal is understanding, not agreement or problem solving. Yet an emotionally injured speaker may not be satisfied until the listener agrees that he or she committed the injury and is appropriately remorseful. If the listener does not agree, communication training brings couples—even couples who communicate perfectly—to an impasse. Similarly, some listeners can't help but be irritated by the speaker's feeling expression, no matter how much editing goes on. In fact, it is natural to be defensive when your partner is upset by your behavior. There are many people who begin therapy saying that all they want is to be heard, understood, or validated. Unfortunately, they do not always know what they want. Many want the other to acknowledge their errors and change in particular and often fundamental ways. Understanding only goes so far.

TRAINING IN PROBLEM-SOLVING SKILLS IN TBCT AND CBCT

While communication training teaches partners how to share their thoughts and feelings, problem-solving skills training teaches partners how to resolve interpersonal conflicts or make difficult decisions. Problem solving is a structured interaction between two people, designed to resolve a particular dispute between them. Usually, but not always, the dispute is a complaint by one person concerning some aspect of the other's behavior. The complaint may be that the partner is doing too much of something, for example, smoking too much or going out with his or her friends too often. Or problems might arise because the partner is not doing something often enough, like spending time together or taking responsibility for household chores. Some relationship disputes involve mutual complaints when both partners object to the other's behavior in a particular situation. For example, when a couple gets together with their friends the husband may complain that his wife withdraws from the conversation, while the wife might complain that her husband talks too much at these gatherings.

Other relationship issues concern difficult decisions that need to be made, usually because partners have different preferences about those decisions. These issues could include decisions around child care, such as the type of arrangement that the couple makes for child care when they are both working; decisions around finances, such as how much to save and spend; or decisions around holiday plans, such as how much time to spend with each of their families over a holiday period.

Limitations of PST

There are several limitations to PST. First, PST is only appropriate when partners have conflict resolution or decision making as their goal. Therapists do not expect, nor would they even recommend, that couples communicate in this way about conflict if their goals were something other than solving the problem or making a difficult decision. Unfortunately, couples in conflict often have little interest in resolution. Their goals might be to be proven right, to have the other acknowledge that they are right, to vent their feelings, or even to hurt their partner's feelings. These goals are all inevitable, natural, and understandable reactions to conflict, but none of these reactions is compatible with solving the problem in such a way as to eliminate the conflict or make a difficult decision. If the goal is to resolve the conflict or make a decision, then PST is indicated. However, if the goal is something else—anything else—then PST is contraindicated.

Second, problem solving is a specialized activity; it is not like any other type of conversation. Therefore, it is not expected to be spontaneous, natural, relaxing, or enjoyable in the way that regular communication often is. This is not to say that problem solving cannot be fun; on the contrary, once couples reap its benefits and become efficient at it, they may find it enjoyable—something that brings them closer together and strengthens commitment to their relationship.

Third, not all problems are amenable to PST; only behaviors for which the partners have control can be targeted for problem solving or decision making. Typically, one has control over shared recreational activities, such as how much time to spend going out together; communication, such as whether it is okay to swear or not with the other; spending or not spending money;

working around the house; parenting; and performing this or that personal activity. Because these are all behaviors that are under voluntary control, they are perfectly reasonable areas about which to problem solve. In contrast, behaviors that are not under voluntary control make poor candidates for PST. One cannot directly control one's trust, sexual desire, love, or any kind of affective experience. Unfortunately, some of the most important areas of relationships are not instrumental. People do not marry or live together in order to divide up money, keep house, or negotiate schedules. The scut work of relationships simply comes with the territory. The passion, romance, intellectual stimulation, humor, trust, comfort, and self-esteem that people seek from their partners cannot be provided on demand.

Fourth, the range and applicability of PST is further restricted by the requirement that a range of solutions or decisions must be possible for a given conflict. Where compromise is impossible, PST tends to break down. Conflicts with only two possible solutions, such as whether to have another child or whether to take a particular job, don't leave room for the brainstorming, negotiation, cost-benefit analyses, and compromise that dominate the solution phase of problem-solving training.

Phases in PST

Because problem solving is a set of skills like the general communication skills discussed above, therapists use the strategies of instruction, modeling, and behavior rehearsal with coaching—including prompting and feedback—to train these skills. As in CT, they also proceed in incremental steps, starting with training in small pieces of PST or starting on small and relatively easy problems to resolve. Below, we present a series of rules or guidelines structured within four phases of PST.

Phase I: Before Beginning PST

1. *Be sure partners have the appropriate problem-solving attitude—a collaborative set.* Successful problem solving requires partners to be collaborative. They need to see that making some sacrifice or some compromise will lead not only to greater satisfaction in their partner but also to a

better relationship. They need to see that a refusal to change is self-defeating for their own personal happiness. As long as the relationship remains distressed, they will both be unhappy. By "giving in" and making some changes the partner wants, they usually find that the short-term cost will be more than outweighed by the advantages of an improved relationship. However, that will only be true if they enter PST with a collaborate attitude.

What are the essential components of that collaborative attitude? First, partners should view the problem as a mutual problem. Even if an issue is raised by only one of them and is of primary concern to only one of them, any relationship problem has implications for them both—if only because of the fact that one person's unhappiness will be bound to affect the other's. Therefore, all relationship problems are mutual problems. Second, partners should view the other's satisfaction as a valuable goal in its own right. Normally couples want to please the other and make the other happy. It is typically only after conflict and struggle that partners become angry and withhold from the other. When that struggle has been diminished, partners may again seek to please the other. Third, partners should see compromise and even sacrifice as a part of a successful relationship. They should see that partners usually have to give up something that they want in other to get other things that they want. They give to get. Of course, no one should give up some central goal or value of their life just for their partner. However, the conflicts that couples face usually do not involve the sacrifice of fundamental goals, key values, or personal integrity. The conflicts center around much more mundane disagreements.

The necessity for collaboration does not mean that partners must always agree to behave in a way that is satisfying to one another. Some requests for change seem unreasonable; at times the problem may be in the mind of the person who registers the complaint more than in the behavior of the person who is the object of the complaint. The method simply depends on each partner remaining open to the possibility of behavior change in response to the other's wishes.

2. *Find the appropriate setting, timing, and agenda.* Problem solving is structured interaction. As such, it should occur only in certain settings and

not in others. The first thing couples should be advised to do when problem solving is to set aside a time and a place in which they can be alone and won't be interrupted. Usually, couples like to hold problem-solving sessions at night, after children either are in bed or absorbed in an activity. This way the couple is less likely to be distracted by children, emails, or their phones.

Couples should not attempt to resolve their disputes at the scene of the crime. When a dispute occurs, they should wait until the next problem-solving session before trying to resolve it. Trying to resolve a grievance when the grievance occurs is usually ill-advised: when partners are emotionally aroused, as they are bound to be when the other does something negative, they are not at their best—they are unlikely to attempt to solve the problem in a constructive manner. Discussing the issue at a neutral time, like during a prearranged problem-solving session, makes it more likely that it will be dealt with effectively. Tackling difficult relationship problems during structured problem-solving sessions brings new skills to bear on these issues. The rules discussed below, if followed, may make some apparently insoluble problems solvable.

Problem-solving sessions should be relatively short—certainly no more than an hour and often much less than an hour. Problem solving is difficult; couples should avoid exhausting themselves. When problem solving goes on a long time, it is usually because it has turned into an argument.

Phase 2: Defining the Problem
Once the couple is in the correct mind-set and has found an appropriate location and time to begin problem solving, the next step is for them to define the problem for discussion.

3. *One problem per problem-solving session.* At the outset of a problem-solving session, partners should decide on an agenda of whose problem is going to be discussed and what problem that will be. A problem-solving session should only address one problem at a time. Often when one mentions a problem, the other counters with a related problem. Soon, every-

thing but the proverbial kitchen sink is brought into the discussion and it devolves into an argument about many problems and who is the worst contributor to the problems.

4. *Keep problem definition and problem solution separate.* A problem-solving session has two distinct, nonoverlapping phases: a problem-definition phase and a problem-solution phase. During the problem-definition phase, a clear, specific statement of the problem is produced, a definition that is understood by both. No attempt is made to solve the problem until both understand exactly what the problem is. Then, during the solution phase, discussion focuses on generating and evaluating possible solutions to the problem, and, finally, on the formation of an agreement designed to resolve the problem.

   The distinction between phases is important because couples' problem-solving communication tends to be chaotic, tangential, and ambiguous. Focused discussion tends to be more efficient. More importantly, perhaps, discussing solutions is positive and forward-looking, whereas problem definition is more apt to be negative and backward-looking. The spirit of collaboration and compromise is dampened by focus on past misdeeds. While an element of this latter focus may be necessary during the definition stage, it should not intrude into the elaboration of solutions unless the partners decide that they are not ready for PST.

5. *In stating a problem, try to begin with something constructive.* The way a problem is first stated sets the tone for the entire discussion. Since most interpersonal problems arise because one partner finds the other's behavior dissatisfying, a statement of the problem requires an implicit or explicit criticism of the other. Yet it is difficult for most people, especially distressed couples, to accept criticism from their partners. Their natural response is to defend themselves or counterattack when they are criticized. To avoid or limit this response, partners voicing a problem need to say it in a way that is least likely to result in the other becoming defensive, so the complainant can maintain the other's cooperation and collaborative spirit. One way of doing this is by beginning the statement of the problem with a constructive remark, such as an expression of appreciation, if it can be done genuinely. It can be particularly helpful

if they mention something positive related to the concern they are bringing up. For example, one might say "I like it when you hold me when we watch TV, but I feel kind of rejected when you aren't affectionate in other situations, like when we are out together in public." This comment would likely go over better than "You say you love me but you are rarely affectionate with me." However, it is not always possible to genuinely praise someone for something related to the problem. Rather than being phony and inventing a compliment, partners can sometimes express appreciation in a more general way in such instances by reminding the other person that they are loved and appreciated, that the relationship is important to them, and that the criticism of their behavior does not signal total rejection. Beyond specific statements of praise or endorsement, the tone that the complainant uses to state the problem is crucial. If the problem is stated in a way that sounds like the complainant is drawing a line in the sand or indicating that the problem is unacceptable and will not be tolerated ever again, the discussion will most likely go poorly.

6. *Describe objective, observable behaviors in specific terms.* When defining a problem, partners should describe the behavior that is bothering them. They should state their complaints or problems in terms of specific words and actions, behaviors that are observable. For example, rather than saying "You don't seem to want to sleep with me anymore," one might say "Most of the time I initiate sex." Or, rather than saying "I get the feeling you aren't interested in what I do" or "You don't care about me," one might say "You seldom ask me how my day was or check in with me to see how I am doing." Notice that in each of the nonbehavioral examples, it is unclear what the problem is, except that the complainant is dissatisfied. It's also not clear what the recipient could do to change. When the complainant is behavioral, on the other hand, the recipient knows exactly what the referent is and communication is much clearer. Sometimes a behavioral example is improved when the complainant identifies the situations in which the behavior occurs. For example, one might say "You don't usually show me physical affection in public, like holding my hand or putting your arm around me."

By focusing on behavior, partners may avoid a common pitfall in describing problems—the use of derogatory adjectives and nouns. For example, one might describe a problem as "You are inconsiderate," or "You are lazy," or "You are cold." These labels are not only vague but provocative. They describe negative attributes of the other's personality rather than specific behaviors of concern. They are likely to lead to defensiveness or counterattack. For example, "So I'm lazy, eh? Well at least I'm not insensitive and cold the way you are." In either case, the problem-solving session has become a debate at best and an argument at worst. If, on the other hand, the complainant can remain focused on maintaining the other person's cooperation, he or she can simply describe the behavior that displeases him or her and forget the labels. For example, instead of the "You are lazy" comment, the complainant might state a specific complaint like "You leave your clothes lying on the floor and leave dirty dishes on the table."

By only describing observable behavior as the problem, partners avoid making inferences about the other's motivations or emotions. Such inferences during problem discussions are usually negative and lead to arguments. For example, one may describe a lack of sex as the problem and claim the other is withholding sex as a punishment. Or one may describe public criticism as the problem and claim the other is trying to humiliate them in front of friends. Then the couple gets into an argument about those motivations of punishment and humiliation and the actual problem behaviors are lost in the discussion. As a result, the couple makes no progress in dealing with these behaviors.

7. *Focus on the present and do not overgeneralize.* Partners should specifically describe the problematic behavior that sometimes occurs in the present. They should avoid giving examples of the times that behavior has occurred in the past. Such examples often lead to arguments about the details of when or why or even if the behavior occurred in that past incident. Most problem behaviors that partners bring up are well known by the other; no examples are needed. In those rare cases that the other is unclear about examples of the problem behavior, the other can ask for a relevant example.

Another pitfall that partners may make in describing a problem is overgeneralization. They may exaggerate the scope of their complaints with words such as "always" and "never." For example, one may say "You never clean up the messes you make," or "You're always late." Not only are these overgeneralizations imprecise, but they are seldom accepted by the partner. In response to an overgeneralized complaint the receiver is likely to dispute the overgeneralization (e.g., "I am not always late!") rather than discuss the problem per se. Whether the problem occurs "all" of the time or some of the time, it is a problem. Debates about frequency are usually not the point. Partners should describe the behavior and avoid discussions about the frequency of its occurrence.

8. *Avoid focusing on the causes of the problem.* Another way that a focus on the past can interfere in problem solving is when partners focus on the causes of the problem behavior. A focus on causes can lead to arguments about the causes and prevent appropriate solutions to the actual problem. For example, "Why" questions by one partner are often perceived as critical by the other and lead to defensive or offensive responses. A question such as "Why don't you clean up the dishes or put away your clothes?" can lead to "Well, I'm busy and don't have much time" or "Why do you run up the credit card debt?" can lead to "Well, if you made more money, it wouldn't be a problem!" Then the partners are in an argument.

However, immediate or proximal causes can sometimes be mentioned by the recipient of the complaint and be helpful in understanding the problem. For example, "I don't intentionally hide my feelings from you; it's just that it seldom occurs to me to share them with you." Or "I have trouble thinking of things to do with the kids. That is one of the reasons I spend so little time with them." Although these factors can be mentioned, may aid understanding, and may figure in the solution to the problem, the focus should not shift to these causes. The danger is that one partner will blame his or her behavior on the immediate cause and thereby deny responsibility for doing anything about it. Immediate causes are factors to be taken into account, not reasons for avoiding a direct focus on the problem.

9. *Describe the feelings that the problem elicits.* The partner who is defining the problem should reveal the emotions, including the soft and hidden emotions that this problem triggers. Almost always, when behavior is objectionable, it is because the behavior (or lack of it) has an emotionally

upsetting impact. If the behavior doesn't have such an impact, it would not be the subject of a problem-solving session. It is important to make these feelings known, in addition to pinpointing the specific behavior that led to the feelings. When the discomfort is disclosed, the partner may be more sympathetic. Partners should not assume that their feelings are obvious. If feelings are stated directly, the other can avoid the hazardous and often not very reliable task of trying to guess what they are. For example, in describing the problem above about clothes and dishes, the complainant could note that "It annoys me when I see clothes on the floor or dirty dishes on the table and makes me feel that I am the housewife who has to take care of those things."

10. *The listener should use the skills of communication training when the speaker defines a problem.* The rules above have pertained primarily to the speaker who is defining a problem for joint discussion. The listener's response is just as important. Listeners have a tendency to rebut the speaker's description of the problem, to challenge whether the issue is really a problem at all, and to defend their behavior in reference to the problem. Instead, the listener should summarize the speaker's problem description, paraphrase or reflect the feelings that it brings about in them, and validate the concern to the extent that they honestly can. For example, the recipient might paraphrase the above complaint by saying, "So a messy house bothers you and makes you feel bad about your role in the family." The listener doesn't need to agree with the speaker to respond with summary, paraphrase, and reflection. For example, perhaps the listener in this example doesn't think the house is very messy and believes that all of their friends with children have houses that are as messy as or messier than their own home. In this case, the listener would not validate that the house is indeed that messy but would still capture the essence of the speaker's problem definition, that the clothes and dirty dishes have an emotional impact on the speaker. The listener should check out whether he or she understands the issue completely, including possible implications of the issue. For example, the listener might say "You didn't say this but it sounds as if you may think that I am the primary creator of the mess?" To which the speaker might reply, "No, I agree that both

of us contribute to the mess but I would like us to address it, because it affects me a lot." In this case, the speaker's clarification of the listener's understanding contained an acknowledgement of each partner's role in the problem, a topic to which we now turn.

11. *Acknowledge your own role in creating, exacerbating, or maintaining the problem.* Both partners should acknowledge their role in the problem. Doing so reduces the chances of a competitive dispute in which each partner blames the other for the problem. If the speaker stating the problem is able to acknowledge some role in it, the listener may have an easier time responding to it. In fact, acknowledging one's role in the problem is one way the speaker can start off the discussion constructively (rule 5 above). For example, if a mother wants to discuss the limited time the father spends taking care of the children, she might acknowledge that she sometimes directs or interferes with his activities with them. Even if the speaker doesn't acknowledge some role in the problem, it can help if the listener acknowledges his or her own role in the problem. If this mother defines a problem solely in terms of the limited amount of time the father spends taking care of the children, ideally he would acknowledge some validity to her claim and some understanding of why that might be upsetting for her, as suggested in the listener rules above. Then maybe she would respond by acknowledging a role that she may play in the problem, such as interfering or directing him when he does take care of the kids. Since most problems are dyadic in nature, with contributions from both partners, this kind of mutual acknowledgement is usually theoretically possible. When done, it promotes collaboration and solution-finding. However, partners should not, and usually can't, accept responsibility disingenuously. They should accept only as much responsibility as they truthfully can. For example, the listener might only be able to say "I can see that you're upset by this issue and I'm willing to work on it with you." Here the listener is at least acknowledging that the partner is upset and expressing his or her willingness to work on the problem.

When both partners clearly contribute to the problem and the listener to the initial problem definition wants to be sure contributions of them both are addressed in the problem-solving session, the couple may define two related problems. For example, the mother above might define the problem of the father's limited time with the children, using the guidelines above. Then the father would define the problem of the mother's interference with his time with the children, using the guidelines above. Then the two have defined what is called a bilateral problem.

Summary of the problem-definition phase. If partners follow all of these guidelines, the complainant will come up with a well-defined problem, which includes a constructive opening statement, a description of the undesirable behavior, a specification of the situations in which the problem occurs, and the emotional consequences of the problem for the partner who was distressed by it. The listener will have shown that he or she understands that problem and the other's feelings about it. Here are some examples of well-defined problems: (a) I love to do things with you and when we have planned activities together, I really feel close to you. But lately on Sundays when neither of us is working, you don't usually help me plan things to do together. I end up feeling like the responsibility for our leisure time is all on my shoulders, and I resent it. (b) I love to make love with you and I feel very special when you initiate sex, but when you let a week go by without initiating or telling me that you'd like to make love with me, I feel rejected. (c) I think you are a wonderful mother and really have good ideas about how to raise the children, but when you break in and discipline Annie while I'm in the middle of disciplining her myself, I get very angry at you. (d) When you open up to me and tell me about your feelings, I really like it and I feel very close to you. The problem is that recently, you have not been asking me about how I am feeling about work or my family and have not been telling me your feelings about things important to you. I tend to turn off to you when we don't talk about important things and I feel distant from you and rather lonely.

Phase 3: Coming to a Solution

12. *Focus on solutions.* Once a couple has agreed on a definition to a problem, the focus should shift to solving it. The discussion should be future-oriented and should answer the question, "What can we do to eliminate this problem and keep it from coming back?" Returns to the problem-

definition phase will get in the way of this future orientation. The most effective way to maintain a focus on solutions and on the future is by brainstorming, whereby partners go back and forth, generating as many possible solutions to the problem as they can think of, without regard to the quality of the solutions. Partners are encouraged to use their imaginations and say anything that comes into their minds, without censoring anything, no matter how silly and unworkable it may seem. All proposed solutions should be written down.

13. *Both partners are responsible for change.* In the spirit of collaboration and cooperation, problem solutions should involve change on the part of both partners—certainly in the case of bilateral problems. However, even when possible solutions clearly point to change on the part of one partner, it is helpful for solutions to include changes by both partners for several reasons. First, partners are more likely to change if they are not doing it alone. Second, it is a rare problem in a relationship in which both partners don't play some role. Recall that the problem-definition phase involved acknowledgement by both partners of their respective roles—whether it be in the initiation, intensification, or maintenance of the problem. Finally, in addition to addressing whatever direct or indirect role they play, partners who are not the target of change can often provide feedback or positive encouragement that will be helpful in the change process. Thus, during brainstorming of solutions, therapists often advise complainants to begin with an offer to change some aspect of their own behavior, prior to requesting a change from the partner. For example, a partner who is distressed at the other's messiness might offer that (a) one place in the home, such as the other's office, might be left messy without complaint as long as the rest of the house was kept orderly or (b) messy dishes left in the morning were okay because the other was always in a hurry to get to work but that the mess would be cleaned in the evening.

During the brainstorming phase, complainants are likely to propose dramatic, immediate, and complete solutions to a problem. Therapists encourage partners to propose more feasible and phased solutions. Even though a partner upset at the other for chronically coming home late because of work might want the other to arrive home at a specified time every workday, such an immediate and dramatic change may not be possible. Instead, the tardy partner might start a process of staged change that includes some flexibility that would be more realistic and ultimately more satisfying for the other. For example, the tardy partner could agree to be home on time at least three of five workdays or agree to be no later than 30 minutes late on any day.

14. *Discuss pros and cons of proposed solutions.* Couples should consider each solution, deciding whether it would contribute to resolving the problem. If the answer is yes, they should then discuss the benefits and costs of implementing that solution. These discussions often go better if the one who proposed the solution speaks first about its benefits and costs. Problem solving is usually a more positive experience if the benefits of a solution are discussed before the costs are enumerated. For example, if one partner had offered a particular solution and the other's first response was, "The thing I don't like about that is . . ." and then went on to list a whole host of reasons the solution wouldn't work, the partner who had offered the solution might feel deflated or angry. The whole tone of the problem-solving session could quickly become very negative. Thus, it usually works better if partners acknowledge the merits of potential solutions before they discuss their limitations. However, both the merits or benefits and the limitations or costs of each solution should be discussed. As a result of this discussion, partners should decide for each solution whether to (a) eliminate it from the list, (b) include it as part of a possible change agreement, or (c) defer a final decision until all proposals have been discussed. This process should be repeated for each item on the list.

15. *Negotiate an agreement.* After discussing the pros and cons of each proposed solution on the list, including the consequences of each proposal for each partner and for the relationship, partners should negotiate a final agreement. Ideally, this agreement includes changes both agree to make. The ability of couples to agree on a mutually acceptable set of solutions and implement the required behavior change is the acid test of effective problem solving. The solution should be spelled out in clear, descriptive, behavioral terms, stating clearly what each spouse is going to do differently. Too often couples agree to vague changes, and subsequently it is unclear exactly

what the agreement was. When each person walks away with a different interpretation of the agreement, future clashes over the terms of the agreement and whether it was complied with frequently occur. Of course, everything cannot be specified in detail, but partners should be careful to specify the behaviors that constitute positive change. Here are some examples of vague agreements alongside more precise agreements:

Vague: Adolfo agrees to come home on time from now on and Marlene won't be on his case.

Precise: On Monday through Friday, Adolfo will be home by 6:30 p.m. If for some reason this is impossible on a particular night, he will let Marlene know by 4:30 p.m., and at that time will tell her when he will be home. Marlene will greet him positively when he arrives home.

Vague: Patty will not be as apprehensive about the future, and will have more confidence in Cosmo.

Precise: Patty will respond positively to Cosmo in conversation about his job when he initiates such conversation. During these conversations, she will not make pessimistic remarks about his future with the company.

The final agreement should be written down, signed, and dated. Thus, partners will have made a formal commitment to carrying out the agreement, and there will be less reliance on memory and thus less distortion by memory. This written agreement should be conveniently posted somewhere in the house so that it can remind partners of what they have agreed to. Sometimes the agreement itself can include reminders, such as Adolfo above agreeing to set his phone alarm so time does not get away from him at work.

Phase 4: Reevaluating the Chosen Solution

When the couple makes the agreement, they should decide to review it at some specified future date to evaluate how well it is working and to determine whether it has successfully solved the problem. Every agreement should have a trial run for a specified period of time. The length of that trial run depends on the frequency of the problem. If problems occur more than once a day, then the solution could be reevaluated after a week. If the problem occurs a few times a week, it might be better to reevaluate after 2–4 weeks. Solutions to problems that occur very sporadically but are impactful when they occur should be evaluated a few days after the problem happens.

At that future time, they should review the agreement and renegotiate those parts that are not working. Sometimes the first agreement will work, and the review will serve to reinforce the changes that have been made. However, often the first agreement will not be the perfect solution and may even create new problems. It is crucial that partners renegotiate the agreement by brainstorming some new ideas or reevaluating the original solutions. Thus, the problem solving can be an ongoing, self-corrective process to address relationship problems. It is important for the therapist to normalize this iterative process as an inherent part of creating deliberate change. Their initial solutions are unlikely to be complete successes; if the problem were that easy to solve, they probably would have solved it long ago. Instead, the initial solution will likely reveal additional information about the problem, its origins, or its most negative impacts—this information can be harnessed to create better and better solutions over time. Unfortunately, couples too often take the failure of an initial solution as evidence that the problem is unsolvable.

Problem-Solving Overview

The example agreements above are quite structured and may seem mechanical and artificial. However, these agreements are attempts to change long-standing habits that have presented problems for the couples, have not changed naturally, and are usually difficult to change. Structure may be necessary at first. Later, after the changes have been in place for a while, they may become more natural and structure may not be needed. Chances are that clarity and structure were missing from their previous attempts to deal with these problems.

In an ideal world, problem solving becomes a natural part of the couple's relationship. Even after partners have solved their major problems in therapy, they should have time put aside for occasional problem-solving sessions.

These *state of the relationship* sessions provide opportunities to deal with any conflict that has arisen since the last problem-solving session and to go over prior agreements and discuss how they are working. If an agreement is not working well or if circumstances have changed such that the agreement is impractical, it should be renegotiated.

CT AND PST IN IBCT

These strategies of communication and problem solving make intuitive sense. They are presumably bolstered by the substantial evidence in support of TBCT and CBCT (e.g., Shadish & Baldwin, 2005). Why are they not first-line interventions in IBCT?

There are both empirical and clinical reasons why IBCT relies on CT and PST in only a secondary way and usually adapts them substantially for use in IBCT. Research has questioned whether couples trained in these approaches continue to use them after therapy has ended. For example, Jacobson, Schmaling, and Holtzworth-Munroe (1987) found that couples receiving PST tended not to practice the skills in a formal way after therapy ended, and whether they did or not failed to predict long-term outcome. Our clinical trial comparing IBCT and TBCT indicated that TBCT couples showed greater improvements in observed communication at the termination of treatment but not by 2-year follow-up (Baucom et al., 2011) and that IBCT produced greater maintenance of relationship satisfaction over this 2-year follow-up period (Christensen et al., 2010). Data from that same clinical trial indicated that IBCT couples reported as much use of these CT and PST skills as TBCT couples at 5-year follow-up, even though, unlike IBCT couples, TBCT couples got extensive training in these skills (Christensen et al., 2010).

In addition to this empirical evidence, there are several clinical and theoretical reasons that we don't rely on CT and PST as first-line interventions. First, we don't believe the primary problem with most distressed couples is a skills deficit. These couples usually have a history of being able to talk well with each other and with other friends and family, as well as problem solve with colleagues, friends, and family. We believe that usually strong negative emotions, rather than the absence of skills per se, interfere with a couple's ability to communicate and problem solve. When partners are angry and resentful, they will have a hard time communicating effectively, no matter how skillful they are in calmer states. They often don't share their true or deeper, vulnerable feelings with each other because they don't feel safe and secure doing so. A primary goal in IBCT is to provide an emotionally safe environment, usually through empathic joining and unified detachment, in which partners can be open and nondefensive. Second, we believe that efforts to improve communication should be targeted at the couple's particular problematic pattern of interaction rather than at some general set of skills. For example, it may be important for a withdrawer to speak up, even if he or she doesn't speak in the ideal "I" statement format, while it may be important for the demander to listen, rather than state again his or her concerns, even if he or she does that in a less than ideal, active listening way. Third, the guidelines or rules often don't fit with the couple's lifestyle or usual way of relating. For example, couples often face problems when they are forced to and they often muddle through and solve problems over time rather than systematically sitting down and going through a step-by-step process. While such a process as envisioned in CT and PST might be useful or better, we have found that few couples will consistently engage in this systematic process. Most couples have busy lives with many interfering and competing factors, making their communication and problem solving much messier than envisioned by CT and PST. Fourth, the guidelines can lead to inauthentic behavior. For example, the guideline to start with a positive when defining a problem can often seem like a "Yes, but" message, and partners hear and respond less to the "Yes" part of the message and more to the "but" part of the message. Finally, there can be iatrogenic effects of the guidelines if partners use them against the other. For example, if one partner is better at adhering to the guidelines, he or she may use that to blame the other for "not doing what the therapist suggested."

In what ways do we rely on CT and PST and how do we incorporate them into IBCT? First, we can use CT and PST as described above. Sometimes couples come in to therapy and request training in communication or problem-solving skills. They may have heard about such training or read about it and think it would be helpful for them. In this case, we would go over the procedures with them, see if they are still interested, and help them focus on parts they think would be most helpful to them. In so doing, we typically emphasize CT more than PST. In TBCT and CBCT, CT comes before PST; if a couple has difficulty with CT, they will usually have greater difficulty with PST.

As an example, an IBCT therapist once worked with a couple that were both artists. The husband was emotionally volatile, would get worked up in an argument and say things that he later regretted, and then would get depressed at his own behavior and his wife's reaction to it. His wife would withdraw in the face of his emotional outbursts but resent that problems were not being addressed. The therapist helped them practice a modified form of CT. They found it helpful to use a concrete object as the floor card indicating who had the floor. The requirement that each had to paraphrase or summarize the other's position to the other's satisfaction before they could state their own views was especially helpful to them in slowing the interaction down and helping them understand each other. They weren't terrific at doing classic "I" statements and didn't limit themselves to those but did find it doable and helpful to limit their talk turns so the other got to speak their piece without waiting too long. After therapy terminated, the couple occasionally came back in for a booster session. They reported that they occasionally relied on this communication technique to deal with their problems, even more than a year after therapy officially ended.

Whatever we teach CT or PST, we are mindful that the couple may fall into some of the traps common with this kind of training. We distinguish between (a) an error in communication that doesn't trigger a strong emotional reaction and can be easily corrected and (b) an error that leads to strong emotions that are better addressed by temporarily abandoning PST. As an example of the first case, perhaps a complainant is not being very specific, we intervene and encourage behavioral specificity, the complainant provides a more specific description, and the couple is able to continue. As an example of the second case, a complainant makes a derogatory comment about the partner, the partner fires back, and both become immediately agitated. In that case we might temporarily abandon PST and instead do empathic joining with both partners, perhaps followed by unified detachment so they can both step back and see how and why their discussions get easily derailed. Then we might return to problem solving with this greater knowledge of what derails them. Thus, we sometimes engage in IBCT strategies as a fallback position while we are doing some CT or PST.

Second, we use parts of CT and PST as needed by the couples, based on their problematic patterns of interaction and what occurs in their interaction in front of us. The rules of CT and PST above were developed because they address common pitfalls in couple communication; these rules are valuable because they alert therapists to potential danger areas. When those pitfalls are a common part of a particular couple's pattern of interaction or a couple is diverted by one of those pitfalls when they are engaged in interaction in therapy, we can use the relevant rules as a means of helping the couple. For example, let's say that a couple often gets derailed when discussing household tasks because they review specific incidents and argue about those incidents (e.g., who did what, how bad the incident was) and argue about the frequency of the incident (e.g., "You never clean the frying pan when you use it"). As IBCT therapists, we would try to help them avoid this pitfall and implement rule 7 above (focus on the present and do not overgeneralize) but without treating it as a rule. We would not usually tell them that this is a rule of good communication or say foul when they break this rule in front of us. Instead, we might help them sit back and reflect with unified detachment how their focus on past incidents or frequency of bad behavior actually prevents them from resolving the problem and leaves them angry with each other. By so doing, we have helped them see an important link in their own behavior: when they discuss household tasks this way, what they don't want to happen usually happens. Thus, we are helping them learn useful information from their own experience rather than telling them a rule they should follow. Once we have had this conversation, we can interrupt occurrences of it in session and say something like, "Wait, it sounds like you guys are starting to talk about past incidents of bad behavior and how often they happen, and as we discussed, that leads you into a bad place. Can you keep the focus on what you each would like to happen, which seems to lead to a better discussion?"

Because we base our use of CT and PST on what the couple needs, given their pattern of interaction and how they interact in front of us (which is often some variation of that pattern), we rarely take couples through a systematic, step-by-step training in all the rules described above. Couples have some skills, they don't need all the rules, and trying to follow all the rules would be cumbersome and difficult for them to maintain. Therefore, unless couples request this kind of training, we want to have them learn only as much as they need to learn and always based on what actually trips them up. As a result, couples don't react as if they have been doing things all wrong and have to learn a whole new way of communication. Also, they rarely will wonder or ask "Why is it important that we do this or not do this?" They have learned why it is important based on their own experience, as highlighted and framed by their therapist.

Let's consider some additional examples of how IBCT selects pieces of CT and PST to use. When one partner says something important because it is new or different, we want to be sure that the other has understood it. We may ask the other to summarize or reflect the statement and then describe their reactions to it. Thus, we are using the summarize part of CT but only for certain important statements rather than having partners summarize each statement that the other has said. As another example, couples will commonly focus on what the other does that they don't like, providing an explanation of why the behavior is so inconsiderate or selfish, leading the partner to be defensive or to counterattack. We might then intervene and encourage the speaker to talk about himself or herself, discussing their own emotional reactions rather than the other's behavior. In this way, we are trying to achieve some of the benefit of "I" statements of feeling without imposing a rigid syntactical format on the speaker.

A final example concerns pieces from PST that we may incorporate as we try to help partners come to doable solutions for their concerns. A common dynamic is that one partner describes a problem, wanting the other to listen and empathize with the problem, but the other provides a solution to the problem. As a result, both the speaker and listener are dissatisfied. After reviewing this process with the couple so that they clearly see it as one of their dysfunctional patterns of communication, we can help them make a clear distinction between problem discussion for the purpose of venting and getting support versus problem discussion for the purpose of problem definition and solution. In IBCT, we feel free to adapt any of the procedures from CT and PST in our work with couples.

Third, we deliberately neglect or directly counter the guidelines of CT and PST when our functional analysis of the couple's communication indicates the positive value of seemingly negative behaviors. For example, the guidelines of CT and PST highlight the value and desirability of positive behavior and of neutral behavior, in contrast to emotionally negative behavior. Certainly many couples get caught in an escalating, negative cycle of interaction that is destructive for them; we help them divert or break that cycle. However, it is not uncommon for one partner to get involved in their life outside the relationship, to take the other for granted, and to distance from the other. That other partner may gradually get more and more upset until they confront the distancing partner angrily. This confrontation may be unpleasant for both in the moment but it may renew their attention to each other and their closeness to each other. Occasionally angry confrontations between partners that lead to greater attention and closeness between them is not unusual in our experience. We would not want to paint this angry partner as the bad guy who uses bad or inappropriate communication techniques. Although we could certainly imagine a better process in which partners are more aware of their drifting from each other and self-correct earlier on and in a more positive way, such a goal may be beyond the reach of many if not most couples. A self-correction through an angry confrontation is better than no or delayed self-correction as long as it leads to a stronger connection between the pair.

Therefore, we neither endorse the strategies of CT and PST wholeheartedly nor do we reject them out of hand. We think those strategies are important for therapists to learn so they know the common pitfalls that prevent couples from talking to each other in constructive ways. However, we rarely use these rules as part of a detailed, step-by-step, systematic training in communication as they were originally envisioned—unless the couple seeks that kind of training. Instead, we use parts of CT and PST as indicated by the couple's pattern of interaction or by how they get stuck as they interact in front of us. We use these rules not as rules of good communication to impose on the couple but rather we work with the couple to help them learn what they do that works and doesn't work. When they implement a rule, they do so because they have gleaned from their own behavior that a change consistent with the rule helps them discuss more constructively. Many specific rules may not be particularly relevant for a couple and we comfortably ignore those rules. Furthermore, we comfortably ignore or even reject any of these rules that may interfere with the way a couple interacts if that interaction, even if not ideal, serves a valuable function for the couple. In fact, we may praise a couple for interaction that doesn't follow the rules, not because it doesn't follow the rules, but because it is their way to self-correct or create greater connection between them.

SUMMARY

In this chapter we reviewed the TBCT and CBCT strategies of communication training (CT) and problem-solving training (PST). Training in both typically consists of some or all of the following components: didactic instruction about the skills, modeling of the skills, behavior rehearsal or practicing of the skills, and coaching or feedback from the therapist. Typically, the training is incremental, starting with easy communication topics or components and advancing to more difficult ones.

CT distinguishes between the roles of speaker and listener and trains partners in how to perform each role. The focus in CT is not on solutions or problem solving but on understanding of each partner's emotional reactions. As speaker, a partner should avoid attacks on the other's character or personality, such as saying "You are lazy" but instead use "I" statements to describe his or her emotional reactions to the other's specific behavior, clarifying if needed the circumstances under which that behavior occurs. The classic "I" statement is of the form "I feel X when you do specific behavior Y in situation Z." As a listener, the partner should attend to the other and paraphrase or reflect what the other has said. Such a summary does not imply agreement, simply understanding. The speaker corrects any misunderstanding until the listener can summarize the message to the speaker's satisfaction. When the speaker comes to a natural stopping point or has a few rounds of message and summary of message, he or she changes roles with the listener so the former listener can get a chance to voice his or her views.

PST is even more structured and complicated, with many more rules than CT. Partners should choose an appropriate time and place when they both want to problem solve a specific issue. Together they define the problem of concern before considering possible solutions. They are to acknowledge relevant positive behavior of the partner even as they define the problem, and they are to each acknowledge their role in creating or maintaining the problem. Once they have defined the problem, they shift to brainstorming possible solutions—ideally, behavior changes that each could do. They consider the pros and cons of these solutions and then negotiate an agreement that they try out. As they see how the solution works, they modify it as necessary.

Although CT and PST are well-formulated interventions that are major parts of the evidence-based treatments of TBCT and CBCT, they are not first-line interventions in IBCT. We reviewed some of the empirical and clinical reasons that make us hesitant to use CT and PST as first-line interventions. Instead, we use them in a more focused and limited way. If couples request such training, we will certainly describe it to them and begin to train them in those skills, always being aware of the pitfalls of such training, such as the difficulty couples have in following the guidelines of CT and PST. We often fall back into empathic joining and unified detachment when couples are unable, even with some coaching, to maintain these guidelines or if they experience them as unhelpful. Most commonly, we adapt specific parts of CT and PST based on the pattern of interaction in which the couple gets stuck or based on their interaction right in front of us. Thus, IBCT does use PST and especially CT, but often not in the way it was originally envisioned.

We have now completed our description of IBCT. In the next section, Part 5, we describe some special considerations and new directions in IBCT. In Chapter 12, we discuss adaptations of IBCT for diverse couples. In Chapter 13, we discuss adaptations of IBCT for intimate partner violence, sexual problems, infidelity, and individual psychopathology. Finally, in Chapter 14, we describe an online intervention program for couples that is based on IBCT.

PART 5

Special Considerations and New Directions in IBCT

12

&

Diversity in Couples: Clinical Considerations in Doing IBCT

THROUGHOUT THIS BOOK, we have used the DEEP analysis to understand individual couples. However, this DEEP analysis can also be used to understand variation across couples. Couples from different cultures, races, ethnicities, religions, and social classes, as well as couples with different sexual orientations sometimes face unique external pressures. For example, same-sex couples may face external resistance or disapproval of their relationships that is not experienced by different-sex couples. Low-income couples may face financial pressures that middle-income and higher income couples don't face. Couples from traditional and patriarchal cultures may face more limiting gender role pressures than couples from more egalitarian cultures. In addition, some differences between partners, emotional sensitivities, or patterns of interaction may be more common in certain types of couples than in others. For example, a man raised in a traditional culture may have stronger preferences for the role he wants his wife to play than a man from a more egalitarian culture. He may have a greater sense of discomfort or shame if his wife works outside the home and makes a higher income than he does. Differences in how openly out to be can be a problem for many same-sex couples, an issue that is never a problem for different-sex couples. Finally, certain patterns of communication are more likely in some types of couples than in others. For example, although the demand/withdraw pattern of communication is common across cultures (Christensen et al., 2006), there is also variation across culture. For example, Rehman and Holtzworth-Munroe (2006) observed American couples, Pakistani couples living in Pakistan, and immigrant Pakistani couples living in America during a conflict task. During demand/withdraw interaction, American women made more aggressive demands while Pakistani women made more unassertive demands. Also, unlike American women, Pakistani women exhibited more withdrawing behavior than their husbands.

In the sections below, we will specifically address how IBCT deals with gender and power issues in different-sex couples, how IBCT deals with issues more commonly encountered in same-sex couples, how IBCT deals with couples that are culturally, racially, ethnically, or religiously different from the dominant group in America, and finally how IBCT deals with social class, particularly low-income couples, who often are culturally, ethnically, racially, or religiously different from the majority group. In each case, we first focus on the relevant clinical issues, how IBCT handles these issues, and then on any relevant research on IBCT with the group in question.

GENDER AND POWER IN IBCT:
INTERACTIONAL EGALITARIANISM

Majorities of both American men and women say they prefer egalitarian marriages over traditional marriages and believe that egalitarian marriages are more satisfying (Rampell, 2014). Yet women continue to do more of the housework and child care even when both partners are employed (Bianchi, Sayer, Milkie, & Robinson, 2012). Should couple therapy in general and IBCT in particular then support egalitarian marriages and help couples achieve the marriages that they say they want?

Yes, IBCT should help couples achieve the marriages that they want. If they want an egalitarian marriage, IBCT should help them achieve that, however they define it. If couples want a traditional marriage, whether out of preference or because of religious or cultural traditions, IBCT should help them achieve that. However, the issue that often confronts couple therapy is when partners disagree about the kind of relationship they want and, in particular, when they disagree about the division of labor in their relationship. In dealing with a dispute such as this, should IBCT come down on the side of the partner wanting a more egalitarian arrangement?

The simple answer is no. In IBCT, we do not normally take positions on the substantive issues that couples disagree about, whether it be about how they manage money or how they divide up the labor. Sometimes we can provide relevant research on the substantive issues about which they disagree. For example, if partners disagree about the use of corporal punishment with their child, we can inform them of the research about the impact of corporal punishment. However, most of the issues on which couples disagree don't have a convincing body of research that would be relevant to them.

Our goal is to help couples discuss their disagreements in a more constructive way than they usually do and thus resolve or reduce the disagreement between them, or at least reduce the tension around that disagreement. In our work with couples, particularly in the way we deal with each partner, it is important that we achieve a kind of interactional egalitarianism by treating each partner equally—whether or not the couple is pursuing an egalitarian relationship. For some couples, the experience of having each partner's perspective valued equally can be empowering in itself.

This notion of interactional egalitarianism seems so simple and straightforward that few if any couple therapists would disagree with it. However, its implementation can be complicated. One partner may set the agenda for therapy and the therapist may inadvertently follow that agenda rather than check with the other person. For example, if a husband announces in the first session "We are here to talk about our sexual relationship," we want to hear what his concerns are, but we would not want to assume that that is why his wife is here. When we turn to her, we would want to make it easy for her to bring up her own agenda so we might say something like "Spouses often come to therapy with different agendas. I wonder what the concerns are that brought you into couple therapy?" Another way that one partner's concerns may dominate discussion is when one partner speaks more assertively or confidently or articulately than the other. Therapists might naturally go in the direction of the concerns of that partner. However, we would want to take the time to expose the concerns of the other, less confident, less assertive, or less articulate partner to be sure we know what her or his concerns are.

A second way we promote interaction egalitarianism is by validating both partners' concerns. We not only want to hear those concerns but we want to validate them. This notion is particularly important in that partners often attempt to minimize, dismiss, or otherwise invalidate the other's concerns. Married women in distressed relationships tend to be unhappier than married men (Jackson, Miller, Oka, & Henry, 2014), and the women usually take the first steps toward seeking couple therapy (Doss, Atkins, & Christensen, 2003). It is not uncommon that women bring their husbands into couple therapy and have a specific agenda for therapy. In contrast, the husband may often communicate that there aren't any problems in the relationship other than his wife's unhappiness. He may also communicate implicitly that his wife's concerns are overreactions to ordinary couple problems and that the real issue is her excessive, negative emotionality about his otherwise normal husband behavior. In this case, we want to avoid colluding with the husband in his dismissal of his wife's reactions, but we don't challenge him directly, for two reasons. First, we don't want to engage in an argument with him or them about the validity of his wife's concern, and second, there probably is some truth in his view about her overreaction. In almost every couple conflict of any duration, there is both a realistic issue and some overreaction or learned sensitivity because they have failed to resolve this issue repeatedly. Instead of challenging his view of her concerns, we refocus his comments on his reactions and concerns. For example, it often is the case that her dissatisfaction is very uncomfortable for him because it communicates to him that he is failing at his role as a good husband. He usually wants to make her happy and often does not completely understand why he so often fails in that. We want to explore his reaction to her reaction and validate that rather than collude with either in dismissing the other's reactions.

In exploring the basis for his wife's dissatisfaction in this example, we want to be open to the very likely possibility that her gendered role in the marriage is in part responsible for her greater distress. As we noted above, women tend to do more housework and child care than their husbands, even when both partners work outside the home (Bianchi et al., 2012). Women also tend to take greater responsibility for managing family life and nurturing family members (Knudson-Martin, 2008). This greater responsibility may be a source for her distress. However, we don't want to jump into a reorganization of family responsibilities; the issues are often more complicated than simply "He needs to do more and then she will be happier." She is sometimes reluctant to give up her role, even if it is stressful, and doesn't trust that he would do the job as well as she does or do it to her liking. He might be willing to do more but not under her supervision. Sometimes what she wants is more appreciation and respect from him for what she does and a greater willingness to help. Sometimes he wants more positive feedback about what he does do but she is resistant to that; after all, she doesn't expect compliments for all she does. This issue, as with most issues in couples, is complicated; simple solutions, such as him doing more of X, may not resolve the problem. However, sometimes simple solutions like him doing more of X are a fundamental part of the resolution. The art of IBCT is facilitating change so that he does more of X willingly and positively instead of begrudgingly because he feels coerced by her and by the therapist.

Third, we treat each partner as being equally worthwhile and usually morally equivalent. Partners often frame their conflicts in moral terms: what one partner wants is what is worthwhile or right while what the other wants is somehow less worthwhile or wrong or at least less right. They may provide evidence in terms of what they think most other couples do or most husbands or most wives do. Partners may solicit our support for the righteousness of their cause directly or indirectly, such as by asking "Don't you think that. . . ." We normally attempt to even the moral plane by framing their conflicts in terms of different preferences, both equally acceptable, and not by privileging one partner's preferences. If a couple's struggles devolve into a conflict between good and evil, it will be more difficult to resolve than one between different preferences. However, sometimes one partner has done something that violates both of their code of values, such as by having an affair. In this case, we don't want to act as if that is not a violation but we don't want to communicate that the act deprives the perpetrator of any moral value or makes the other forever the moral superior. We will deal with this complicated issue in Chapter 13 when we discuss affairs.

Particularly relevant to the issue of moral equality are the issues of fairness and debts. Often one partner will argue that they have sacrificed more for the relationship than the other partner has and thus are owed by the partner. The sacrificing partner may have a compelling case, such as a partner who supported the other through advanced training or education or who stayed home with the kids while the other advanced in his or her career. Yet the nonsacrificing partner also has an opinion and point of view that is important to hear. We do not weigh in on the issue no matter how compelling the case. We know that joining with the sacrificing partner to pressure a resistant partner to pay his overdue debts is not likely to lead to much satisfaction by either. Instead, we try to facilitate a constructive discussion of the issue, using the strategies we have detailed in earlier chapters. For example, the couple's previous decisions were not made in a vacuum and rarely were they made unilaterally. Often both endorsed their decisions at some level, such as a decision for one partner to work while the other got advanced training. We try to move the couple away from what is often their separate, accusatory views of the other—that the benefitting partner is selfish and got more than their share, and that the sacrificing partner is complaining unfairly about a decision they fully cooperated with. In a constructive discussion without accusation and defensiveness, the beneficiary may be more inclined to show the sacrificing partner appreciation for what was done and accommodation and support for what the sacrificing partner wants to do now.

Fourth, we treat each partner's views and opinions as equally important, even if one partner has a legitimate claim to greater expertise or competence. One partner may be more educated or come from a higher social class and thus assume that their preferences and tastes are more sophisticated and should have more weight. One partner may have attended more relevant classes or consulted with more experts on child development, parenting, interpersonal communication, or marriage and thus may want a greater say in decisions about matters relevant to that expertise. We don't directly challenge the expertise but communicate that both partners' opinions are valuable and often add that for most issues, the science is not so compelling as to preclude all other opinions, including the partner's opinion. Thus, we try to help them make joint decisions even if one partner has claim to greater experience, sophistication, or expertise.

Fifth, we treat each partner as equally important and thus deserving of equal respect, courteousness, and responsiveness. This may seem obvious, but it is easy to be more responsive to one than the other. For example, if one partner has more status or prestige than the other or makes more money than the other and thus is the one who pays our bills, we may unconsciously treat that partner as more important. For example, if the husband is a judge or lawyer or successful businessman and speaks with authority, we may be more responsive to him, allowing him to interrupt his partner or talk over her. We may be more persuaded by his arguments. If he is busy as well as important, we may defer to his schedule, asking him if a particular time works without checking with his wife or doing only a perfunctory check with her. There are many ways in which we can inadvertently communicate that one is more important than the other. We must always try to treat the two members of the couple equally.

Consider an IBCT case in which the husband was a powerful attorney. Although his wife was also an attorney, she was not a litigator and was in a lower status and much lower paid position. The husband had a big, domineering personality, a characteristic that often worked well for him in business but not so well in his personal relationships; his wife alternated between intimidated accommodation and passive resistance to him. The husband also took a challenging, argumentative, critical approach toward therapy and the therapist. Here the challenge was not to treat the husband better than the wife; the challenge was to avoid countering the husband's argumentativeness and joining in a mutual defense pact with the wife. However, the husband's aggressive behavior, although well-honed in his business, was also a defense. He struggled with considerable anxiety, realized that his colleagues and staff did not like him, and was extremely sensitive to his wife's reactions toward him. It was not easy to create a space where he could expose some of his vulnerabilities. Had the therapist taken the response that others often took with him, meeting his aggressive argument in kind or joining with others against him, that space would not have been created.

Finally, we are concerned about the psychological health of both partners equally and attuned to the likelihood that the psychological health of one or both may be directly related to the state of the relationship. One partner's depression or anxiety may be strongly related to issues in the marriage. That does not mean, of course, that the partner is responsible or to blame for the depression or anxiety. However, changes in the relationship can positively affect the psychological state of both partners. In Chapter 13, we will consider the issue of psychopathology in one partner, particularly depression, and how relationship intervention can positively affect that.

Why do we so insist in IBCT on interactional equality? The reasons are partly ethical and partly strategic. Ethically, we believe all people have fundamentally equal value even though they differ in their status, their income, and their prestige. As such they deserve equal treatment. However, strategically, we believe that partners often get into struggles over who is more important, who is more knowledgeable or competent, who is more morally right, whose reactions are more appropriate, or whose positions are more reasonable. By taking a position of interactional equality, we try to undermine those struggles.

However, there are some important caveats here. If the couple is not in conflict about who is more competent or knowledgeable, then we normally don't challenge that. If the less expert partner is happy to defer to the other's opinion on the relevant matter and doesn't resist the role of uninformed or less informed assistant, then we would not interfere with their roles in this. The exception might be if both were cooperating in a way to silence the less expert partner, who really does have a different view but doesn't feel entitled to express it. Similarly, if both partners agree that one partner tends to overreact, we would not challenge that, assuming that there is a reality basis for that view. The exception would be if both were cooperating in a way to dismiss the more reactive partner's reactions entirely. It is common that the reactive partner does have strong reactions but also that those reactions have validity. Finally, if both partners believe that one engaged in an immoral act, we would not counter that, assuming that that view has a basis in reality. The exception would be if both were cooperating in a way to dismiss the feelings or views of that partner who did the immoral act. Even if someone did something wrong, they are entitled to opinions and feelings. They don't give up their voice simply because of an error or moral failing.

The existing research data suggests that men and women respond equally well to IBCT. The major clinical trial of IBCT saw little difference between the response of men and women (Christensen et al., 2004; Christensen et al., 2010). In a nationally representative clinical trial of the online program that is an adaptation of IBCT (to be discussed in Chapter 14), women tended to report greater reductions in negative relationship qualities than did men (Doss et al., 2016); in that same sample, men were more likely to deteriorate in relationship satisfaction than women (Doss, Roddy, Nowlan, Rothman, & Christensen, 2019). However, results with a larger sample of low-income couples did not reveal any gender differences (Doss et al., 2020). Encouragingly, there is no evidence that the online program benefits women less than men. These data certainly indicate that IBCT and its emphasis on interactional equality have benefits for both and that the benefits for one don't come at the expense of the historically less powerful partner, the woman.

IBCT WITH SAME-SEX COUPLES

Same-sex couples consist of either two males or two females who self-identify as gay or lesbian, as bisexual, or as pansexual. We should not assume that two males in a romantic relationship are necessarily both gay or that two females in a romantic relationship are necessarily both lesbian.

All couples, whether they are different-sex or same-sex, face common issues around communication, intimacy, division of labor, and the like. Research has shown considerable similarity between same-sex and different-sex couples, such as similar scores on standardized measures of love, satisfaction, and relationship adjustment (Peplau & Fingerhut, 2007). Kurdek (2005, p. 253) summarized this point as follows: "despite external differences in how gay, lesbian and heterosexual couples are constituted, the relationships of gay and lesbian partners appear to work in much the same way as the relationships of heterosexual partners." Therefore, in IBCT we approach the problems of same-sex couples in much the same way as we approach the problems of different-sex couples. We endorse the point made by Green and Mitchell

(2008, p. 663) that it is important for therapists to "remain open to the possibility that a given same-sex couple's problems have little or nothing to do with the partners being lesbian or gay." We certainly don't want to assume that the problems of a same-sex couple are just because they are gay, lesbian, or bisexual (Shelton & Delgado-Romero, 2013).

However, there are special issues that affect same-sex couples that we should take into consideration in our work with them and that may well affect their functioning: stigma and discrimination that they may experience for being a same-sex couple, sexual norms and boundaries that may be different from different-sex couples, gender-linked roles considering both are the same gender, and the challenge of having children. We will discuss each of these in turn.

Public acceptability of same-sex relationships has increased dramatically over the last 50 years. A clear marker of that change was the decision in 2015 by the United States Supreme Court to legalize same-sex marriage. Despite this clear progress, some religious groups consider same-sex unions morally wrong. Others object, not so much from religious or moral convictions, but from a sense that those unions are unnatural or deviant or perverted in some way. Thus, partners in a same-sex relationship may experience a variety of negative reactions from others, ranging from whispers, insinuations, and social rejection to bullying and physical assault. If they travel to certain other countries, their relationship will be considered criminal. In this country, much of the discrimination that same-sex couples experience "is presumptive and exclusionary rather than overly aggressive, and it contributes to a feeling of marginality and invisibility" (Green & Mitchell, 2008, p. 665). Even if partners don't experience overt discrimination from families and friends, the support they do get is often limited or absent, and same-sex couples often fail to reap one of the primary benefits of marriage: acceptance as a couple within one's social, work, and familial community.

It is always important for us as IBCT therapists to be accepting and supportive of the customs and behaviors of couples who come for therapy unless they are damaging or destructive, such as engaging in heavy alcohol or drug use or harsh physical punishment of children. It is especially important, given the stigma that is often attached to same-sex couples, that we be affirmative of their relationship—that we view their relationship as legitimate, as important, and as valuable as any different-sex romantic relationship. If we have a hard time accepting same-sex unions and find, for example, the sexual practices of a gay couple disgusting or detestable, we will likely implicitly communicate that in the way we treat or respond to the couple. Those implicit actions, however minimal, may impair our ability to be good therapists. We agree with Green and Mitchell (2008, p. 675) that "the single most important prerequisite for helping same-sex couples is the therapist's personal comfort with love and sexuality between two women or two men." Thus, we would recommend that any therapist who cannot honestly be affirmative of same-sex unions refer those couples to therapists who can.

Even if we feel we can treat same-sex couples with the same value and respect we give to different-sex couples, it is important to avoid heterosexist bias. If a woman calls us about couple therapy, it is important that we not assume she is calling for herself and her husband. Similarly, if a man calls, we should not assume he wants treatment for him and his female partner. If a male partner in a different-sex relationship has had an affair, we should not assume that that affair was with another woman. Our questionnaires should be neutral about the sexual composition of the couple. Instead of having a heading on a demographic questionnaire be "husband" and "wife" or "man" and "woman," we could have the heading be "Partner A" and "Partner B." In these subtle and not-so-subtle ways, we can communicate that we don't have a heterosexist bias.

In working with same-sex couples and addressing the issue of bias against them, we first focus on assessment, paying special attention to the second E in the DEEP analysis, namely the external stressors that affect the partners individually and as a couple. We focus not only on the common stressors of work and money but also on minority stress that may come from bias and discrimination by family, friends, and workplace colleagues, or simply from the limited support that comes from those sources. Even news reports of discrimination or violence against gays and lesbians can be stressful for same-sex couples, reminding them of their limited acceptability in the world. We find out whether partners have experienced different levels of support or bias from their social networks.

In assessing the first E in the DEEP analysis, we are attentive to the possibility of internalized homophobia, in which one or both partners have reacted to the bias in the world around them by questioning themselves and blaming themselves for their struggles. In our feedback session with a same-sex couple, we would go over the DEEP analysis and offer our conceptualization of their situation, namely that they are experiencing real stressful circumstances in a heterosexist world. During the active phase of therapy, we would use the usual strategies of empathic joining and unified detachment to deal with their stressors and the way they handle them. Out of these discussions or from a focus on deliberate change, the couple might decide to cultivate a more supportive social network to help ease that stress.

A related interpersonal issue that comes up for same-sex couples concerns how out to be—a common "D" or difference in the DEEP understanding. One partner may be much more comfortable displaying their status as a same-sex couple at work, on social media, or in public than the other. For example, one may want to engage in open displays of physical affection in public, such as holding hands or kissing while the other is uncomfortable about that. Again, we would use our strategies of empathic joining, unified detachment, tolerance building, and deliberate change to address these issues. In Chapter 7, we discussed a video available through the American Psychological Association in which an IBCT therapist, Christopher Martell, works with a male same-sex couple dealing with this issue. Martell uses unified detachment to help them see that they are working as a team to fight bias and discrimination, albeit in very different ways. They had not realized it before and the realization eased the tension that they felt.

Another issue that confronts therapists dealing with same-sex couples is sexuality and sexual boundaries. Most heterosexual couples endorse the norm of monogamy. Partners may violate that norm by having an affair, a topic we will discuss in the next chapter, but they generally endorse the norm. However, nonmonogamy is much more likely to be present with same-sex couples—especially among men (Haupert, Gesselman, Moors, Fisher, & Garcia, 2017). In working with same-sex couples, we should not assume that they endorse monogamy as a norm or the ideal. A comparison of men in same-sex monogamous relationships with those in same-sex nonmonogamous relationships found no difference between the groups on various indicators of relationship health (Whitton, Weitbrecht, & Kuryluk, 2015). However, what we should be aware of is that partners may have different understandings of their sexual boundaries, ambiguity in their definitions of those boundaries, and inconsistent adherence to those boundaries, all of which can create problems for them (Green & Mitchell, 2008). Therefore, for some couples, IBCT would involve discussion of the sexual boundaries that the couple desires and clarification of those boundaries. We should also note that sexual nonmonogamy may be much more than a simple preference for some couples or for some individuals. The choice may serve functions that both reflect and affect the relationship, such as when one wants many sexual partners to confirm his attractiveness or because he fears that the current relationship may end anytime. As with other relationship domains, we try to create a safe, nonjudgmental place where partners can explore what they want and how they feel about it through empathic joining and unified detachment. As a result of those discussions, they may decide to redefine the sexual boundaries they have or to more affirmatively endorse their existing ones (Martell & Prince, 2005).

The fact that same-sex couples are both male or both female can be both a blessing and a curse. On the positive side, same-sex relationships can free partners from the rigidity of gender roles. Stereotypes of same-sex couples suggest that same-sex partners take on feminine and masculine roles, with one being more the "husband" and the other more the "wife." While this may be true for some couples, most contemporary same-sex couples don't divide up roles and tasks in that way (Peplau & Fingerhut, 2007). In fact, the research indicates that same-sex couples work out the division of labor in the relationship in a more egalitarian way than do different-sex couples (Peplau & Fingerhut, 2007).

On the negative side, a same-sex relationship can mean that both partners adhere to the same gender-linked role. Two women can both accommodate or try to please the other too much, neglecting their own needs, or both can be reluctant to initiate sex. Two men can compete over leadership in their sexual relationship or in career success or have difficulty being nurturing. Also, same-sex partners do not have gender roles to guide them in their formation of their relationship, such as the division of labor or roles in the relationship. They may have to go through a period of experimentation to determine who does what (Green & Mitchell, 2008).

Like their different-sex counterparts, same-sex couples often want to have children. A recent estimate indicates that 114,000 same-sex couples in the United States had children, consisting of about equal numbers of male couples and female couples. Same-sex couples are more likely to have adopted children or had foster children than different-sex couples but an estimated 68% have biological children (S. K. Goldberg & Conron, 2018). Obviously, the process is more complicated for same-sex couples than for different-sex couples. To have a biological child, female couples must obtain a sperm donor; male couples must obtain a surrogate. Before doing so, they must decide on who of the two will be the biological parent. Even adoption and foster parenting is more complicated for same-sex couples because of the stigma against parenting by them. Some states and adoption agencies refuse to work with same-sex couples. Same-sex couples may thus seek couple therapy to decide on whether to have children, to decide on whether to have a biological, adopted, or foster child, or to help them through the process of adoption or foster parenting. The usual strategies of IBCT can assist them with these difficult issues.

We believe that IBCT can work as well with same-sex couples as with different-sex couples. At present, we only have anecdotal data to support that contention with regard to traditional face-to-face therapy. However, results indicate that the online adaptation of IBCT, discussed in Chapter 14, is equally effective for same-sex and different-sex couples (Hatch et al., in press).

IBCT WITH OTHER DIVERSE COUPLES

The most common married couple in the United States consists of a white male and white female. Because of the growth of Hispanic and Asian populations in the United States, the percentage of newlyweds who are both Hispanic or both Asian has increased dramatically from 1980 to 2015 while the percentage of newlyweds who are both white have decreased (https://www .pewsocialtrends.org/2017/05/18/1-trends-and-patterns-in-intermarriage/).

However, the rate of intermarriage has also increased dramatically; in 2015 one in six newlyweds were married to someone of a different race or ethnicity (https://www.pewresearch.org/fact-tank/2019/02/13/8-facts-about-love-and -marriage/). Also, the rate of religious intermarriage has increased dramatically so that 39% of marriages since 2010 have been between partners with different religious faiths (https://www.pewresearch.org/fact-tank/2015/06 /02/interfaith-marriage/). Therefore, as couple therapists we are increasingly likely to work with couples from a different ethnic, cultural, racial, or religious background than us. We are also increasingly likely to work with couples consisting of partners of different ethnicities, cultures, races or religious backgrounds. What kinds of adaptations or accommodations should we make to work with these increasingly diverse couples?

Ideally, we would have some familiarity with the racial, ethnic, cultural, and religious background of our clients so we don't make inappropriate assumptions about them or engage in behavior that is potentially offensive to them. For example, in working with couples from cultural backgrounds that emphasize close family ties, we would not want to assume that those ties necessarily represent unhealthy enmeshment. We would not want to offer to shake the hand of a different-sex member of an orthodox Jewish couple, because cross-sex physical contact is forbidden to all but people married to each other. If we have little or no familiarity with the background of couples who seek help from us, we can of course refer them to a couple therapist who is from that background or has greater familiarity with it than we do. However, often that is not possible. We can read about the culture of people from particular backgrounds. For example, there are excellent books that discuss couple therapy with people from various ethnic, racial, and religious backgrounds (e.g., Kelly, 2017). If a white therapist works in an area where there are lots of African American couples or lots of Mexican American couples, getting familiar with the traditions of that group makes sense. However, these writings on the traditions of particular groups pose a danger of stereotyping. There is considerable variability in the practices of any group; many couples who come from a particular background have been strongly influenced by mainstream American culture and therefore have a unique mix of practices. Also, for therapists who work in large, diverse urban areas, a goal of becoming knowledgeable about all the relevant traditions of the couples who might come for couple therapy is unreasonable. Therefore, it is a good strategy to always assume as little as possible about couples we see and be open to learning from them their own, often unique, traditions and practices.

To guide us in our work with diverse couples, it is helpful to consider the dimensions on which the couples we see may differ from us and the couples we typically see. These are also the dimensions on which couples consisting of partners from different races, different ethnicities, different cultures, and different religions (i.e., mixed couples) may differ. Hofstede's cultural dimensions theory (Hofstede, 1980, 2011; Hofstede & Minkov, 2010) is an influential, empirically based theory based on values surveys done throughout the world. In its current form, Hofstede proposes six important cultural dimensions that differentiate cultures across the world. Although this theory is not without its criticisms (e.g., McSweeney, 2002) and it defense (e.g., Hofstede, 2002), it can serve as our guide to possible cultural dimensions on which couples and partners in mixed couples may differ from each other. We will discuss each of the six dimensions in terms of its meaning for family relations and for couple therapy. Specifically, we will discuss how these dimensions suggest the kinds of struggles that couples may have and the kinds of sensitivities that may underlie them.

The first dimension is power distance, which indicates that cultures differ in the extent and acceptability of the social hierarchy. In high power distance cultures, unequal power and authority is accepted as a given whereas in low power distance cultures authority is questioned and must be earned, such as through education or expertise. In high power distance cultures, parents have strong authority over their children and teach their children obedience, while in low power distance cultures, parents are more likely to treat children more as equals. Similarly, in high power distance cultures, elders garner more respect and fear than in low power distance cultures. A couple from a high power distance culture is liable to see the therapist as an expert and expect him or her to tell them the right way to behave. A couple from a low power distance culture is more likely to question the therapist and view his or her advice with skepticism. A couple consisting of partners from cultures very different in power distance may disagree about the importance of following the counsel of authority figures in their life, such as religious leaders, physicians, or therapists.

A second dimension is individualism versus collectivism. In individualistic cultures, the emphasis is on "I"—people are expected to take care of themselves and their immediate family, personal expression and achievement are rewarded, and ties with others besides the immediate family are loose. In collectivistic cultures, the emphasis is on "we"—people belong to extended family groups and owe a loyalty to that group, the success and harmony of the group is valued over individual achievement, and ties with others are close. A couple from an individualistic culture may experience more isolation than a couple from a collectivist culture experiences, but the latter may experience more social pressure from their group and more shame if they violate some norm of the group. In a couple consisting of partners from cultures different in individualism or collectivism, the partner from the individualistic culture may not understand or may disparage the feelings of family obligation that the other feels. For example, in our clinical trial of couple therapy, a Chinese husband felt he needed to bring his mother to America and have her live with him and his wife once his father had passed away. His wife, although Chinese, was more acculturated and Western in her outlook, and could not fathom the possibility of her mother-in-law living in their own home.

A third dimension is uncertainty-avoidance, which refers to tolerance for ambiguity. In strong uncertainty-avoidance societies, there is an emphasis on clarity, structure, rules, and the absolute truth. In low uncertainty-avoidance societies, there is greater tolerance for ambiguity, deviance, and even a certain amount of chaos. There is an emphasis on the relativism of truth and a dislike of rules. A couple from a high uncertainty-avoidance culture may seek structure and rules from the therapist about how to have a good relationship while a couple from a low uncertainty-avoidance culture may resist such rules. A couple consisting of partners from cultures different in uncertainty-avoidance may disagree about the importance of rules and how strictly they should be enforced. One may seek greater structure and clarity and definitiveness in the relationship while the other feels constrained by that.

A fourth dimension is masculinity-femininity, defined at the societal rather than the individual level. In Hofstede's view, a masculine society emphasizes maximum differentiation between male and female social roles while a feminine society deemphasizes such role differentiation. A masculine society emphasizes assertiveness, achievement, and material success while a feminine society emphasizes cooperation, caring for others, and quality of life. A couple from a masculine culture may seek help with their struggles over family tasks so they can perform them more efficiently and successfully while a couple from a feminine culture may seek help to restore passion and meaning into their relationship. Partners from cultures different in masculinity-femininity may differ on what they want from life and their relationship, with one valuing work success over relationships and the other valuing relationships over work success.

A fifth dimension on which cultures differ is long-term orientation versus short-term orientation. Long-term orientation cultures emphasize the future: the best things are yet to happen; perseverance and thrift are emphasized. In contrast, short-term orientation cultures emphasize the past and present: consumption and spending are valued. Couples from cultures with a long-term orientation may be anxious about the future and want to engage in appropriate planning and saving to ensure a good future. Couples from short-term orientation cultures may value traditions and emphasize enjoyment of the present. Partners from cultures different in short-term versus long-term orientation may disagree about how much to save for the future versus how much to enjoy life now.

A sixth and final dimension on which cultures differ is indulgence versus restraint. Cultures high on restraint emphasize strict adherence to social norms, emphasize order in the society, deemphasize leisure, and have stricter norms around sexual behavior while cultures high on indulgence emphasize individual freedom, leisure, and pleasure; have loser adherence to social norms; and have more lenient norms around sex. Couples from cultures high in restraint may struggle with the demands of social norms, particularly if one or both have difficulty behaving consistently with those norms. Couples from cultures high in indulgence may struggle over whose freedom and whose desires should dominate when those desires differ. Partners from cultures different in restraint versus indulgence may struggle over how closely to follow existing norms.

Implications for IBCT

These six dimensions alert us to possible areas where couples may struggle, because they differ on these important dimensions, or because they have difficulty following the dictates of the culture, or because being raised in a culture emphasizing a particular dimension may lead to certain vulnerabilities. Thus, these dimensions alert us to possible differences and emotional sensitivities in our DEEP analysis. In addition, if a couple is from a culture quite different from the culture in which they currently live, they may also experience external stress as a result. For example, a woman in a Muslim couple may experience social rejection because she wears a hijab; an orthodox Jew may experience rejection because he wears a yarmulke. A mixed-race couple of a black man and a white woman may experience some rejection from both whites and blacks. Thus, cultural differences can add to the external stress component of the DEEP analysis.

One key factor that is often similar across many couples from minority races, ethnicities, cultures, and religions is social class and low household incomes. Black couples have significantly lower household incomes than white couples do. Immigrant couples generally have lower household incomes than couples who have been in America for generations. In addition to whatever social rejection they experience for their particular cultural practices, people from minority cultures often have the heavy burden of financial stress. They may have conflicts about how to spend the little money that they have. They may have little time together for relaxation because they are working more than one job. Thus, a key factor in the DEEP analysis is the external stress that these couples experience.

We have seen throughout this book how the DEEP analysis can incorporate important features in couples that are key to understanding their distress. Now we have shown how the *differences, emotional sensitivities,* and *external stress* components of the DEEP analysis can also incorporate those features of couples from different races, cultures, ethnicities, and religions. We have not focused much on the *patterns* component of the DEEP analysis because we believe that patterns of interaction, because they are ways that couples use to solve the common problems of intimacy posed by differences, emotional sensitivities, and external stressors, have considerable cross-cultural consistency. Certainly, the limited evidence we have is consistent with that notion (Christensen et al., 2006). Even when a particular culture is quite different from the American culture, a familiar pattern is apparent, though in somewhat modified form (Rehman & Holtzworth-Munroe, 2006). Therefore we believe the conceptual framework of the DEEP analysis can be used with diverse couples.

What about treatment strategies in IBCT? Should they be modified to accommodate diverse couples? We believe that the strategies of empathic joining, unified detachment, and direct change can be used across diverse couples. Also, the approach of interactional egalitarianism can be especially important in working with couples from diverse cultures, particularly from patriarchal cultures. In those cases, we respect the hierarchy that the couple endorses, such as the view that the man is the head of the household. We may give him appropriate respect, such as by soliciting his views first. However, we ensure that we give full attention to his wife's views. If he tends to dismiss those views as unimportant, we might try to promote aspects of their cultural beliefs that would counter that tendency. For example, we might discuss how strong men and powerful leaders are able to listen the views of those they care about and love.

Sometimes IBCT strategies must be modified in small and large ways to accommodate diverse couples. A small way in which the strategies might be modified is when the therapist takes a more active role in fostering change than normal because both partners in the couple come from a culture in which they see the therapist as the expert who will teach them the right way to get along. It doesn't mean that we abandon empathic joining or unified detachment. However, we may be more explicit about the rationale of our acceptance interventions and more didactic in our delivery. If consistent with the couple's desires, we may also engage in teaching the couple communication and problem-solving skills earlier in the course of treatment and see if that is beneficial for them. A large way in which treatment strategies may be modified is when the therapist sees that external stressors are playing a major role in a couple's difficulties and engages in concrete practical steps to ameliorate that situation. We give a rather dramatic example of that below.

Ray and Myrna were an African American couple from an inner city area that had come under the control of gangs and drug dealers. They sought couple therapy because they were in conflict over whether or not their son Matthew should go to the police: a local gang had taken a contract out on his life. Myrna was terrified that her son would end up dead if the family didn't handle this without involving the police, while Ray felt equally strongly that Matthew's only chance, "slim instead of none," as he put it, was to involve the police. Although there were themes with this couple as there are with all couples, and it would have been possible to do IBCT as it is typically done, under the circumstances it seemed inappropriate for the therapist to conduct couple therapy as usual.

As enthusiastic as we are about IBCT, we recognize that not all problems are best solved by psychotherapy. The therapist has several options in a situation like this. One of them is to conduct couple therapy as if the primary problem were between the partners. He or she could focus on the theme of conventionality versus nonconformity that characterized many of the conflicts faced by the couple. Myrna tended to be mistrustful of the dominant power structure and felt that they were better off expecting nothing from it and operating according to the rules of the streets. Ray recognized that neither state nor federal institutions were likely to be helpful; nevertheless, he had licked a drug habit that he had picked up as a teenager, he had a job, and he still believed that social conformity with the dominant culture was the better alternative. One could construct a DEEP analysis to capture the differences between them, the fears each had, the very real social stressors they faced, and the pattern of interaction in which they often got stuck. One could try to help them discuss the issue in a more constructive way through empathic joining and unified detachment. Or one could take a more directive stance and try to guide them through the immediate crisis, brainstorming with them possible solutions, evaluating those solutions, and then attempting to implement them. To work with them in this way without recognition of the existential threat they faced would be insensitive to say the least. Their son could be murdered. Under such circumstances, the normal response for a parent is to be terrified and marital conflict is natural. There was another option—for the therapist to recognize that the presenting problem here was far more than a couple conflict and to seek consultation and support.

Myrna's position about the police was not based on psychopathology around authority issues. She had good, reality-based reasons to be skeptical about the police being willing and able to save their son's life. Knowing when to seek consultation is a clinical skill in and of itself. In this case, the consultation had to come from someone who knew the culture of the inner city and understood the interrelationships among community institutions and between those institutions and the larger culture. A common mistake made by therapists in these situations is to make assumptions based on their own experience as privileged professionals and to give advice based on what they would do if the lives of their own children were in danger. If therapists are not knowledgeable about the dire situation in which their clients are in, they need to know where to go in order to get such consultation.

In the case of Myrna and Ray, the therapist brought in a community leader (a paraprofessional with no advanced degree) who took over, with the therapist continuing to follow up and provide continuity of care. The African American community activist negotiated the interested parties through the crisis, and the police were never involved. Once the parents and the son felt safe, other factors in the environment required attention. There was a teenage pregnancy to deal with: their daughter needed to decide whether to have an abortion, but she would not talk to the parents about it. If she was going to carry the child, she needed housing, welfare, and prenatal care. The therapist was able to bring the teenager into the office, help her with decision making, and mobilize the family to deal with the practical issues at hand. When these crises were dealt with, communication between partners improved and the couple, grateful to the therapist for help, decided to discontinue therapy. This is clearly not the typical couple therapy case, but it illustrates the adaptability of therapy when external forces have a powerful and dangerous impact on the couple and the family.

The existing data on IBCT suggest it is effective for diverse couples. In a study by Jean Yi (2007), the results from ethnic minority couples were compared with the results from white, non-Hispanic couples from the clinical trial of IBCT versus TBCT. Over 5 years of follow-up data, results from the two groups were comparable with the possible exception of African American women, who tended to perform more poorly. Also, the nationwide clinical trial of the online program adapted from IBCT, the OurRelationship program, performed similarly in minority couples as in white couples and in low-income couples as in middle-income and upper income couples. However, Hispanic and low-income couples were less likely to complete the program (Georgia Salivar, Roddy, Nowlan, & Doss, 2018).

SUMMARY

In this chapter, we have described how IBCT flexibly addresses the various needs of diverse couples. We first reviewed how IBCT handles gender and power issues. Although we do not normally take a position on the substantive issues on which couples disagree, even when differential power is related to those issues, such as with disputes about the division of labor in the house, we do promote what we call interactional equality. Our goals are a) to attend to both partners' concerns equally, b) validate those concerns equally, c) treat each partner as equally worthwhile and generally morally equivalent, d) view each partner's opinions as equally important, e) give each partner equal respect and courtesy, and f) show equal concern for both partners' psychological health, being open to the possibility that that health may be related to issues in the marriage. We gave illustrations of how we implement those goals, the occasional exceptions to those goals, and the frequent challenges to their implementation.

In working with same-sex couples, we first emphasized the similarity between same-sex and different-sex couples. The appearance in couple therapy of a same-sex couple may have little or nothing to do with their status as same-sex couples. However, it is extremely important that a therapist who works with these couples is comfortable with love and sexual intimacy between partners of the same sex and does not communicate heterosexist bias toward them. These couples do have certain special issues that may be a part of their relationship distress, such as the stigmas they may experience, differences in their comfort with being out, norms of nonmonogamy, allocation of roles in the relationship without the advantages and disadvantages of different sex-role stereotypes, and complications around having children. We discussed how some of these issues can contribute to the DEEP analysis with same-sex couples and how IBCT intervention strategies can address them.

We also addressed couples that differ racially, ethnically, culturally, religiously, and financially from the traditional white, middle-class couple of Christian heritage as well as the increasingly common intermarriage of partners who are different from each other in one or more of these ways. We noted that it is certainly helpful to have familiarity with the culture of the couples we see or to refer them to a therapist who does have this familiarity, but it is increasingly difficult for therapists who work in urban areas with a diverse population to either be familiar with the particular subculture or know a good therapist who is. Thus, we must often be open to learning from our clients about their traditions and customs. We reviewed six cultural dimensions from Hofstede's cultural dimensions theory (Hofstede, 1980; 2010, 2011) as a way to think about dimensions on which the couples we see may be different from us or how partners in an intermarriage may be different from each other: power distance, individualism versus collectivism, uncertainty-avoidance, masculinity-femininity, long-term versus short-term orientation, and indulgence versus restraint. We discussed how these dimensions might inform our DEEP analysis and affect our interventions in IBCT.

In each of these areas of diversity, we reviewed data showing the effectiveness of IBCT. IBCT and its online adaptation is similarity effective for men and women in different-sex relationships, is similarly effective across ethnic and racial groups, and is similarly effective for low-income couples and higher income couples. Additionally, the online adaptation of IBCT has been shown to be equally effective for couples in same-sex and different-sex relationships.

13

❈

Special Problems in Couple Therapy: Violence, Sexual Problems, Infidelity, and Psychopathology

ONE OF CHRISTENSEN'S STATISTICS instructors in graduate school once told the class that most good things in the world are positively correlated with each other and most bad things in the world are positively correlated with each other, at about a correlation of .30. He was obviously making an overgeneralization but capturing an important truth. With regard to couples, the negative quality of relationship dissatisfaction is associated with poorer mental and physical health in the partners, with sexual problems, with specific problematic acts such as infidelity, and with dangerous acts such as violence. In this chapter we will examine the particular issues of intimate partner violence, sexual problems, infidelity, and psychopathology. These issues appear in couple therapy frequently, raise special concerns, and require adaptations or alterations of typical IBCT.

INTIMATE PARTNER VIOLENCE (IPV) AND IBCT

The definition of intimate partner violence (IPV) always refers to physical acts of aggression such as slapping, kicking, and beating but often includes sexual violence such as the use of force or threats of violence to obtain sex. In addition, IPV can sometimes be defined to include psychological abuse, such as insults, humiliation, and intimidation (sometimes stalking is included in this category) and controlling behaviors, such as isolating the partner, monitoring the partner, and preventing their free movement. Sometimes psychological or emotional abuse and controlling behaviors are excluded because they are more difficult to define. For example, the WHO report on violence against women included only sexual and physical violence (Garcia-Moreno et al., 2013).

The prevalence of IPV is unfortunately high. The Centers for Disease Control's survey of a nationally representative sample of the U.S. population found the lifetime prevalence of severe IPV was 24% in women and 14% in men while 2.7% of women and 2.0% of men experienced severe IPV in the last 12 months (Breiding, Chen, & Black, 2014). Not surprisingly, there is a link between relationship dissatisfaction and IPV. A meta-analysis of 32 studies found significant negative associations with small-to-moderate effect sizes between relationship satisfaction and partner aggression. The associations were stronger for male than for female perpetrators and stronger for female than for male victims (Stith, Green, Smith, & Ward, 2008). Thus, distressed couples are more likely to have experienced IPV. A sample of distressed couples who were recruited for our clinical trial of IBCT were empirically classified into three categories of moderate-to-severe violence, low-level violence, and no violence; only 20% were in the no-violence category (Simpson, Doss, Wheeler, & Christensen, 2007).

The prevalence of sexual violence and stalking are also unfortunately high. Nearly 10% of women have been raped by their partner and 2.2% of men have been made to penetrate their partner in their lifetime. Additionally, almost 16% of women and 8% of men have experienced sexual violence other than rape by an intimate partner. The lifetime prevalence of stalking by an intimate partner "in which the victim felt very fearful or believed that they or someone close to them would be harmed or killed" was 10.7% for women and 2.1% for men (Breiding et al., p. 17). In most cases of sexual violence or stalking, physical violence is also present. For example, in examining those women who reported lifetime intimate partner rape, physical violence, and stalking, only 2.6% reported stalking only and only 4.4% reported rape only.

Psychological aggression is, not surprisingly, the most common intimate partner violence. In their category of psychological aggression, the CDC report includes both expressive aggression, which refers to verbal acts, such as insulting or humiliating the partner or calling the partner a name and coercive control, which includes diverse acts such as destroying something of importance, keeping the partner from having money, threatening to hurt the partner or self, and making decisions for the other. Over 48% of both men and women report a lifetime prevalence of at least one incident of psychological aggression with over 40% of women reporting both expressive aggression and coercive control and over 30% of men reporting expressive aggression and over 40% reporting coercive control. However, women report more of every kind of incident of coercive control except for the item "kept track of by demanding to know where you were and what you were doing," which men reported more frequently.

IPV clearly exists on a continuum, ranging from angry, harsh language directed at the other to violent assault that leads to injury and sometimes death. Along that continuum, Johnson and Ferraro (2000) distinguished situational couple conflict from battering, or what they labeled as "intimate terrorism." Situational couple conflict, the most common kind of intimate partner violence, is infrequent, less severe, and mutual, whereas battering or intimate terrorism is severe, frequent, and primarily unidirectional. Many couples with situational violence seek couple therapy; these partners are rarely violent outside the home or otherwise involved in criminal behavior. Couples with intimate terrorism are often involved in the criminal justice system and domestic violence shelters; the perpetrators (usually men) are often antisocial and have criminal behavior beyond IPV, such as violence outside the home. Existing data certainly support the heterogeneity of IPV—it comes in many forms and frequencies—but division into these two categories is overly simplistic. For example, there can be severe mutual violence between partners.

Even if violence is mutual between heterosexual partners, the impact is likely to be different. Women in heterosexual relationships are more likely to be injured in violent confrontations, more likely to be victims of sexual violence and severe coercive control, and more likely to be afraid of their partner (Rowe & Jouriles, 2019).

Appropriateness of IBCT for Couples with IPV

Because of the prevalence and danger of IPV, we believe that all couple therapists have an ethical obligation to assess for IPV. Therapists need to determine whether the couple can participate safely and appropriately in couple therapy. Couples can participate safely as long as the provocative discussions that often occur in couple therapy will not trigger a dangerous episode of IPV or that dangerous episodes of violence do not occur during the course of therapy, whether triggered by therapeutic discussions or not. Couples can participate appropriately in couple therapy as long as they feel free to express themselves without fear of physical reprisal. As we noted in Chapter 4, our general guidelines for determining if a couple can participate safely and appropriately are that (a) there has been no violence leading to injury in the last year and (b) there is no ongoing fear of physical reprisal.

As we discussed in Chapter 4, we assess for violence through both questionnaire and interview. Our Couple Questionnaire has the items below that we believe constitute the *minimal* questionnaire assessment that should be conducted, namely, items assessing any incidents of physical aggression in the last year by self or partner and any fear of physical reprisal for voicing one's views:

Many people, at one time or another, get physical with their partners when they are angry. For example, some people threaten to hurt their partners, some push or shove, and some slap or hit. Please indicate approximately how many times the behaviors in a, b, and c have occurred in the last year. Therapists will review your responses and discuss them with you as relevant.

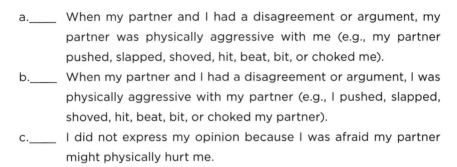

a.____ When my partner and I had a disagreement or argument, my partner was physically aggressive with me (e.g., my partner pushed, slapped, shoved, hit, beat, bit, or choked me).

b.____ When my partner and I had a disagreement or argument, I was physically aggressive with my partner (e.g., I pushed, slapped, shoved, hit, beat, bit, or choked my partner).

c.____ I did not express my opinion because I was afraid my partner might physically hurt me.

Our focus in these items is on physical violence since that can be literally life threatening. We ask about physical violence in the last year since recent incidents are most predictive of future incidents. We don't have questionnaire items about sexual coercion or stalking since they usually occur only in couples that also have physical violence. Also, we expect that these incidents will be revealed in the individual interview if they do occur. Similarly, we don't have questionnaire items about psychological aggression because we expect that they will come out in the individual or joint discussions. Also, couple therapy is normally not counterindicated just because psychological aggression is present. We do ask about physical intimidation because we want to be sure that partners are not afraid to voice their views or to describe incidents in their relationship, such as incidents of sexual coercion, stalking, or psychological aggression. Certainly one can do a more thorough questionnaire assessment, using measures such as the Conflict Tactics Scale (Straus et al., 1996) and depending on the population, one might choose to do that. However, for ordinary couple therapy, we think these few items are usually sufficient as initial screening items.

At the beginning of the individual interview, we always examine the Couple Questionnaire and ask about IPV. Even if partners mark zero on all three items above, we may say something like "So there are no incidents or issues with physical violence or fear of physical violence in the relationship?" just to confirm the absence of violence. If the client indicates any incident of physical violence, we follow up with detailed questions about the specific incidents of violence that occurred. We need to determine how serious the incidents were. In our efforts to evaluate seriousness, we ask them to describe the specific violent behaviors that occurred in the most serious incident of violence. Although any kind of violence should be unacceptable in relationships, there are many degrees of violence. We don't want to overreact to an incident of pushing or shoving or underreact to an incident of choking or beating. If there has been violence in the last year, we want to investigate if there has been a pattern of violence throughout the relationship. If there are children in the home, we want to enquire about their exposure to incidents of violence, which would make violence doubly concerning and potentially reportable to child protective services. We also follow up on the question about fear of physical reprisal. We need to know if partners will be hesitant to be open about their views or feelings during therapy out of fear of physical reprisal by the partner. In couples with a history of severe IPV, it is not uncommon to experience fear even if there has not been recent violence (as the perpetrator is able to use the threat of violence to maintain control). Finally, if there has been violence or if there is fear of physical reprisal, and we have followed up thoroughly, we may also ask if there are other incidents of concern to them. An open-ended question may elicit other concerning incidents such as incidents of sexual coercion, coercive control, or stalking.

There is a strong link between alcohol consumption and physical violence (Foran & O'Leary, 2008), with a stronger link between alcohol use and male-to-female violence than for alcohol use and female-to-male violence. This link for men is stronger in clinical samples and for more serious alcohol use (Foran & O'Leary, 2008). Thus, if there are reports of physical violence, we may ask about alcohol use and whether that use is associated with the violent episodes. Such information may help us make appropriate referrals or deal more effectively with the couple if we decide we can see them in therapy.

In our early clinical trials of IBCT and in the first edition of this book, we took a very conservative position on IPV, focusing only on male-to-female violence and erring on the side of excluding couples from treatment when they might have been able to participate safely. For example, in our clinical trial (Christensen et al., 2004), we excluded couples if they ever had had a serious incident of violence no matter how long ago, and we excluded couples if they had multiple incidents of minor violence without injury, such as pushing, shoving, or grabbing. Subsequent data from several sources have made us question this decision. First, we followed up couples who were excluded from our clinical trial due to IPV. Of the 97 couples excluded, 55 partners were assessed 2 years after exclusion from the study. Three quarters of these females were still married to and living with their partners; about a third had sought couple therapy in the community and that therapy was associated with improved relationship satisfaction. Thus, the couples we excluded largely stayed together, and some sought couple therapy and got some benefit from it, despite being told by us that couple therapy was inappropriate for them (DeBoer, Rowe, Frousakis, Dimidjian, & Christensen, 2012).

A second source was data that cast doubt on the underlying assumption that IPV was almost exclusively an issue of males being violent to their female partners. Research indicated that females and males often perpetrated equal frequencies of violence in heterosexual relationships (e.g., Dutton, 2012) although differences in severity and impact exist. Also, same-sex relationships, including lesbian relationships, evidenced violence at similar levels as different-sex relationships (Simpson & Jouriles, 2019). Given these data, it was important, at the very least, that we assess IPV from each partner to the other in different-sex and same-sex relationships.

A third source was data on the effectiveness of treatment for IPV. We were reluctant to promote couple therapy for couples with IPV, not only because therapy sessions could lead to strong emotional arousal that might precipitate violence, but also because a couple therapy approach might convey social acceptability for a violent relationship, might promote joint responsibility for the violence, and might not be effective in countering the violence. However, recent studies have shown that traditional couple therapy (Nowlan, Georgia, & Doss, 2017) as well as couple therapy oriented toward reducing violence can be effective in decreasing intimate partner violence (Rowe & Jouriles, 2019; Stith & McColllum, 2011; Zarling, Lawrence, & Marchman, 2015). These latter programs typically screen couples carefully to ensure that partners have not experienced significant injury, they do not fear physical retribution for voicing their views, and partners are willing to take responsibility for their own violence. Thus, they include some couples that we would have excluded from our clinical trial, such as a couple that had experienced minor injuries such as scrapes or bruises, as long as partners were willing to take responsibility for their violence and seek a nonviolent relationship. These programs emphasize safety and focus on interventions designed to alter violence (e.g., time-out, nonviolence contracts, interaction patterns leading to violence).

Given these data and considerations, we now assess for violence from each partner toward the other and are now more open to accepting couples into treatment we might have excluded earlier. We certainly want to continue to exclude couples with battering and always prioritize the safety of any victims of violence. However, when faced with a couple that seeks to improve their relationship but in which there has been violence, including minor injury, we must consider the following factors: (a) the danger that conflict in the relationship holds for one or both partners, (b) the commitment that partners have to staying together and improving their relationship, and (c) the availability of effective alternative treatments [e.g., the effective couple-based interventions above are not widely available; the court-mandated batterer programs are only minimally effective (Cantos & O'Leary, 2014) and may be inappropriate for partners in couples who come for couple therapy]. If partners are committed to staying together and improving their relationship, as was the case in most of the couples we rejected, if alternative effective treatment is not available, and if future physical risk is small, we now accept these couples into a modified version of IBCT.

Adapting IBCT for Couples with IPV

What kinds of adaptations do we make? First, we make sure that both partners endorse a goal of a completely nonviolent relationship. We communicate that we work with couples who were previously violent but can only continue to work with couples if they end the violence. Second, we make sure that partners are willing to take personal responsibility for their previous violent acts, rather than blaming the partner for a provocative but nonviolent action that triggered the violence and that they take personal responsibility for behaving nonviolently in the future, no matter how provocative their partner's nonviolent behavior is. Third, we make violence a focus of treatment in the following ways: (a) we establish a nonviolence contract, (b) we establish a safety plan for what partners will do if violence occurs or is feared (e.g., who the person might call or stay with for the night), (c) we teach time-out methods as a way of defusing escalating conflict, (d) we focus on the patterns of interaction that lead to violence, and (e) each week our first order of business is to investigate provocative incidents that could lead or have led to violence between partners in the past. Let's consider each of these strategies in turn.

First, we make a nonviolence contract. Although this contract can be oral or written, a written contract is liable to be more effective. Both partners agree that they will not have any kind of physical contact when one or both are angry at the other ("no angry touching"). They also agree not to threaten each other with violence. Finally, they agree to report any incidents of violence to the therapist using the Weekly Questionnaire or calling us if it is urgent. Couples may be hesitant to report violence out of shame or out of fear that a report could jeopardize therapy. We certainly won't continue seeing couples in therapy if they are unable to bring any dangerous levels of violence under control, but we don't immediately terminate therapy if the couple reports a violent episode, depending on the nature of that episode.

If there is a risk for dangerous levels of violence, we also can create a safety plan for one or both partners. A safety plan indicates what partners can do if they fear violence, if they see that a situation is escalating toward violence, or if violence occurs. We help them decide on a safe place where they can go, such as the home of a family member or friend or a hotel. We encourage them to call police if violence occurs or if they fear violence and escape to the safe place is difficult or impossible. We may give them the National Domestic Violence Hotline, which is available 24 hours in both English and Spanish (800-799-SAFE and TTY 800-787-3224), and the website of this hotline (http://www.thehotline.org/).

During treatment, we first focus on the pattern of escalation that leads to violence. As with all patterns of interaction, each partner contributes to the escalation. When going over this pattern, we make sure not to conflate this fact with responsibility for violence. We communicate that they are both responsible for escalation but only the person who engages in violence is responsible for that violence. Based on the pattern of escalation, we explore with both partners realistic actions each could take as conflict escalates so as to reduce the likelihood of further escalation. For example, one partner's attempt to de-escalate through time-out by suddenly walking out of the room might be very provocative for the other but that same partner signaling that he or she is getting really upset and proposing they discuss the issue later might enable them both to de-escalate better. In that context, we usually teach the time-out technique discussed in Chapter 9.

Finally, we use the Weekly Questionnaire to monitor the occurrence of any violence and the occurrence of provocative incidents (i.e., the negative events on the questionnaire) that could lead to violence. We use our strategies of empathic joining, unified detachment, and direct change to discuss these incidents so the couple has a better understanding of them and better control over them.

If these efforts are not successful in controlling the violence, and particularly if the violence increases, then we might engage the couple in serious discussions about the viability of their relationship. If the three of us working together cannot bring the violence under control, then the relationship needs different or more powerful intervention or serious discussion about the advisability of maintaining a relationship that could be dangerous to one or both. In our work with violent couples, we communicate that we can work with couples who were previously violent, but we cannot work with couples who continue to be violent.

Effectiveness of IBCT with IPV

What is evidence for the effectiveness of IBCT with violent couples? As noted earlier, in our clinical trial of IBCT we had conservative criteria for exclusion on the basis of violence. Nevertheless, 45% of the 134 couples in our clinical trial reported physical violence in the year prior to seeking therapy. A comparison of the violent with the nonviolent couples indicated no differences in their improvement on either relationship or individual outcomes. Couples maintained low levels of physical aggression during and after treatment. Furthermore, psychological aggression decreased as relationship and individual functioning improved (Simpson et al., 2008). Similarly, in the online adaptation of IBCT, couples randomized to the intervention were significantly less likely to engage in physical violence than couples randomized to a wait-list control condition (Doss, Roddy, Llabre, Georgia Salivar, & Jensen-Doss, 2020). Additionally, presence of physical violence at the beginning of the program did not moderate program effectiveness (Roddy, Georgia, & Doss, 2018).

SEXUAL PROBLEMS AND IBCT

Sexual problems in intimate relationships are special, even unique, for several reasons. First, these problems are fundamental, going to the heart of the relationship, in ways that other problems do not. Partners usually form romantic relationships such as marriage in large part because of their sexual attraction to each other. Sexual intimacy is what distinguishes romantic relationships from other types of intimate relationships such as friends and family. Even in sexually open relationships, there are usually boundaries that restrict sexual activity. For example, partners may engage in group-sex activities, such as threesomes, but prohibit dyadic sexual activity with another partner. Therefore, the appearance of sexual problems raises questions about the fundamental viability of the relationship: is my partner no longer attracted to me? Can our relationship survive? Will we be unable to have sex and thus biological children?

A second reason that sexual problems are unique is that they raise questions about one's fundamental worth as a romantic partner—questions that are often tied to one's gender. If a male can't perform sexually, he may question his own worth as a male and his value in the relationship. If a female does not seem to be attractive to her partner, she may question her own worth as a woman and her value in the relationship. A third reason that sexual problems are unique, related to the second, is that these problems are often associated with shame and embarrassment. Partners may be reluctant to reveal that they have these problems or may want to spare their partner's feelings and not mention that their partner has a problem. Consider as a contrast a problem with in-laws. Although conflicts around in-laws can be serious and difficult, they do not go to the fundamental attraction between two partners, they do not threaten partners' self-worth in such a basic way, and they are not likely to be such a source of shame or embarrassment.

Not only are sexual problems unique, they are relatively common. A national survey of mature adults in the United States aged 40–80 years found that over a quarter of men and a third of women reported one or more sexual problems: early ejaculation in men and lack of desire in women were the most common problems (Laumann, Glasser, Neves, & Moreira, 2009). A national probability survey in Great Britain of individuals aged 16–74 found that about 25% reported an imbalance in sexual interest; 17% of women and 18% of men reported that their partner had a sexual problem (K. R. Mitchell et al., 2013). In our study of IBCT and TBCT, 28% of couples reported problems with sex or physical affection as one of their primary reasons for seeking couple therapy (Doss et al., 2004). Additionally, both men's and women's sexual dissatisfaction was predictive of them taking a more active role in seeking couple therapy (Doss et al., 2003).

Treatment of Sexual Problems in IBCT

Many kinds of sexual problems can be treated with IBCT, but others require specialized treatment. Perhaps the most common sexual problems are disagreements about frequency and type of sexual activity. One partner may want sex more often than the other or be more adventuresome than the other. These kinds of issues can usually be treated using the typical strategies of IBCT, even when one partner's desires are unusual and involve a fetish. For example, an IBCT therapist worked with a couple where the man liked to cross-dress. His wife knew about this before their marriage and generally accepted it. However, because he sometimes liked to cross-dress in public, she was concerned it would not remain private. Thus, the couple argued about the situations in which he could cross-dress, and the therapist used IBCT strategies to help them with that conflict. Another issue that can be treated with typical IBCT interventions is sexual distancing or sexual alienation because of relationship distress. One or both partners withdraw sexually, not because of some dysfunction but because of their anger and resentment.

However, there are some issues that require specialized treatment. The presence of a sexual dysfunction such as erectile disorder, female orgasmic disorder, and desire disorders require particular expertise and sometimes coordination with medical specialists. This treatment can certainly be integrated with IBCT but includes assessment and intervention procedures different from IBCT. Also, special expertise—and likely a different treatment than IBCT—is necessary to treat paraphilic disorders, particularly if they involve illegal behavior such as pedophilic and exhibitionistic disorder, and where the goal is termination of the behavior.

Regardless of whether couples present in IBCT with sexual problems, the assessment phase of IBCT should include screening of the sexual functioning of the couple. Because partners may be embarrassed about their sexual problems or not want to subject their partner to embarrassment, it is sometimes better to ask about sexual difficulties in the individual session. We recommend having a questionnaire item about sexual satisfaction, such as in our Problem Areas Questionnaire. This questionnaire asks partners to rate their dissatisfaction with a number of common areas of concern for couples, including "sex relations" and asks them to circle the top three areas of concern. Partners may be more willing to indicate problems on a questionnaire than to voice them out loud. Furthermore, if partners indicate dissatisfaction on the item like that on the Problem Areas Questionnaire, it is natural for us to do follow-up in the individual session. Depending on how the partner responds to this question, we can do a thorough assessment of the nature of their sexual difficulty.

In working with sexual problems, our goal is satisfaction, not sexual performance. We are not trying to train sexual athletes, only responsive partners. In fact, our goal should not be the sex of film actors, novel writers, or porn stars but "good enough sex (GES)" (McCarthy, 2015). McCarthy argues that "GES is not 'settling' or accepting mediocre sex. GES is about celebrating exceptional sex, relishing good sex, enjoying okay or run of the mill sex, accepting mediocre or dissatisfying sex, and addressing and changing dysfunctional sex" (p. 121).

In working to achieve that goal, we should be aware that couples with sexual problems often have several common characteristics. They often have very narrow definitions of sex, in which sex means intercourse with orgasm. We want to broaden that definition so that sex means any intimate contact that is pleasurable to them both. Also, couples with sexual difficulties often have limited or no communication about sex so that open discussion in the safe forum of couple therapy can by itself be very helpful for them, letting them know each other's likes and dislikes. In addition, these couples often have stereotyped roles and attitudes about sex, such as having the man be the primary or only initiator or beliefs that the man should always be ready for sex. We want to broaden those roles and attitudes if that can increase their satisfaction. Finally, we can usually assume that couples with sexual problems will have ingrained patterns of avoidance of sex. Because their problems are associated with failure, pain, shame, and embarrassment, one or both may actively avoid sexual situations.

Annon (1976) described the PLISSIT model for intervention in sexual problems, particularly sexual dysfunctions. This staged or stepped model of care describes four levels of intervention: Permission-giving, Limited Information, Specific Suggestions, and finally Intensive Sex Therapy. In IBCT, we can certainly do the first three levels. Regarding permission-giving, we take the position, typical among sex therapists, that any sexual activity between consenting adult partners that is pleasurable is good, even if it is unusual. Partners may feel concerned that their particular practices are deviant or sick but if they don't involve coercion or children and are pleasurable, we generally endorse them and try to relieve the partners of their concerns. At the second level, we can sometimes provide partners with information that is useful or reassuring to them, for example, telling them that most men masturbate occasionally or that it is common for partners to have occasional fantasies of sex with other people. At the third level, we can sometimes provide specific suggestions to partners that can be helpful. For example, two IBCT co-therapists once worked with a married couple in which the husband was experiencing erectile problems. When he would lose his erection, both he and his wife would feel a sense of failure and end the sexual session in disappointment. The cotherapists told the couple that men sometimes lose their erections but can sometimes regain them and suggested that the couple stay in the sexual situation and continue to fondle and enjoy each other. Even if he didn't regain his erections, they could still have a positive time together. They followed that suggestion, he regained his erection, and they had a positive sexual experience. As a result, they soon ended treatment. Finally, as

IBCT therapists we can engage in sex therapy if we have the appropriate training and expertise or have the appropriate supervision available; or we can refer out. For descriptions of sex therapy and couple therapy for sexual problems, see Binik and Hall (2014), McCarthy (2015), and Weeks and Gambescia (2015).

If a couple has stopped having sex or dramatically reduced their frequency of sex because of the anger and resentment one or both feel toward the other, IBCT typically begins by focusing on the presenting problems that have led to the anger and resentment. Using typical IBCT strategies, we try to rebuild the emotional connection between partners. Sometimes this leads naturally to a resumption of sex between partners. However, many times the relationship improves but sexual contact remains limited or absent. Partners may have gotten out of the habit of being sexual with each other and they may feel some awkwardness or discomfort about resuming sexual contact. In that situation, we help them address their sexual relationship directly. It is usually helpful in these situations to collaborate with the couple and develop a series of exercises for them to do in the privacy of their home that promote nondemand, pleasurable physical contact. These exercises typically start with low-level pleasurable touching with the goal of exploration and pleasure, not arousal (e.g., touching and massages fully clothed or only partially nude and avoiding breasts and genitals) and progress gradually toward more sensual exploration and touching (e.g., nude massages with oil but avoiding breasts and genitals) and erotic touching (e.g., including breasts and genitals). This gradual progression of exercises, with debriefing with the therapist and open communication between partners, can counteract their discomfort and avoidance and lead to a resumption of physical and sexual contact.

We don't have a lot of data on the impact of IBCT on sexual functioning. In our clinical trial, women in IBCT experienced significant reductions in sexual dissatisfaction (within-group Cohen's $d = -0.65$) and increases in sexual frequency (within-group Cohen's $d = 0.25$); however, men in IBCT did not significantly improve on either dimension (Rothman et al., under review). An examination of client responses to our open-ended questions about what they liked and didn't like about couple therapy indicated that a number of respondents indicated that they would have liked a greater focus on their sexual relationship. In retrospect, we believe that our therapists may have focused too much on the core issues of the couple and the specific conflicts around those issues and not paid enough attention to their sexual relationship.

INFIDELITY AND IBCT

To most laypeople, infidelity refers to sexual intimacy, usually intercourse, with someone other than the partner. Infidelity researchers often use an expanded definition that includes emotional as well as sexual intimacy. For example, Glass (2002) defines infidelity as "a secret, sexual, romantic, or emotional involvement that violates the commitment to an exclusive relationship" (p. 489). In IBCT, we use an even more expanded definition of infidelity because we want to capture the violations that can occur in relationships that are not sexually exclusive. Our definition would be "a secret sexual, romantic, or emotional involvement that violates the couple's shared understanding of their commitment to each other." For example, a same-sex male relationship might allow sexual contact with other men as long as that sexual contact is not repeated with the same other man. Thus, infidelity could occur if one partner started having repeated, secret sexual contact with another man but not if the sexual contact was not repeated. Often partners in open relationships have not spelled out in detail what kind of contact constitutes a violation, and one partner may engage in behavior that he or she thinks is okay, while the other, upon learning of it, may believe it constitutes a violation. Thus, one partner may believe that infidelity has occurred while the other insists that it has not. A similar issue occurs in couples who are committed to monogamy when one partner believes only sexual intercourse with another person constitutes infidelity while the other believes viewing pornography or intimate physical contact with another that does not include intercourse constitutes infidelity.

Infidelity in couples is relatively common. Existing data suggest that about one quarter of all men and about a fifth of all women in heterosexual relationships report having sex outside the relationship (Mark, Janssen, & Milhausen, 2011). Infidelity is also the most frequently cited reason for divorce (Allen & Atkins, 2012). According to therapists' reports, about one third of couples who begin couple therapy do so because of an affair (Whisman, Dixon, & Johnson, 1997). Thus, couple therapists must be prepared to deal with infidelity.

Assessment of Infidelity in IBCT

Given the prevalence of infidelity and the secret nature of it, a critical question is when and how to assess for it. If infidelity or related issues around trust are a presenting problem for the couple, they will mention it in the first joint session or bring it up in the individual session. If infidelity or trust is not an issue for the couple, then we do not routinely investigate infidelity. Our hands are normally full with the presenting problems, and we don't want to create or raise issues for the couple unless the issue is importantly related to the presenting problem. For example, if a couple's presenting problem is a sexual concern, in which the wife seems consumed with whether her husband is attracted to her, his earlier affair might clearly be relevant to the problem. However, if a couple does not mention infidelity or trust as an issue and their concerns are unrelated to trust, a probe about any past infidelity is not called for. The exception to this guideline is if we suspect that there is current, undisclosed infidelity—a current, competing, secret relationship that occupies a partner's energy but has not been revealed to the other. If we suspect that, then we do want to assess and confront infidelity.

As we discussed in Chapter 4, we assure the client at the beginning of the individual session that we will keep information confidential from the partner if the client indicates that he or she wants a piece of information kept secret. Then, when we go over the rating scales on commitment to the relationship from the Couple Questionnaire, we enquire about commitment in general and often about any current, competing relationship in particular. If we have any reason to think that a partner may be in a competing relationship, we may say during this discussion of commitment something like "When couples are having serious trouble in their relationship, one or both partners may secretly seek the comfort or companionship or connection with another person. Do you think your partner is involved in a secret relationship? Are you involved in such a relationship?" If the client mentions a past secret relationship that is clearly over, we can certainly discuss that relationship, the client's feelings about it such as guilt or longing, and the client's views on sharing it with the partner. We don't take a position on whether clients should or should not share a past infidelity with the partner. Sometimes such sharing can be helpful to the relationship, sometimes harmful. We want such a decision to be in the hands of the client.

However, if the client is having a current, secret, competing relationship, we want to assess that in detail so we can determine the client's investment in the relationship, his or her awareness of the barrier that this competing relationship creates for therapy, and his or her willingness to end the relationship or reveal it to the partner. Our position is that we cannot do couple therapy when a partner is in a secret, competing relationship with someone else. The partner must end the relationship, reveal it to the partner, or both. However, we don't impose that rule or even mention that concern right away. Usually partners are aware of the problem posed by a competing relationship and have struggled with what to do about it. We want to join them in that struggle, helping them discuss the ambivalence and guilt that they may feel, and ideally lead them to the decision that they need to end the relationship or share it with the partner in order for couple therapy to proceed.

These kinds of situations are very difficult and often uncomfortable. They require modifications to the usual assessment plan. For example, we may need to have more than one individual session with the involved partner. We may need to postpone the feedback session so that the involved partner fully ends the affair first. We need to keep discussing the possibility of the involved partner revealing the affair to the uninformed and possibly suspicious partner. If an uninformed partner discovers an affair, it is almost always more problematic for the maintenance of the relationship than if the involved partner reveals the affair.

If a partner is involved in a current, secret affair and insists after discussion with us that he or she can and does want to maintain the secret relationship while working on the current relationship, we can at that point indicate that we are not able to do couple therapy. Doing so would violate our implicit commitment to both partners that we are here to improve their relationship and think it can be improved. Certainly if the uninvolved partner ever discovered the secret relationship, he or she would understandably feel betrayed by us.

In our experience, it is rare that a couple reaches this point. In fact, we are aware of only one example of this situation. An IBCT therapist was working with a couple in which the wife revealed in the individual session that she was in a lesbian relationship with a woman friend. She planned to stay with her husband and wanted to improve her relationship with him but was not willing to give up or disclose her lesbian relationship. The therapist explained his position to her, which she understood. He made sure she had referrals for individual therapy. The couple never returned for further sessions. If the husband had called and inquired about couple therapy, the therapist would have told him that his wife decided not to pursue couple therapy and that she could best explain why. Thus, the therapist would have maintained the woman's confidentiality as was promised. However, the husband never called. Presumably his wife told him that she was not interested in therapy anymore, didn't like the therapist, or both.

The more common issue with current, secret affairs is that partners do not reveal them to us. In our clinical trial, some partners did not reveal their ongoing affairs to us, and later these affairs were discovered by the spouse. In most of these cases, the couple divorced (Atkins et al., 2005; Marín et al., 2014). Not surprisingly, the other was not sympathetic to the partner when the two had gone through couple therapy while the partner had continued the competing relationship and not revealed it.

Working with Infidelity in IBCT

The most difficult situation therapeutically with current, secret affairs is when the involved partner agrees to end the relationship but wants to keep it secret from the partner. In those situations, we want to be sure that the involved partner is committed to ending the relationship. Ending a relationship that has been emotionally meaningful or sexually fulfilling is not easy, and the partner of the client in that relationship may resist or protest the ending, no matter how intent the client is on ending it. Therefore, we not only want to be sure the client is committed to ending the relationship but that the client ends the relationship prior to the feedback session. Furthermore, we want to periodically assess whether the client has reinitiated their relationship with the affair partner. We discuss during the individual session and set up during the feedback session a process by which we will meet individually with each partner periodically during treatment to assess progress. Typically, we set up these meetings as brief, individual sessions prior to the joint session. We discuss with each partner his or her views about the progress of couple therapy. With the partner who had an affair, we ask about contact with the affair partner. If the involved partner is successful in ending the relationship, we can end these check-ins. However, if the involved partner reveals occasional slip-ups, we need to discuss revelation of the affair or the termination of couple therapy even if the partner insists on an intent to end the affair. Fortunately, these situations don't present themselves very often.

The more common therapeutic situation is when infidelity has been revealed or discovered and the couple comes to therapy to cope with that. In our work with these kinds of couples, we should know that affairs come in all shapes and sizes. There are affairs in which affair partners had an emotionally involved, romantic connection with each other that expressed itself fully in sexual contact. There are affairs in which affair partners had an emotionally involved, romantic connection with each other but they limited their sexual contact in deference to the existing marriage or committed relationship. There are purely sexual affairs with little or no emotional involvement and emotional affairs with little or no sexual involvement. Similarly, there are many different motives for an affair. Sometimes a partner may fall in love with a coworker even though there were no serious problems in the marriage or other committed relationship. Sometimes partners seek out others because of problems or limitations in the relationship. Sometimes partners seek out affairs to validate their attractiveness or out of anger at the partner for having an affair of their own or because of other affronts.

Just as there are many kinds of affairs and reasons for them, there are many kinds of reactions to those affairs. When trusting and unsuspecting partners discover an affair, they may experience a kind of interpersonal trauma at this betrayal. Their sense of security in the world is shattered and they may experience PTSD-like symptoms. They are faced with big questions and looming decisions: can they ever trust this person again? Should they stay with this person they loved and trusted or should they end this relationship? Other partners who have been distrusting and suspected an affair may feel a sense of validation and anger when they get confirmation of an affair. Their partner had dismissed their distrust and questions and had made them feel they were silly or overreacting, and now they see their suspicions were warranted. Affairs may challenge the self-worth of the betrayed partner, making him or her wonder about his or her attractiveness, or judgment, or ability to maintain a relationship. These strong reactions may occur even if there was no overt affair. Discovery that the other secretly looked at pornography can be upsetting. An IBCT therapist once worked with a couple in which the wife discovered the husband masturbating to porn and experienced it as a betrayal almost as bad as if he were discovered having sex with another woman.

The betrayed partner is not the only one who may have strong feelings or face major questions. The partner involved in the affair usually feels some guilt about the affair along with a strong desire to justify the affair and redeem his or her sense of still being a good person. If the affair was an important relationship, the involved partner may feel conflicted about whether to stay with the existing partner or leave for the affair partner. If the involved partner decides to stay with the existing partner, he or she may feel a sense of loss of the affair partner and worry about whether the relationship with the existing partner can ever be fully restored.

In working with couples in which one or both partners have had an affair, there are several important principles that we follow. First, we take a nonjudgmental approach to participating partners (i.e., the ones who had the affair) as well as to their injured partners. That doesn't mean we condone affairs, but our focus is on how the partners react to affairs, not how we react. It is much more important for the outcome of the relationship whether the participating partners genuinely view their affairs as violations of their code of conduct than if we do. If we judge the participating partners, they may be more defensive and find it harder to voice their own self-evaluation. Second, we promote the notion that both members are responsible for problems in the relationship but only the person who had the affair is responsible for dealing with those problems by having an affair. This principle counteracts the tendency for participating partners to blame the relationship for their actions or the tendency of injured partners to defend themselves and the relationship (e.g., defend their lack of sexual interest during the relationship). Third, we promote the notion that there are always reasons for human behavior, including affairs, but those reasons are not justifications or excuses for that behavior. Injured partners may want to know why the participating partners had an affair and participating partners often want to explain why they had an affair. That conversation can be helpful as long as neither conflates reasons with justifications or excuses.

If a couple comes to therapy in the immediate aftermath of the discovery or disclosure of infidelity, there may be strong emotions and high conflict that demand immediate attention. Rather than doing a leisurely assessment over three sessions, we may need to problem solve with the couple in the very first session. Partners may need a short-term separation to cool the high conflict and prevent any children from exposure to that conflict. There could be health issues that demand immediate attention, such as the possibility of a sexually transmitted disease or the possibility of pregnancy. Both partners may vacillate between a desire to end the relationship immediately or a desire to reconcile. In this situation, we almost always recommend that they delay any such important decision. They can choose to separate or divorce at any point and should not make that decision in the immediate aftermath of discovery or disclosure when emotions are high.

Once conflict is contained and any health issues are addressed, we can proceed with our assessment. Individual sessions are extremely important when an affair is involved because partners may be more open in these sessions than in joint sessions. For example, participating partners may be more forthcoming about the nature of their affairs and their willingness to end them completely. Injured partners may be more open about their desire to stay in the relationship even if they threaten to leave when they are with their partner. In the feedback session, we can provide a tentative DEEP analysis focused on the affair. For example, a key difference between the two that long predated the affair may have been that the participating partner was always more sociable and flirtatious than the injured partner. In terms of emotional sensitivities, the injured partner may have experienced cheating in previous relationships that make him or her especially sensitive to infidelity. The participating partner may have often been considered and considered himself or herself the less morally upright of the two and this affair simply affirms that status. Often, there were external factors that influenced the affair, such as alcohol consumption, frequent travel, or working intensely on a project with a coworker. Finally, the partners may be in a negative pattern of interaction that prevents them from constructively discussing the affair. For example, in a common interaction pattern in the aftermath of the affair, the injured partner overwhelms the participating partner with accusatory questions and negative evaluations while the participating partner minimizes the affair and gives limited and sometimes misleading or false information about the affair.

As part of the feedback session, we typically present a plan for treatment. With infidelity, the steps usually involve discussion of what happened, its meaning, and its impact on both partners. Because these are often very charged discussions, we often suggest that they be done exclusively during therapy sessions and encourage couples not to discuss them at home. As a result of these discussions, partners can make a decision on whether to leave or stay in the relationship and how to close the door on the relationship with the affair partner, if that relationship has not been completely ended. Further discussion often focuses on understanding why the affair happened and dealing with the ongoing issue of trust.

During the active phase of therapy, we rely on empathic joining and unified detachment, as well as direct change strategies, all adapted for the issue of infidelity. For example, during discussions of what happened, we guide injured partners away from accusatory questions and explore with them the concerns behind the question. Usually injured partners want to know information in order to evaluate the threat of the other relationship. Did they confess their love to each other? Did they discuss marriage? Injured partners may also want to know the extent of the personal injury, such as the extent to which their own feelings were ignored. Did they make love at the couple's home, in their own bed? Did they engage in sexual activities that the participating partners wouldn't do with them? Sometimes injured partners want information that will embarrass the participating partner, such as wanting

them to state how often they had sex. Finally, there is often some information that injured partners don't want to know, such as the details of the sexual relationship. If we can shift injured partners from accusatory questions
to revelations about what they want to know and why, the discussion can
become constructive and less fraught.

We also work with the participating partners to shift them away from
their natural inclination to minimize their involvement or to only give *stag-
gered disclosure*. Once we have gotten injured partners to describe what they
want to know, we find out whether participating partners are willing to share
that information and any reluctance they have about sharing. Then we can
encourage them to share the relevant information along with any fears they
have about the sharing, warning them of the danger of incomplete or partial
disclosure and encouraging them to round up when they give information
(so they err by overestimation rather than by underestimation). We frame
the injured partner's questions as a way to understand what happened—
perhaps as a first step to moving on—rather than as a form of punishment.
We also encourage the participating partner to reveal any feelings they have
about what they have done, such as guilt or shame. With both injured and
participating partners, we are generous with our validation and empathy, as
this is a difficult process for both. However, by working this way with both
injured and participating partners, we shift the discussion from challenging questions and defensive answers to factual and emotional revelations by
both. When participating partners are able to show genuine remorse, injured
partners are more likely to understand and forgive. When injured partners
can describe their emotional injuries rather than attack, the participating
partners can be less defensive, more empathic, and more openly remorseful. Thus, these conversations can open the way to possible forgiveness and
reconciliation.

When partners have decided, at least tentatively, to stay together and
injured partners are willing to close the door on the other relationship, we
try to facilitate discussions about how to do that so partners can act together.
Although these discussions also rely on empathic joining and unified detachment, they also emphasize concrete change. For example, injured partners
may want to be a part of the breakup process, such as seeing the letter or

email the participating partners write or listening in on the phone conversation that the participating partners make. As another example, injured partners often want to punish or expose the affair partners, such as disclosing the affair to their unsuspecting spouses or sending affair partners an attacking letter. We facilitate discussions about these actions so partners can act as a team when they close the door on that competing relationship.

When couples decide to stay together, the most challenging issues are ongoing issues of trust. Will injured partners ever trust the participating partners? Will participating partners always be under scrutiny? We can help them create a trusting relationship only by helping them meet the challenges to that trust that they face in their daily life, such as the participating partners working late or going away on a business trip or the injured partners going on a business trip and leaving the participating partners home alone. We facilitate discussion of these challenges, ideally discussing upcoming events that might be difficult and planning actions that might make those events easier. In this process, it is often helpful if participating partners are willing to make extra efforts at reassurance, such as by calling in to check in when they are away or working late, in order to build back trust. Some of the most challenging issues concern contact with the former affair partner. Sometimes that person still works at the office of the participating partner, goes to the same church, or will be at the same school function. Discussion about how to handle those meetings in a way that is limited but socially acceptable can help both partners deal with the difficult social interactions that they present.

Our description has focused on the most positive outcomes, namely partners forgiving and reconciling, ending previous relationships with affair partners, and building trust. Of course, sometimes partners are not able to do this and move toward separation or divorce. We may help them achieve that separation in the most constructive way possible and, if they have children together, work with them to facilitate coparenting arrangements. Perhaps the most complicated scenario is when partners stay together but infidelity continues or is likely to continue. For example, an IBCT therapist worked with a couple in which the husband would occasionally have sexual encounters when he was away on business trips. These would create temporary havoc in the relationship but the husband wanted to continue his marriage to his wife and she wanted to remain with him. Despite the efforts in couple therapy and in his individual therapy, he was not willing or able to end his occasional affairs. It was thus important in this case for both partners, particularly the wife, to be aware of the ongoing pattern of affair, temporary upset, recovery, and another affair so they could decide what they wanted to do. It also seemed important not to soften the wife's anger too much or encourage her forgiveness and her hope that things would be different. Her anger seemed to reduce the frequency although it did not eliminate his indiscretions.

Effectiveness of IBCT with Infidelity

The evidence from our research on IBCT provides encouragement for couple therapy if there has been infidelity. If partners are not continuing a secret affair, then therapy seems to help couples with infidelity as much as it helps couples who are in therapy for other reasons than infidelity (Atkins et al., 2005). Even at a 5-year follow-up, couples with infidelity who stayed together were as improved as those couples without infidelity who stayed together. However, couples with infidelity were more than twice as likely to separate than couples without infidelity (Marín et al., 2014). Infidelity is often a trigger for the termination of the relationship. However, many couples who have experienced infidelity can benefit from IBCT, stay together, and improve their relationship.

INDIVIDUAL PSYCHOPATHOLOGY
AND COUPLE THERAPY

Individual psychopathology is very common, with estimates from the National Institute of Mental Health that about 20% of the U.S. population suffers from a diagnosable mental disorder (https://www.nimh.nih.gov/health/statistics/mental-illness.shtml). Not surprisingly, individual psychopathology goes hand in hand with couple discord. Research in large, population-based samples links discord with mood, anxiety, and substance use disorders (Whisman, 2007). Longitudinal studies indicate that relationship discord precedes depressive episodes (Whisman & Bruce, 1999) and the development of alcohol use disorders (Whisman, Uebelacker, & Bruce, 2006). In addition, longitudinal research has indicated that depressive symptoms predict increases in relationship distress (Whisman & Uebelacker, 2009). Thus, relationship discord and individual psychopathology have reciprocal influences on each other and raise the question of how to deal with individual psychopathology in doing IBCT.

Assessment of Psychopathology in IBCT

Despite the link between relationship discord and individual psychopathology, we do not regularly conduct diagnostic assessments of each partner to see if they meet criteria for any disorder. However, we obtain basic information about each person, such as whether they are on medication and whether they are currently in treatment or have had past treatment for a disorder. During our individual sessions with each partner, we learn about their individual history that might be relevant to their current problems including their past or current treatment for a disorder. Even if neither partner has ever been on psychiatric medication or been in psychotherapy, one or the other may voice concerns about themselves or the other, such as concerns about alcohol or drug use, depressive reactions, or anxiety reactions. Furthermore, even if partners never mention concerns related to psychopathology, during the course of therapy we may learn of extreme reactions that each has had to the other and to their stressors that suggest psychopathology. Thus, we learn about individual psychopathology that is related to their couple problems, and we can proceed with a diagnostic assessment as indicated.

Individual pathology can exist in a good relationship and discord can exist without the presence of individual pathology. When individual pathology exists in an otherwise positive relationship, couple therapy per se is not required but a couple-based intervention can still be helpful. For example, Baucom, Shoham, Mueser, Daiuto, and Stickle (1998) described partner-assisted interventions, in which the partner is recruited to help the patient by encouraging and reinforcing their efforts to combat their disorder, and disorder-specific interventions in which the relationship can be altered in fundamental but focal ways that will facilitate recovery from the disorder. In the first case, a couple intervention might educate partners about depression and have the partner encourage the depressed patient to engage in positive activities and cheer on those activities. In the second case, a couple intervention might educate partners about agoraphobia and help these partners gradually alter their accommodation to an agoraphobic patient, such as cases in which the partner takes on all manner of household responsibilities so the patient does not need to go outside. For recent examples of these interventions see Fischer and Baucom (2019).

When individual psychopathology exists alongside a distressed relationship, the therapeutic situation is more challenging. This is where IBCT is relevant and thus our focus in this section.

IBCT for Couples with Individual Psychopathology

If a partner openly acknowledges individual psychopathology, the therapeutic challenge is easier—even if he or she insists, most likely correctly, that the relationship makes it worse. The partner who has a disorder, whom we will call the patient for ease of distinction, may be willing to participate in a relevant, evidence-based treatment for that disorder before, while, or after participating in couple therapy. Thus, the couple may benefit from the effects of both interventions. However, often diagnosis itself may be a source of conflict. The partner may blame the patient for the diagnosis, insist that the patient seek treatment, and claim that only then will the relationship improve. The patient may insist that it is the partner who actually needs treatment or that the relationship and the way the partner treats him or her is responsible for any pathology on the patient's part. In some cases, the patient may claim a diagnosis but the partner is suspicious of the mental health profession or concerned about finances and insists that the patient is overreacting or babying himself or herself. These conflicts about diagnosis prevent improvement of both the patient's condition and the relationship.

When there is a conflict about diagnosis, we don't want to weigh in on one side or the other except in extreme situations, which we discuss below. If we insist, as experts in the field, that one partner has or does not have a diagnosis, our judgment will validate the views of one of the two, perhaps alienate the other, and often intensify conflict between the pair. Instead, we focus on the conflict between them about the diagnosis, which impairs their ability to work together as a couple on problematic behavior between them. Then we zero in and identify the major problematic behavior pattern that exists between them. For example, an anxious partner may express concerns that strike the other one as extreme but initially lead the other to provide reassurance; when that reassurance does not ameliorate the anxiety, the other criticizes the anxious partner for his or her anxiety. Or, as another example, a depressed partner may be irritable and negative and the other withdraws and avoids the depressed partner who then escalates his or her negativity to get a response from the other who then does respond with exasperation and criticism, which is somewhat reinforcing for the depressed patient because it at least provides connection. In working with these couples, we choose words that describe the relevant behaviors but that are not offensive for either. For example, sometimes partners can admit to feeling anxious or feeling depressed as long as they don't believe that indicts them with a disorder. If those words are too provocative, we can talk about them being concerned and seeking reassurance or feeling down and hopeless and wanting someone to listen to them. The key is to accurately describe the pattern between them, using words that are not diagnostically loaded and are often provided by the couple themselves.

There are certainly types of individual pathology for which IBCT is not appropriate. If the individual psychopathology is life threatening, as with serious suicidal tendencies, then immediate attention to that pathology is essential. Couple therapy might be able to be of assistance as well but only after the immediate danger has been ameliorated, such as with medication, hospitalization, or therapy. Adult anorexia is another example of a life-threatening individual pathology. Couple therapy has been shown to be helpful with this disorder but only as part of a comprehensive approach to the disorder that involves individual therapy, nutrition counseling, and medical management (e.g., Baucom et al., 2017). If individual psychopathology means the patient cannot participate appropriately in couple therapy, then obviously that is another situation in which IBCT is inappropriate. For example, if one partner is actively psychotic, the psychotic ideation needs to be addressed first. Similarly, if one partner has serious drug or alcohol abuse or dependency, the condition may be life threatening (e.g., driving under the influence) or make the partner an unsuitable candidate for couple therapy (e.g., the partner is often inebriated or comes to therapy inebriated). However, couple therapy can enhance substance disorder treatment when it is part of a comprehensive approach that includes individual treatment and often medication (see McCrady & Epstein, 2015).

Whether any individual pathology is openly acknowledged or is a source of conflict, we use our conceptual framework of the DEEP analysis to understand the relationship and help the partners understand it. Let's consider an example of a depressed female partner in a conflicted different-sex relationship. Even in the early days of their relationship, long before any depressive episode, perhaps he was the optimistic one and she the pessimistic one. Sometimes that difference served as a nice balance between them, in that he could always see the positive but she could anticipate the negative in a situation. He could often lift her mood whereas her attention to possible negative outcomes prevented them from snap decisions and led to more deliberate actions. Other times it was a source of conflict, in that neither felt their views were validated by the other. She would sometimes see him as naïve and "head in the sand" while he would see her as a "Debbie Downer" and both would tire of the others' views. She may have had a depressed mother who made her familiar with, but sensitive to, the possibility of being depressed. She would never want to become the irritable, angry woman she saw her mother as being. Because of his history, he had no experience dealing with strong negative feelings and would feel inadequate if he could not alter the mood of those close to him with his optimistic attitude. The stress of young children and careers may have contributed substantially to her depression and reduced his tolerance of her moods. Now he avoids engaging with her when he senses her being down, which makes her feel alone. When she voices her concerns with him, often escalating them in order to get his attention, he insists she see someone for her depression and maybe get some medication. She feels those comments by him as efforts to dismiss her—"I don't want to deal with you. Get professional help." She resists those efforts in part as resistance to him and in part because she does not want to see herself as a depressed person, following in the footsteps of her mother.

Done appropriately in the feedback session, a DEEP analysis like that above can reduce the conflict a couple has over diagnosis and give them a common way to think about their dilemma. It can prepare the way for our usual interventions of empathic joining, unified detachment, and direct change. For example, during empathic joining we would try to facilitate her voicing what goes on when she is down, that not only does she feel down but she feels bad about herself for feeling down and feels lonely in her sadness and uncertain whether he is interested in hearing about it. For him, we would try to facilitate what goes on with him, such as his sense of helplessness when she feels down. If these discussions work, she would not feel alone but connected during them and he would not feel so helpless but experience that listening to her and not trying to correct her feelings actually makes her feel better. Thus, the discussions themselves could bring about the changes that each wants. During unified detachment discussions, we would help them walk through the behavioral sequence that occurred, such as during a recent incident, when they didn't handle her being down well, and also walk them through the behavioral sequence that occurred when they had a recent incident when they handled her being down better. As a result of both these empathic joining and unified detachment discussions, which often happen together, the partners might make spontaneous changes in their behavior that better the situation. However, we could also hold discussions with them about how they might be able to respond differently in ways that would alter their usual pattern. Depending on how these discussions go and how her depression evolves, we could help them problem solve, as a team, about what additional steps might be helpful for her depression, such as individual therapy or medication.

Effectiveness of IBCT for Couples
with Psychopathology

In our clinical trial of IBCT versus TBCT, we did diagnostic interviews of each partner and found that 15.6% of partners met criteria for a current DSM-IV diagnosable disorder while 56% of partners met criteria for a lifetime diagnosable disorder (Atkins et al., 2005). We also measured a variety of mental health symptoms and functioning to create a mental health index.

Neither the diagnosis nor our mental health index was related to amount of improvement in relationship satisfaction at termination (Atkins et al., 2005), at 2-year follow-up (Baucom, Atkins, Simpson, & Christensen, 2009), or 5-year follow-up (Baucom, Atkins, Rowe, & Christensen, 2015). Furthermore, the mental health index improved during treatment as relationship satisfaction improved (Christensen et al., 2004). Thus, the available evidence on in-person IBCT suggests it can be effective for couples with a partner suffering from current or past psychopathology. This data is buttressed by the data on our online program in IBCT, which we will describe in the next chapter. In nationwide clinical trials, partners improved not only in relationship satisfaction but in depression, anxiety, and problematic alcohol use—especially when people entered the program with problems in those domains (Doss et al., 2016; Roddy et al., in press). Moreover, these effects were maintained for at least a year after treatment (Doss et al., 2019; Roddy, Knopp, Georgia Salivar, & Doss, in press).

SUMMARY

In this chapter, we reviewed four special problems in couple therapy: intimate partner violence, sexual problems, infidelity, and individual psychopathology. We briefly reviewed some demographic data on the prevalence of these problems and their clear link with relationship discord. Then we described the accommodations that IBCT makes in treating each of these problems and the impact of IBCT on these problems.

IPV requires careful assessment to determine if couples can participate safely and appropriately in IBCT. Although the general guideline is the absence of any injury from physical violence in the last year and no current fear of physical violence in retaliation for voicing one's views, determining if this guideline has been met can be tricky. The commitment that the couple has to staying together and the availability of alternative treatment, as well as the risk for violence, can also affect the decision on whether to treat a couple with IPV. If a couple with some level of violence is considered for IBCT, the couple must endorse the goal of a nonviolent relationship and accept personal responsibility for any violence. If a couple accepts these conditions, IBCT therapist may have them sign a no-violence contract, develop safety plans, and focus therapeutic efforts on provocative incidents, helping them develop strategies of de-escalation during those incidents. Constant monitoring of any violent incidents is a part of any IBCT treatment. If a couple is unable to control violence through couple therapy, then the therapist is in a strong position to encourage the ending of their couple relationship. If the couple is not able to end violence with the help and monitoring of a trusted third party, they are unlikely to be able to do so on their own.

Sexual problems are somewhat different from other problems that trouble couples in that they may call into question the fundamental connection between partners, may raise serious concerns about one's self-worth as a sexual partner, and may be associated with shame and embarrassment. In doing IBCT, we always want to assess for sexual difficulties, through both questionnaire and interview. If there are sexual problems, we need to assess them to determine whether they can be treated in IBCT or require special expertise. Sexual dysfunctions or paraphilic disorders usually require specialized treatment and expertise. Conflicts about frequency or type of sex, as well sexual distancing because of anger and resentment, can be treated with IBCT. We briefly reviewed how IBCT handles these sexual difficulties.

IBCT uses a broad definition of infidelity, describing infidelity as a secret emotional or sexual relationship that violates the couple's mutual understanding of their commitment to each other. Thus, infidelity can even occur in sexually open relationships if one partner has sex in ways that violate their understanding, such as by having sex with a mutual friend. In our assessment of couples, we are concerned about current infidelity rather than past infidelity unless past infidelity is an ongoing issue of the partners. We want to learn of any current infidelity and we promise partners confidentiality from the other but will only conduct couple therapy if partners end any current, competing relationship or reveal it to the partner. These incidents of current infidelity present a difficult but fortunately infrequent challenge for the therapist. The more common situation is when partners present with past or current infidelity as a presenting problem. In describing our work with these kinds of couples, we reviewed several important principles, such as the notion that both partners are responsible for problems in their relationship but only the partner participating in an affair is responsible for engaging in that affair. We also reviewed the major challenges that couples face and how we help in IBCT, such as deciding to stay or leave, ending the competing relationship, and handling the ongoing issue of trust.

Individual psychopathology is often part of a distressed relationship, with a reciprocal influence between the two. However, individual psychopathology can exist in a good relationship and there are couple-based approaches that use the relationship to assist individual therapy (e.g., Fischer & Baucom, 2019). IBCT is more appropriate for couples in distress who also have individual pathology. We reviewed assessment and treatment issues when partners have both relationship distress and problems with individual functioning and when they disagree about whether one has a mental disorder. As always, we do the DEEP analysis and try to alter the pattern of communication between couples, particularly the pattern that exists when one partner exhibits pathology-related behavior, such as depressive or anxious behavior.

Finally, for each of these four problems we reviewed data from our IBCT clinical trial that supports the effectiveness of IBCT for couples with each of these special problems as well as sometimes suggests changes in the way we do IBCT. We also briefly mentioned relevant data from our nationwide clinical trial of an online version of IBCT. In the next chapter, we look at that online program in depth and present a model for how it can be integrated into a condensed format of IBCT.

14

&

OurRelationship.com and IBCT: A Model for Integration

THE OURRELATIONSHIP PROGRAM is an online self-help program based on IBCT principles that can be completed on a computer, tablet, or smartphone. It is a stand-alone online program but, like the IBCT self-help book, *Reconcilable Differences* (Christensen et al., 2014), can be used as homework to introduce or reinforce many of the concepts couples learn during sessions. It can also be the foundation for an abbreviated form of IBCT, which is especially useful when therapists are initially learning IBCT or when financial or logistical concerns limit the duration of treatment.

The OurRelationship program consists of three phases—Observe, Understand, and Respond—that comprise the OUR acronym. In the **O**bserve phase, couples get objective feedback on their general relationship functioning (e.g., overall happiness, relative amounts of positives versus negatives) and are guided through identifying one or two central relationship problems (i.e., core issues) that they want to focus on. In the **U**nderstand phase, couples develop a DEEP understanding of their core issues, including receiving detailed, objective feedback on important **D**ifferences (e.g., personality, attachment styles, emotional expressiveness) and **E**xternal stress. In

Emotions, couples explore their surface and hidden emotions and how these emotions are triggered by previous experiences. Next, in the **P**atterns activity, couples identify their patterns of communication during and following an argument about their core issues. Finally, in the **R**espond phase of OurRelationship, couples are introduced to the distinction between acceptance and change and identify specific changes to improve their issues. During each phase, partners initially work alone and then come together and share their work with each other in a conversation guided by the program. Throughout the program, couples watch videos of demographically diverse example couples and learn key information through a combination of narrated animation and text. The program requires a total of 6–8 hours of time from each partner, typically done over the course of several weeks. We describe the program in more detail in the remainder of the chapter.

There are several versions of the OurRelationship program that therapists may find useful. There are versions for partners to do together as well as versions that an individual can do on his or her own. The OurRelationship program is currently available in English and in Spanish with or without a coach. When couples or individuals opt to do the program with a coach, they have four brief video or phone calls with a staff member to answer technical questions, keep them on schedule, and help them apply the program to the specifics of their relationship. Finally, we are currently working on developing a version of the program tailored to same-sex couples and translating the program into additional languages. Therapists can find out more information about the programs currently available, pricing, and resources to help them integrate the program into their practice at www.OurRelationship .com/therapists.

EVIDENCE FOR THE EFFECTIVENESS OF THE OURRELATIONSHIP PROGRAM

To date, the OurRelationship program has been shown to be effective in three nationwide randomized controlled trials involving over 1400 couples (Doss et al., 2016; Doss et al., 2020; Roddy, Rothman, & Doss, 2018)— more couples than have been involved in all randomized controlled trials of in-person couple therapy combined. Additionally, the OurRelationship program has been tested on large samples of low-income couples and racial or ethnic minority couples, indicating that it can be useful to groups that have not historically been served by couple therapy. Below, we review the evidence for the OurRelationship program in more detail.

We want to be careful to note upfront that these studies have tested the OurRelationship program supported by one to four 15-minute calls with a coach (typically a student in a masters or doctoral graduate program). To date, we have not yet tested the effectiveness of the OurRelationship program integrated into a course of treatment with an IBCT therapist. However, we would expect this integration to be even *more* effective than our previous studies for a number of reasons. First, the dosage is significantly higher and provides the opportunity for therapists to intervene during the key conversations couples have with each other (in the online version, couples have those conversations on their own). Second, because therapists know their couples better than online coaches, therapists can tailor the OurRelationship content to the specific needs of the couple. Finally, the increased alliance and rapport between couples and therapists can facilitate completion of the activities in a way that the online coaches cannot.

Effects on Relationship Functioning

The OurRelationship program has been shown to improve relationship functioning in three separate randomized clinical trials (Doss et al., 2016; Doss et al., 2020; Roddy, Rothman, & Doss, 2018). Here, we will focus on results of the OurRelationship program compared to a no-treatment wait list control group, as those offer the strongest experimental evidence. All of the effects we describe below were statistically significant in their respective studies; however, we focus here on between-group Cohen's d because this metric places the focus on the magnitude of the effect. For comparison, the between-group effects of couple therapy on relationship satisfaction are typically within the medium to large range (Cohen's d = 0.59 to 0.84; Shadish & Baldwin, 2003, 2005), with the major clinical trial of IBCT having a within-group effect size at treatment termination of 0.90 (Christensen et al., 2010).

Compared to a control group, couples experienced significantly greater improvements during the OurRelationship program in relationship satisfaction (d = 0.53 to 0.69), emotional intimacy (d = 0.46), relationship confidence or break-up potential (d = 0.47 to 0.53), and communication conflict (d = -0.78), and greater reductions in intimate partner violence (d = -0.28). Although the OurRelationship program has not been directly compared with couple therapy, these effect sizes indicate that when this program is delivered in conjunction with four 15-minute coach calls, it is either just as effective or almost as effective as most couple therapies. Furthermore, our studies have shown that the effects of the OurRelationship program last for at least a year after the end of treatment (Doss et al., 2019; Roddy, Knopp, Georgia Salivar, & Doss, in press).

Effects on Individual Mental and Physical Health

The OurRelationship program has also been shown to significantly improve both mental health and physical health. However, the magnitude of these effects often differs by whether an individual had problems in these areas. Unlike relationship distress, in which the vast majority of couples presented in the distressed range, many individuals did not have serious mental or physical health problems when beginning the program. Therefore, we present effects separately for all individuals and those individuals who began the program in the distressed range.

In both nationally representative samples (Doss et al., 2016) and samples of low-income couples (Roddy, Rhoades, & Doss, in press), the OurRelationship program has been shown to improve depressive symptoms (all individuals: d = -0.36 to -0.50; initially distressed individuals: d = -0.42 to -0.71) as well as anxious symptoms (all individuals: d = -0.21 to -0.36; initially distressed individuals: d = -0.42 to -0.94). Participants also reported decreases in perceived stress (all individuals: d = -0.42; initially distressed individuals: d = -0.48), anger (all individuals: d = -0.23; initially distressed individuals: d = -0.39), and problematic alcohol use (all individuals: d = -0.11; initially distressed individuals: d = -0.33).

Couples participating in the OurRelationship program also report significantly greater improvements in other domains of individual functioning than do couples in a control group. Specifically, couples in the program experience improvements in perceived health (all individuals: $d = 0.12$ to 0.23; initially distressed individuals: $d = 0.42$ to 0.51), insomnia (all individuals: $d = -0.24$; initially distressed individuals: $d = -0.41$), quality of life (all individuals: $d = 0.18$; initially distressed individuals: $d = 0.44$), and work functioning (all individuals: $d = 0.19$; initially distressed individuals: $d = 0.57$). As we previously mentioned, we expect that the addition of sessions with an IBCT therapist following the protocol described in this chapter will increase the program's effects on relationship functioning, mental health, and physical health behaviors.

WAYS THE OURRELATIONSHIP PROGRAM CAN SUPPLEMENT A THERAPY PRACTICE

There are four primary ways in which we believe the OurRelationship program can be helpful to IBCT therapists, their practice, and the clients they treat. Notably, none of these uses requires the therapist to access client data on the OurRelationship site—instead relying on couples to access their own data on their own devices (either during or outside of session). This approach minimizes security and HIPPA-compliance concerns because the program serves as a self-help resource rather than a therapist-provided service.

To Supplement Individual Therapy

It is not uncommon for relationship issues to arise during individual therapy focused on other topics. Rather than referring out for couple therapy, therapists can encourage an individual client of theirs to complete either the couple or individual version of the OurRelationship program. In the individual version, clients complete the program without their partner and are provided with suggestions for how to share what they've learned with their partner at the end of the program. As described in more detail below, the therapist could review key concepts and expand upon program content at key moments during the program (e.g., after each of the three program phases).

As Homework During Couple Therapy

Instead of using *Reconcilable Differences*, as we encourage in other parts of this book, the OurRelationship program could be used to conduct assessments and provide feedback. Additionally, the program could be used to introduce key concepts or skills—which might be especially helpful for clients who would benefit from video examples. Using the program, rather than the book, might make it more likely that both members of the couple complete the homework assignment.

Integrated into a Course of Couple Therapy

Perhaps the most powerful way to use the OurRelationship program is to integrate it into standard practice, replacing some face-to-face sessions with the online program. There are at least three reasons to take such an approach.

First, couples are often limited in the number of face-to-face sessions they can afford, either because of insurance restrictions (e.g., limits on number of sessions or the therapist being out of network) or because they are not able to afford to pay out of pocket for a full course of treatment. In those situations, supplementing in-person sessions with the online program can be an alternative to reducing therapists' hourly rate or providing a shortened version of typical IBCT that might have limited effectiveness.

Second, some couples have restrictions on the number of in-person sessions they can attend because of scheduling difficulties (e.g., different work schedules; limited child care), because they are located a long distance from a therapist's office, because one or both partners travel often, or because the couple themselves are in a long-distance relationship (and therefore both partners are only sporadically in the same location as the therapist). It is possible for therapists to use the OurRelationship program as part of telehealth services and never have an in-person session. The existing research on telehealth generally—and the OurRelationship program specifically—would suggest that such an approach could be an effective and exciting way for IBCT therapists to increase the reach of their services.

Third, some couples make a tentative call to a therapist for the first time and are hesitant to get involved (e.g., never done it before, it is costly, time-consuming). In our provision of the OurRelationship program, a common reason for seeking help online is that one partner—often the man—is reluctant to seek help for their relationship. In these situations, the OurRelationship program could be used as a first step; the couple might find sufficient benefit from the program so that is all they need or, once they have experience with the program and have overcome their initial hesitation, the couple might want to continue to make gains during in-person therapy. Thus, a therapist could use the OurRelationship program as a way of getting a foot in the door when one or both members of the couple are initially reluctant about therapy.

As a Way to Get Started Providing IBCT

When we train therapists in IBCT within the Department of Veterans Affairs (VA), we conduct an intensive initial training followed by 6 months of weekly supervision with an expert IBCT consultant—including the consultant listening to tapes of actual sessions and providing feedback. Unfortunately, most readers of this book will not have that same level of training in IBCT. Therefore, we suggest that therapists who are beginning to implement IBCT consider integrating the OurRelationship program into their practice, following the structure we provide in this chapter. As we describe below, couples who complete the program will have already started to conceptualize their relationship difficulties in an IBCT framework, which will facilitate the therapist's conceptualization and feedback. Additionally, the program will help structure the couple's conversations of difficult topics.

ASSESSMENT AND FEEDBACK PHASE OF IBCT INTEGRATED WITH OURRELATIONSHIP

In this section, we describe the OurRelationship program in greater detail and introduce an eight-session framework for integrating the OurRelationship program into IBCT. We believe this eight-session model will provide the optimal balance of effectiveness and ease of attendance for most couples.

However, we recognize that some couples may need fewer or additional sessions; after outlining the eight-session structure, we include ideas on how to reduce this model to as few as four sessions and suggest ways in which additional sessions could be added.

To illustrate this material, we imagine how Hank and Maria—the couple we met in Chapter 1—could have utilized the OurRelationship program during this eight-session model of IBCT. Because Hank does not have a very positive view of the mental health field in general—which has only been reinforced in his view by therapists' inability to diagnose their son James, if indeed he has a diagnosis at all—Hank was reluctant to begin couple therapy. However, he acquiesced to Maria and agreed to participate in a brief, eight-session course of IBCT supplemented by the OurRelationship program.

IBCT Session 1: Initial Meeting and Program Introduction

When incorporating the OurRelationship program into IBCT, we recommend therapists begin with an initial, conjoint session—much as described in Chapter 4. In that session therapists would get an understanding of the couple's one or two core issues as well as their relationship strengths. Consistent with their presentation in Chapter 1, Maria described her concerns about their son James' developmental delays and how Hank did not support her in her parenting; in fact, she complained that Hank seemed to undermine the support she provided to James by being overly strict and harsh. Hank countered that Maria was too permissive with James, making James' difficulties worse. However, Hank's primary concern that he voiced was that Maria spent little time and energy on their romantic relationship—especially their sexual relationship.

When using the OurRelationship program, there are three additional tasks—not described in Chapter 4—for the therapist to accomplish at the end of this initial session. First, the therapist should introduce the OurRelationship program to couples and describe how it will be used as an integral part of treatment. To facilitate this discussion, therapists can download and print a description at www.OurRelationship.com/therapists.

Second, the therapist should help the couple decide whether they want to work on one or two core issues during the OurRelationship program. After discussing the presenting problems, the therapist usually has a good sense of whether there is one core issue or whether there are two distinct issues. If there are more than two distinct issues, we encourage couples to wait to address those additional issues until after the first two issues are tackled. We generally find it is useful to combine issues A and B in the following situations:

- If issue A is a subset of issue B.
- If A and B have the same polarization process.
- If fixing issue A would naturally create significant improvements in issue B.
- If the therapist is confident that the same DEEP understanding underlies both A and B.

In contrast, there are at least two instances in which therapists should encourage couples to treat A and B as two core issues, even if they meet some of the same characteristics above:

- One or both partners do not see the connection between the two issues or pushes back at the idea of combining them.
- One or both partners will likely refuse to consider changes in core issue A unless changes in core issue B are also being considered.

Consistent with their initial presentation, Maria chose "Coparenting conflict" and Hank chose "Lack of physical affection and warmth/intimacy" as their core issues. For Maria and Hank, it was important for the therapist to keep their core issues distinct for two reasons. First, the content of them—and their DEEP understandings—are different. One could imagine Hank feeling there was not sufficient emotional and physical intimacy even if they agreed on how to coparent James. Similarly, improvements in their romantic relationship are unlikely to fully address Maria's coparenting concerns. Second, neither Maria nor Hank would probably be willing to fully commit to the changes the other was wanting without seeing that their own issues and desired changes would be addressed. If couples are undecided about whether to focus on a single core issue or work on two core issues simultaneously, we generally recommend couples focus first on a single core issue. Doing so will help them move more efficiently through the online program and, if they still would like to work on the other core issue, they can do so in the optional Strengthen phase of the program described below.

Third, the therapist should assign the couple to do the Observe phase before returning for individual sessions. For couples with less familiarity with technology, it may be helpful to demonstrate how to access and navigate the program.

OurRelationship Program: Observe Phase

Assessment and feedback. Couples begin the program in the Observe phase—the "O" of OUR. After viewing some instructions on how to use the program, each member of the couple completes a brief assessment about their relationship—a quick assessment of overall relationship satisfaction (a four-item version of the Couple Satisfaction Index, described in Chapter 4) and separate brief assessments of relationship negatives (e.g., conflict, negativity) and positives (e.g., affection, closeness). The individual then receives feedback on these three areas in the form of graphs and text tailored to their answers.

Maria saw that her global relationship satisfaction was in the distressed red range—similar to couples who seek couple therapy or file for divorce. She read that it was important for her to take action (e.g., seeking therapy) to improve her relationship. Additionally, her ratings of both the positive and negative domains of her relationship were in the red range. Hank saw similar feedback to Maria, although his global relationship satisfaction was in the red/yellow range. His ratings of positivity were in the red range but negativity was in the yellow range; therefore, the program encouraged him to focus on improving positives—rather than reducing negatives—during the program.

Selecting a label for their core issue and positives activities. Next, the program helps each member of the couple select a label for their relationship problem that they want to improve—the core issue that is identified at the end of the conjoint session. Each partner is asked to write a brief label of this issue as well as a longer description of it into the program. These labels and descriptions are saved to their account. Consistent with their presentation in the initial joint meetings, Maria labeled her issue "Coparenting conflict" and Hank labeled his issue as "Lack of intimacy/warmth."

After picking their core issue, each partner is then asked to choose one-to-five activities that they would enjoy doing with their partner in the next couple of weeks. These can be things that the couple used to do together—but have stopped—or new things they want to try out. We emphasize that they should not be related to the core issue or something that has caused fights in the past. Individuals are informed that they will share these activity ideas with their partner in the next activity, with what they wrote as possible activities displayed on the screen.

Maria and Hank selected some good possibilities during this activity including meeting up for lunch two times per week on weekdays, when James is at preschool and getting a babysitter two times per month so they can go out to dinner and a movie. Each also selected some activities that overlap somewhat with their core issues, so the therapist would need to ensure that these would not cause a fight before encouraging them. For example, Hank chose "Watch a movie on the TV before bed on Friday nights." As Maria often falls asleep in James' bed at night, it would be important that Maria was committed to this idea. Similarly, Maria chose "Go to the park as a family," which could trigger some of Hank's concerns about being left out when Maria and James are together. It would be important to ensure that Hank would enjoy this activity.

Speaker and listener communication skills. To help couples prepare for the conversation to share their ideas for positive activities, the program introduces couples to the speaker-listener conversation structure (described in Chapter 11). Additionally, couples learn about tips for things they can do as both the speaker and the listener to help the conversation go well.

Conversation to share ideas for positive activities. In this activity, the positive activities that each member chose are displayed on the screen and, using a speaker-listener structure, the program encourages the couple to discuss their ideas. At the end of the conversation, they are also encouraged to select a few fun activities to do together before their next session with the therapist as well as a few activities they could do over a longer period of time—but before the end of the treatment. The purpose of this conversation is twofold. First, it allows couples to get an initial experience with the speaker-listener structure with a low-conflict topic; this practice will enable them to use that structure more effectively with conflictual topics later in therapy. Second, it gives the couple an opportunity to improve some of the positives in their relationship. Earlier versions of the OurRelationship program lacking these positives did not create increases in positives during the program (Doss et al., 2016; although positives did increase in the year following the program: Doss et al., 2019).

IBCT Session 2: Individual Meetings with Both Partners

After couples complete the Observe phase, we recommend having two, 20-minute individual sessions with each member of the couple. In the individual sessions, as described in Chapter 4, it continues to be important to assess for severe intimate partner violence and ongoing mental health issues that may be contraindicators for couple therapy. The OurRelationship program has been shown to help couples with mild-moderate IPV and mental health difficulties—and even create meaningful improvements in both (Doss et al., 2020; Roddy, Georgia, & Doss, 2018; Roddy, Rhoades, & Doss, in press); therefore, the same exclusionary criteria for IBCT can be applied to provision of the OurRelationship program. Because of the reduced time available for the individual sessions, we recommend omitting continued assessment of the core issues, as the couple will have an opportunity to form a DEEP understanding during the program. For their part, both Hank and Maria denied intimate partner violence resulting in fear or injury, severe mental health difficulties, or ongoing affairs during their individual meetings.

In the final 10 minutes (of the 50 minute-long appointment), we suggest therapists bring both partners together to describe the Understand phase of the OurRelationship program. At this point, the couple and therapist will also need to decide whether the couple will share their DEEP understandings with each other during the next conjoint session or during a structured conversation as part of the program (described below). For couples who are unlikely to get into an argument during this structured conversation, sharing their DEEP understandings before the next therapy session as part of the online program can allow that therapy session to focus on debriefing the conversation (utilizing unified detachment or empathic joining, as appropriate) and reviewing the specific content of their DEEP understandings. On the other hand, for couples who are likely to get into an argument or might be dismissive of their partner's perspectives, it might be best to have the sharing occur with the therapist present.

Finally, if time permits, it can be helpful to review the ideas the couple came up with for fun activities they can do together and see how those activities went (consistent with our broad goal in IBCT to catch positive behavior). Additionally, we can use this opportunity to ensure they have a specific plan to do some of the fun activities in the upcoming week. As described previously, we would want to make sure that some of the ideas for positive activities Maria and Hank came up with would not trigger conflict related to their core issues. We would also want to make sure that they had a shared, concrete plan—for example, the specific days and times to meet for lunch—and had thought through any barriers that might get in the way.

OurRelationship Program: Understand Phase

The primary goal of the Understand phase is to help couples develop a DEEP understanding (as described in Chapter 3) of the core issue they picked. If the couple chose to work on two core issues, each person first focuses on the core issue they picked before then developing a DEEP understanding of the core issue their partner picked. At the end of the phase, the couple again meets with their therapist to share their DEEP understandings; if two issues are selected, it will likely require two 50-minute sessions to complete the sharing.

DEEP Activities. Each member of the couple completes activities on the four DEEP components individually, separate from their partner. The activities follow a similar structure—initial education on the topic (accompanied by animations and videos of example couples) followed by a section allowing them to select how that DEEP component applies to the core issue that the individual picked.

In the Differences activity, individuals are introduced to the first video example couple, who illustrate both similarities and differences. The program then displays graphs and descriptions of how these couples score on measures of common differences (e.g., personality, emotional expressiveness, attachment styles). Then, individuals are asked to consider their own relationship and are shown how they *and* their partner score in these same domains. (These scores are populated from the individual's and partner's responses to the standardized assessment in the Observe phase.) Sometimes, the *lack* of differences can also be meaningful to couples. For example, Hank was surprised to see that he and Maria scored similarly on their level of desired closeness. After viewing this feedback, individuals also have an opportunity to explore numerous other potential differences or similarities (e.g., parenting styles, sexual preferences) that can cause problems in some relationships. Finally, both partners are asked to pick the difference or similarity that is most related to their core issue and write brief descriptions about why they chose this domain and give a recent example. For their core issues, Maria chose differences in parenting style (strict versus accommodating) and Hank chose differences in sexual desire.

In the Emotions chapter, individuals meet a different video couple and see how the couple tends to express surface, hard emotions instead of the underlying hidden, soft, or vulnerable emotions. They have a chance to learn how the couple's conversations go much better when the couple is able to identify and then share their hidden, soft, or vulnerable emotion with their partner. Individuals also get an understanding of how previous experiences can make the hidden emotions so painful by seeing examples from the video couple. Turning to their own relationship, users are then asked to identify the surface emotions they and their partner typically show during the core issue and speculate about what underlying emotions they might both be feeling. Individuals are also encouraged to identify any previous experiences—either from earlier in this relationship or earlier in their lives—that might explain why their hidden emotions are especially powerful for them. As in the Differences chapter, all of this information is saved by the program.

After going through this activity, Hank was able to identify that he feels unloved when Maria does not respond to his bids for emotional or sexual closeness—and that this feeling is especially painful because of his previous relationship that ended because of him feeling like a third wheel to his partner's child. For her part, Maria feels alone and isolated when Hank challenges her parenting of James—made all the more painful because of the contrast with her memories of how her own parents came together to care for her disabled brother.

Next, in the External stress chapter, couples see a third example couple and learn how common external stressors exacerbate this couple's core issue. Individuals then receive graphical and text feedback on their *and* their partner's level of perceived stress (as rated in the Observe phase by both members of the couple). Couples are then asked to identify a few things that are causing them stress individually and a few things that are causing their partner's stress. While Maria and Hank have some other stressors in their lives (especially money concerns), they both selected James' developmental delays as the biggest source of external stress for both of their core issues. The chapter on Patterns of communication covers two broad categories of communication around the core issue—patterns the couple experience *during* conversations about their core issue and patterns of recovery *after* those conversations. As in other DEEP activities, individuals see an example video couple illustrating these often problematic patterns before being asked to identify the types of patterns they experience with their own core issue. During conversations about the core issue, for example, users are asked to pick the behavior that they and their partner tend to do most often: criticize or blame, avoid or withdraw, monitor or investigate, or calmly discuss. Following an argument about their core issue, users are asked to consider their patterns of recovery method, recovery speed, and the role of apologies.

Over time, both Hank and Maria have started avoiding communication around their core issues. Maria assumes that Hank will not be supportive of her parenting decisions and no longer asks for his assistance or his opinions regarding James. Although Hank will occasionally make bids for sexual activity, he typically does not initiate anymore because he assumes Maria will not be interested. They also have important differences in the way they recover from an argument about these issues. Hank tends to want to "just move on" relatively quickly after a fight and doesn't feel that anyone needs to apologize; his priority is to get back to normal with as minimal fuss as possible. Maria, in contrast, doesn't really want to be around Hank until she's recovered emotionally from the fight and wants the guilty party (usually Hank!) to apologize before she can get back to normal. Not surprisingly, they sometimes get into a second fight about how they dealt with the first fight, with Hank accusing Maria of holding the first fight over his head and Maria countering that Hank is trying to minimize the conflict.

Polarization over time. After developing a DEEP understanding of their core issue, the next chapter encourages individuals to consider how the DEEP components have changed over time. We introduce the idea of polarization and illustrate through video and audio of our example couples how those couples' issues became more challenging over time.

DEEP understanding of a partner's core issue. If the couple chose to work on two different core issues, then both people are asked to develop a DEEP understanding of the core issue their partner chose. Because individuals are already familiar with the components of the DEEP understanding, this chapter does not contain the educational components and video examples from earlier chapters. It focuses instead on asking users to select the options or write the responses about their own relationship related to the second core issue.

Because Hank and Maria were working on two core issues, they both had an opportunity to think about the other's core issue at this point. The activity on Emotions, in particular, was impactful for both of them. In thinking about her hidden or soft emotion, Maria teared up because it has been such a long time since she had felt excited to have sex with Hank—and she really missed that; it used to be something she loved about him and their relationship. For his part, the Emotions activity enabled Hank to realize what really bothered him about the way Maria parented James wasn't the parenting at all—it was how it made him feel that Maria didn't care about him, that somehow James was all that mattered.

Sharing DEEP understandings (optional). If the couple chooses to share their DEEP understanding with each other before the next therapy session, they will complete an activity that will allow them to have a conversation following the speaker-listener structure. Specifically, what each person picked or wrote about for each of the DEEP components is displayed on the screen and they are asked to talk about it with their partner. The partner then has a chance to paraphrase before then presenting his or her perspective on that component. If couples choose to work on two core issues, they will have two separate conversations—one for each core issue.

IBCT Session 3: Feedback Following the Understand Phase

The primary function of this session is to solidify couples' DEEP understandings and describe the intervention phase. In this way, this session broadly functions as the feedback session, with many of the same goals as described in Chapter 5. However, the specific content of this session will depend on whether couples choose to share their DEEP understandings through the online activity or wait to share with the therapist present.

If couples will share their DEEP understandings during the session. Note: If the couple is working on two core issues, it will be necessary for the therapists to schedule two feedback sessions—one for each core issue—because the couples' conversation to share each of their DEEP understandings will likely be longer than 30 minutes per core issue.

In session, the couple can log into the program (using their own smartphone, tablet, or laptop computer) and launch the DEEP conversation activity. Following instructions on the screen, the couple can share with each other what they've written into the program. Once the first person has shared what he or she chose as the biggest difference related to the core issue, the partner is asked to paraphrase. If preferred, the therapist can ask couples to skip the paraphrasing step and just use the device to help each partner remember what they chose or wrote in the program.

Then, the couple switches roles and the partner becomes the speaker. When this happens, the new speaker should take the mobile device (which is functioning as the "floor card" discussed as part of Communication Training in Chapter 11) and read what he or she chose as the biggest difference. If desired by the therapist, the other person is then asked to paraphrase.

After both partners are done sharing their perspectives on Differences, we would then add any observations or information that we found relevant in our own formulation of the couple. We generally encourage therapists to allow both partners to share what they wrote in the program before opening up the session to a broader conversation designed to facilitate unified detachment. Specifically, we would then utilize some of the unified detachment strategies, described in detail in Chapter 7. For example, the therapist could highlight how these differences really are normal, natural, and understandable. The therapist could explore whether those differences had always been present or had evolved over time because of changing life situations. The therapist could encourage the couple to consider whether these same differences are also a source of strength or enjoyment in other areas of their relationship—either currently or in the past.

After this discussion, the couple would share what they wrote in the Emotions chapter, following the same structure as described for Differences. They would continue in this same way for the External stress and Patterns of communication chapters. After each of these sections of the DEEP understanding, as with the Differences section, the therapist could offer additional information that might enhance the couple's understanding. For example, the therapist might bring up material from the individual sessions to enhance the understanding of the origin of one or both of the partner's sensitivities. Or the therapist might help the couple articulate more clearly the patterns of interaction and recovery that occur around their core issue.

It is important for us to note here that, even during these structured conversations, we want to continue to prioritize powerful emotions either partner is experiencing in the session. For example, sharing of vulnerable, hidden emotions can often create powerful emotions—especially if these hidden emotions haven't been shared before. If this occurs, the therapist should allow the speaker-listener structure to fade into the background and instead focus on the emotions in the room, using empathic joining techniques. For example, in their discussion of Maria's core issue, Hank revealed that he worried Maria's focus on James meant that she didn't love him anymore. His complaints of Maria coddling James by taking so much time to put him to bed and falling asleep with James weren't so much about coddling James as they were about not being able to spend time with her. After Hank shared those vulnerable emotions in the speaker role, we would quickly transition to empathic joining. As the therapist, we would likely reflect how powerful those feelings were for Hank (i.e., heightening the emotion) before asking Maria to share what it was like to hear Hank share that with her. Only after the empathic joining intervention had run its course would we move on to discussion of the Patterns of communication.

Finally, toward the end of the session, we return to the enjoyable activities the couple elected to do together at the end of the Observe phase. Because the therapy sessions are focused on the core issues they chose to focus on, including a brief discussion of fun activities will perhaps help the couple remember their relationship strengths and help the session end on a positive note. As with all therapy homework, it is also important to follow up to promote compliance with the assignment. We want to assess whether the couple has engaged in those activities. If so, did they find them enjoyable? If not, what barriers kept them from doing so? Do they want to recommit to continuing to do those activities together? If not, what other activities can they select?

At the end of the session, or the end of the second session, if the couple chose to work on two core issues, we discuss the next steps in therapy with the couple (described below).

If couples have already shared their DEEP understandings through the program. In this situation, we typically like to start with a debriefing of the conversations they had with each other. If the conversation went poorly, we respond with unified detachment or a combination of unified detachment and empathic joining. With unified detachment, we help the couple understand which components of the DEEP model got them into trouble. For example, did they get sucked back into their typical Pattern? Did a Difference or External stress make sharing difficult? Or did surface emotions, rather than the softer hidden emotions, derail the conversation? If the conversation went poorly and one or both are still upset by it or a discussion of the conversation leads to such upset, we use empathic joining the explore the emotions that got triggered for each and use unified detachment to detail the sequence that led to the upset. We also want to link this upset to the sensitivities and patterns of the DEEP analysis. On the other hand, if the conversation went well, we respond with empathic joining, exploring the positive emotions that partners may have felt. Generally, this involves asking couples to tell us about the best part of the conversation and following up with questions like "What was it like for you to share that with your partner?" and "What was it like for your partner to share that with you?"

After debriefing the conversation, we ask couples to tell us what they picked for their DEEP components. As described in the previous section, we follow up with each of the DEEP components—either to offer our own perspectives on what they chose or to flesh out the couple's conceptualization of each of the components. For example, after couples share the differences they picked, we might enquire about the origins of those differences, if their effect has changed over time, or whether those problematic differences are related to any strengths of the partner or of the relationship. During these conversations, we're always on the lookout for opportunities to engage the couple in empathic joining around any emotions that emerge in session.

After completing the DEEP understanding phase of session 3, we describe for couples what the intervention phase will look like, similarly to what was described in the feedback session in Chapter 5. For example, we introduce the Weekly Questionnaire and discuss how it will focus our treatment efforts. We also mention to the couples that we will ask them to do the Respond phase of the OurRelationship program but only after we have completed a couple of treatment sessions.

INTERVENTION PHASE OF IBCT INTEGRATED WITH OURRELATIONSHIP

IBCT Sessions 4 and 5: IBCT Intervention Sessions

As described in Chapter 5, we use the Weekly Questionnaire to begin each session, helping couples apply their DEEP understandings to the most salient positive and negative events in the past week as well as deal with challenging issues and upcoming events. Armed with their DEEP understandings, couples start to view their relationships in more accurate ways. They may start to see new avenues to improve their relationship—and may even begin to implement some of these changes on their own. They may also continue to struggle with long-standing issues. Therefore, what a couple needs at this point varies greatly from couple to couple. As IBCT therapists, we are accepting of these challenges and meet a couple where they are—offering empathic joining, unified detachment, or tolerance interventions as appropriate (and as described in Chapters 6–8).

Within an eight-session framework, our hope would be that a couple's collaborative set is strong enough by the fifth session that we could begin to consider adding some deliberate change strategies to our acceptance interventions. If so, at the end of session five, we introduce the Respond phase of the OurRelationship program and assign it to be completed before the following session. In the Respond phase, couples work toward making specific, deliberate changes to improve their relationship. Therefore, a couple's success in the Respond phase is dependent on many of the considerations described in Chapter 9 (Deliberate Change). For example, if couples do not have a collaborative approach to the activities and are more interested in scoring points off each other than working together to jointly problem solve, the Respond phase will not be very effective. Therefore, if we do not believe couples have this collaborative set (i.e., attitude) and we have additional therapy sessions available to us, we recommend conducting additional sessions of treatment before assigning the Respond activities.

As with the Understand phase, therapists should work with couples at this point to decide whether they will have a conversation with each other about the changes they came up with before the next therapy session (facilitated by the program) or whether they will wait to share those changes only during the therapy session. Couples with strong collaborative sets and those who were successful sharing their DEEP understandings as part of the program are likely good candidates for having those conversations on their own.

OurRelationship Program: Respond Phase

Acceptance versus change. In the first chapter of the phase, couples are introduced to the concepts of acceptance and deliberate change using a modified version of the serenity prayer—distinguishing between things that are largely outside of their direct control (e.g., their natural differences and hidden emotions that are triggered) from things that are under their control (e.g., their patterns of communication, how they cope with external stress, and facets of their core issue). These concepts are illustrated with video and audio from the example couples.

Deliberately changing patterns. With a better understanding of the limits of deliberate change, couples are ready to make a plan for those changes. In the first activity in this section, couples see tips to improve their communication patterns that are tailored for their specific communication behaviors. For example, if the user typically demands and their partner typically avoids, the user will see ideas on how they could communicate in a way that engages the partner without him or her feeling attacked or defensive. Thinking about their typical patterns after a fight (e.g., one person wants to talk about a fight while the other just wants to move on and not dwell on it), users view tips on how to successfully navigate these differences and facilitate recovery. After viewing all these tips, users select up to three things they and their partner can change in their patterns of communication during and after a fight. Because Maria and Hank both tended to avoid—both during and often after a fight—they saw tips on how to constructively engage with each other more. Maria really liked the idea of scheduling a weekly "relationship meeting" so they could be sure to discuss issues that were bothering them. Hank, realizing that he often didn't reveal what he was thinking or feeling when an issue came up, decided to commit to sharing with Maria how he felt even if it risked starting a fight.

Improving the user's core issue. Of course, just as in IBCT more generally, sometimes couples need to enact deliberate change targeted at the core issue itself. To aid in this process, the OurRelationship problem provides a library of tips on numerous common problems. Couples can view as many or as few of these topics as they like and then pick up to three things they plan to change in their own behavior and up to three things they would like their partner to change in his or her behavior. Among other changes, Hank decided to ask Maria to fall asleep with him in their own bed rather than James' bed most nights. Maria decided to ask Hank to come with her to James' next appointment with his pediatrician so that Hank could hear for himself what the doctor said about James' developmental delays.

Improving the partner's core issue. If the couple chose to work on two core issues, the individual is also asked to pick things that they as well as their partner can change to improve their partner's core issue. As with their own core issue, users are able to browse a library of tips for common problems before picking things to change and writing those into the program. For Hank's core issue, "lack of intimacy/warmth," Maria offered to snuggle more often when they were watching TV but also wrote that she would like Hank to recognize that snuggling usually wouldn't lead to sex. For Maria's core issue, "coparenting conflict," Hank wrote that he would try not to criticize Maria's parenting in front of James and asked that Maria consult him on major parenting decisions before putting those decisions into action.

Sharing ideas for deliberate change (optional). If the couple chose to share their ideas for change with each other before the next therapy session, they will complete an activity which will allow them to have a conversation following the speaker-listener structure. Specifically, what each person selected and wrote about is displayed on the screen and they are asked to talk about it with their partner. If couples chose to work on two core issues, they will have two separate Respond conversations—one for each core issue.

IBCT Session 6: Reviewing Changes
from the Respond Phase

The primary purpose of this session is to assist couples in deciding on spe-cific behavioral changes that will improve their core issues or components of their DEEP understandings under their control—usually their patterns and portions of their external stress. However, as with session 3, the specific content of this session will depend on whether couples have already shared their changes with each other as part of the online program. Below, we first present a suggested structure assuming that couples did not already have a conversation.

If couples will share their ideas for change during the session. In the Respond phase, each member of the couple will have identified things they can change and things their partner can change in three areas: (a) their patterns of communication when the core issue comes up, (b) their patterns of recovery following an argument regarding the core issue, and (c) the core issue itself. If the couple chose to work on two separate core issues, then they will have two separate conversations—which we suggest doing in two therapy sessions.

Reviewing solutions. After orienting couples to the session, we recommend therapists ask couples to log into the program on the couple's phone or on the therapist's tablet or laptop and open the Respond conversation activity. Con-sistent with the structure described in Chapter 11, this activity structures this portion of problem solving by having couples share what they wrote in the program using a speaker-listener structure.

After both partners share their ideas for changing their patterns during the core issue (i.e., the first of three components), we either remain within the typical problem-solving structure or transition to IBCT acceptance interventions depending on the needs of the couple. If the couple is demon-strating a good collaborative alliance, then we use this as an opportunity to flesh out the ideas they came up with. Would certain changes bene-fit from being further defined or separated into their component pieces? Are there potential changes the couple omitted that we could tentatively introduce into the brainstorming process? Ideally, we should use Socratic questioning, so that the changes aren't construed as the therapist's ideas. On the other hand, if the couple has lost their collaborative set or powerful emotions have become the focus, we shift to either unified detachment or empathic joining. When the couple is ready, we then encourage them to progress to the next step.

Selecting solutions to try. Having shared their ideas on how they and their partner could change, the couple is now ready to select changes they both want to try. If things have been going well, we use this as an opportunity to *catch the positive* and have them reflect on what it has been like for them to work so collaboratively. If it has been difficult, then unified detachment or empathic joining or a combination of the two is usually called for before moving on. Once couples are ready, the online activity takes the couple through sharing each of their changes for recovery from their core issue and subsequently selecting solutions to try. The sequence is repeated one last time for changes to the core issue itself. As with the first time through, we encourage therapists to celebrate the successes that couples experience when they do it well or switch to unified detachment and empathic joining when they no longer seem able to work together collaboratively.

Setting a time to reevaluate. An important final step in the problem-solving process is deciding on a time to revisit the deliberate changes the couple selected and revising those changes as necessary. If a core issue occurs several times a week or more, a week is usually sufficient to know whether the changes are working. On the other hand, if the core issue happens only once a week or less, the couple might want to reevaluate in a month.

Assigning remaining OurRelationship activities as homework. Finally, the therapist would assign the remaining activities in the OurRelationship program focused on the difficulties of deliberate change.

If couples have already shared their ideas for change through the program. In this situation, we recommend asking generally how the conversation went. When the conversation went poorly, it is important to return to acceptance techniques before—or instead of—pushing forward to get the couple to work together on deliberate change. If the conversation went well, it can also be helpful to start the session with acceptance. For example, unified detachment can be useful in helping couples understand why they were successful in working together to come up with viable solutions—reinforcing the new patterns that are emerging. Empathic joining can be helpful in facilitating the expression of the positive feelings that each experienced in successfully tackling a difficult issue. Following discussion of the general tenor of the conversation, we turn to the specific changes they identified. With our DEEP understanding of this couple in mind, we help couples evaluate whether the changes they selected will be helpful. Are they specific and behavioral? Will they be too difficult to implement? Even if implemented, will they create important changes in the underlying issues rather than just improving derivative problems? Also, is the responsibility for change at least somewhat mutual? We encourage couples to select something both of them can change so that they have a shared responsibility to enact the change. Even if couples agree that one partner is the primary person who needs to change, the other partner can commit to a change that will facilitate the primary person's efforts.

OurRelationship Program: Acting on Your Plan

As homework, we encourage couples to complete the Acting on Your Plan activity before the next session. In Chapter 9, we elaborated a number of ways in which deliberate change is so difficult. Couples completing the Respond phase will encounter those same problems. To prevent and partially inoculate couples against common difficulties that come with deliberate change, individuals are asked to consider the types of difficulties they and their partners may encounter when enacting the changes they picked. For example, couples learn about problems that arise when one partner doesn't recognize that the problem is occurring, when one partner becomes emotional or stressed, when the change feels awkward or fake, and when the change is harder or more complicated than they expected.

IBCT Session 7: Integrating Acceptance and Change

In this session, we focus on whether couples have begun to make the changes they agreed to. Most couples are not able to fully implement their selected changes. Even if couples were able to implement the changes, those changes may not have had the intended effects. Not surprisingly, Maria and Hank had mixed success in their initial attempts at change. Early in the week, Maria twice returned to their bed rather than falling asleep in James' bed. However, James got a cold in the latter part of the week and Maria didn't want to leave James' bed too early for fear of waking him; as a result, she fell asleep there. Hank was understandably excited by Maria's initial return but then was disappointed when the change was short-lived. Both listed on their Weekly Questionnaire a recent argument about whether Maria was "really trying" to improve their relationship.

In these situations, we first highlight and reinforce the fact that they tried—itself an important change in their relationship. Next, we explore barriers to change. If couples did the OurRelationship homework described above, we ask them whether the likely barriers they identified in the activity were indeed the ones that interfered with their change efforts. Then we use unified detachment and empathic joining to debrief their change efforts. For Hank and Maria, it was important to do empathic joining around Hank's disappointment as well as Maria's frustration with Hank's disappointment. Additionally, unified detachment helped them understand why this change was difficult for both of them. Following these acceptance interventions, we turn to problem solving around the barriers the couple encountered. Should the couple try the changes they picked again? Or is there enough evidence that different changes are needed?

Of course, some couples are able to implement important changes and are already experiencing the positive impacts of these changes. With these couples, we want to first celebrate these changes, asking them to describe the attempted change and result in detail. Next, we expand the focus and encourage the couple to consider why they were successful in these changes (when they had likely unsuccessfully attempted to fix the problem in the past), tying the success to their DEEP understanding when possible. Finally, if time remains, we help them identify strategies that they can use to maintain these changes or successfully introduce additional changes they selected. We will also again normalize for the couples that deliberate change is hard and prepare them for the inevitable slip-ups.

IBCT Session 8: Discussing Changes,
Celebrating, and Tolerating Future Problems

In our last session with a couple, we want to celebrate the gains that they have made, anticipate that there will continue to be challenges, and make a plan for the future.

Changes during treatment. We usually begin this termination session by presenting objective measures of change in the couples' relationship. Because we have been tracking their relationship satisfaction on the Weekly Questionnaire, we are able to show couples how their satisfaction has changed—or not—during treatment. Beyond this general indication of change in satisfaction, we focus on specific changes they may have made. We can review our DEEP analysis of their core issue or issues and discuss if they made some changes in their patterns of interaction around these issues, in their way of recovering from arguments, or in the core issues themselves. We discuss this feedback and these changes honestly and openly; if couples have not benefited from treatment, that is important information and informs what we do in the remainder of the session.

Celebrating improvements or providing hope. If couples have experienced improvements during treatment, we ask couples to reflect on how they're feeling differently about their relationship. On the other hand, when couples do not report notable improvements, we highlight the fact that the partners have been willing to work collaboratively to tackle important problems in their relationship; most couples run from those problems, but they faced them head on; that takes courage. It also shows that they value their relationship and care for each other. We also want to instill hope that this experience marks an important turning point in their relationship. We might ask: if you remember to think about your DEEP understandings when your core issue arises, how might that change things? If you could keep doing the changes you decided on, how would your relationship change?

Keeping it going. Finally, we talk with the couple about the things they want to take away from this experience. Which parts of their DEEP understanding are going to be most helpful for them to keep in mind? What changes to their patterns or core issues are going to be most important for them to continue? What barriers are they likely to encounter in doing that? Also, we want to revisit the positive activities they have been doing together. Have they been enjoying them? How can they remember to make time to keep doing them? Are there other ideas they want to try?

Finally, we talk with couples about additional resources that are available to them in the OurRelationship program. In the optional Strengthen phase, couples can complete activities to reevaluate the changes that they picked, work on an additional core issue not discussed during therapy, or follow the structure of the speaker-listener or problem-solving conversations to discuss any topic they would like.

ALTERNATIVE STRUCTURES FOR INTEGRATION WHEN MORE OR FEWER SESSIONS ARE POSSIBLE

In this chapter, we have assumed an eight-session course of IBCT. However, there may be situations in which a briefer or longer course of treatment is indicated. If couples are able to attend just 1–3 sessions, we would recommend that they complete the OurRelationship program with a coach rather than working with an IBCT therapist. With four sessions, we would have one initial conjoint session (session 1, above), two combined individual sessions (session 2, above), one feedback session (session 3 plus description of the Respond phase), and a final session to debrief the changes they picked plus a brief termination portion (session 6 above, finished with brief coverage of material in session 8). With five sessions, we would add back in session 4 to allow couples to apply their DEEP understanding before moving on to selecting changes to improve their relationship. With six sessions, we would likely omit sessions 5 and 7. With seven sessions, we would omit session 7. For any length of treatment shorter than eight sessions, we would strongly encourage couples to share their DEEP understandings and potential changes with each other through the online activities, allowing the therapy sessions to focus on reactions to those conversations and ideas they generated.

If couples can attend more than eight sessions, we would proceed with the first three sessions as described above, which would take couples through assessment and feedback as well as the Observe and Understand phases of OurRelationship. Then we would proceed with sessions 4 and 5 as described but add additional IBCT intervention sessions as needed prior to assigning the Respond phase. We can also extend the number of sessions after the Respond phase to ensure that changes are solidified or to handle difficult couples who have had gotten stuck in their efforts to create change. Thus, with more sessions available, we can strategically decide on when to introduce the Respond phase (and the follow-up Acting on Your Plan activity).

SUMMARY

In this chapter, we presented the OurRelationship program—an online intervention for relationship distress based on IBCT principles—that can be integrated into a therapy practice in a number of ways. Specifically, we discussed how the program could be used to supplement individual therapy, as homework during a traditional course of IBCT, or integrated into an abbreviated version of IBCT of four sessions or more. We also suggested that integration of the OurRelationship program can be a good way for therapists who are newly learning IBCT to get started.

Next, we reviewed the three nationwide randomized clinical trials that have been conducted on the OurRelationship program, involving over 1400 couples. Results from these studies, which only involved one-to-four 15-minute calls with a coach—not in-person sessions with a therapist, repeatedly demonstrate that the OurRelationship program creates significant gains in a number of domains of relationship functioning including satisfaction, emotional intimacy, communication conflict, intimate partner violence, and break-up potential. Additionally, the program has been shown to create significant improvement in depressive and anxious symptoms, perceived stress, perceived health, alcohol abuse, and insomnia. When provided with the added support, dosage, and tailoring made possible through in-person sessions with a therapist, we expect the OurRelationship program would be even more effective.

We spent the majority of the chapter describing an eight-session version of IBCT, which is organized around the three phases of the OurRelationship program—Observe, Understand, and Respond. Following the initial conjoint intake session, the couple is asked to complete the Observe phase before their individual sessions. In this phase, couples complete online activities that provide feedback on general relationship functioning (e.g., relationship satisfaction) and help them select an issue they would like to focus on during treatment (i.e., their core issue).

Following the individual session, each member of the couple separately completes the Understand phase of the OurRelationship program. In this phase, couples develop a DEEP understanding of their relationship. In the Differences chapter, individuals view objective feedback on how they and their partner differ on key constructs such as personality, emotional expressiveness, and attachment styles. They select the difference that is most related to their core issue and write about a recent example. In the Emotions chapter, couples learn about hidden and surface emotions and select the hidden and surface emotions that both they and their partner experience during the core issue. In the External stress chapter, users view objective feedback on their and their partner's level of perceived stress and have a chance to select external stressors that are making their core issue worse. Finally, in the Patterns of communication chapter, users learn about the importance of communication and select the patterns they get into when dealing with their core issue as well as patterns during recovery from the core issue. After the couple completes the online activities, they have a session in which they share the DEEP understandings they developed with their partner. This session serves many of the same roles as the traditional IBCT feedback session but is more client-led.

In the third and final phase of the program, the Respond phase, therapists integrate the online activities with in-person sessions to help couples differentiate appropriate targets for acceptance or change. Individuals then have an opportunity to identify things they and their partners can change to improve their patterns of communication and the core issues they selected. To aid in these problem-solving exercises, the OurRelationship program provides tips and information tailored to the specific patterns and core issues the couple selected.

In sum, we encourage IBCT therapists to consider integrating the OurRelationship program into their practice when a full course of IBCT is not feasible for logistical, insurance, or other reasons. We expect it will be the most effective way to deliver IBCT in a brief format.

Afterword

ONE OF CHRISTENSEN'S INSTRUCTORS, and one of the founders of behavior therapy, Cyril Franks, was fond of saying, "When all is said, it is rarely done." His point was of course to emphasize action rather than words. Now that we have said all that we have to say in this book, it is up to you, the reader, to do the action of implementing Integrative Behavioral Couple Therapy.

In this book, we have described the theoretical principles of IBCT and how those principles are similar to and different from other evidence-based treatments for couples. We have described the evidence in support of IBCT. However, most of the book has been a detailed description, with numerous examples, of how to do IBCT. Yet, even if you follow the guidelines and principles we have set out, much of couple therapy will be a matter of your judgment and discretion. We want that to be the case. Our approach is contingency-shaped rather than rule-governed. Therefore, we must always be responsive to our clients, adapting our principles and our behavior to their unique situations and behavior.

Consider the simple example of a compliment. If one member of a couple genuinely compliments the other on some constructive action, we would usually see that as a step forward and want to encourage it. However, partners can respond in many ways to compliments. The recipient may be embarrassed by the compliment, may not trust that it is genuine, may feel it as a jinx to further positive action, or experience it as a pressure that they will now be expected to do the constructive action on a regular basis. In these cases we would not want to just encourage what happened and assume it will eventually have a positive impact. Instead, we would want to help the partner explore his or her reactions to the compliment and help the one who complimented explore his or her reactions to those reactions. In so doing, we help them understand each other better, be more emotionally connected, and often experience a mutually positive reaction—a kind of dyadic reinforcement. However, it is impossible to outline every possible client reaction to a situation—even one as seemingly simple and positive as a compliment. That is where this manual ends and your clinical judgment, conceptualization, and relationship with the individual couple takes over. Indeed, only when we are responsive to what our clients are feeling, and are willing to explore what it means to them as individuals, do we begin to offer our clients that individualized acceptance and change necessary to extract themselves from their polarization and set them on a new path.

We know that IBCT can bring about positive change in a majority of couples. However, we also know that it is no panacea. Some couples will remain distressed or will go on to separation and divorce. Yet, we can be helpful even for these couples. When going through the worst of times, we humans can benefit from having someone understand and accompany our journey, no matter how difficult or painful it is. And, if we can prevent the couple from doing additional harm—to each other or to their children—we will have buffered them from one of life's most potent stressors.

Research on couples and on IBCT continues. When the next version of this book is written, ideally not as far in the future as the previous book was in the past, it will have new insights on the complex workings of couples. In the meantime, this book can guide clinicians seeking to implement Integrative Behavioral Couple Therapy. In addition, the IBCT website (https://ibct.psych .ucla.edu/) contains regularly updated information about IBCT, upcoming workshops on IBCT, questionnaires used in IBCT, citations to the clinical and scientific literature on IBCT, and a list of therapists throughout the United States who have completed training in IBCT. Their training, usually done through the VA or directly by Christensen or Jacobson, included extensive observation of the therapists' actual sessions with couples. Thus, we have confidence that these therapists not only understand IBCT, but can implement it.

Appendix

RESEARCH ON IBCT AND OURRELATIONSHIP.COM

Atkins, D. C., Berns, S. B., George, W., Doss, B., Gattis, K., & Christensen, A. (2005). Prediction of response to treatment in a randomized clinical trial of marital therapy. *Consulting and Clinical Psychology, 73,* 893–903.

Atkins, D. C., Dimidjian, S., Bedics, J. D., & Christensen, A. (2009). Couple discord and depression in couples during couple therapy and in depressed individuals during depression treatment. *Journal of Consulting and Clinical Psychology, 77,* 1089–1099.

Atkins, D. C., Eldridge, K., Baucom, D. H., & Christensen, A. (2005). Infidelity and behavioral couple therapy: Optimism in the face of betrayal. *Consulting and Clinical Psychology, 73,* 144–150.

Baucom, B. R., Atkins, D. C., Simpson, L. E., & Christensen, A. (2009). Prediction of response to treatment in a randomized clinical trial of couple therapy: A 2-year follow-up. *Consulting and Clinical Psychology, 77,* 160–173.

Baucom, B. R., Atkins, D. C., Simpson, L. E., & Christensen, A. (2015). Prediction of treatment response at 5-year follow-up in a randomized clinical trial of behaviorally based couple therapies. *Consulting and Clinical Psychology, 83,* 103–114.

Baucom, B. R., Sheng, E., Christensen, A., Georgiou, P. G., Narayanan, S. S., & Atkins, D. C. (2015). Behaviorally-based couple therapies reduce emotional arousal during couple conflict. *Behavior Research and Therapy, 72,* 49–55.

Baucom, K. J. W., Baucom, B. R., & Christensen, A. (2015). Changes in dyadic communication during and after integrative and traditional behavioral couple therapy. *Behavior Research and Therapy, 65,* 18–28.

Baucom, K. J. W., Sevier, M., Eldridge, K. A., Doss, B. D., & Christensen, A. (2011). Observed communication in couples 2 years after integrative and traditional behavioral couple therapy: Outcome and link with 5-year follow-up. *Consulting and Clinical Psychology, 79,* 565–576.

Benson, L. A., Doss, B. D., & Christensen, A. (2018). Online intervention for couples affected by generalized anxiety disorder. *European Journal of Counselling Psychology, 7,* 1–13.

Benson, L. A., Sevier, M., & Christensen, A. (2013). The impact of behavioral couple therapy on attachment in distressed couples. *Marital and Family Therapy, 39,* 407–420.

Christensen, A. (2010). A unified protocol for couple therapy. In K. Hahlweg, M. Grawe-Gerber, & D. H. Baucom (Eds.), *Enhancing couples: The shape of couple therapy to come* (pp. 33–46). Göttingen, Germany: Hogrefe.

Christensen, A., & Doss, B. D. (2017). Integrative behavioral couple therapy. *Current Opinion in Psychology, 13,* 111–114.

Christensen, A., Atkins, D. S., Berns, S., Wheeler, J., Baucom, D. H., & Simpson, L. E. (2004). Traditional versus integrative behavioral couple therapy for significantly and chronically distressed married couples, *Consulting and Clinical Psychology, 72,* 176–191.

Christensen, A., Atkins, D. C., Yi, J., Baucom, D. H., & George, W. H. (2006). Couple and individual adjustment for two years following a randomized clinical trial comparing traditional versus integrative behavioral couple therapy. *Consulting and Clinical Psychology, 74,* 1180–1191.

Christensen, A., Atkins, D. C., Baucom, B., & Yi, J. (2010). Marital status and satisfaction five years following a randomized clinical trial comparing traditional versus integrative behavioral couple therapy. *Consulting and Clinical Psychology, 78,* 225–235.

Christensen, A., & Glynn, S. (2019). Integrative Behavioral Couple Therapy. In B. H. Fiese (Editor-in-chief), *APA handbook of contemporary family psychology: Vol. 3. Family therapy and training* (pp. 275–290). Washington, DC: American Psychological Association.

Cordova, J. V., Jacobson, N. S., & Christensen, A. (1998). Acceptance versus change interventions in behavioral couple therapy: Impact on couples' in-session communication. *Marriage & Family Counseling, 24,* 437–455.

Doss, B. D., Benson, L. A., Georgia, E. J., & Christensen, A. (2013). Translation of Integrative Behavioral Couple Therapy to a web-based intervention. *Family Process, 52,* 139–152.

Doss, B. D., Cicila, L. N., Georgia, E. J., Roddy, M. K., Nowlan, K. M., Benson, L. A., & Christensen, A. (2016). A randomized controlled trial of the web-based OurRelationship program: Effects on relationship and individual functioning. *Consulting and Clinical Psychology, 84,* 285–296.

Doss, B. D., Knopp, K., Roddy, M. K., Rothman, K., Hatch, S. G., & Rhoades, G. K. (2020). Online programs improve relationship functioning for distressed low-income couples: Results from a nationwide randomized controlled trial. *Consulting and Clinical Psychology*.

Doss, B. D., Roddy, M. K., Llabre, M. M., Georgia Salivar, E., & Jensen-Doss, A. (2020). Improvements in coparenting conflict and child adjustment following an online program for relationship distress. *Family Psychology*.

Doss, B. D., Roddy, M. K., Nowlan, K. M., Rothman, K., & Christensen, A. (2019). Maintenance of gains in relationship and individual functioning following the online OurRelationship program. *Behavior Therapy, 50*, 73–86.

Doss, B. D., Thum, Y. M., Sevier, M., Atkins, D. C., & Christensen, A. (2005). Improving relationships: Mechanisms of change in couple therapy. *Consulting and Clinical Psychology, 73*, 624–633.

Gattis, K. S., Simpson, L. E., & Christensen, A. (2008). What about the kids?: Parenting and child adjustment in the context of couple therapy. *Family Psychology, 22*, 833–842.

Georgia Salivar, E. J., Roddy, M. K., Nowlan, K. M., & Doss, B. D. (2018). Effectiveness of the OurRelationship program for underserved couples. *Couple and Family Psychology: Research and Practice, 7*, 212–226.

Georgia Salivar, E. J., Rothman, K., Roddy, M. K., & Doss, B. D. (2020) Relative cost effectiveness of in-person and internet interventions for relationship distress. *Family Process*.

Jacobson, N. S., Christensen, A., Prince, S. E., Cordova, J., & Eldridge, K. (2000). Integrative Behavioral Couple Therapy: An acceptance-based, promising new treatment for couple discord. *Consulting and Clinical Psychology, 68(2)*. 351–355.

Marín, R. A., Christensen, A., & Atkins, D. C. (2014). Infidelity and behavioral couple therapy: Relationship outcomes over 5 years following therapy. *Couple and Family Psychology: Research and Practice, 3*, 1–12.

Nowlan, K. M., Roddy, M. K., & Doss, B. D. (2017). The online OurRelationship program for relationally distressed individuals: A pilot randomized controlled trial. *Couple and Family Psychology: Research and Practice, 6*, 189–204.

Roddy, M. K., & Doss, B. D. (in press). Relational and psychological mechanisms of change in low income couples' perceived health.

Roddy, M. K., Knopp, K., Georgia Salivar, E., & Doss, B. D. (in press). Maintenance of relationship and individual functioning gains following online relationship programs for low-income couples.

Roddy, M. K., Nowlan, K. M., Christensen, A., & Doss, B. D. (2016). Integrative behavioral couple therapy: Theoretical background, empirical research, and dissemination. *Family Process, 55*, 408–422.

Roddy, M. K., Nowlan, K. M., & Doss, B. D. (2017). A randomized controlled trial of coach contact during a brief online intervention for distressed couples. *Family Process, 56*, 835–851.

Roddy, M. K., Rhoades, G. K., & Doss, B. D. (in press). Effects of ePREP and OurRelationship on low-income couples' mental health and health behaviors: A randomized controlled trial. *Prevention Science.*

Roddy, M. K., Rothman, K., Cicila, L. N., & Doss, B. D. (2019). Why do couples seek relationship help online? Description and comparison to in-person interventions. *Marital and Family Therapy, 45,* 369–379.

Roddy, M. K., Rothman, K., & Doss, B. D. (2018) A randomized controlled trial of different levels of coach support in an online intervention for relationship distress. *Behaviour Research and Therapy, 110,* 47–54.

Roddy, M. K., Stamatis, C. A., Rothman, K., & Doss, B. D. (2020). Mechanisms of change in a brief, online relationship intervention. *Family Psychology, 34,* 57–67.

Sevier, M., Atkins, D. H., Doss, B. D., & Christensen, A. (2015). Up and down or down and up? The process of change in constructive couple behavior during traditional and integrative behavioral couple therapy. *Marital and Family Therapy, 41,* 113–127.

Sevier, M., Eldridge, K., Jones, J., Doss, B., & Christensen, A. (2008). Observed communication and associations with satisfaction during traditional and integrative behavioral couple therapy. *Behavior Therapy, 39,* 137–150.

Simpson, L.E., Doss, B.D., Wheeler, J., & Christensen, A. (2007). Relationship violence among couples seeking therapy: Common couple violence or battering? *Marital and Family Therapy, 33,* 270–283.

Simpson, L. E., Atkins, D. C., Gattis, K. S., & Christensen, A. (2008). Low-level relationship aggression and couple therapy outcomes. *Family Psychology, 22,* 102–111.

Wimberly, J. D. (1998). An outcome study of integrative couples therapy delivered in a group format [Doctoral dissertation, University of Montana, 1997]. *Dissertation Abstracts International: Section B: The Sciences and Engineering, 58*(12), 6832B.

References

Allen, E., & Atkins, D (2012). The association of divorce and extramarital sex in a representative U.S. sample. *Family Issues, 33*, 1477–1493.

Annon, J. (1976). The PLISSIT model. *Sex Education and Therapy, 2*, 1–15.

Atkins, D. C., Berns, S. B., George, W., Doss, B., Gattis, K., & Christensen, A. (2005). Prediction of response to treatment in a randomized clinical trial of marital therapy. *Consulting and Clinical Psychology, 73*, 893–903.

Atkins, D. C., Eldridge, K., Baucom, D. H., & Christensen, A. (2005). Infidelity and behavioral couple therapy: Optimism in the face of betrayal. *Consulting and Clinical Psychology, 73*, 144–150.

Baucom, B. R., Atkins, D. C., Rowe, L. S., & Christensen, A. (2015). Prediction of treatment response at 5-year Follow-up in a Randomized Clinical Trial of Behaviorally Based Couple Therapies. *Consulting and Clinical Psychology, 83*,103–14.

Baucom, B. R., Atkins, D. C., Simpson, L. E., & Christensen, A. (2009). Prediction of response to treatment in a randomized clinical trial of couple therapy: A 2-year follow-up. *Consulting and Clinical Psychology, 77*, 160–173.

Baucom, B. R., McFarland, P. T., & Christensen, A. (2010). Gender, topic, and time in observed demand/withdraw interaction in cross- and same-sex couples. *Family Psychology, 24*, 233–242.

Baucom, D. H., & Epstein, N. (1990). *Cognitive behavioral marital therapy*. New York: Brunner/Mazel.

Baucom, D. H., Epstein, N., Kirby, H, S., & LaTaillade, J. J. (2015). Cognitive-Behavioral Couple Therapy. . In A. S. Gurman, J. L. Lebow, & D. K. Snyder (Eds.), *Clinical handbook of couple therapy* (5th ed., pp. 23–60). New York: Guilford.

Baucom, D. H., Epstein, N., & Rankin, L. A. (1995). Cognitive Aspects of Cognitive-

Behavioral Marital Therapy. In N. S. Jacobson & A. S. Gurman (Eds.), *Clinical handbook of couple therapy* (pp. 65–90). New York: Guilford Press.

Baucom, D. H., Hahlweg, K., & Kuschel, A. (2003). Are waiting-list control groups needed in future marital therapy outcome research? *Behavior Therapy, 34*, 179–188.

Baucom, D. H., Kirby, J. S., Fischer, M. S., Baucom, B. R., Hamer, R., & Bulik, C. M. (2017). Findings from a couple-based open trial for adult anorexia nervosa. *Family Psychology, 31*, 584–591.

Baucom, D. H., Shoham, V., Mueser, K. T., Daiuto, A. D., & Stickle, T. R. (1998). Empirically supported couple and family interventions for marital distress and adult mental health problems. *Consulting and Clinical Psychology, 66*, 53–88.

Benson, L. A., McGinn, M. M., & Christensen, A. (2012). Common principles of couple therapy. *Behavior Therapy, 43*, 25–35.

Berg, I. K. (1994). *Family-based services: A solution-focused approach.* New York: Norton.

Bianchi, S. M., Sayer, L. C., Milkie, M. A., & Robinson, J. P. (2012). Housework: Who did, does or will do it, and how much does it matter? *Social Forces, 91*, 55–63.

Binik, Y. M., & Hall, K. S. K. (2014). *Principles and practice of sex therapy, fifth edition.* New York: Guilford.

Breiding, M. J., Chen, J., & Black, M. C. (2014). *Intimate partner violence in the United States-2010.* Atlanta, GA: National Center for Injury Prevention and Control, Centers for Disease Control and Prevention.

Cantos, A. L., & O'Leary, K. D. (2014). One size does not fit all in treatment of intimate partner violence. *Partner Abuse, 5(2)*, 204–236.

Caprariello, P. A., & Reis, H. T. (2011). Perceived partner responsiveness minimizes defensive reactions to failure. *Social Psychological and Personality Science, 2*(4), 365–372.

Christensen, A. (2010). A unified protocol for couple therapy. In K. Hahlweg, M. Grawe-Gerber, & D. H. Baucom (Eds.). *Enhancing couples: The shape of couple therapy to come* (pp. 33–46). Göttingen, Germany: Hogrefe.

Christensen, A., Atkins, D. C., Baucom, B., & Yi, J. (2010). Marital Status and Satisfaction Five Years Following a Randomized Clinical Trial Comparing Traditional Versus Integrative Behavioral Couple Therapy. *Consulting and Clinical Psychology, 78*, 225–235.

Christensen, A., Atkins, D. S., Berns, S., Wheeler, J., Baucom, D. H., & Simpson, L. E. (2004). Traditional versus integrative behavioral couple therapy for significantly and chronically distressed married couples, *Consulting and Clinical Psychology, 72*, 176–191.

Christensen, A., Atkins, D. C., Yi, J., Baucom, D. H., & George, W. H. (2006). Couple and individual adjustment for two years following a randomized clinical trial comparing traditional versus integrative behavioral couple therapy. *Consulting and Clinical Psychology, 74*, 1180–1191.

Christensen, A., Dimidjian, S., & Martell, C. R. (2015). Integrative Behavioral Couple Therapy. In A. S. Gurman, J. L. Lebow, & D. K. Snyder (Eds.), *Clinical handbook of couple therapy* (5th ed., pp. 61–94). New York: Guilford.

Christensen, A., Eldridge, K., Catta-Preta, A. B., Lim, V. R., & Santagata, R. (2006). Cross-cultural consistency of the demand/withdraw interaction in couples. *Marriage and the Family, 68,* 1029–1044.

Christensen, A., Doss, B. D., & Jacobson, N. S. (2014). *Reconcilable Differences.* New York: Guilford.

Christensen, A. & Glynn, S. (2019). Integrative Behavioral Couple Therapy. In B. H. Fiese (Editor-in-Chief) *APA Handbook of Contemporary Family Psychology: Vol. 3. Family Therapy and Training* (pp. 275–290). Washington, DC: American Psychological Association.

Christensen, A., Jacobson, N.S., & Babcock, J.C. (1995). Integrative behavioral couple therapy. In N.S. Jacobson & A.S. Gurman (Eds.), *Clinical Handbook of Marital Therapy* (2nd ed., pp. 31–64). New York: Guilford.

Cooper, D., Yap, K., & Batalha, L. (2018). Mindfulness-based interventions and their effects on emotional clarity: A systematic review and meta-analysis. *Affective Disorders, 235,* 265–276.

Davis, M. H. (2018). *Empathy: A Social Psychological Approach.* New York: Routledge.

Davis, J. R, & Gold, G. J. (2011). An examination of emotional empathy, attributions of stability, and the link between perceived remorse and forgiveness. *Personality and Individual Differences, 50,* 392–397.

DeBoer, K. M., Rowe, L. S., Frousakis, N. N., Dimidjian, S., & Christensen, A. (2012). Couples excluded from a therapy trial due to intimate partner violence: Subsequent treatment-seeking and occurrence of IPV. *Psychology of Violence, 2*(1), 28–39.

de Shazer, S. (1982). *Patterns of brief family therapy.* New York: Guilford.

Doss, B. D., Atkins, D. C., & Christensen, A. (2003). Who's dragging their feet: Husbands and wives seeking marital therapy. *Marital and Family Therapy, 29,* 165–177.

Doss, B. D., Cicila, L. N., Georgia, E. J., Roddy, M. K., Nowlan, K. M., Benson, L. A., & Christensen, A. (2016). A randomized controlled trial of the web-based OurRelationship program: Effects on relationship and individual functioning. *Journal or Consulting and Clinical Psychology, 84,* 285–296.

Doss, B. D., Knopp, K., Roddy, M. K., Rothman, K., Hatch, S. G., & Rhoades, G. K. (in press). Online programs improve relationship functioning for distressed low-income couples: Results from a nationwide randomized controlled trial. *Consulting and Clinical Psychology.*

Doss, B. D., Roddy, M. K., Llabre, M. M., Georgia Salivar, E., & Jensen-Doss, A. (in press). Improvements in coparenting conflict and child adjustment following an online program for relationship distress. *Family Psychology.*

Doss, B. D., Roddy, M. K., Nowlan, K. M., Rothman, K., & Christensen, A. (2019). Maintenance of gains in relationship and individual functioning following the online OurRelationship program. *Behavior Therapy, 50*, 73–86.

Doss, B. D., Simpson, L. E., & Christensen, A. (2004). Why do couples seek marital therapy? *Professional Psychology, 35*, 608–614.

Doss, B. D., Thum, Y. M., Sevier, M., Atkins, D. C., & Christensen, A. (2005). Improving relationships: Mechanisms of change in couple therapy. *Consulting and Clinical Psychology, 73*, 624–633.

Dovidio, J. F., Piliavin, J. A., Schroeder, D. A., & Penner, L. A. (2006). *The social psychology of prosocial behavior*. New Jersey, NJ: Lawrence Erlbaum.

Dutton, D. G. (2012). The case against the role of gender in intimate partner violence. *Aggression and violent behavior, 17*, 99–104.

Ekers, D., Webster, L., Van Straten, A., Cuijpers, P., Richards, D., & Gilbody, S. (2014). Behavioural activation for depression: An update of meta-analysis of effectiveness and sub group analysis. *PloS One, 9*(6):e100100.

Epstein, N., Werlinich, C. A., & LaTaillade, J. J. (2015). Couple therapy for partner aggression. In A. S. Gurman, J. L. Lebow, & D. K. Snyder (Eds.), *Clinical handbook of couple therapy* (5th ed., pp. 389–411). New York: Guilford.

Epstein, N., & Baucom, D. H. (2002). *Enhanced cognitive-behavioral therapy for couples: A contextual approach*. Washington, DC: American Psychological Association.

Erbas, Y., Ceulemans, E., Lee Pe, M., Koval, P., & Kuppens, P. (2014). Negative emotion differentiation: Its personality and well-being correlates and a comparison of different assessment methods. *Cognition and Emotion, 28*, 1196–1213.

Fincham, F. D., Paleari, F. G., & Regalia, C. (2002). Forgiveness in marriage: The role of relationship quality, attributions, and empathy. *Personal Relationships, 9*, 27–37.

Finkel, E. J., Slotter, E. B., Luchies, L. B., Walton, G. M., &. Gross, J. J. (2013). A brief intervention to promote conflict reappraisal preserves marital quality over time. *Psychological Science, 24*(8), 1595–1601.

Fischer, M. S., & Baucom, D. H. (2018). Couple-based interventions for relationship distress and psychopathology. In J. N. Butcher, J. Hooley, & P. C. Kendall (Eds.), *Psychopathology: Understanding, Assessing and Treating Adult Mental Disorders*. Washington, DC: American Psychological Association, 661–686.

Foran, H. M., & O'Leary, K. D. (2008). Alcohol and intimate partner violence: A meta-analytic review. *Clinical Psychology Review, 28*, 1222–1234.

Funk, J. L., & Rogge, R. D. (2007). Testing the ruler with item response theory: Increasing precision of measurement for relationship satisfaction with the Couples Satisfaction Index. *Family Psychology, 21*, 572–583.

Garcia-Moreno, C., Pallitto C., Devries, K., Stockl, H., Watts, C., & Abrahams, N. (2013). *Global and regional estimates of violence against women: Prevalence and health effects of intimate partner violence and non-partner sexual violence.* Geneva, Switzerland: World Health Organization.

Georgia Salivar, E. J., Roddy, M. K., Nowlan, K. M., & Doss, B. D. (2018). Effectiveness of the OurRelationship program for underserved couples. *Couple and Family Psychology: Research and Practice, 7,* 212–226.

Glass, S. P. (2002). Couple therapy after the trauma of infidelity. In A. S. Gurman & N. S. Jacobson (Eds.), *Clinical handbook of couple therapy* (3rd ed. pp. 488–507). New York: Guilford Press.

Goldberg, L. R. (1993). The structure of phenotypic personality traits. *American Psychologist, 48,* 26–34.

Goldberg, S. B., Tucker, R. P., Greene, P. A., Davidson, R. J., Wampold, B. E.,, Kearney, D. J., Simpson, T. L. (2018). Mindfulness-based interventions for psychiatric disorders: A systematic review and meta-analysis. *Clinical Psychology Review 59,* 52–60.

Goldberg, S. K., & Conron, K. J. (2018). How many same-sex couples in the U.S. are raising children? https://williamsinstitute.law.ucla.edu/research/parenting/how -many-same-sex-parents-in-us/

Goldman, A., & Greenberg, L. (1992). Comparison of integrated systemic and emotionally focused approaches to couples therapy. *Consulting and Clinical Psychology, 60,* 962–969.

Goldman, R. N., & Greenberg, L. S. (2007). Integrating love and power in Emotion-Focused Couple Therapy. *European Psychotherapy, 7,* 117–135.

Green, R. J., & Mitchell, V. (2008). Gay and lesbian couples in therapy: Minority stress, relational ambiguity, and families of choice. In A. S. Gurman (Ed.), *Clinical handbook of couple therapy* (4th ed., pp. 662–680). New York: Guilford.

Greenberg, L., & Johnson, S. M. (1988). *Emotionally focused therapy for couples.* New York: Guilford Press.

Gu, J., Strauss, C., Bond, R., & Cavanagh, K. (2015). How do mindfulness-based cognitive therapy and mindfulness-based stress reduction improve mental health and wellbeing? A systematic review and meta-analysis of mediation studies. *Clinical Psychology Review, 37,* 1–12.

Hatch, S. G., Rothman, K., Roddy, M. K., Dominguez, R.M., Le, Y., & Doss, B. D. (in press). Heteronormative relationship education for same-gender couples. *Family Process.*

Haupert, M. L., Gesselman, A. N., Moors, A. C., Fisher, H. E., & Garcia, J. R. (2017). Prevalence of experiences with consensual nonmonogamous relationships: Findings from two national samples of single Americans. *Sex and Marital Therapy, 43,* 424–440.

Hayes, A. M. (2015). Facilitating emotional processing in depression: The application of exposure principles. *Current Opinion in Psychology, 4,* 61–66.

Hayes, A. M., Ready, C. B., & Yasinski, C. (2015). Application of exposure and emotional processing theory to depression: Exposure-based cognitive therapy. In N. C. Thoma & D. McKay (Eds.), *Working with emotion in cognitive behavioral therapy: Techniques for clinical practice* (pp. 146–174). New York: Guildford.

Hayes, S. C., Strosahl, K. D., & Wilson, K. G. (2012). *Acceptance and commitment therapy: The process and practice of mindful change* (2 ed.). New York: Guilford Press.

Hofstede, G. (1980). *Culture's consequences: International differences in work-related values*. Beverly Hills, CA: Sage.

Hofstede, G. (2002). Dimensions do not exist: A reply to Brendan McSweeney. *Human Relations, 55,* 1355–1361.

Hofstede, G. (2011). Dimensionalizing cultures: The Hofstede Model in context. *Online Readings in Psychology and Culture, 2*(1). https://doi.org/10.9707/2307-0919.1014

Hofstede, G., Hofstede, G. J., & Minkov, M. (2010). *Cultures and organizations: Software of the mind* (Rev. 3rd ed.). New York: McGraw-Hill.

Hoyt, M. F. (2015). Solution-Focused Couple Therapy. In A. S. Gurman, J. L. Lebow, & D. K. Snyder (Eds.), *Clinical handbook of couple therapy* (5th ed., pp. 300–332). New York: Guilford.

Jackson, J. B., Miller, R. B., Oka, M., & Henry, R. G. (2014). Gender differences in marital satisfaction: A meta-analysis. *Marriage and Family, 76,* 105–129.

Jacobson, N. S., & Christensen, A. (1996). *Acceptance and change in couple therapy: A therapist's guide to transforming relationships*. New York: Norton.

Jacobson, N. S., Christensen, A., Prince, S. E., Cordova, J., & Eldridge, K. (2000). Integrative Behavioral Couple Therapy: An acceptance-based, promising new treatment for couple discord. *Consulting and Clinical Psychology, 68,* 351–355.

Jacobson, N. S., & Margolin, G. (1979). *Marital therapy: Strategies based on social learning and behavior exchange principles*. New York: Brunner/Mazel.

Jacobson, N. S., Schmaling, K. B., & Holtzworth-Munroe, A. (1987). A component analysis of behavioral marital therapy: Two-year follow-up and prediction of relapse. *Marital and Family Therapy, 13,* 187–195.

Johnson, S. M. (2008). Emotionally focused couple therapy. In A. S. Gurman (Ed.), *Clinical handbook of couple therapy* (4th ed., pp. 107–137). New York: Guilford.

Johnson, S. M. (2015). Emotionally focused couple therapy. In A. S. Gurman, J. L. Lebow, & D. K. Snyder (Eds.), *Clinical handbook of couple therapy* (5th ed., pp. 97–128). New York: Guilford.

Kabat-Zinn, J. (2013). *Full catastrophe living: Using the wisdom of your body and mind to face stress, pain, and illness* (Rev. ed.). New York: Bantam.

Karney, B. R., & Bradbury, T. N. (2000). Attributions in marriage: State or trait? A growth curve analysis. *Personality and Social Psychology, 78,* 295–309.

Kaplan, J. S., & Tolin, D. F. (2011). Exposure therapy for anxiety disorders. *Psychiatric Times, 28*(9).

Kashdan, T. B., Barrett, L. F., & McKnight, P. E. (2015). Unpacking emotion differentiation: Transforming unpleasant experience by perceiving distinctions in negativity. *Current Directions in Psychological Science, 24*, 10–16.

Kelley, H., Berscheid, E., Christensen, A., Harvey, J., Huston, J., Levinger, G., McClintock, E., Peplau, L.A., & Peterson, D. (1983). *Close Relationships.* San Francisco: W.H. Freeman.

Kelley, H., Berscheid, E., Christensen, A., Harvey, J., Huston, J., Levinger, G., McClintock, E., Peplau, L. A., & Peterson, D. (2002). *Close Relationships.* Clinton Corners, NY: Percheron Press.

Kelly, S. (2017). *Diversity in couple and family therapy: Ethnicities, sexualities, and socioeconomics.* Santa Barbara, CA: Praeger.

Khoury, B., Lecomte, T., Fortin, G., Masse, M., Therien, P., Bouchard, V., Chapleau, M., Paquin, K., & Hofmann, S. G. (2013). Mindfulness-based therapy: A comprehensive meta-analysis. *Clinical Psychology Review, 33*, 763–771.

Knudson-Martin, C. (2008). Gender issues in the practice of couple therapy. In A. S. Gurman (Ed.), *Clinical handbook of couple therapy* (4th ed., pp. 641–661). New York: Guilford.

Kurdek, L. A. (2005). What do we know about gay and lesbian couples? *Current Directions in Psychological Science, 14*, 251–254.

Laumann, E., Glasser, D., Neves, R., & Moreira, E. D. (2009). A population-based survey of sexual activity, sexual problems and associated help-seeking behavior patterns in mature adults in the United States of America. *International Journal of Impotence Research, 21*, 171–178.

Laurenceau, J. P., Rivera, L. M., Schaffer, A., & Pietromonaco, P. R. (2004). Intimacy as an interpersonal process: Current status and future directions. In D. Mashek & A. Aron (Eds.), *Handbook of closeness and intimacy* (pp. 61–78). Mahwah, NJ: Lawrence Erlbaum.

Lebow, J. L., Chambers, A. L., Christensen, A., & Johnson, S. M. (2012). Marital distress. *Marital and Family Therapy, 38*, 145–168.

Liberman, R. P. (1970). Behavioral approaches to family and couple therapy. *American Journal of Orthopsychiatry, 40*, 105–118,

Malle, B. F. (2006). The actor-observer asymmetry in attribution: A (surprising) meta-analysis. *Psychological Bulletin, 132*, 895–919.

Marín, R. A., Christensen, A., & Atkins, D. C. (2014). Infidelity and behavioral couple therapy: Relationship outcomes over 5 years following therapy. *Couple and Family Psychology: Research and Practice, 3*, 1–12.

Mark, K. P., Janssen, E., & Milhausen, R. R. (2011). Infidelity in heterosexual couples: Demographic, interpersonal, and personality-related predictors of extradyadic sex. *Archives of Sexual Behavior, 40*, 971–982.

Markman, H. J., Stanley, S. M., & Blumberg, S. L. (2010). *Fighting for your Marriage.* New York: Wiley.

Martell, C. & Prince, S. (2005). Treating infidelity in same-sex couples. *Journal of Clinical Psychology, 61*, 1429–1438.

McCarthy, B. (2015). *Sex made simple: Clinical strategies for sexual issues in therapy.* Eau Claire, WI: PESI Inc.

McCrady, B. S. & Epstein, E. E. (2015). Couple therapy and alcohol problems. In A. S. Gurman, J. L. Lebow, & D. K. Snyder (Eds.), *Clinical handbook of couple therapy* (5th ed., pp. 555–584). New York: Guilford.

McSweeney, B. (2002). Hofstede's model of national cultural differences and their consequences: A triumph of faith – a failure of analysis. *Human Relations, 55,* 89–117.

Miller, W. R., & Rollnick, S. (2013). *Motivational Interviewing: Helping People Change* (3rd ed.). New York: Guilford.

Mitchell, A. E., Castellani, A. M., Sheffield, R. L., Joseph, J. I., Doss, B. D., & Snyder, D. K. (2008). Predictors of intimacy in couples' discussions of relationship injuries: An observational study. *Family Psychology, 22*, 21–29.

Mitchell, K. R., Mercer, C. H., Ploubidis, G. B., Jones, K. G., Datta, J., Field, N., Copas, A, J., Tanton, C., Erens, B., Sonnenberg, P., Clifton, S., Macdowall, W., Phelps, A., Johnson, A. M., & Wellings, K. (2013). Sexual functioning in Britain: Findings from the third National Survey of Sexual Attitudes and Lifestyles (Natsal-3). *The Lancet, 382,* 30, 1817–1829.

Nowlan, K. M., Georgia, E. J., & Doss, B. D. (2017). Long-Term effectiveness of treatment-as-usual couple therapy for military veterans. *Behavior Therapy, 48,* 847–859.

O'Leary, K. D. (2008). Couple therapy and physical aggression. In A. S. Gurman (Ed.), *Clinical handbook of couple therapy* (4th ed., pp. 478–498). New York: Guilford.

O'Leary, K. D., & Williams, M. C, (2006). Agreement about acts of physical aggression in marriage. *Family Psychology, 20,* 656–662.

Patterson, G. R., & Hops, H. (1972). Coercion, a game for two: Intervention techniques for marital conflict. In R. E. Ulrich & P. Mounjoy (Eds.), *The experimental analysis of social behavior* (pp. 424–440). New York: Appleton.

Pavey, L., & Greitemeyer, T., & Sparks, P. (2012). "I help because I want to, not because you tell me to": Empathy increases autonomously motivated helping. *Personality & Social Psychology Bulletin, 38,* 681–689.

Peplau, L. A., & Fingerhut, A. W. (2007). The close relationships of lesbians and gay men. *Annual Review of Psychology, 58,* 405–424.

Prochaska, J. O., & DiClemente, C. C. (1983). Stages and processes of self-change of smoking: Toward an integrative model of change. *Consulting and Clinical Psychology, 51(3),* 390–395.

Prochaska, J. O., DiClemente, C. C., & Norcross, J. C, (1992). In search of how people change: Applications to addictive behaviors. *American Psychologist, 47,* 1102–1114.

Rampell, C. (2014). What men (and women) want in a marriage, today vs. yesterday.

Washington Post, retrieved from https://www.washingtonpost.com/news/rampage/wp/2014/12/09/what-men-and-women-want-in-a-marriage-today-vs-yesterday/

Rathgeber, M., Bürkner, P., Schiller, E., & Holling, H. (2019). The efficacy of emotionally focused couples therapy and behavioral couples therapy: A meta-analysis. *Journal of Marital and Family Therapy, 45*, 447–463.

Rehman, U. S., & Holtzworth-Munroe, A. (2006). A cross-cultural analysis of the demand–withdraw marital interaction: Observing couples from a developing country. *Consulting and Clinical Psychology, 74*, 755–766.

Reis, H. T., & Shaver, P. (1988). Intimacy as an interpersonal process. In S. Duck (Ed.), *Handbook of personal relationships* (pp. 367–389). Chichester, UK: Wiley & Sons.

Roddy, M. K., Georgia, E. J., & Doss, B. D. (2018). Couples with intimate partner violence seeking relationship help: Associations and implications for self-help and online interventions. *Family Process, 57*, 293–307.

Roddy, M. K., Knopp, K., Georgia Salivar, E., & Doss, B. D. (2020). Maintenance of relationship and individual functioning gains following online relationship programs for low-income couples.

Roddy, M. K., Rhoades, G. K., & Doss, B. D. (in press). Effects of ePREP and OurRelationship on low-income couples' mental health and health behaviors: A randomized controlled trial. *Prevention Science*

Roddy, M. K., Rothman, K., & Doss, B. D. (2018) A randomized controlled trial of different levels of coach support in an online intervention for relationship distress. *Behaviour Research and Therapy, 110*, 47–54.

Rohrbaugh, M. J., & Shoham, V. (2015). Brief strategic couple therapy. In A. S. Gurman, J. L. Lebow, & D. K. Snyder (Eds.), *Clinical Handbook of Couple Therapy* (5th ed., pp. 335–357). New York: Guilford.

Rothman, K., Cicila, L. N., McGinn, M. M., Hatch, S. G., Christensen, A., & Doss, B. D. (under review). Trajectories of sexual satisfaction during and after couple therapy for relationship distress.

Rowe, L. S., & Jouriles, E. N. (2019). Intimate partner violence and the family. In B. H. Fiese (Editor-in-chief), *APA handbook of contemporary family psychology: Vol. 2. Applications and broad impact of family psychology* (pp. 399–416). Washington, DC: American Psychological Association.

Segal, Z. V., Williams, J. M. G., & Teasdale, J. D. (2013). *Mindfulness-based cognitive therapy for depression* (2nd ed.), New York: Guildford.

Shadish, W. R., & Baldwin, S. A. (2003). Meta-analysis of MFT interventions. *Marital and Family Therapy, 29*, 547–570.

Shadish, W. R., & Baldwin, S. A. (2005). Effects of behavioral marital therapy: A meta-analysis of randomized controlled trials. *Consulting and Clinical Psychology, 73*, 6–14.

Shelton, K., & Delgado-Romero, E. A. (2013). Sexual orientation microaggressions: The experience of lesbian, gay, bisexual, and queer clients in psychotherapy. *Psychology of Sexual Orientation and Gender Diversity, 1*, 59–70.

Simpson, L. E., Atkins, D. C., Gattis, K. S., & Christensen, A. (2008). Low-level relationship aggression and couple therapy outcomes. *Family Psychology, 22*, 102–111.

Simpson, L. E., Doss, B. D., Wheeler, J., & Christensen, A. (2007). Relationship violence among couples seeking therapy: Common couple violence or battering? *Marital and Family Therapy, 33*, 270–283.

Skinner, B. F. (1966). *The behavior of organisms: An experimental analysis.* Englewood Cliffs, NJ: Prentice Hall.

Snyder, D. K. (1997). *Marital Satisfaction Inventory—Revised (MSI–R) manual.* Los Angeles: Western Psychological Services.

Snyder, D. K., & Halford, W. K. (2012). Evidence-based couple therapy: Current status and future directions. *Family Therapy, 34,* 229–249.

Snyder, D. K., Simpson, J., & Hughes, J. N. (2006). *Emotion regulation in couples and families: Pathways to dysfunction and health.* Washington, DC: American Psychological Association.

Snyder, D. K., & Wills, R. M. (1989). Behavioral versus insight-oriented marital therapy: Effects on individual and interspousal functioning. *Consulting and Clinical Psychology, 57,* 39–46.

Spanier, G. B. (1976). Measuring dyadic adjustment: New scales for assessing the quality of marriage and similar dyads. *Marriage and the Family, 38*, 15–28.

Starr, L. R., Hershenberg, R., Li, Y. I., & Shaw, Z. A. (2017). When feelings lack precision: Low positive and negative emotion differentiation and depressive symptoms in daily life. *Clinical Psychological Science, 5*, 613–631.

Stith, S. M., & McCollum, E. E. (2011). Conjoint treatment of couples who have experienced intimate partner violence. *Aggression and Violent Behavior, 16*, 312–318.

Stith, S. M., Green, N. M., Smith, D. B., & Ward, D. B. (2008). Marital satisfaction and marital discord as risk markers for intimate partner violence: A meta-analytic review. *Family Violence, 23*, 149–160.

Stith, S. M., Rosen, H., McCollum, E. E., & Thomsen, C. J. (2004). Treating intimate partner violence within intact couple relationships: Outcomes of multi-couple versus individual couple therapy. *Marital and Family Therapy, 30*, 305–318.

Straus, M. A., Hamby, S. L., Boney-McCoy, S., & Sugarman, D. B. (1996). The Revised Conflict Tactics Scales: Development and preliminary psychometric data. *Family Issues, 17*, 283–316.

Stuart, R. B. (1969). Operant-interpersonal treatment for marital discord. *Consulting and Clinical Psychology, 33*(6), 675–682.

Stuart, R. B. (1980). *Helping couples change: A social learning approach to marital therapy.* New York: Guilford.

Torre, J., & Lieberman, M. (2018). Putting feelings into words: Affect labeling as implicit emotion regulation. *Emotion Review, 10,* 116–124.

van der Velden, A. M., Kuyken, W., Wattar, U., Crane, C., Pallesen, K. J., Dahlgaard, J., Fjorback, L. O., & Piet, J. (2015). A systematic review of mechanisms of change in mindfulness-based cognitive therapy in the treatment of recurrent major depressive disorder. *Clinical Psychology Review, 37,* 26–39.

Weeks, G. R., & Gambescia, N. (2015). Couple therapy and sexual problems. In A. S. Gurman, J. L. Lebow, & D. K. Snyder (Eds.), *Clinical handbook of couple therapy* (5th ed., pp. 635–656). New York: Guilford.

Weiss, R. L., & Birchler, G. R. (1978). Adults with marital dysfunction. In M. Hersen & A. S. Bellack (Eds.), *Behavior therapy in the psychiatric setting.* Baltimore: Williams & Williams.

Weiss, R. L., Hops, H., & Patterson, G. R. (1973). A framework for conceptualizing marital conflict, technology for altering it, some data for evaluating it. In L. A. Hamerlynck, L. C. Handy, & E. J. Mash (Eds.), *Behavior change: Methodology, concepts, and practices* (pp. 309–342). Champaign, IL: Research Press.

Whisman, M. A. (2007) Marital distress and DSM-IV psychiatric disorders in a population-based national survey. *Abnormal Psychology, 116,* 638–643.

Whisman, M. A., & Bruce, M. L. (1999) Marital distress and incidence of major depressive episode in a community sample. *Abnormal Psychology, 108,* 674–678.

Whisman, M. A., Dixon, A. E., & Johnson, B. (1997). Therapists' perspectives of couple problems and treatment issues in couple therapy. *Family Psychology, 11*(3), 361–366.

Whisman, M. A., & Uebelacker, L. A. (2009) Prospective associations between marital discord and depressive symptoms in middle-aged and older adults. *Psychology and Aging, 24,* 184–189.

Whisman, M. A., Uebelacker, L. A., & Bruce, M. L. (2006) Longitudinal association between marital discord and alcohol use disorders. *Family Psychology, 20,* 164–167.

Whitton, S. W., Weitbrecht, E. M., & Kuryluk, A.D. (2015). Monogamy agreements in male same-sex couples: Associations with relationship quality and individual well-being. *Couple and Relationship Therapy, 14,* 39–63.

Wile, D. B. (1981). *Couples therapy: A nontraditional approach.* New York: Wiley.

Wills, T. A., Weiss, R. L., & Patterson, G. R. (1974). A behavioral analysis of the determinants of marital satisfaction. *Consulting and Clinical Psychology, 42,* 802–811.

Wimberly, J. D. (1998). An outcome study of integrative couples therapy delivered in a group format. (Doctoral dissertation, University of Montana, 1997). *Dissertation Abstracts International: Section B: The Sciences and Engineering, 58(12-B),* 6832.

Yi, J. C. (2007). Ethnic minorities in couple therapy: A five-year follow-up (Order No. 0819365). Available from *ProQuest Dissertations & Theses Global.* (304806978). Retrieved from https://search.proquest.com/docview/304806978?accountid=14512

Index